JavaScript
Complete

Steven Holzner

McGraw-Hill
New York • San Francisco • Washington, D.C. • Auckland
Bogotá • Caracas • Lisbon • London • Madrid • Mexico City
Milan • Montreal • New Delhi • San Juan • Singapore
Sydney • Tokyo • Toronto

McGraw-Hill

A Division of The McGraw·Hill Companies

1 2 3 4 5 6 7 8 9 0   DOC/DOC   9 0 3 2 1 0 9 8

P/N 047158-4

PART OF ISBN 0-07-913736-9

*The sponsoring editor for this book was Michael Sprague and the production
supervisor was Pamela Pelton. It was set in Century Schoolbook by Douglas &
Gayle Limited.*

Printed and bound by R. R. Donnelley & Sons Company.

McGraw-Hill books are available at special quantity discounts to use as
premiums and sales promotions, or for use in corporate training programs.
For more information, please write to Director of Special Sales, McGraw-Hill,
11 West 19th Street, New York, NY 10011. Or contact your local bookstore.

This book is printed on recycled, acid-free paper containing a mini-
mum of 50% recycled de-inked fiber.

To Nancy, as always!

ACKNOWLEDGMENTS

I would like to thank those who have helped me through the process of creating this book: My editor, Michael Sprague and the other folks at Mc-Graw-Hill without whom this book may not have been published. I also would like thank the production staff at Douglas & Gayle.

CONTENTS

Contents

INTRODUCTION

Welcome to JavaScript! In this book, Web pages will come alive with animation, check boxes, radio buttons, graphics, styles, cookies, animated styles, images, and more—all thanks to JavaScript.

JavaScript is a lightweight *scripting language* that you write directly into your Web pages. Web browsers understand the JavaScript you've placed in your pages, and they execute the statements you have written, giving you the power to control your Web pages from behind the scenes. As we'll see in this book, that control can be dramatic, letting us do everything with Web pages from handling buttons and setting colors to rewriting the Web page entirely from scratch as the user watches.

We'll get a guided tour of JavaScript in this book. Before starting that tour, let's take a moment to see what's ahead.

What's in This Book?

In this book, we'll see JavaScript from first to last, starting with the basics and working up through the infrastructure of the language—up to the advanced topics, producing some truly powerful and exciting Web pages.

We'll spend time first making sure we understand the internals of JavaScript before proceeding because we'll need a good foundation to build on. After mastering the fundamentals, we'll see where the real power is—interacting with JavaScript's environment, the Web browser itself—making use of what the browser has to offer us.

You might have seen some impressive pages on the Web, and you'll see how to write a lot of them here. In fact, the theme in this book is seeing JavaScript at work—and seeing what it can do for you—so we've filled this book with bite-sized, fully working examples: nearly 90 of them. These examples are complete and concise—not the code fragments you see in many books on programming, and not the convoluted code monsters you see in other books that run on for hundreds of lines. Our examples are specifically designed to be clear and to the point.

In this book, each example is designed to illustrate one programming point that you can use, without a lot of needless extra code. Here are some of the topics we'll cover in examples:

■ Creating Web pages that remember users by name

■ Using cookies

■ Using check boxes

- Rewriting Web pages on the fly
- Creating graphics animation
- Using radio buttons
- Using JavaScript style sheets
- Initializing Web pages
- Using select controls
- Using text areas
- Rewriting Web pages from Java using JavaScript
- Displaying dialog boxes
- Using cascading style sheets (CSS)
- Connecting JavaScript to Java
- Controlling Java applets from JavaScript
- Loading graphics on a Web page in response to user requests
- Giving the user thumbnail previews of Web pages
- Rewriting Web pages in other frames
- Highlighting hyperlinks when the mouse moves over them
- Using buttons and text boxes
- Displaying prompt boxes
- Customizing Web pages according to time of day
- Handling the mouse
- Displaying alert boxes
- Using JavaScript from Java
- Creating style classes
- Opening new browser windows
- Uploading files to your server
- Reading keys the user types directly
- Controlling windows with keystrokes
- Displaying confirm boxes
- Creating and using JavaScript style functions
- Determining the user's last Web location
- Using the history object to navigate back and forth
- Navigating the Web browser from code

- Layering images on the screen
- Supporting dragging and dropping of Web page elements
- Using the Internet Explorer DirectAnimation controls
- Using ActiveX controls
- Using Netscape layers
- Creating scriptlets
- Using the sequencer ActiveX control for animation
- Creating JavaScript objects
- Using the built-in window, document, navigator, and location objects
- Determining which browser and version your page is running in
- Passing arguments to dialog boxes
- Creating image maps
- Using JavaScript: URLs

That's just a partial list, but you can see there's a great deal of programming power coming up. Before digging into these topics, however, we should make sure we're prepared.

What You'll Need

Two main browsers support JavaScript: Netscape Navigator and Microsoft Internet Explorer (although Microsoft's version of JavaScript is really called *JScript*, as we'll see). This book is targeted at version 4.0 of both browsers.

Until now, JavaScript books have been aimed almost exclusively at Netscape Navigator, which has been understandable because Netscape is the company that created JavaScript in the first place. That's no longer a viable approach, however, because Microsoft Internet Explorer gives us literally hundreds of programming possibilities that Netscape Navigator doesn't support (and of course the reverse is true as well).

With the introduction of such items as scriptlets, DirectAnimation, structured graphics, dynamic styles and much more, version 4.0 of Internet Explorer can't be ignored. This is the first book that explores the two browsers on an equal footing, finding as much JavaScript power in Internet Explorer as in Netscape Navigator.

You'll need one or both of these browsers to get the full measure from this book; you can download Internet Explorer from the Microsoft site, `http://www.microsoft.com`, or a beta version of Netscape Navigator from the Netscape site, `http://www.netscape.com`. These downloads are free. You can also buy a release version of Netscape Navigator from software vendors.

Besides a browser, you'll need some way of creating Web pages with scripts (that it, JavaScript code in HTML <SCRIPT> elements). Although many Web page editors are great at creating HTML, not many excel at allowing you to edit your own scripts. We'll keep our examples short, which means you can use a normal text editor—even Windows WordPad —to create Web pages. (In fact, there are now Web page editors especially built to edit JavaScript, and they can be of considerable help.) Please note that if you use a word processor such as Microsoft Word to create Web pages, you must save your documents as simple text, not as formatted word processor files.

JavaScript is directed at the Web, of course, so to put the results of your labors to work, you should have a Web connection—such as an Internet Service Provider (ISP)—and some way of uploading your Web pages to that ISP. Only when your Web pages are installed on the Web can users download and make use of them. On the other hand, both the browsers we'll work with in this book can read Web pages from disk, so you can develop your pages entirely offline.

That's really it—we're ready to go. We will get started at once in Chapter 1, "Welcome to JavaScript!" where we begin putting JavaScript to work.

1

Welcome to JavaScript!

Welcome to our book on JavaScript. In this book, we're going to take a guided tour of what JavaScript has to offer us, which is a great deal. JavaScript is the language you embed in your Web pages to make things happen. With JavaScript, your Web pages come alive, responding to the user and making things happen.

For example, in this book, we'll see how to handle mouse clicks and mouse movements in our Web pages, highlighting hyperlinks when the user moves the mouse over them. We'll see how to make check boxes, buttons, and other HTML controls active in our Web page. We'll see how to support graphics animation, dynamic rewriting of Web pages, jumping to new Web pages, cookies, image maps, and much more.

Many people have the idea that JavaScript is a elementary language, capable of some basic functions, but not much more. That, however, is not true. JavaScript is a powerful language that can manipulate your Web pages and perform tasks that you can't do in other languages, as we'll see. We'll see how far you can go with JavaScript in this book.

Many people also have the idea that JavaScript is a scripting version of Java, but that's also not so.

JavaScript Is Not Java

The Java language and the JavaScript language are related, but the connection is not as close as you might think. Java is a product of Sun Microsystems, and JavaScript is a product of Netscape.

NOTE: *In fact, the original name for JavaScript was not JavaScript at all, but LiveScript.*

You create Java applets and applications by compiling them into .class bytecode files with the Java compiler. If you want to use an applet, you embed a reference to it in a Web page using the <APPLET> HTML tag and download the .class file with the Web page. An applet can have some space in a Web page that you set aside for it, and it can display graphics and text to the user in that space.

On the other hand, you write JavaScript directly into a Web page by using the <SCRIPT> HTML tag, like this:

```
<SCRIPT LANGUAGE = Javascript>

    function ChangeImage()
    {
        document.form1.IMG1.src = "gif/image2.gif"
    }

</SCRIPT>
```

The JavaScript itself is downloaded with the Web page and interpreted by the Web browser. Note that this means JavaScript is browser-dependent —some browsers don't even support JavaScript yet. However, Microsoft's Internet Explorer and Netscape's Navigator both support JavaScript in their latest versions, so most people browsing the Web can handle JavaScript in some form.

Unlike Java, JavaScript doesn't work directly with graphics and text; JavaScript works with the HTML elements in a Web page. Note that although JavaScript does not deal with graphical elements directly, Web browsers do—and we can control Web browsers with JavaScript, as we'll see. In this way, we'll be able to take advantage of JavaScript's considerable power.

That's how JavaScript works, then—you embed the JavaScript you want to use in a Web page, and it's downloaded when users open the Web page in their browsers. This picture is complicated, however, by the number of versions of JavaScript on the Web now: JavaScript 1.0, 1.1, and 1.2. In fact, there's a version of JavaScript on the Web that, strictly speaking, isn't JavaScript at all—it's Microsoft's JScript.

Two Browsers, Two JavaScripts

The two main Web browsers today are Netscape Navigator and Microsoft Internet Explorer. Because JavaScript is a Netscape product, you might suspect that Microsoft's version would be different, and you'd be correct. When JavaScript first came out—so the legend goes—Netscape was slow to supply the specification to Microsoft, and Microsoft simply reverse-engineered JavaScript, creating its own version named *JScript*.

For most purposes, JavaScript and JScript are close enough that you don't have to worry about the differences, but there are indeed differences (see Appendix A). We'll point out differences to watch for as we progress in the book.

Netscape Navigator 2.0 was the first version to support JavaScript, and that version of JavaScript was version 1.0. Navigator 3.0 supports JavaScript 1.1, and Navigator 4.0 supports the current version, JavaScript 1.2.

TIP: *You can find Netscape's JavaScript documentation—the JavaScript handbook—at:*

`http://www.netscape.com/eng/mozilla/3.0/handbook/javascript/`

However, the JavaScript handbook is behind the times, because it covers only JavaScript for the Netscape Navigator 3.0, and the current version is 4.0. You can find information on the most recent JavaScript version—JavaScript 1.2—at:

`http://developer.netscape.com/library/documentation/communicator/`

The keywords used in JavaScript 1.2 appear in Table 1-1.

Table 1-1 The JavaScript keywords.

abs	acos	action	alert	alinkColor
anchor method	Anchor object	anchors	appCodeName	Applet
applets	appName	appVersion	Area	arguments array
arguments property	Array	asin	atan	atan2
back	bgColor	big	blink	blur
bold	Boolean	border	break	Button
caller	ceil	charAt	Checkbox	checked
clearTimeout	click	close (document object)	close (window object)	closed
comment	complete	confirm	constructor	continue
cookie	cos	current	Date	defaultChecked
defaultSelected	defaultStatus	defaultValue	description	document
domain	elements array	elements property	embeds array	enabledPlugin
encoding	escape	eval	exp	fgColor
filename	FileUpload	fixed	floor	focus
fontcolor	fontsize	for	for..in	Form object
form property	forms	forward	Frame	frames
Function	function	getDate	getDay	getHours
getMinutes	getMonth	getSeconds	getTime	getTimezoneOffset
getYear	go	hash	height	height
Hidden	history array	history object	host	hostname
href	hspace	if..else	Image	images
index	indexOf	isNaN	italics	javaEnabled
join	lastIndexOf	lastModified	length	link method
Link object	linkColor	links	LN10	LN2
location	log	LOG10E	LOG2E	lowsrc

lowsrc	Math	max	MAX_VALUE	method
MimeType	mimeTypes	min	MIN_VALUE	name
NaN	navigator	NEGATIVE_INFINITY	new	next
next	Number	onAbort	onBlur	onChange
onClick	onError	onFocus	onLoad	onMouseOut
onMouseOver	onReset	onSelect	onSubmit	onUnload
open (document object)	open (window object)	opener	Option	options
parent	parse	parseFloat	parseInt	Password
pathname	PI	Plugin	plugins	port
POSITIVE_INFINITY	pow	previous	prompt	protocol
prototype	Radio	random	referrer	refresh
reload	replace	reset method	Reset object	return
reverse	round	scroll	search	select method
Select object	selected	selectedIndex	self	setDate
setHours	setMinutes	setMonth	setSeconds	setTime
setTimeout	setYear	sin	small	sort
split	sqrt	SQRT1_2	SQRT2	src
status	strike	String	sub	submit method
Submit object	substring	suffixes	sup	taint
taintEnabled	tan	target	Text object	text property
Textarea	this	title	toGMTString	toLocaleString
toLowerCase	top	toString	toUpperCase	type
typeof	unescape	untaint	URL	userAgent
UTC	value	valueOf	var	vlinkColor
void	vspace	while	width	window object
window property	with	write	writeln	

The current version of JScript is 3.0 (for Internet Explorer 4.0). Internet Explorer 3.0 supported JScript 1.0, Microsoft Internet Information Server 1.0 supported JScript 2.0, and both Internet Information Server 4.0 and Internet Explorer 4.0 support JScript 3.0. The keywords used in JScript 3.0 appear in Table 1-2.

TIP: *The Microsoft JScript documentation comes in the Microsoft Internet Software Development Kit—the Inet SDK—which you can find at:*

`http://www.microsoft.com/msdn/sdk/inetsdk/asetup/first.asp`

Having so many different versions of JavaScript around is a problem for many programmers, so there have been efforts to standardize JavaScript. In fact, there's a tentative JavaScript standard now, referred to as *ECMA-262*, the JavaScript Language Specification. This standard is a document of the European standards body ECMA, and it's available at the Netscape Web site. As of this writing, ECMA-262 is not yet official, so we will deal with both JavaScript and JScript throughout the book.

Table 1-2 The JScript keywords.

$1...$9 Properties	abs Method	acos Method	Add Method
AddFolders Method	Addition Operator (+)	anchor Method	arguments Property
Array Object	asin Method	Assignment Operator (=)	atan Method
atan2 Method	atEnd Method	AtEndOfLine Property	AtEndOfStream Property
Attributes Property	AvailableSpace Property	big Method	Bitwise AND Operator (&)
Bitwise Left Shift Operator (<<)	Bitwise NOT Operator (~)	Bitwise OR Operator (|)	Bitwise Right Shift Operator (>>)
Bitwise XOR Operator (^)	blink Method	bold Method	Boolean Object
break Statement	BuildPath Method	caller Property	@cc_on Statement
ceil Method	charAt Method	charCodeAt Method	Close Method
Column Property	Comma Operator (,)	// (Single-line Comment Statement)	/*..*/ (Multiline Comment Statement)
CompareMode Property	Comparison Operators	compile Method	Compound Assignment Operators
concat Method (Array)	concat Method(String)	Conditional Compilation	Conditional Compilation Variables
Conditional (trinary) Operator (?:)	constructor Property	continue Statement	Copy Method
CopyFile Method	CopyFolder Method	cos Method	Count Property
CreateFolder Method	CreateTextFile Method	Data Type Conversion	Date Object
DateCreated Property	DateLastAccessed Property	DateLastModified Property	Decrement Operator(--)
Delete Method	delete Operator	DeleteFile Method	DeleteFolder Method
Dictionary Object	dimensions Method	Division Operator (/)	do...while Statement
Drive Object	Drive Property	DriveExists Method	DriveLetter Property
Drives Collection	Drives Property	DriveType Property	E Property
Enumerator Object	Equality Operator (==)	escape Method	eval Method
exec Method	Exists Method	exp Method	File Object

continues

7

Table 1-2 The JScript keywords. (continued)

FileExists Method	Files Collection	Files Property	FileSystem Property
FileSystemObject Object	fixed Method	floor Method	Folder Object
FolderExists Method	Folders Collection	Folders Collection	fontsize Method
for Statement	for...in Statement	FreeSpace Property	fromCharCode Method
Function Object	function Statement	GetAbsolute-PathName Method	GetBaseName Method
GetDate Method	GetDay Method	getDrive Method	getDriveName Method
GetExtensionName Method	GetFile Method	GetFileName Method	GetFolder Method
GetFullYear Method	GetHours Method	GetItem Method	GetMilliseconds Method
GetMinutes Method	GetMonth Method	GetParentFolder-Name Method	GetSeconds Method
GetSpecialFolder Method	GetTempName Method	GetTime Method	GetTimezoneOffset Method
GetUTCDate Method	GetUTCDay Method	GetUTCFullYear Method	GetUTCHours Method
GetUTCMilliseconds Method	GetUTCMinutes Method	GetUTCMonth Method	GetUTCSeconds Method
getVarDate Method	getYear Method	Global Object	global Property
Greater than Operator (>)	Greater than or equal to Operator(>=)	Identity	@if Statement Operator (===)
if..else Statement	ignoreCase Property	Increment Operator (++)	index Property
indexOf Method	Inequality Operator (!=)	Infinity Property	input Property
isFinite Method	isNaN Method	IsReady Property	IsRootFolder Property
italics Method	item Method	Item Property	Items Method
Join Method	Key Property	Keys Method	Labeled Statement
lastIndex Property(RegExp)	lastIndex Property (Regular Expression)	lastIndexOf Method	lastMatch Property

lastParen Property

lbound Method

leftContext Property

length Property (Array)

length Property(Function)

length Property(String)

Less than Operator (<)

Less than or equal to Operator (<=)

Line Property

link Method

LN2 Property

LN10 Property

log Method

LOG2E Property

LOG10E Property

Logical AND Operator (&&)

Logical NOT Operator (!)

Logical OR Operator (||)

Math Object

Logical AND Operator (&&)

max Method

MAX_VALUE Property

min Method

MIN_VALUE Property

MIN_VALUE Property

Modulus Operator (%)

Move Method

MoveFile Method

moveFirst Method

MoveFolder Method

moveNext Method

multiline Property

Multiplication Operator (*)

Name Property

NaN Property (Global)

NaN Property(Number)

NEGATIVE_INFINITY Property

new Operator

Nonidentity Operator (!==)

Number Object

Object Object

OpenAsTextStream Method

OpenTextFile Method

Operator Precedence

ParentFolder Property

parse Method

parseFloat Method

parseInt Method

Path Property

PI Property

POSITIVE_INFINITY Property

pow Method

prototype Property

random Method

Read Method

ReadAll Method

ReadLine Method

RegExp Object

Regular Expression Object

Regular Expression Syntax

Remove Method

RemoveAll Method

return Statement

reverse Method

rightContext Property

RootFolder Property

round Method

ScriptEngine Function

ScriptEngine-BuildVersion Function

ScriptEngineMajorVersion Function

ScriptEngineMinor-Version Function

SerialNumber Property

@set Statement

setDate Method

setFullYear Method

setHours Method

setMilliseconds Method

setMinutes Method

setMonth Method

setSeconds Method

setTime Method

setUTCDate Method

setUTCFullYear Method

setUTCHours Method

setUTCMilli-seconds Method

setUTCMinutes Method

continues

Table 1-2 The JScript keywords. (continued)

setUTCMonth Method	setUTCSeconds Method	setYear Method	ShareName Property
ShortName Property	ShortPath Property	sin Method	Size Property
Skip Method	SkipLine Method	slice Method (Array)	slice Method (String)
small Method	sort Method	source Property	sqrt Method
SQRT1_2 Property	SQRT2 Property	strike Method	String Object
sub Method	SubFolders Property	substr Method	substring Method
Subtraction Operator (-)	sup Method	switch Statement	tan Method
test Method	TextStream Object	this Statement	toArray Method
toGMTString Method	toLocaleString Method	toLowerCase Method	toString Method
TotalSize Property	toUpperCase Method	toUTCString Method	typeof Operator
Type Property	ubound Method	Unary Negation Operator (-)	unescape Method
Unsigned Right Shift (>>>) Operator	UTC Method	valueOf Method	var Statement
VBArray Object	void Operator	VolumeName Property	while Statement
with Statement	Write Method	WriteBlankLines Method	WriteLine Method

What Does JavaScript Look Like?

Let's see some JavaScript at work right now. There's an easy way to do that with Netscape Navigator, and executing some JavaScript will give us a chance to see what it looks like.

To execute a single line of JavaScript without a Web page, you simply choose Open Page from the File menu. This choice displays the Open Page dialog box. Then type `javascript:` into the text box in the Open Page dialog box, and click the Open button to open a `javascript typein` frame in the Navigator, as shown in Figure 1-1.

Here, we'll type in this line of JavaScript, causing the browser to open an alert dialog box with the message `Hello from JavaScript!` in it:

```
alert("Hello from JavaScript!");
```

Type this line into Navigator now and press the Enter key. This opens an alert box with our message in it, as shown in Figure 1-1. Now we've executed our first line of JavaScript!

One thing we should note here is that the preceding line of JavaScript ends with a semicolon (;), which is the standard for both Java and JavaScript. However, JavaScript is much looser about this requirement than Java, so you can end your lines of code with or without a semicolon.

NOTE: *Although formal usage includes the semicolon at the end of Java-Script statements, we will not insist on that usage in this book. So much Java-Script on the Internet is written without semicolons that practically speaking, either way—with or without semicolons—is considered acceptable in all but the most formal situations.*

Figure 1-1
Typing JavaScript in directly.

Now that we've executed one line of JavaScript, let's write our first Web page using JavaScript.

Our First JavaScript Example

We could start our first JavaScript Web page by displaying a header indicating what this page is:

```
┌──────────────────────────────────┐
│                                  │
├──────────────────────────────────┤
│                                  │
│                                  │
│                                  │
│                                  │
│                                  │
│        Our First JavaScript Example │
│                                  │
│                                  │
│                                  │
│                                  │
└──────────────────────────────────┘
```

Then we can use JavaScript to write text directly in the Web page, which the browser will display like this:

```
┌──────────────────────────────────┐
│                                  │
├──────────────────────────────────┤
│                                  │
│ Hello and welcome to JavaScript! │
│                                  │
│                                  │
│        Our First JavaScript Example │
│                                  │
│                                  │
│                                  │
│                                  │
│                                  │
└──────────────────────────────────┘
```

To embed JavaScript in a Web page, we have to know how to use the <SCRIPT> tag, so let's take a look at that tag now.

Using the <SCRIPT> Tag

Here's how you use the <SCRIPT> tag in Netscape Navigator:

```
<SCRIPT
    LANGUAGE="LanguageName"
    SRC="Location">
  .
  .
  .
 Script statements go here...
  .
  .
</SCRIPT>
```

In this case, we set the LanguageName variable to JavaScript. The SRC attribute can specify the location of a separate file that holds the JavaScript; such files have a .js suffix, like this: calculator.js.

NOTE: *To download .js files, your Web server should map .js files to the MIME type "application/x-javascript."*

You can also indicate the version of JavaScript you want to use. To use JavaScript version 1.0 (first appeared in Navigator 2.0), use the default language name, "JavaScript":

```
<SCRIPT LANGUAGE = "JavaScript">
```

To indicate that you're using JavaScript 1.1 (which first appeared in Navigator 3.0), use "JavaScript1.1" as the scripting language:

```
<SCRIPT LANGUAGE = "JavaScript1.1">
```

To indicate that you want to use JavaScript 1.2 (Navigator 4.0), set the language to "JavaScript1.2":

```
<SCRIPT LANGUAGE = "JavaScript1.2">
```

Here's how to use the <SCRIPT> tag in Internet Explorer:

```
<SCRIPT
    EVENT=string
    FOR=string
    ID=string
    IN=string
    LANGUAGE=JAVASCRIPT | VBSCRIPT
    LIBRARY=string
```

```
    TITLE=string>
    .
    .
Script statements go here...
    .
    .
</SCRIPT>
```

Notice that you can set the language to either "JavaScript" (that setting, in Internet Explorer, is the same as "JScript") or "VBScript," which is Microsoft's competing scripting language that's based on its Visual Basic product.

Handling Browsers That Don't Handle JavaScript

While we're discussing the <SCRIPT> tag, we should mention one more thing—a lot of older browsers don't support scripting, so all your script is in danger of appearing, uninterpreted, directly in your Web page's display in those browsers. You can avoid this by enclosing all the script statements in an HTML comment this way:

```
<SCRIPT LANGUAGE = JavaScript>
<!- Hide the script from browsers that don't sup-
port JavaScript
    .
    .
    .
// ->
</SCRIPT>
```

Note that we preface the end of the comment with a double slash (//). This symbol indicates that this line is a JavaScript *comment* (the same convention used in Java and C++) and should be ignored by JavaScript. If we omitted the //, JavaScript would try to interpret the HTML end-of-comment characters ("—>") and generate an error.

Now that we've taken a look at the <SCRIPT> tag, let's put it to work in our example.

Writing to a Web page From JavaScript

Our goal in this example is to write this text in a Web page:

```
┌─────────────────────────────────────────────┐
│                                             │
├─────────────────────────────────────────────┤
│                                             │
│  Hello and welcome to JavaScript!           │
│                                             │
│                                             │
│                                             │
│             Our First JavaScript Example    │
│                                             │
│                                             │
│                                             │
│                                             │
│                                             │
│                                             │
└─────────────────────────────────────────────┘
```

Let's create this Web page, which we'll call hello.htm, now. We begin with with the <HTML> tag and set up the page's head:

```
<HTML>

<HEAD>
<TITLE>Our first JavaScript Example</TITLE>
   .
   .
   .
```

Next, we'll use the <SCRIPT> tage to set up our JavaScript area in the Web page:

```
<HTML>

<HEAD>
<TITLE>Our first JavaScript Example</TITLE>

<SCRIPT LANGUAGE = JavaScript>
   .
   .
   .
</SCRIPT>

</HEAD>
```

We'll perform the actual writing to the Web page with one line, which looks like this (don't worry about the actual statement at this point; we're just exploring the mechanics of setting up a JavaScript-enabled Web page):

```
<HTML>

<HEAD>
<TITLE>Our first JavaScript Example</TITLE>

<SCRIPT LANGUAGE = JavaScript>

document.writeln("Hello and welcome to JavaScript!")

</SCRIPT>

</HEAD>
```

NOTE: *In this example, we're using the JavaScript* document object *to write our message to the Web page with that object's writeln() (that is, "write line")* method. *We'll learn all about objects and methods soon.*

TIP: *The writeln() method writes your data to the Web page and then skips to a new line. If you don't want to skip to a new line, use write().*

All that's left is the <H1> header that appears in the Web page to indicate what this page is all about:

```
<HTML>

<HEAD>
<TITLE>Our first JavaScript Example</TITLE>

<SCRIPT LANGUAGE = JavaScript>

document.writeln("Hello and welcome to JavaScript!")

</SCRIPT>

</HEAD>


<BODY>

<CENTER>
<H1>
Our First JavaScript Example
</H1>
</CENTER>

</BODY>

</HTML>
```

That's all there is to it! Open Hello.htm in a Web browser, as shown in Figure 1-2. As you can see, JavaScript has produced our message and written it directly to the Web page's HTML as text we can see. Our first example is a success.

The code for this Web page, Hello.htm, is shown in Listing 1-1.

Figure 1-2
Our first JavaScript example.

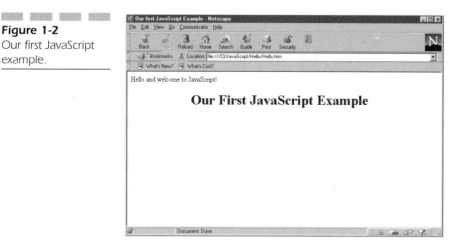

Listing 1-1
Hello.htm.

```
<HTML>

<HEAD>
<TITLE>Our first JavaScript Example</TITLE>

<SCRIPT LANGUAGE = JavaScript>

document.writeln("Hello and welcome to JavaScript!")

</SCRIPT>

</HEAD>

<BODY>

<CENTER>
<H1>
Our First JavaScript Example
</H1>
</CENTER>

</BODY>

</HTML>
```

As we've seen in this example, you can use JavaScript to write directly to a Web page. In fact, we'll be doing a lot of that in this chapter and the next one as we get a good grounding in JavaScript's infrastructure.

However, in addition to simply putting lines of text into Web pages, JavaScript can work directly with HTML controls (text boxes, scrollbars, buttons, and so on are called *controls*). Before getting serious and dealing only with text output for a while (so we can see how programming constructs like conditionals and loops work in JavaScript), let's take a moment to get a quick overview of how JavaScript works with HTML controls in a Web page.

JavaScript Works With HTML Controls

Let's say that we have a Web page with an image and a button in it:

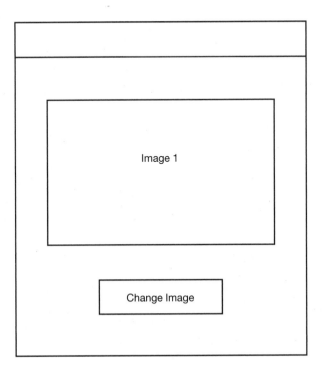

We can script our page to watch when the user clicks the button. When he or she does, we can load in a new image and display it:

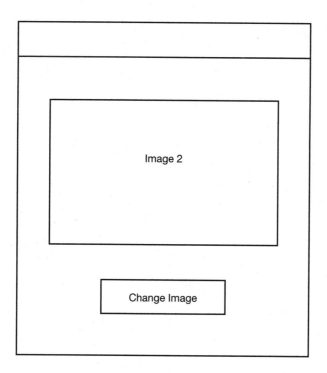

In this way, we'll get an sneak preview of how JavaScript can work with HTML controls. Don't pay too much attention to the details here—this is just a glimpse of what's coming after we have covered a lot of JavaScript techniques.

This new Web page will be called img.htm. First, we add the original image to our Web page, naming it "IMG1" with the <IMG> Name attribute:

```
<HTML>

<TITLE>IMG example</TITLE>

<BODY>

<CENTER>
<FORM NAME = form1>

<IMG NAME = "IMG1" SRC = "gif/image1.gif" WIDTH = 236
     HEIGHT = 118>
<BR>
<BR>
     .
     .
     .
```

Next, we add the button by using the HTML <INPUT> tag (we'll learn all about this tag in Chapters 3, "Forms: Text Boxes and Buttons," and 4, "Forms: Check Boxes and Radio Buttons"):

```
<HTML>

<TITLE>IMG example</TITLE>

<BODY>

<CENTER>
<FORM NAME = form1>

<IMG NAME = "IMG1" SRC = "gif/image1.gif" WIDTH = 236
     HEIGHT = 118>
<BR>
<BR>
<INPUT TYPE = BUTTON Value = "Change Image" onClick =
     "ChangeImage()">

</FORM>
</CENTER>
     .
     .
     .
```

Note that we've set the button's onClick attribute to ChangeImage(). This is the name of a JavaScript *function*, which (as we'll see in Chapter 2, " JavaScript Program Control and Objects"), is a way of naming a section of JavaScript code. In this case, we create the ChangeImage() function in a script like this:

```
<HTML>

<TITLE>IMG example</TITLE>

<BODY>

<CENTER>
<FORM NAME = form1>

<IMG NAME = "IMG1" SRC = "gif/image1.gif" WIDTH = 236
     HEIGHT = 118>
<BR>
<BR>
<INPUT TYPE = BUTTON Value = "Change Image" onClick =
     "ChangeImage()">
```

```
</FORM>
</CENTER>

</BODY>

<SCRIPT LANGUAGE = Javascript>
    function ChangeImage()
    {
        .
        .
        .
    }
</SCRIPT>

</HTML>
```

Finally, we load the new image into the Web page with one line of Java-Script (we're resetting the SRC attribute of the IMG1 image from image1.gif to image2.gif):

```
<HTML>

<TITLE>IMG example</TITLE>

<BODY>

<CENTER>
<FORM NAME = form1>

<IMG NAME = "IMG1" SRC = "gif/image1.gif" WIDTH = 236
    HEIGHT = 118>
<BR>
<BR>
<INPUT TYPE = BUTTON Value = "Change Image" onClick =
    "ChangeImage()">

</FORM>
</CENTER>

</BODY>

<SCRIPT LANGUAGE = Javascript>
    function ChangeImage()
    {
        document.form1.IMG1.src = "gif/image2.gif"
    }
</SCRIPT>

</HTML>
```

Open the Web page in a browser now, as shown in Figure 1-3. You can see the first image in our Web page.

Now click the Change Image button; when you do, the browser replaces the image with a second image, as shown in Figure 1-4. Our Web page is a success! Now we've gotten a preview of how JavaScript works with HTML controls, so we'll cover the details of this process later.

The listing for this Web page, img.htm, is shown in in Listing 1-2.

Figure 1-3
Our IMG Web page.

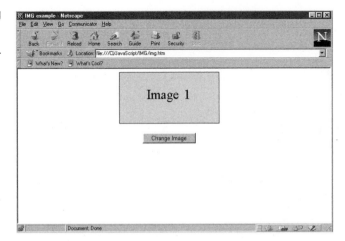

Figure 1-4
Clicking the button loads a new image.

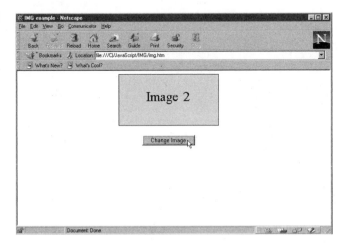

```
<HTML>

<TITLE>IMG example</TITLE>

<BODY>

<CENTER>
<FORM NAME = form1>

<IMG NAME = "IMG1" SRC = "gif/image1.gif" WIDTH = 236
     HEIGHT = 118>
<BR>
<BR>
<INPUT TYPE = BUTTON Value = "Change Image" onClick =
     "ChangeImage()">

</FORM>
</CENTER>

</BODY>

<SCRIPT LANGUAGE = Javascript>
    function ChangeImage()
    {
        document.form1.IMG1.src = "gif/image2.gif"
    }
</SCRIPT>

</HTML>
```

Now that we've gotten a look at what we can do in JavaScript, let's start building our JavaScript programming power by paying attention to the details. The first detail we'll handle is working with data in our programs.

Handling Data in JavaScript

The attraction of computers, from a programmer's point of view, is that they can manipulate data and then present that data to the user. In the remainder of this chapter, we'll explore how we can manipulate data with JavaScript as we build our understanding of the language's infastructure.

Using Variables

Let's say we wanted to keep track of today's date, the 31st, in a program. We can do that with *variables*, which are named storage locations in a program. In this case, we set up a variable named "date" in a JavaScript program:

```
<SCRIPT>

var date;

</SCRIPT>
```

Setting up a variable like this is called *declaring* the variable. Now we're free to put data into that variable; we use the = assignment operator to place the number 31 into the variable:

```
<SCRIPT>

var date;

date = 31;

</SCRIPT>
```

The date variable now holds the value 31, and we can retrieve (or change) that data simply by referring to the variable by name.

You work on variables by using *operators*; for example, we just saw that you can set the data in a variable with the = assignment operator. Here's how to use the addition operator (+) to add two numbers, 30 and 1, and place the result, 31, into the date variable:

```
<SCRIPT>

var date;

date = 30 + 1;

</SCRIPT>
```

The available JavaScript operators are shown in Table 1-3. These operators cover most standard mathematical operations.

Table 1-3 The JavaScript operators.

Computational	Logical	Bitwise	Assign.	Misc. Descr.	Sym.	Descr.	Sym.	Descr.	Sym.
Unary negation	−	Logical NOT	!	Bitwise NOT	~	Assignment	=	delete	delete
Increment	++	Less than	<	Bitwise Left Shift	<<	Compound Assignment	OP=	typeof	typeof
Decrement	−−	Greater than	>	Bitwise Right Shift	>>			void	void
Multiplication	*	Less than or equal to	<=	Unsigned Right Shift	>>>				
Division	/	Greater than or equal to	>=	Bitwise AND	&				
Modulo arithmetic	%	Equality	==	Bitwise XOR	^				
Addition	+	Inequality	!=	Bitwise OR						
Subtraction	-	Logical AND	&&						
		Logical OR	||						
		Conditional (trinary)	?:						
		Comma	,						
		Identity	===						
		Nonidentity	!==						

We can also add the data in variables with the + operator. The following code, for example, shows how we declare two variables, number30 and number1, place the numbers 30 and 1 in those variables, and add the values in those variables, placing the result in the date variable:

```
<SCRIPT>

var date;
var number30, number1;

number30 = 30;
number1 = 1;

date = number30 + number1;

</SCRIPT>
```

TIP: *Note that here we declare two variables, number30 and number1, on the same line. JavaScript allows you to declare multiple variables on the same line in this way—just separate them with a comma.*

You can place a value in a variable when you declare it, like this:

```
<SCRIPT>

var date = 31;          <-

</SCRIPT>
```

In fact, you don't even have to declare a variable to be able to use it in JavaScript. Here, for example, we "declare" the variable named date simply by using it—the first time you use an undeclared variable, JavaScript declares it for you:

```
<SCRIPT>

var number30, number1;

number30 = 30;
number1 = 1;

date = number30 + number1;

</SCRIPT>
```

There's a reason you might want to stick to a policy of declaring all variables before using them, however; it has to do with the variable's _-1scope_-0.

Variable Scope

The *scope* of a variable in a JavaScript program is made up of the parts of the program in which the variable is "visible"—that is, you can refer to and use it. If you declare a variable in a script but outside any code block (any code set off by the { and } characters, as we'll see later), then that variable is *global*, which means you can refer to it anywhere in the program.

In fact, you can declare a variable in a script in the head of a page and another variable in a script in the body of the page. If both are global variables, you can refer to both variables anywhere in your scripts, like this:

```
<HTML>

<HEAD>
<SCRIPT>

var date = 31;

</SCRIPT>
</HEAD>

<BODY>

var year = 1998;

date = 1;                   //date is global.

</BODY>

</HTML>
```

However, if you declare variables in a code block (that is, within curly braces), then that variable is *local* to that code block, which means you can refer to it only in that code block or in code blocks that the present code block encloses.

Keeping variables local is very useful for restricting what goes in the global variable "space"—if you have dozens of global variables, you might unintentionally end up with two that have the same name, and they'll conflict with one another. If you restrict your variables to local scope, you won't have to worry about them getting set inadvertently in other parts of the program.

TIP: *In fact, one of the big advantages of object-oriented programming (OOP) is that you can make data local in new ways, which is especially useful in longer programs to keep the global variable space cleaner.*

When you use a variable without first declaring it, JavaScript makes that variable a global variable, which might not be what you intended. For that reason, it's usually best to make it your practice to declare variables before using them—that way, if you want to make a variable local, you won't end up with a global variable by mistake.

Variable Types

JavaScript is call a *loosely typed* language, which means you can use the "var" keyword to declare variables of all kinds of data types. For example, you can declare a variable like this in a script:

```
<SCRIPT>

var date = 31;

</SCRIPT>
```

Now the date variable holds the value 31. However, you can switch the type of data in that variable in the program, if you like. Here, we place a text string—"Today is the 31st"—into the date variable:

```
<SCRIPT>

var date = 31;
date = "Today is the 31st";      <-

</SCRIPT>
```

You can't do this in a strongly typed language like Java. There, you have to declare variables' types (such as integer or floating point) when you declare the variable. In JavaScript, we can simply use "var" to declare all our variables, no matter what we're going to place in those variables.

The types of data you can place in a variable in JavaScript 1.2 are number, Boolean, string, function, and object. A number is just as we've seen—values like 31 or 3.14159. Boolean variables take values of true or false and are usually flags to keep track of conditions, such as the variable dataIsReady. Strings are enclosed in quotation marks in JavaScript, such as "Here is the text." We'll cover functions and objects in the next chapter.

JScript recognizes six types of data: numbers, strings, objects, Booleans, null, and undefined. The null data type simply holds a value of 0, and the undefined data type is a special one that indicates a variable has not yet been set to any particular value.

Variable Naming Conventions

JavaScript programmers usually follow the Java naming convention for variables. If you have a variable name that is one word, like *date*, the convention is to make it all lowercase letters. If you have a variable made of two or more words, like *TheData*, the convention is to capitalize only the initial letter of the second and subsequent words, like this: theData, theOtherData, and theDataThatGoesHere.

Now that we've gotten a look at variables in theory, let's put what we've seen to work. We'll do that in an example named "var.htm" next.

The var Example

Our first variable example is a very simple one—we'll just declare a variable, place a number in it, and display the number in a Web page after reading it back from the variable. This process will make what we've been talking about more concrete and show how we can display numeric values.

We'll display a header in our Web page to show what this example is all about:

A var statement Example.

We'll also declare a variable named "number," place a value of 4 in it, and then display that value this way:

```
The number is 4.



                        A var statement Example.



```

Let's create this Web page, var.htm, now. We start the usual way, with the <HTML> tag, a title in the head section, and a header showing what the page is all about:

```
<HTML>

<HEAD>

<TITLE>
A var Statement Example
</TITLE>

<HEAD>

<BODY>

<CENTER>
<H1>
A var Statement Example.
</H1>
</CENTER>

</BODY>

</HTML>
```

Next, we add the <SCRIPT> section, declare our number variable, and place a value of 4 in that variable:

```
<HTML>

<HEAD>
```

```
<TITLE>
A var Statement Example
</TITLE>

<SCRIPT LANGUAGE = JavaScript>

var number = 4

   .
   .

</SCRIPT>

<HEAD>

<BODY>

<CENTER>
<H1>
A var Statement Example.
</H1>
</CENTER>

</BODY>

</HTML>
```

Now we're ready to display the value in the variable in our Web page, but how do we do that?

Displaying the Value in a Variable

So far, we've used `document.writeln()` to display text in JavaScript, but the value in our variable is a number. How do we display that?

It turns out that we can display the value in a variable with `document.writeln()` simply by referring to it by name—in code, that looks like this:

```
<HTML>

<HEAD>

<TITLE>
A var Statement Example
</TITLE>

<SCRIPT LANGUAGE = JavaScript>
var number = 4

document.writeln("The number is " +  number + ".")
```

```
</SCRIPT>

<HEAD>

<BODY>

<CENTER>
<H1>
A var Statement Example.
</H1>
</CENTER>

</BODY>

</HTML>
```

TIP: *Note that strings, like other JavaScript data types, can use the + operator. For example, you can create the text "Happy New Year!" this way: var HNY = "Happy " + "New " + "Year!";.*

Open the var.htm example now, as shown in Figure 1-5. As you can see, we've placed data into a variable and read that data again, displaying it in our Web page. Now we're using variables in JavaScript.

Listing 1-3 shows the code for this Web page.

Our var example is fine as far as it goes, but it's not very useful. It's important to be able to not only store and display data in a program, but also work with that data, so we'll start working with our data next.

Figure 1-5
The var example uses variables.

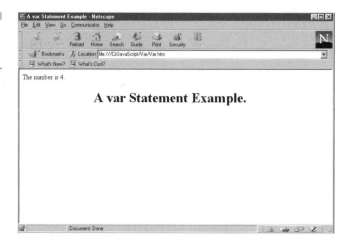

Listing 1-3
Var.htm.

```
<HTML>

<HEAD>

<TITLE>
A var Statement Example
</TITLE>

<SCRIPT LANGUAGE = JavaScript>
var number = 4

document.writeln("The number is " +  number + ".")


</SCRIPT>

<HEAD>

<BODY>

<CENTER>
<H1>
A var Statement Example.
</H1>
</CENTER>

</BODY>

</HTML>
```

Controlling Your Program: the if Statement

The first step in working with our data will be to examine that data and take action based on its value. We'll examine the value of our data first with the JavaScript if statement.

The if statement lets you test a certain condition like this:

```
if(conditional){
     .
     .
     .
     code block
     .
     .
     .
}
```

Here, *conditional* is a JavaScript statement or Boolean variable that can be true or false. Such statements usually use the logical operators that were shown in Table 1-3. For example, if you want to check whether the value in the variable named "number" is equal to 4, you can test it by using the equality logical operator: if(number == 4).

TIP: *Notice that to test whether the number variable was equal to 4, we used the equality operator, if(number == 4), not the assignment operator, if(number = 4). The latter expression is a mistake, although it's a common one. Make sure to use == and not = when you want to test for equality.*

If the conditional expression is true, then the code in the code block that follows the if statement is executed; otherwise, it's not. This gives us control over the flow of our program, so we can make decisions based on our data. Let's take a look at an example using the if statement now.

The if Example

We'll start our if example Web page with a header indicating which example it is. Then we will set up our variable named "number" as we did in the previous example, and place a value of 4 in it. We'll use a series of if statements to test the value in the number variable, like this:

```
if(number == 1){
    document.writeln("The number is 1.")
}
if(number == 2){
    document.writeln("The number is 2.")
}
if(number == 3){
    document.writeln("The number is 3.")
}
if(number == 4){
    document.writeln("The number is 4.")
}
```

Only one of these if statements will execute its code block, and we'll see the result in our Web page:

```
The number is 4.


                    An if statement Example.




```

Let's put this Web page together now. We start with the page itself and the header indicating which example it is:

```
<HTML>

<HEAD>

<TITLE>
An if Statement Example
</TITLE>

<HEAD>

<BODY>

<CENTER>
<H1>
An if Statement Example.
</H1>
</BODY>
</CENTER>

</HTML>
```

Next, we add the <SCRIPT> section where we declare our variable and check the value in that variable with a series of if statements:

```
<HTML>

<HEAD>

<TITLE>
An if Statement Example
</TITLE>

<SCRIPT LANGUAGE = JavaScript>
var number = 4
```

```
if(number == 1){
    document.writeln("The number is 1.")
}
if(number == 2){
    document.writeln("The number is 2.")
}
if(number == 3){
    document.writeln("The number is 3.")
}
if(number == 4){
    document.writeln("The number is 4.")
}
if(number == 5){
    document.writeln("The number is 5.")
}
if(number == 6){
    document.writeln("The number is 6.")
}
if(number == 7){
    document.writeln("The number is 7.")
}

</SCRIPT>

<HEAD>

<BODY>

<CENTER>
<H1>
An if Statement Example.
</H1>
</BODY>
</CENTER>

</HTML>
```

Only one of the preceding if statements will execute its code block—the one that tests `if number == 4`.

We've used a lot of if statements here just to check whether the value in the number variable is equal to 4. However, we can use ranges of possible values to cut this process down to size—for example, we can check whether the value in number is less than 3 or greater than or equal to 3 by using the "less than" logical operator:

```
<HTML>

<HEAD>

<TITLE>
```

```
An if Statement Example
</TITLE>

<PRE>
<SCRIPT LANGUAGE = JavaScript>
var number = 4

if(number == 1){
    document.writeln("The number is 1.")
}
if(number == 2){
    document.writeln("The number is 2.")
}
if(number == 3){
    document.writeln("The number is 3.")
}
if(number == 4){
    document.writeln("The number is 4.")
}
if(number == 5){
    document.writeln("The number is 5.")
}
if(number == 6){
    document.writeln("The number is 6.")
}
if(number == 7){
    document.writeln("The number is 7.")
}


if(number < 3){
    document.writeln("The number is less than 3.")

</SCRIPT>
</PRE>

<HEAD>

<BODY>

<CENTER>
<H1>
An if Statement Example.
</H1>
</BODY>
</CENTER>

</HTML>
```

The conditional expression `number < 3` is true if the value in number is less than 3. Other common logical operators include the greater than operator (`number > 3`), the less than or equal to operator (`number <= 3`), and the greater than or equal to operator (`number >= 3`).

TIP: *Note that now that our script is printing multiple lines in the Web page, we use <PRE> tags to make sure the Web browser doesn't automatically wrap those lines together.*

So far, then, we've checked whether the value in number is less than 3, but what if it's greater than 3? As it stands, our program won't report that.

Using an else Statement

We haven't used the second part of the if statement yet, but we will now. If the conditional in the if statement isn't true, the if statement's code block isn't executed. However, we can follow the if statement with an else statement, and that statement's code block is executed if the conditional is false. For example, if the number is not less than 3, we can still execute the code in an else statement as shown in the following code, where we indicate that the value is greater than or equal to 3:

```
<HTML>

<HEAD>

<TITLE>
An if Statement Example
</TITLE>

<PRE>
<SCRIPT LANGUAGE = JavaScript>
var number = 4

if(number == 1){
    document.writeln("The number is 1.")
        .

        .

        .
if(number < 3){
    document.writeln("The number is less than 3.")
}else{
    document.writeln("The number is greater than or equal
      to 3.")
}

</SCRIPT>
</PRE>

<HEAD>
```

```
<BODY>

<CENTER>
<H1>
An if Statement Example.
</H1>
</BODY>
</CENTER>

</HTML>
```

Now we'll report on the number this way in our Web page:

The number is 4.
The number is equal to or greater than 3.

An if statement Example.

That's the general way to use an if statement—with an if statement and an (optional) else statement:

```
if(conditional){
    .
    .
    .
code block
    .
    .
    .

}
else{
    .
    .
    .
code block
    .
    .
    .

}
```

Open this Web page now, as shown in Figure 1-6. As you can see, we've checked the value in our variable two ways with if statements.

The code for this Web page, if.htm, is shown in Listing 1-4.

Figure 1-6
The if Web page uses
the if statement.

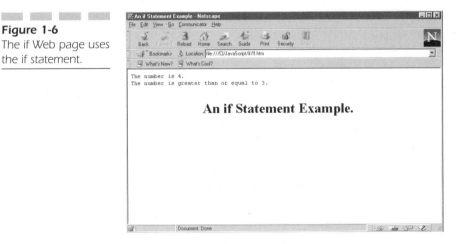

Besides the if statement, there's another conditional statement we'll take a look at now: the switch statement.

Listing 1-4
If.htm.

```
<HTML>

<HEAD>

<TITLE>
An if Statement Example
</TITLE>

<PRE>
<SCRIPT LANGUAGE = JavaScript>
var number = 4

if(number == 1){
    document.writeln("The number is 1.")
}
if(number == 2){
    document.writeln("The number is 2.")
}
if(number == 3){
    document.writeln("The number is 3.")
}
if(number == 4){
    document.writeln("The number is 4.")
}
if(number == 5){
    document.writeln("The number is 5.")
}
if(number == 6){
    document.writeln("The number is 6.")
```

```
}
if(number == 7){
    document.writeln("The number is 7.")
}


if(number < 3){
    document.writeln("The number is less than 3.")
}else{
    document.writeln("The number is greater than or equal
      to 3.")
}

</SCRIPT>
</PRE>

<HEAD>

<BODY>

<CENTER>
<H1>
An if Statement Example.
</H1>
</BODY>
</CENTER>

</HTML>
```

Controlling Your Program: The switch Statement

JavaScript switch statements work much like if statements because you use them to determine what statements are executed after performing an equality test. Here's what a generic switch statement looks like:

```
switch(test){

    case value1:
            .

            .

            .
        statements
            .

            .

            .
    break;
```

```
case value1:
            .

            .

            .
     statements
            .

            .

            .
     break;
case value1:
            .

            .

            .
     statements
            .

            .

            .
     break;
default:
            .

            .

            .
     statements
            .

            .

            .
     break;


}
```

You place a variable or expression in the switch statement—we used the variable named "test"—and if the value is equal to the value in one of the case statements (value1, value2, and so on in the preceding example), the statements following that case statement are executed, up to the break statement. If no case matches the value in the variable we're looking at, the (optional) default statement is executed.

TIP: *Note that if you omit the break statement at the end of a switch case, execution simply keeps going with the code in the next case statement.*

Let's create a switch statement example now. We'll place a header in our Web page as usual. Then we'll examine our number variable using a switch statement, displaying the value in the number variable this way:

```
The number is 4.



           A switch Statement Example.
```

Let's write this example, switch.htm, now. We start by declaring our variable, number, and setting up the switch statement:

```
<HTML>

<HEAD>

<TITLE>
A switch Statement Example
</TITLE>

<SCRIPT LANGUAGE = JavaScript>

var number = 4

switch(number){
        .
        .
        .
```

First, we'll check whether the number is 1; if so, we display that fact:

```
<HTML>

<HEAD>

<TITLE>
A switch Statement Example
</TITLE>

<SCRIPT LANGUAGE = JavaScript>

var number = 4

switch(number){
    case 1:
        document.writeln("The number is 1.")
        break
```

.
.
.

Then we add the other case statements this way:

```
<HTML>

<HEAD>

<TITLE>
A switch Statement Example
</TITLE>

<SCRIPT LANGUAGE = JavaScript>

var number = 4

switch(number){
    case 1:
        document.writeln("The number is 1.")
        break
    case 2:
        document.writeln("The number is 2.")
        break
    case 3:
        document.writeln("The number is 3.")
        break
    case 4:
        document.writeln("The number is 4.")
        break
    case 5:
        document.writeln("The number is 5.")
        break
    case 6:
        document.writeln("The number is 6.")
        break
    case 7:
        document.writeln("The number is 7.")
        break
    default:
        document.writeln("The number is not in the range
     1-7.")
        break
}

</SCRIPT>

<HEAD>

<BODY>

<CENTER>
```

```
<H1>
A switch Statement Example.
</H1>
</CENTER>

</BODY>

</HTML>
```

That's it—now open this page, as shown in Figure 1-7. As you can see, the only case statement that was executed was the one comparing the number variable to 4. Our switch statement example is a success!

The code for this page, switch.htm, is shown in Listing 1-5.

Figure 1-7
The switch statement Web page.

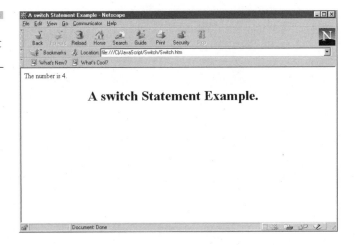

Listing 1-5
Switch.htm.

```
<HTML>

<HEAD>

<TITLE>
A switch Statement Example
</TITLE>

<SCRIPT LANGUAGE = JavaScript>
var number = 4

switch(number){
    case 1:
        document.writeln("The number is 1.")
        break
    case 2:
```

continues

Listing 1-5.
continued

```
          document.writeln("The number is 2.")
          break
     case 3:
          document.writeln("The number is 3.")
          break
     case 4:
          document.writeln("The number is 4.")
          break
     case 5:
          document.writeln("The number is 5.")
          break
     case 6:
          document.writeln("The number is 6.")
          break
     case 7:
          document.writeln("The number is 7.")
          break
     default:
          document.writeln("The number is not in the range
     1-7.")
          break
}

</SCRIPT>

<HEAD>

<BODY>

<CENTER>
<H1>
A switch Statement Example.
</H1>
</CENTER>

</BODY>

</HTML>
```

CONCLUSION

That's it for our first chapter. We've gotten a start in JavaScript by exe-cuting a single line of JavaScript, creating our first JavaScript example, getting a preview of how JavaScript works with HTML elements, seeing how to store our data in variables, and learning how to use the if and switch statements to work with our data.

We'll continue our JavaScript exploration in the next chapter, when we start working with more powerful JavaScript: loops, functions, objects, and more. Let's turn to that chapter now.

2

JavaScript Program Control and Objects

In this chapter, we'll dig deep into JavaScript's infrastructure, seeing how to control the operation of our programs in detail. There's a great deal to cover in this chapter: learning about new statements like the for, while, and do-while statements; using and creating JavaScript functions; passing arguments to functions; reading values returned from functions; working with JavaScript objects; creating custom objects; and even working with Internet Explorer scriptlets, which let scripts act like Web page objects.

There's a lot of information in this chapter, so we'll start at once by taking a look at a popular JavaScript statement: the for statement. It's one of the JavaScript statements that let you handle *loops*. Loop statements let you handle large amounts of data by working on each piece of data, item by item, as we'll see.

Program Control: The for Statement

The first loop statement we'll look at is the for statement, which generally looks like this:

```
for (initialization; test; increment)
    statement
```

Here, *initialization* is an initialization statement that usually starts a loop *index* of some sort; *test* is a conditional statement involving the loop index that, while true, permits the loop to continue; and *increment* is a JavaScript statement executed after each loop (the increment statement is usually used to increment—or decrement—the loop index).

Although only one statement is listed in the preceding code example for the body of the loop, such a statement can be a compound statement made up of many lines of JavaScript. A compound statement is a code block surrounded by curly braces ({ and }).

Let's see an example of a for loop to make this new programming construction clear. We'll create a new Web page called "for.htm." In the scripting section of this Web page, we'll set up a variable named "number" and set it equal to 4. Then we'll loop repeatedly until the loop index—a variable we'll increment each time through the loop—is equal to the value in the number variable, at which point we'll display that result.

We'll start the for example by setting up our number variable and setting it equal to 4:

```
<HTML>

<HEAD>

<TITLE>
A for Statement Example
</TITLE>

<SCRIPT LANGUAGE = JavaScript>

var number = 4
        .
        .
        .
```

NOTE: *As we develop our JavaScript code, it's worth repeating our policy on semicolons. Although the formal JavaScript specification originally required a semicolon at the end of each statment, no popular Web browser now requires those semicolons. As a result, it's become as acceptable not to use semicolons as to use them. In fact, these terminating semicolons often give beginning programmers some trouble, and for that reason, we will not require them in this book. (If, however, you have no trouble remembering to use a semicolon at the end of each statement and prefer to do so, by all means use them in your code.)*

Next, we set up our for loop. We'll declare a loop index variable named `loop_index`. Each time we loop, we'll increment `loop_index` by 1 and compare it to the value in number. We'll loop while the `loop_index` is less than or equal to 7. Here's how we set up our for loop, declare the `loop_index` variable, loop while `loop_index` is less than or equal to 7, and increment `loop_index` at the end of each loop by using the JavaScript increment operator (++):

```
<HTML>

<HEAD>

<TITLE>
A for Statement Example
</TITLE>

<SCRIPT LANGUAGE = JavaScript>

var number = 4

for(var loop_index = 0; loop_index <= 7; loop_index++){
    .
    .
    .
}
```

NOTE: *We declared the `loop_index` variable in the for statement itself to make `loop_index` local to the body of the for loop, but you can declare `loop_index` outside the loop if you like. In fact, because JavaScript automatically declares variables, you don't need to declare `loop_index` at all; you can simply use it (but that would make `loop_index` a global, not local, variable).*

TIP: *The increment operator (++) and the decrement operator (–) are popular ones. These operators can work as prefix or postfix operators. A prefix operator looks like this: x = ++y. Here, the value in y is incremented and then assigned to x. On the other hand, a postfix operator, such as x = y++, is applied only after the rest of the expression is evaluated. In this case, x is assigned the original value in y, and then y is incremented.*

We can place an if statement in the loop's body this way, where we check to see whether the value in the number variable is equal to the `loop_index`, and if so, we display that fact in the Web page:

```
<HTML>

<HEAD>

<TITLE>
A for Statement Example
</TITLE>

<SCRIPT LANGUAGE = JavaScript>

var number = 4

for(var loop_index = 0; loop_index <= 7; loop_index++){
    if(number == loop_index){
        document.writeln("The number is " +  loop_index +
    ".")
    }
}

</SCRIPT>

<HEAD>

<BODY>

<CENTER>
<H1>
A for Statement Example.
</H1>
</CENTER>

</BODY>

</HTML>
```

Now open this page, as shown in Figure 2-1. As you can see, we've looped over the possible values of the number variable and displayed the value when the loop index is equal to it. Our for loop example is a success!

The code for this Web page, `for.htm`, is shown in Listing 2-1.

Figure 2-1
Our for statement
example uses a
for loop.

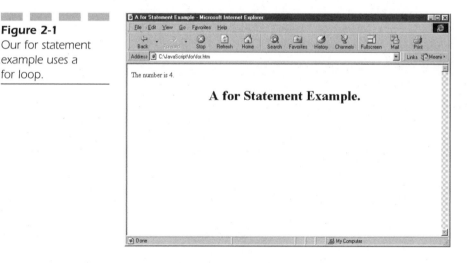

Listing 2-1
For.htm.

```
<HTML>

<HEAD>

<TITLE>
A for Statement Example
</TITLE>

<SCRIPT LANGUAGE = JavaScript>
var number = 4

for(var loop_index = 0; loop_index <= 7; loop_index++){
    if(number == loop_index){
        document.writeln("The number is " + loop_index +
    ".")
    }
}

</SCRIPT>

<HEAD>

<BODY>

<CENTER>
<H1>
A for Statement Example.
</H1>
</CENTER>

</BODY>

</HTML>
```

There are even more powerful ways of controlling loops—we can *break* a loop if we need to.

Using Breaks

You can use the break statement to end a loop, if necessary (execution then continues with the line of code following the loop). For example, we can test a `loop_index` repeatedly, breaking the loop if that index gets too large:

```
for (var loop_index = 0; loop_index < 1000000; loop_
    index++){
    if(loop_index > 10000){
        break
    }
}
```

NOTE: *The break statement breaks only the current loop; if the current loop is nested inside another loop, that outer loop still continues.*

Using Labeled Breaks

In JavaScript 1.2, you can use *labeled* breaks, which let you label the loop you want to break. For example, if we have a loop within a loop, we can break both loops if we label the outer loop (here, we've used the label "OuterLoop"):

```
OuterLoop:
for (var loop_index1 = 0; loop_index1 < 1000000; loop_
    index1++){
    for (var loop_index2 = 0; loop_index2 < 1000000;
    loop_index2++){
        if(loop_index > 10000){
            break OuterLoop
        }
    }
}
```

We've gotten an introduction to loops, particularly the for loop. We'll take a look at another type of JavaScript loop next—the while loop.

Program Control: The while Statement

We've seen that loops like the for loop use a test expression and keep looping while that expression is true. The while statement works in much the same way; this loop keeps executing its statement (which might hold many lines of JavaScript) while a particular expression is true:

```
while (expression)
    statement
```

Let's take a look at a while loop example; we can call this new Web page `while.htm`. We'll keep looping and incrementing a loop index until that loop index equals the value in our number variable. Because the while loop will keep executing while the loop index doesn't equal the value in number, we can report on the comparison each time through the loop.

The while loop will terminate when the loop index equals the value in number, so we'll add code after the while loop to display the value in the loop index, which now equals the value of the number we've been looking at:

```
The number is not 0.
The number is not 1.
The number is not 2.
The number is not 3.
However, the number is 4.




                    A While Statement Example.
```

Let's put this to work. We start by declaring our number variable and our loop index:

```
<HTML>

<HEAD>

<TITLE>
A while Statement Example
</TITLE>

<PRE>
<SCRIPT LANGUAGE = JavaScript>

var number = 4
var loop_index = 0
        .
        .
        .
```

NOTE: *The JavaScript while loop doesn't require a loop index at all, although we use one in this example. You can test any expression that evaluates to true or false in a while loop.*

Now we set up the while loop. In this loop, we want to keep looping while the loop index is not equal to the value in the variable number, so we use the *1inequality operator*, !=, which evaluates to true as long as the two elements it's comparing are not equal:

```
<HTML>

<HEAD>

<TITLE>
A while Statement Example
</TITLE>

<PRE>
<SCRIPT LANGUAGE = JavaScript>

var number = 4
var loop_index = 0

while(loop_index != number){
    .
    .
    .
}
```

TIP: *You can use the logical Not operator (!) to flip the logical value of an expression. For example, if dataIsReady is a Boolean variable whose value is true (set this way: var dataIsReady = true), then this expression is false:*

```
!dataIsReady
```

Each time through the loop, we'll report that the loop index is not equal to the number variable. Then we increment the loop index for the next time through the while loop:

```
<HTML>

<HEAD>

<TITLE>
A while Statement Example
</TITLE>

<PRE>
<SCRIPT LANGUAGE = JavaScript>

var number = 4
var loop_index = 0

while(loop_index != number){
        document.writeln("The number is not " +  loop_
    index + ".")
        loop_index++
}
```

At the conclusion of the while loop, `loop_index` is equal to the value in number, so we display that value this way:

```
<HTML>

<HEAD>

<TITLE>
A while Statement Example
</TITLE>

<PRE>
<SCRIPT LANGUAGE = JavaScript>

var number = 4
var loop_index = 0

while(loop_index != number){
        document.writeln("The number is not " +  loop_
    index + ".")
        loop_index++
}
```

```
document.writeln("However, the number <I>is</I> " +
     loop_index + ".")

</SCRIPT>

</PRE>
<HEAD>

<BODY>

<CENTER>
<H1>
A while Statement Example.
</H1>
</CENTER>

</BODY>

</HTML>
```

TIP: *We can display our text in italics by using the <I> tags when we print out that text onto the Web page. In the same way, you can print any other HTML tag by using* `document.writeln()`.

That's it—now open the Web page. As shown in Figure 2-2, the while loop executes until the loop index is incremented to the value in the number variable, at which point the while loop stops and we report that value. Our while statement example is working!

Listing 2-2 shows the code for this page, `while.htm`.

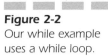

Figure 2-2
Our while example uses a while loop.

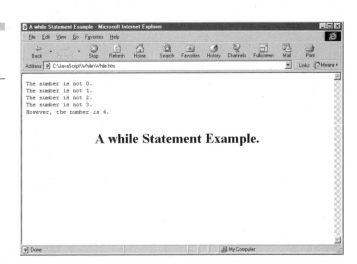

Listing 2-2
`While.htm.`

```
<HTML>

<HEAD>

<TITLE>
A while Statement Example
</TITLE>

<PRE>
<SCRIPT LANGUAGE = JavaScript>
var number = 4
var loop_index = 0

while(loop_index != number){
        document.writeln("The number is not " +  loop_
    index + ".")
        loop_index++
}

document.writeln("However, the number <I>is</I> " +
    loop_index + ".")

</SCRIPT>

</PRE>
<HEAD>

<BODY>

<CENTER>
<H1>
A while Statement Example.
</H1>
</CENTER>

</BODY>

</HTML>
```

There's another type of while statement—the *do-while* statement, which we'll explain next.

Program Control: The do-while Statement

The do-while statement is much like the while statement, but there's one crucial difference—the test expression is at the end of the loop, not at the beginning, like this:

```
do
    statement
while (expression);
```

The structure of the do-while loop—with the test expression at the end —ensures that (unlike the while loop) the loop's statement is executed at least once. This method is useful if the expression you're going to test depends on some code executed in the body of the loop (which wouldn't be executed before the expression test was made in a while loop).

In fact, we can perform the same set of operations as we did with the while loop, presenting the same result.

In this case, we just need to replace the while loop from the previous example with a do-while loop, like this:

```
<HTML>

<HEAD>

<TITLE>
A do-while Statement Example
</TITLE>

<PRE>
<SCRIPT LANGUAGE = JavaScript>
var number = 4
var loop_index = 0

do{
        document.writeln("The number is not " +  loop_
    index + ".")
        loop_index++
}while(loop_index != number)

document.writeln("However, the number <I>is</I> " +
    loop_index + ".")

</SCRIPT>

</PRE>
<HEAD>

<BODY>

<CENTER>
<H1>
A do-while Statement Example.
</H1>
</CENTER>
```

```
</BODY>

</HTML>
```

That's all there is to it—now open the page, as shown in Figure 2-3. You can see the same result as in the previous example—the program keeps looping until the loop index is equal to the value in the number variable.

The code for this page, do-while.htm, is shown in Listing 2-3.

Figure 2-3
Our do-while example uses a do-while loop.

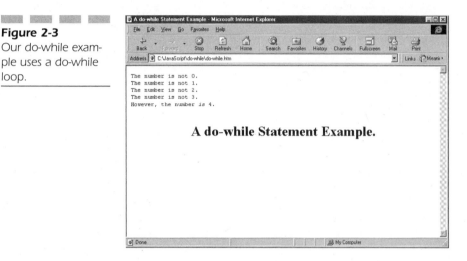

Listing 2-3
Do-while.htm.

```
<HTML>

<HEAD>

<TITLE>
A do-while Statement Example
</TITLE>

<PRE>
<SCRIPT LANGUAGE = JavaScript>
var number = 4
var loop_index = 0

do{
        document.writeln("The number is not " +  loop_
    index + ".")
        loop_index++
}while(loop_index != number)
```

continues

Listing 2-3
Continued.

```
document.writeln("However, the number <I>is</I> " +
    loop_index + ".")

</SCRIPT>

</PRE>
<HEAD>

<BODY>

<CENTER>
<H1>
A do-while Statement Example.
</H1>
</CENTER>

</BODY>

</HTML>
```

That completes our look at loops for the moment. Now that we've gained some JavaScript power, we're ready to work with the next step up in JavaScript programming: functions.

All About JavaScript Functions

JavaScript functions are all about compartmentalizing your code into easy-to-handle chunks. For example, you might have 50 lines of Java-Script designed to capitalize text strings. If you need to use this code a dozen times in a program, you could insert it each time, but that would make your program 600 lines longer.

A far better idea is to place the 50 lines of code into a *function* that you can then call—calling a function means the code in that function is executed. By using a function, you add only the code needed to create the function—the 50 lines of code we mentioned, for example—and the dozen one-line calls to the function. We'll see how this works in a moment.

Here's the general form of a function in JavaScript (the square braces, [and], indicate an optional value):

```
function functionName([argument1 [, argument2 [, ...
    argumentn]]])
{
```

```
        statements
}
```

You declare a function by using a function statement, indicating the function's name and the arguments that function can take. *Arguments* are variables or other items (such as objects, which are coming up later in this chapter) that the function can operate on. For example, if we had a function named `adder()` that adds two values, we can pass the values to add to `adder()` this way:

```
adder(addMe1, addMe2)
```

Functions can also return values. For example, the `adder()` function should return the sum of the two arguments passed to it, so we can add two values like this:

```
var addMe1, addMe2, sum

addMe1 = 1
addMe2 = 3

sum = adder(addMe1, addMe2)
```

The preceding code is functionally the same as this:

```
var addMe1, addMe2, sum

addMe1 = 1
addMe2 = 3

sum = addMe1 + addMe2
```

NOTE: *The code in functions isn't executed until the function is called, which means that, unlike the code we've developed so far, the code in the functions we write isn't executed as soon as the page is loaded into the Web browser. There are, however, special functions you can set up to run as soon as the page is loaded, as we'll see.*

Let's put together an example, `function.htm`, using functions to make it clearer. In this case, we'll create a function that returns a particular value: 4. Every time we call this function, it will return 4. We can report the value we get when we call this function in the Web page, as shown here:

```
┌──────────────────────────────────────────────┐
│                                              │
├──────────────────────────────────────────────┤
│  The number is 4.                            │
│                                              │
│                                              │
│                                              │
│                A function Example.           │
│                                              │
│                                              │
│                                              │
│                                              │
│                                              │
│                                              │
└──────────────────────────────────────────────┘
```

Let's put this to work now in `function.htm`. Here, we'll set up a function named `getNumber()` that returns a value of 4, so we call that function when we display our message in the Web page:

```
<HTML>

<HEAD>

<TITLE>
A function Example
</TITLE>

<SCRIPT LANGUAGE = JavaScript>

    document.writeln("The number is " +  getNumber() +
    ".")
        .
        .
        .
```

Now we'll set up the `getNumber()` function:

```
<HTML>

<HEAD>

<TITLE>
A function Example
</TITLE>

<SCRIPT LANGUAGE = JavaScript>
```

```
        document.writeln("The number is " +  getNumber() +
          ".")


function getNumber()
{
    .
    .
    .
}
</SCRIPT>
```

The code in this function is executed when we call the function; in this case, we simply want to return a value of 4. You return values from a function with the `return()` statement, as follows:

```
<HTML>

<HEAD>

<TITLE>
A function Example
</TITLE>

<SCRIPT LANGUAGE = JavaScript>

        document.writeln("The number is " +  getNumber() +
          ".")


function getNumber()
{
    return(4)
}
</SCRIPT>

<HEAD>

<BODY>

<CENTER>
<H1>
A function Example.
</H1>
</CENTER>

</BODY>

</HTML>
```

Now open `function.htm`, as shown in Figure 2-4. As you can see, the `getNumber()` function did indeed return a value of 4.

Listing 2-4 shows the code for this page, `function.htm`.

Figure 2-4
The function exam-
ple calls a function.

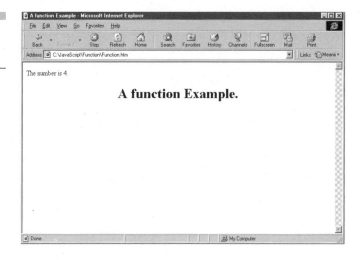

Listing 2-4
Function.htm.

```html
<HTML>

<HEAD>

<TITLE>
A function Example
</TITLE>

<SCRIPT LANGUAGE = JavaScript>

    document.writeln("The number is " +  getNumber() +
    ".")


function getNumber()
{
   return(4)
}
</SCRIPT>

<HEAD>

<BODY>

<CENTER>
<H1>
A function Example.
</H1>
</CENTER>

</BODY>

</HTML>
```

Our first function example was a simple one—`getNumber()` took no arguments and simply returned a value of 4. Let's see how to handle arguments passed to functions next.

Handling Arguments in Functions

In this next example, we'll pass two arguments to the `getNumber()` function and place code in that function to add the two arguments and return the sum. We can call this new example `args.htm`.

Visually, the result will be the same as before, but in this case the `getNumber()` function takes two arguments and adds them, returning a sum that we can display.

In this Web page, `args.htm`, we call `getNumber()` and pass two values (1 and 3) to that function:

```
<HTML>

<HEAD>

<TITLE>
A function Argument Example
</TITLE>

<SCRIPT LANGUAGE = JavaScript>

    document.writeln("The number is " +  getNumber(1, 3) +
    ".")
        .
        .
        .
```

In the `getNumber()` function, we can read the values passed to us and add them. Let's take a look at that process now.

Handling Arguments in Functions

Handling arguments in a function is easy. You just give a name to the arguments passed to the function in the function declaration—here, we'll call those arguments a and b:

```
<HTML>

<HEAD>

<TITLE>
```

```
A function Argument Example
</TITLE>

<SCRIPT LANGUAGE = JavaScript>

    document.writeln("The number is " +  getNumber(1, 3) +
    ".")


function getNumber(a, b)
{
    .

    .

    .

}
</SCRIPT>
```

Now we're free to refer to those arguments as a and b in the body of the function. In particular, we want to add the values in a and b and return their sum, which we do like this:

```
<HTML>

<HEAD>

<TITLE>
A function Argument Example
</TITLE>

<SCRIPT LANGUAGE = JavaScript>

    document.writeln("The number is " +  getNumber(1, 3) +
    ".")


function getNumber(a, b)
{
    return(a + b)
}
</SCRIPT>

<HEAD>

<BODY>
<H1>
A function Argument Example.
</H1>
</BODY>

</HTML>
```

Open args.htm now, as shown in Figure 2-5. The getNumber() function got the values it's supposed to work with—1 and 3—and added those values, displaying the result in the Web page. Now we're able to pass arguments to and return values from JavaScript functions.

The code for this page, **Args.htm**, is shown in Listing 2-5.

Figure 2-5
This Web page includes a function that adds the arguments passed to it.

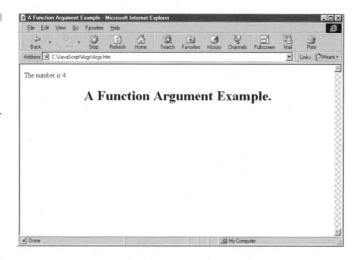

Listing 2-5
Args.htm.

```
<HTML>

<HEAD>

<TITLE>
A function Argument Example
</TITLE>

<SCRIPT LANGUAGE = JavaScript>

    document.writeln("The number is " +  getNumber(1, 3) +
    ".")


function getNumber(a, b)
{
    return(a + b)
}
</SCRIPT>

<HEAD>

<BODY>
<H1>
A function Argument Example.
</H1>
</BODY>

</HTML>
```

TIP: *In JavaScript, you can actually call a function with fewer arguments than you've declared the function with. That's OK as long as you don't try to read values from arguments that weren't passed to you (they'll return a value of "undefined," but you can use the new typeOf operator to check whether you're dealing with such a value).*

TIP: *You can also pass more arguments to a function than the function is set up to take. To read such arguments, you can use the arguments array, which is available in every function (we'll see how arrays work later in this chapter). The first argument passed to the function is the first entry in the arguments array, and you refer to it as* `functionName.arguments[0]`, *the second argument as* `functionName.arguments[1]`, *and so on (using square brackets is how you use arrays, as we'll see soon).*

Now that we've worked our way though handling functions in JavaScript, we're ready to step up to the next level: objects, which are central to JavaScript programming.

Object-Based Programming in JavaScript

You might notice that the heading for this section is "Object-Based Programming in JavaScript," not "Object-Oriented Programming in JavaScript." JavaScript doesn't support true *object-oriented programming* (OOP) of the Java and C++ kind. However, JavaScript does use and rely on objects, so JavaScript is usually referred to as object-based, not object-oriented.

So what's an object? We'll look into that now.

What's an Object?

The idea of objects in programming really gained popularity with C++. The C language had been in wide use for a long time and had reached several significant limitations when it came to working with larger programs.

In small programs, you can easily manage a few functions and variables in the global space. However, when the number of functions and variables grows in larger programs with thousands of lines, the global space can become unwieldy. Imagine trying to work with hundreds of data items over hundreds of pages of code and trying to keep them all in mind as you program.

As programs got bigger and bigger, it became important to be able to divide them up conceptually into objects rather than variables and functions. An *object* is a grouping of both variables and functions constructed in such a way that all the functions and data internal to that object stay internal and are not "visible" outside that object.

Creating self-contained objects was a great advance in programming because it allows you to divide a program naturally into parts that act more autonomously, which is the way we think of parts of a program anyway (for example, this part handles the screen display, this part handles the data processing, and so on).

You can see how useful this approach is if you consider a machine like a refrigerator. You don't want to be bothered by the process of temperature regulation and pump activation yourself—you want the refrigerator to handle all that. Because the refrigerator does handle all data and functions internally, you can think of it handily as one useful object: a refrigerator, instead of a collection of hundreds of separate items. This conceptualization technique made handling larger programs much easier.

For example, imagine that part of a program handled display on the screen. That process could be very complex, involving setting screen registers, checking scan modes, and so on, but there's no reason the rest of the program needs to know about all that. Instead, you could wrap all those functions and data together—a process known as *encapsulation*—into a single object named, say, "display."

This object would have both internal data and functions and external data and functions. The internal data and functions—referred to as *private*—handle the details of working with the screen, and the externally available data and functions—referred to as *public*—let the rest of the program send data to the screen easily. For example, one such public function could be called `writeln()`, which writes a line of text on the screen. To write such a line of text, then, you could use the display object like this:

```
display.writeln("Hello from JavaScript!")
```

That's the way you use an object's public functions, with the dot (.) operator. In fact, we've already seen an object that operates just like that: the document object. All along we've been displaying lines of text on the screen—`document.writeln("Hello from JavaScript!")`—using the JavaScript document object. This object has many useful built-in variables—called *properties*—and built-in functions—called *methods*—that we can use. One such method is `writeln()`, and that's the method we've been using to display text.

What Are Object Methods?

It takes a little while to get used to object terminology. The built-in functions of an object are called *methods*; the internal methods of an object (inaccessible from outside the object) are called *private methods* (only the internal parts of the object use the private methods and variables in the object). The externally available methods of an object are called its *public methods*.

As mentioned, we've been using the `writeln()` public method of the document object, so we've already gotten a start on the terminology.

What Are Object Properties?

Besides calling functions' methods, you call an object's variables' properties in JavaScript. For example, if our display object had a public property (like methods, properties can be both public and private) named "src" that held the name of an image to display, we could set that property this way, just like setting a variable:

```
display.src = "gif/image2.gif"
```

We have already seen this process at work in the previous chapter when we got a preview of working with HTML controls in our `img.htm` page. When the user clicked a button, we changed the src property of the <IMG> tag to "gif/image2.gif." We gave the <IMG> element the name IMG1 in that program, and when you refer to an image element by name in JavaScript, that element is considered an object. That means we set the src property of IMG1 to "gif/image2.gif" this way:

```
IMG1.src = "gif/image2.gif"
```

However, it turns out that's not really enough information for Java-Script; we need to locate the IMG1 object in the context of the whole Web page. IMG1 was actually embedded in a *form* (form1) in our page (forms are how we'll enclose controls in Web pages, as we'll see in the next chapter), so IMG1 was a *member object* of form1. The form1 object, in turn, was a member object of the document object, so we actually used this line to set the <IMG> element's src property:

```
document.form1.IMG1.src = "gif/image2.gif"
```

In this way, we see that objects can enclose other objects and the dot operator is used to refer to such member objects.

Built-in JavaScript Objects

We've discussed a few of the objects built into JavaScript —document, form, and image objects—and you might be wondering what other objects are already built in. You can find a list of the built-in objects in Netscape Navigator in Table 2-1, along with their methods, properties, and events. We include the objects' events here, as a matter of reference, but we won't get to them until the next chapter. However, we should note here that JavaScript events occur in response to a user action, such as clicking a button or using the mouse; some of the JavaScript objects are set up especially to deal with such events.

The matching table—if complete—for Internet Explorer would take dozens of pages, because there are many dozens of built-in objects in Internet Explorer. In fact, all HTML tags have an associated object in Internet Explorer (that's not so in Netscape Navigator, where only a few HTML tags have objects you can use with them), so we'd have to list all possible HMTL tags in such a table just to start. To get an object overview for Internet Explorer, however, we've listed some selected objects along with their properties, methods, and events for Internet Explorer in Table 2-2.

Table 2-1 Netscape Navigator Objects

Object	Properties	Methods	Event Handlers
Anchor	none	none	none
Anchors Array	length,	none	none
Applet	none	All public methods of the applet	none
Applets Array	length	none	none
Area	hash, host, hostname, href, pathname, port, protocol, search, target	none	onMouseOut, onMouseOver
Array	length, prototype	join, reverse, sort	none
Boolean	prototype	eval, toString, valueOf	
Button	form, name, type, value	blur, click, focus	onBlur, onClick, onFocus
Checkbox	checked, defaultChecked, form, name, type, value	blur, click, focus	onBlur, onClick, onFocus
Date	prototype	getDate, getDay, getHours, getMinutes, getMonth, getSeconds, getTime, getTimezoneOffset, getYear, parse, setDate, setHours, setMinutes, setMonth, setSeconds, setTime, setYear, toGMTString, toLocaleString, toString, UTC, valueOf	none
Document	alinkColor, Anchor, anchors, Applet, applets, Area, bgColor, cookie, domain, embeds, fgColor, Form, forms, Image, images, lastModified, linkColor, Link, links, referrer, title, URL, vlinkColor	close, open, write, writeln	none
FileUpload	form, name, type, value	blur, focus	onBlur, onChange, onFocus
Form	action, Button, Checkbox, elements, encoding, FileUpload, Hidden, length, method, name, Password, Radio, Reset, Select, Submit, target, Text, Textarea	reset, submit	onReset, onSubmit
Forms Array	length	none	none

Object	Properties	Methods	Event Handlers
Frame	frames, name, length, parent, self, window	blur, clearTimeout, focus, setTimeout	onBlur, onFocus
Frames Array	length	none	none
Function	arguments, caller, prototype	eval, toString, valueOf	none
Hidden	name, type, value	none	none
History	current, length, next, previous	back, forward, go	none
History Array	length	none	none
Image	border, complete, height, hspace, lowsrc, name, prototype, src, vspace, width	none	onAbort, onError, onLoad
Images Array	length	none	none
Link and Area	hash, host, hostname, href, pathname, port, protocol, search, target	none	onClick, onMouseOut, onMouseOver
Links Array	length	none	none
Location	hash, host, hostname, href, pathname, port, protocol, search	reload, replace	none
Math	E, LN2, LN10, LOG2E, LOG10E, PI, SQRT1_2, SQRT2	abs, acos, asin, atan, atan2, ceil, cos, exp, floor, log, max, min, pow, random, round, sin, sqrt, tan	none
MimeType	description, enabledPlugin, type, suffixes	none	none
MimeTypes Array	length	none	none
Navigator	appCodeName, appName, appVersion, mimeTypes, plugins, userAgent	javaEnabled, taintEnabled	none
Number	MAX_VALUE, MIN_VALUE, Nan, NEGATIVE_INFINITY, POSITIVE_INFINITY	eval, toString, valueOf	none

continues

Table 2-1 Continued.

Object	Properties	Methods	Event Handlers
Option	defaultSelected, index, prototype, selected, text, value	none	none
Options Array	length	none	none
Options Array Elements	defaultSelected, index, length, selected, selectedIndex, text, value	none	none
Password	defaultValue, form, name, type, value	blur, focus, select	onBlur, onFocus
Plugin	description, filename, length, name	none	none
Plugins Array	length	refresh	none
Radio	checked, defaultChecked, form, length, name, type, value	blur, click, focus	onBlur, onClick, onFocus
Reset	form, name, type, value	blur, click, focus	onBlur, onClick, onFocus
Select	form, length, name, options, selectedIndex, text, type	blur, focus	onBlur, onChange, onFocus
String	length, prototype	anchor, big, blink, bold, charAt, fixed, fontcolor, fontsize, indexOf, italics, lastIndexOf, link, small, split, strike, sub, substring, sup, toLowerCase, toUpperCase	none
Submit	form, name, type, value	blur, click, focus	onBlur, onClick, onFocus
Text	defaultValue	blur, focus, select form, name, type, value	onBlur, onChange, onFocus, onSelect
Textarea	defaultValue, form, name, type, value	blur, focus, select	onBlur, onChange, onFocus, onSelect
Window	closed, defaultStatus, document, Frame, frames, history, length, location, name, opener, parent, self, status, top, window	alert, blur, clearTimeOut, close, confirm, focus, open, prompt, setTimeOut	onBlur, onError, onFocus, onLoad, onUnload

Table 2-2 Selected Internet Explorer Objects

Object	Properties	Methods	Event Handlers
All	length	item, tags	none
Anchors	length	none	none
Applets	length	item, tags	none
Area	className, docHeight, docLeft, docTop, docWidth, parentElement, sourceIndex, tagName, coords, href, id, name, noHref, shape, style, target, title	scrollIntoView, contains, getMember, setMember	onafterupdate, onbeforeupdate, onblur, onclick, ondblclick, onfocus, onhelp, onkeydown, onkeypress, onkeyup, onmousedown, onmousemove, onmouseout, onmouseover, onmouseup
Array	length, prototype	concat, join, reverse, slice, sort	none
Body	className, docHeight, docLeft, docTop, docWidth, parentElement, sourceIndex, tagName, align, aLink, background, bgColor, bgProperties, id, leftMargin, link, scroll, style, text, title, topMargin, vLink	removeMember, scrollIntoView, contains, getMember, setMember	onafterupdate, onbeforeupdate, onblur, onclick, ondblclick, onfocus, onhelp, onkeydown, onkeypress, onkeyup, onmousedown, onmousemove, onmouseout, onmouseover, onmouseup, onscroll
Boolean	prototype	none	none
Button	className, docHeight, docLeft, docTop, docWidth, parentElement, sourceIndex, tagName, accessKey, dataFld, dataFormatAs, dataSrc, disabled, title	removeMember, scrollIntoView, contains, getMember, setMember	onafterupdate, onbeforeupdate, onblur, onclick, ondblclick, onfocus, onhelp, onmousedown, onmousemove, onmouseout, onmouseover, onmouseup
Date	constructor, prototype	getDate, getDay, getFullYear, getHours, getMilliseconds, getMinutes, getMonth, getSeconds, getTime, getTimezoneOffset, and many more	none
Dialog	width, height, dialogArgs, returnValue	close	none

continues

Table 2-2 Continued.

Object	Properties	Methods	Event Handlers
Document	alinkColor, linkColor, vlinkColor, mimeType, title, bgColor, link, vLink, aLink, cookie, lastModified, charset, location, referrer, fgColor, activeElement, strReadyState, domain, URL, fileSize, fileCreatedDate, fileModifiedDate, fileUpdatedDate	close, open, clear, write, writeln, rangeFromText, rangeFromElement, execCommand, queryCommandEnabled, queryCommandText, elementFromPoint, queryCommandSupported, queryCommandState, queryCommandIndeterm, createElement	onclick, onmouseover, ondblclick, onkeypress, onmousedown, onmousemove, onmouseup, onkeydown, onkeyup, onmouseout, onreadystatechange, onhelp, onbeforeupdate, onafterupdate
Event	keyCode, fromElement, toElement, button, cancelBubble, srcElement, x, y, shiftKey, ctrlKey, altKey, returnValue	none	none
Frame	className, docHeight, docLeft, docTop, docWidth, parentElement, sourceIndex, tagName, borderColor, frameBorder, height, id, marginHeight, marginWidth, name, noResize, scrolling, src, title, width	removeMember, scrollIntoView, contains, getMember, setMember	onfocus, onload, onunload
Form	className, docHeight, docLeft, docTop, docWidth, parentElement, sourceIndex, tagName, action, id, , name, style, target, title	removeMember, scrollIntoView, contains, getMember, setMember	ondblclick, onhelp, onmousedown, onmousemove, onmouseout, onmouseover, onmouseup, onreset, onsubmit
Forms	length	item, tags	none
Frames	length	item	none
Function	arguments, caller	none	none
History	length	back, forward, go	none
Images	length	item, tags	none

Object	Properties	Methods	Event Handlers
Input	dataFld, dataSrc, className, docHeight, docLeft, docTop, docWidth, parentElement, sourceIndex, tagName, accessKey, align, disabled, id, language, maxLength, name, readOnly, size, style, tabIndex, title, type, value	removeMember, scrollIntoView, contains, getMember, setMember	onafterupdate, onbeforeupdate, onblur, onchange, onclick, ondblclick, onfocus, onhelp, onkeydown, onkeypress, onkeyup, onmousedown, onmousemove, onmouseout, onmouseover, onmouseup , onselect
Links	length	item, tags	none
Location	hash, host, hostname, href, pathname, port, protocol, search	reload, replace	none
Math	E, LN2, LN10, LOG2E, LOG10E, PI, SQRT1_2, SQRT2	abs, acos, asin, atan, atan2, ceil, cos, exp, floor, log, max, min, pow, random, round, sin, sqrt, tan	none
MimeType	description, enabledPlugin, name, suffixes,	none	none
navigator	appName, appVersion, appCodeName, userAgent, cookieEnabled, javaEnabled	none	none
Number	MAX_VALUE, MIN_VALUE, NaN, NEGATIVE_INFINITY, POSITIVE_INFINITY	none	none
Object	prototype, constructor	toString, valueOf	none
plugins	length	item, tags	none
String	length, prototype	anchor, big, blink, bold, charAt, charCodeAt, concat, fixed, fontcolor, fontsize, fromCharCode, indexOf, italics, lastIndexOf, link, match, replace, search, slice, small, split, strike, sub, substr, substring, sup, toLowerCase, toUpperCase	none

continues

Table 2-2 Continued.

Object	Properties	Methods	Event Handlers
style	background, borderTopColor, borderRightColor, borderBottomColor, borderLeftColor, borderTopWidth, borderRightWidth, borderBottomWidth, borderLeftWidth, visibility, font, textDecoration, verticalAlign, textTransform, backgroundColor, backgroundImage, backgroundRepeat, backgroundAttachment, fontSize, fontFamily, fontWeight, lineHeight, color, letterSpacing, fontStyle, textAlign, textIndent, marginLeft, marginRight, marginTop, marginBottom, display, clear, left, top, width, height, borderLeftStyle, borderRightStyle, borderTopStyle, borderBottomStyle, textDecorationUnderline, textDecorationOverline, textDecorationLineThrough, fontVariant, cssText, border, margin, zIndex, overflow, posTop, posLeft, posWidth, posHeight	getMember	none
Table	dataSrc, className, docHeight, docLeft, docTop, docWidth, parentElement, sourceIndex, tagName, align, background, bgColor, border, borderColor, borderColorDark, borderColorLight, cellPadding, cellSpacing, cols, frame, height, id, rules, style, title, width	removeMember, scrollIntoView, contains, getMember, setMember,	onafterupdate, onbeforeupdate, onclick, ondblclick, onhelp, onkeydown, onkeypress, onkeyup, onmousedown, onmousemove, onmouseout, onmouseover, onmouseup
window	name, length, parent, self, top, status, defaultStatus, opener, closed	item, navigate, blur, focus, alert, confirm, prompt, setTimeout, clearTimeout, close, open, scroll, showModalDialog	onfocus, onload, onunload, onblur, onhelp

There are several types of built-in objects in our Web browsers: element objects, like the one we've used for the <IMG> tag; scripting objects, such as the document object; and objects built into JavaScript itself, like the Math, Date, String, and Array (JavaScript 1.1 and later) objects. We'll explore the element and scripting objects throughout this book (in fact, Chapter 8, "Using the Document Object in JavaScript," focuses solely on the document object), so while we're discussing the internals of JavaScript, let's take a look at two of the useful built-in JavaScript objects: the String and Array objects.

Built-in Objects: The String Object

You handle text strings with the String class in JavaScript. This class has all kinds of string-manipulation methods built in, as you can see in Table 2-3 for the JScript String object and Table 2-4 for the JavaScript 1.2 String object.

Table 2-3

The JScript 3.0 String object's methods.

anchor	match
big	replace
blink	search
bold	slice
charAt	small
charCodeAt	split
concat	strike
fixed	sub
fontcolor	substr
fontsize	substring
fromCharCode	sup
indexOf	toLowerCase
italics	toString
lastIndexOf	toUpperCase
link	valueOf

Table 2-4

The JavaScript 1.2
String object's
methods.

anchor	big
blink	bold
charAt	eval
fixed	fontcolor
fontsize	indexOf
italics	lastIndexOflink
small	split
strike	sub
substring	sup
toLowerCase	toUpperCase
toString	valueOf

Let's create a String object ourselves and put some of those methods to work. We'll create a new Web page for this purpose, `string.htm`, and use the String object's bold() method and length property to display some of our text in bold and indicate the length of the string in characters.

We start by setting up our String object this way:

```
<HTML>

<HEAD>

<TITLE>
A String Example
</TITLE>

<SCRIPT LANGUAGE = JavaScript>

var string = "Here is some text!"
        .
        .
        .
```

Now we've created our String object, which we've named "string." We're ready to display the string by using the document object's `writeln()` method. To do that, we can make the string bold with its `bold()` method and find the string's length with its length property, as shown here:

```
<HTML>

<HEAD>
```

```
<TITLE>
A String Example
</TITLE>

<SCRIPT LANGUAGE = JavaScript>

var string = "Here is some text!"

document.writeln("This string: " + string.bold() + " is " +
        string.length + " characters long.")


</SCRIPT>

<HEAD>

<BODY>

<CENTER>
<H1>
A String Example.
</H1>
</CENTER>

</BODY>

</HTML>
```

Now open the page, as shown in Figure 2-6. As you can see, we've been able to use the String object's `bold()` method and length property.

The code for this page, `string.htm`, is shown in Listing 2-6.

Figure 2-6.
Our String object example.

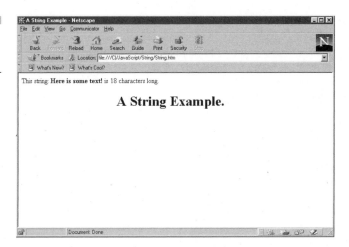

Listing 2-6
`String.htm.`

```
<HTML>

<HEAD>

<TITLE>
A String Example
</TITLE>

<SCRIPT LANGUAGE = JavaScript>
var string = "Here is some text!"

document.writeln("This string: " + string.bold() + " is " +
      string.length + "
characters long.")


</SCRIPT>

<HEAD>

<BODY>
<H1>
A String Example.
</H1>
</BODY>

</HTML>
```

The String example gave us our start with using objects, but we should note that it made things easy for us in a way that doesn't happen with most JavaScript objects.

Using the new Operator

The String object actually doubles as a variable type in JavaScript, so we could declare our String object just as we could any other variable:

```
var string = "Here is some text!"
```

Usually, when you declare a new object, however, you use the *new operator* (even though it's a word, not a symbol like + or −, the new operator is a true operator). Treating the String object as a true object, we'd declare it this way:

```
var string = new String("Here is some text!")
```

TIP: *The counterpart of the new operator is the delete operator in JavaScript. If you want to get rid of an object (and so free up its memory allocation), delete it this way:* `delete theObject`. *You can also delete objects by setting them to* null *with the assignment operator (=).*

Here we indicate that we're creating a new String object that should be initialized to "`Here is some text!`" In fact, the expression `String("Here is some text!")` is actually a call to a special method: the String class's *constructor*.

Object Constructors

When you declare an object, it's usually convenient to initialize it at the same time. For example, when we declare our object named string, we initialize it to "`Here is some text!`" at the same time by passing that text to the String object's constructor. An object's constructor is a special method —which has the same name as the object, such as `String()` or `Array()` — that you pass initialization information to. In the case of our String object, we pass the text "`Here is some text!`" to the constructor.

We could also have passed nothing to the constructor and iniitialized the string object later, like this:

```
var string = new String()
string = "Here is some text!"
```

Now that we've gotten the terminology down and worked with the String object, let's move on to the next JavaScript object: the Array object.

Built-in Objects: the Array Object

In programming, you use arrays to manage indexed data items. For example, you might have an array of numbers named `numbers[]` (you use square brackets with arrays just as you use parentheses with functions):

numbers [ ]

```
| 5 | 7 | 1 | 3 | 4 | 8 |
```

Each location (sometimes called a *slot* in JavaScript) in the array can be referred to by an index, which starts at 0:

numbers [ ]

index ⟶   0   1   2   3   4   5

```
| 5 | 7 | 1 | 3 | 4 | 8 |
```

In this way, you can handle the data in an array by referring to each item by index—the first item is `numbers[0]`, the next is `numbers[1]`, and so on. This is perfect for working with data in a loop because you can use the loop index as the array index as well, as shown here:

```
for(var loop_index = 0; loop_index < maxValue; loop_
    index++){
    if(numbers[loop_index] == 4){
        document.writeln("Found it!")
    }
}
```

Let's see an example now called `array.htm`. We'll store the strings `"Hello "`, `"from "`, and `"JavaScript!"` in an array, and then loop over that array, displaying each string in succession; the results will give us `"Hello from JavaScript!"` on the screen.

We'll use the JavaScript Array object in this example; that object's JScript 3.0 methods are listed in Table 2-5 and its JavaScript 1.2 methods are in Tale 2-6.

Table 2-5	concat	join
The JScript 3.0 Array object's methods.	reverse	slice
	sort	toString
	valueOf	

Table 2-6	eval	join
The JavaScript 1.2 Array object's methods.	reverse	sort
	toString	valueOf

Let's create this example now. We begin by declaring our new Array object, which we'll call `message[]`:

```
<HTML>

<HEAD>

<TITLE>
An Array Example
</TITLE>

<SCRIPT LANGUAGE = JavaScript>

var message = new Array()
          .
          .
          .
```

Next, we fill the array with the strings we want to use:

```
<HTML>

<HEAD>

<TITLE>
An Array Example
</TITLE>

<SCRIPT LANGUAGE = JavaScript>

var message = new Array()

message[0] = "Hello "
message[1] = "from "
message[2] = "JavaScript!"
          .
          .
          .
```

Now we can assemble the message we want to display from the three array elements, and we do that in a loop:

```
<HTML>

<HEAD>

<TITLE>
An Array Example
</TITLE>

<SCRIPT LANGUAGE = JavaScript>

var message = new Array()

message[0] = "Hello "
message[1] = "from "
message[2] = "JavaScript!"

for(var loop_index = 0; loop_index < 3; loop_index++){
     document.write(message[loop_index])
}

</SCRIPT>

<HEAD>

<BODY>

<CENTER>
<H1>
An Array Example.
</H1>
</CENTER>

</BODY>

</HTML>
```

NOTE: *To make sure our three-part message was printed on one line, we used the document object's* `write()` *method, instead of* `writeln()` *because* `writeln()` *skips to the next line after writing its text and* `write()` *doesn't.*

That's it—open this page now, as shown in Figure 2-7. As you can see in that figure, we've been able to fill an array with our strings, then loop over that array and display those strings, one after the other, to create our message.

TIP: *Some languages let you create multidimensional arrays, but JavaScript doesn't. Instead, you can create arrays of Array objects to do the same thing.*

The code for this page, `array.htm`, is shown in Listing 2-7.

Figure 2-7
Our array example
uses JavaScript
arrays.

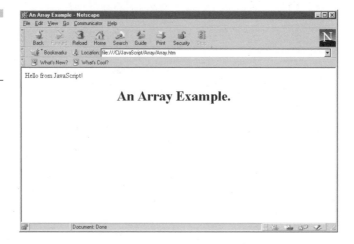

Listing 2-7
`Array.htm.`

```
<HTML>

<HEAD>

<TITLE>
An Array Example
</TITLE>

<SCRIPT LANGUAGE = JavaScript>

var message = new Array()

message[0] = "Hello "
message[1] = "from "
message[2] = "JavaScript!"

for(var loop_index = 0; loop_index < 3; loop_index++){
    document.write(message[loop_index])
}

</SCRIPT>

<HEAD>

<BODY>
```

continues

```
<CENTER>
<H1>
An Array Example.
</H1>
</CENTER>

</BODY>

</HTML>
```

Now that we've see a few of the built-in objects available in JavaScript, let's take a look at some of the built-in ways of handling objects. The first technique we'll look at is using the JavaScript for-in statement.

Using the for-in Statement

You can loop over all the elements of an object or an array with the for-in statement:

```
for (variable in [object | array])
    statement
```

This statement is especially made to allow you to work easily with objects and arrays. Let's put together an example called `for-in.htm`. In this example, we can display all the properties of the document object like this:

The properties of the document object:
title = A for-in Statement Example
URL=file:///cl/JavaScript/for-in/for-in.htm

A for-in Statement Example.

We start this new page by indicating that we're going to display the elements of the document object:

```
<HTML>

<HEAD>

<TITLE>
A for-in Statement Example
</TITLE>

<PRE>
<SCRIPT LANGUAGE = JavaScript>

document.writeln("The properties of the document object:")
         .
         .
         .
```

We set up the for-in statement this way, using a variable we'll call element:

```
<HTML>

<HEAD>

<TITLE>
A for-in Statement Example
</TITLE>

<PRE>
<SCRIPT LANGUAGE = JavaScript>

document.writeln("The properties of the document object:")

for(var element in document){
     .
     .
     .
}

</SCRIPT>
     .
     .
     .
```

Now we can use the element variable as a loop index and refer to the properties of the document object as document[element] because you can treat an object name as an indexed array of its internal members:

```
<HTML>

<HEAD>

<TITLE>
A for-in Statement Example
</TITLE>

<PRE>
<SCRIPT LANGUAGE = JavaScript>

document.writeln("The properties of the document object:")

for(var element in document){
    document.writeln(element + " = " + document[element])
}

</SCRIPT>
</PRE>

<HEAD>

<BODY>

<CENTER>
<H1>
A for-in Statement Example.
</H1>
</CENTER>

</BODY>

</HTML>
```

The result of this program is shown in Figure 2-8. As you can see, we're displaying the properties of the document object one by one in that page.

It's instructive to open this page in both Netscape Navigator and Internet Explorer; doing so highlights a major difference between the two browsers—the immense number of programming objects available in Internet Explorer (sometimes it seems as though there's almost too many of them). Here's what you get in Netscape Navigator when you open the for-in.htm page:

```
The properties of the document object:
location = file:///C|/JavaScript/for-in/for-in.htm
forms = [object FormArray]
links = [object LinkArray]
anchors = [object AnchorArray]
applets = [object AppletArray]
```

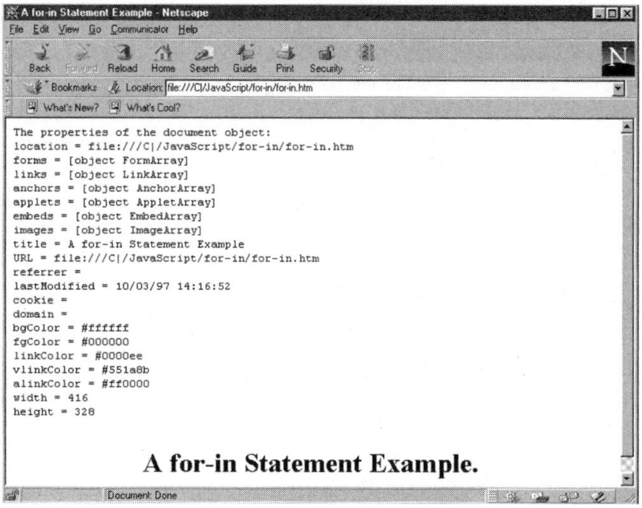

Figure 2-8
This example lists the
document object's
properties.

Figure 2-8
This example lists the
document object's
properties.

```
embeds = [object EmbedArray]
images = [object ImageArray]
title = A for-in Statement Example
URL = file:///C|/JavaScript/for-in/for-in.htm
referrer =
lastModified = 10/03/97 14:30:08
cookie =
domain =
bgColor = #ffffff
fgColor = #000000
linkColor = #0000ee
vlinkColor = #551a8b
alinkColor = #ff0000
width = 416
height = 328
```

Here's what the same page returns in Internet Explorer:

```
The properties of the document object:
activeElement = [object]
alinkColor = #0000ff
all = [object]
anchors = [object]
applets = [object]
bgColor = #ffffff
body = [object]
cookie =
defaultCharset = iso-8859-1
domain =
embeds = [object]
```

```
fgColor = #000000
fileCreatedDate = Monday, September 29, 1997
fileModifiedDate = Friday, October 03, 1997
fileSize = 413
fileUpdatedDate =
forms = [object]
frames = [object]
images = [object]
lastModified = 10/03/97 18:30:08
linkColor = #0000
fflinks = [object]
location = file:///C:/JavaScript/for-in/for-in.htm
mimeType = Microsoft HTML Document 4.0
nameProp = A for-in Statement Example
onafterupdate = null
onbeforeupdate = null
onclick = null
ondblclick = null
ondragstart = null
onerrorupdate = null
onhelp = null
onkeydown = null
onkeypress = null
onkeyup = null
onmousedown = null
onmousemove = null
onmouseout = null
onmouseover = null
onmouseup = null
onreadystatechange = null
onrowenter = null
onrowexit = null
onselectstart = null
parentWindow = [object]
plugins = [object]
protocol = File
ProtocolreadyState =
interactivereferrer =
scripts = [object]
security = This type of document does not have a security
     certificate.
selection = [object]
styleSheets = [object]title = A for-in Statement Example
URL = file:///C:/JavaScript/for-in/for-in.htm
vlinkColor = #800080
```

Listing 2-8 shows the code for this page, `for-in.htm`.

There's another important JavaScript programming construct made to work with objects—the *with* statement—and we'll take a look at it now.

```
<HTML>

<HEAD>

<TITLE>
A for-in Statement Example
</TITLE>

<PRE>
<SCRIPT LANGUAGE = JavaScript>

document.writeln("The properties of the document object:")
for(var element in document){
    document.writeln(element + " = " + document[element])
}

</SCRIPT>
</PRE>

<HEAD>

<BODY>

<CENTER>
<H1>
A for-in Statement Example.
</H1>
</CENTER>

</BODY>

</HTML>
```

Using the with Statement

If you want to use many of an object's properties in a program, you might consider the with statement. You set up a code block with this statement, specifying the object whose properties and methods you want to refer to in that code block:

```
with (object)
    statement
```

Inside the code block, you can then refer to the object's properties and methods without referring to the object—for example, you can use `writeln()` instead of `document.writeln()`. Let's put together an example, `with.htm`, that uses the with statement. We can display a few properties of the document object, such as the foreground and background color, using the with statement.

We start our new page, `with.htm`, by setting up the with statement and indicating that the object we want to use is the document object—note that we set up a code block (delimited by { and }) after the with statement:

```
<HTML>

<HEAD>

<TITLE>
A with Statement Example
</TITLE>
<PRE>

<SCRIPT LANGUAGE = JavaScript>

with(document){
    .
    .
    .

}

</SCRIPT>
```

Now that we've set up our with statement and its code block, we can refer to the foreground color (fgColor) and background color (bgColor) by name, without having to use their full names (that is, `document.fgColor`):

```
<HTML>

<HEAD>

<TITLE>
A with Statement Example
</TITLE>
<PRE>

<SCRIPT LANGUAGE = JavaScript>

with(document){
    document.writeln("The document foreground color is " +
        fgColor + ".")
```

```
        document.writeln("The document foreground color is " +
          bgColor + ".")
    }

    </SCRIPT>

    </PRE>
    <HEAD>

    <BODY>

    <CENTER>
    <H1>
    A with Statement Example.
    </H1>
    </CENTER>

    </BODY>

    </HTML>
```

Now open the page, as shown in Figure 2-9. As you can see, our with statement is working—we don't have to refer to an object's properties or methods with its full name, which saves us a little bit of programming time. The code for this page, with.htm, is shown in Listing 2-9.

Figure 2-9
The with statement makes working with objects easier.

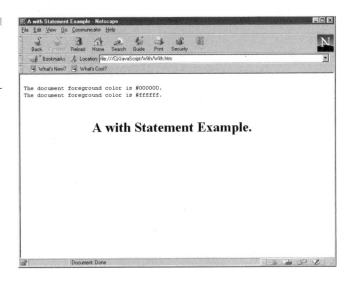

Listing 2-9
with.htm.

```
<HTML>

<HEAD>

<TITLE>
A with Statement Example
</TITLE>
<PRE>

<SCRIPT LANGUAGE = JavaScript>

with(document){
    document.writeln("The document foreground color is " +
      fgColor + ".")
    document.writeln("The document foreground color is " +
      bgColor + ".")
}

</SCRIPT>

</PRE>
<HEAD>

<BODY>

<CENTER>
<H1>
A with Statement Example.
</H1>
</CENTER>

</BODY>

</HTML>
```

We've already covered a lot of ground on the built-in objects we have to work with in this chapter. Now we're ready for the next step—creating our own JavaScript objects.

Creating Custom Objects

To see how creating your own objects in JavaScript works, we'll create a new example called object.htm. In this example, we'll create an object that stores a string of text—"Custom objects!"—and supports a method —display()—that we can call to write that string to our Web page.

Now we're ready to create our custom object, but how exactly do we do that?

Setting Up a Custom JavaScript Object in Code

You create a custom object by using the *function* keyword in JavaScript. For example, we can name our object "text" and have the string we store in that object passed to us as an argument in the object's constructor. Setting that up looks like this in JavaScript:

```
<HTML>

<HEAD>

<TITLE>
A Custom Object Example
</TITLE>

<SCRIPT LANGUAGE = JavaScript>

    function text(textString)
    {
        .
        .
        .
    }
```

We want to store the text string passed to us as a property of the object, so we'll explain that next.

Creating an Object Property

We can name our new object property textString. Here's how we create it:

```
<HTML>

<HEAD>

<TITLE>
A Custom Object Example
</TITLE>

<SCRIPT LANGUAGE = JavaScript>
```

```
function text(textString)
{
    this.textString = textString
        .
        .
        .
}
```

Here we take the argument passed to us and store it in a new property named `textString`. Note our use of the *this* keyword in the preceding code. This particular keyword refers to the current object, and it's very useful (we can't refer to the present object by name yet because we haven't given it a name or even declared it).

Now we've set up the textString property in the text object. The next step is to print out the string in that property on a Web page, and we'll do that by creating a new method for our object.

Creating an Object Method

You can associate a JavaScript function with an object, making it a method of our object, the same way we set up our textString property. That is, if we want to add a `display()` method to the text object, we do so like this:

```
<HTML>

<HEAD>

<TITLE>
A Custom Object Example
</TITLE>

<SCRIPT LANGUAGE = JavaScript>

    function text(textString)
    {
        this.textString = textString
        this.display = display
    }
```

Next, we have to write the `display()` method itself. We do that by simply displaying the text from the textString property in a Web page:

```
<HTML>

<HEAD>
```

```
<TITLE>
A Custom Object Example
</TITLE>

<SCRIPT LANGUAGE = JavaScript>

    function text(textString)
    {
        this.textString = textString
        this.display = display
    }

    function display()
    {
        document.writeln("The text is: " +
    this.textString)
    }
```

That's it—our new object is ready to go. To actually work with new objects of the text type (JavaScript doesn't support true OOP, so we will refer to an object's *type*, instead of the standard OOP terminology of an object's *class*), we need to declare those objects.

Instantiating the Object

The process of declaring and initializing objects is called *instantiation*. To instantiate a text object, we use the new operator, passing the string we want to store in that object (such as "Custom objects!") to the object's constructor:

```
<HTML>

<HEAD>

<TITLE>
A Custom Object Example
</TITLE>

<SCRIPT LANGUAGE = JavaScript>

    function text(textString)
    {
        this.textString = textString
        this.display = display
    }

    function display()
    {
```

```
    document.writeln("The text is: " +
 this.textString)
 }

 theText = new text("Custom objects!")
       .
       .
       .
```

Now we're free to call the object's `display()` method, just as we would for any other object:

```
<HTML>

<HEAD>

<TITLE>
A Custom Object Example
</TITLE>

<SCRIPT LANGUAGE = JavaScript>

    function text(textString)
    {
        this.textString = textString
        this.display = display
    }

    function display()
    {
        document.writeln("The text is: " +
    this.textString)
    }

    theText = new text("Custom objects!")

    theText.display()

</SCRIPT>

<HEAD>

<BODY>

<CENTER>
<H1>
A Custom Object Example.
</H1>
</CENTER>

</BODY>

</HTML>
```

That completes the example—our custom object is ready to go. Open the page now, as shown in Figure 2-10. As you can see, the object was created with the text we placed in it, and the `display()` method correctly displays that text. Now we have the power to create our own objects in JavaScript.

The code for this page, `object.htm`, is shown in Listing 2-10.

Figure 2-10
We create and use a custom JavaScript object.

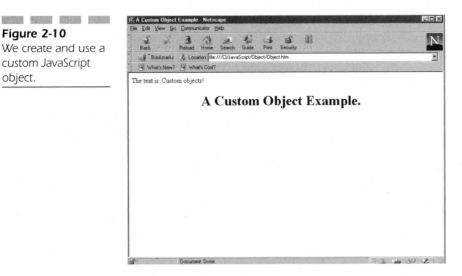

Listing 2-10
`Object.htm`.

```
                        <HTML>

<HEAD>

<TITLE>
A Custom Object Example
</TITLE>

<SCRIPT LANGUAGE = JavaScript>

    function text(textString)
    {
        this.textString = textString
        this.display = display
    }

    function display()
    {
        document.writeln("The text is: " +
    this.textString)
    }
```

continues

Listing 2-10
Continued.

```
        theText = new text("Custom objects!")
        theText.display()

</SCRIPT>

<HEAD>

<BODY>

<CENTER>
<H1>
A Custom Object Example.
</H1>
</CENTER>

</BODY>

</HTML>
```

One reason you might want to create your own objects in JavaScript is to pass arguments to functions by reference, not value. Normally, in JavaScript, what's really passed to functions are copies of the arguments you pass, not the arguments themselves. This is called *calling by value*. However, if you want a function to change a variable you pass to it, you need to pass a reference to that variable, not just a copy of the variable; you do that by *calling by reference*. The trick is that objects are always passed by reference in JavaScript, so you can enclose the value you want to pass by reference in an object:

```
function dataObject(value)
{
    this.value = value
}
```

Then when you pass that object to a function, that function can work on the actual value of the argument, not just on a copy of it:

```
function increment(obj)
{
    obj.value++
}
```

The last topic we'll explore in this chapter is an Internet Explorer topic: scriptlets. Internet Explorer supports an <OBJECT> tag, which is typically used for ActiveX controls; however, starting with Internet Explorer 4.0 final edition (but not supported in either of the two preview editions), you can use the <OBJECT> tag with scripts to create objects.

Using Internet Explorer Scriptlets

As mentioned, you can now use the <OBJECT> tag in Internet Explorer to create an object from a script. We'll take a look at this process in a new Web page named `scriptlet.htm`. We'll create an object from a script and then set a property of that object to the words "`Hello from scriptlets!`". We'll be able to read that property's text back and display the text.

We'll start this example by creating the script for the object in a file named `s.htm`. The object we'll create will have one property—a string named textString—and one method to retrieve that string, called `get_textString()`. To make sure the property and method are public (so they can be accessed by scripts in the Web page where our new object will be embedded), we must preface their names with `public_`:

```
<SCRIPT LANGUAGE = JScript>

public_textString = ""

function public_get_textString()
{
    return textString
}

</SCRIPT>
```

NOTE: *In the scriptlet example, we use <SCRIPT LANGUAGE = JScript>, not <SCRIPT LANGUAGE = JavaScript>. Because scriptlets are a Microsoft invention, they require using JScript, not standard JavaScript.*

Now we will create a new object from the code in `s.htm`. To do that, we create a new Web page, `scriptlet.htm`, and place the <OBJECT> tag in it:

```
<HTML>

<HEAD>
<TITLE>
A Scriptlet Example
</TITLE>
</HEAD>

<BODY>

<OBJECT
        .
        .
        .
```

```
</OBJECT>
      .
      .
      .
```

This type of object is different from a scripting object. The objects you create with the <OBJECT> tag are HTML objects, so we specify the height and width of our new object in the Web page (we won't display anything in our object's space in the Web page), as well as giving it a name ("Scriptlet1") and indicating that the code for this scriptlet is in `s.htm`:

```
<HTML>

<HEAD>
<TITLE>
A Scriptlet Example
</TITLE>
</HEAD>

<BODY>

<OBJECT
width=200
height=100
NAME="Scriptlet1"
TYPE="text/x-scriptlet"
DATA="s.htm">
</OBJECT>
      .
      .
      .
```

Note also that we give a MIME type ("text/x-scriptlet") for the scriptlet so Internet Explorer will know how to handle the text in the `s.htm` file. (You specify MIME types for all documents transferred over the Web; your *Internet Service Provider* (ISP) has a large "map" of MIME types that it applies to the documents it handles, based on those document's filename extensions.)

Now the new HTML object is ready, and we can refer to it as Scriptlet1. In this case, we'll place some text—`"Hello from scriptlets!"`—into the scriptlet's textString property and then read it back, displaying it this way:

```
<HTML>

<HEAD>
<TITLE>
A Scriptlet Example
</TITLE>
</HEAD>
```

```
<BODY>

<OBJECT
width=200
height=100
NAME="Scriptlet1"
TYPE="text/x-scriptlet"
DATA="s.htm">
</OBJECT>

<SCRIPT LANGUAGE = JScript>

Scriptlet1.textString = "Hello from scriptlets!"

document.writeln(Scriptlet1.textString)

</SCRIPT>

<BR>
<BR>
<BR>

<CENTER>
<H1>
A Scriptlet Example.
</H1>
</CENTER>

</BODY>
</HTML>
```

Open the `scriptlet.htm` page. As shown in Figure 2-11, we've loaded our text string into the scriptlet's textString property and read it back. Now we're supporting scriptlets in our Web pages!

Figure 2-11
Using scriptlets in a
Web page.

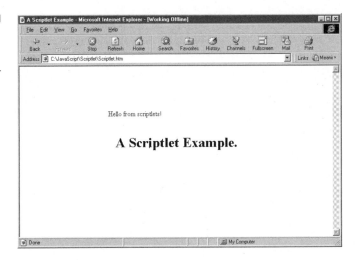

The code for this page, `scriptlet.htm`, is shown in Listing 2-11, and Listing 2-12 shows the code for the scriptlet itself, `s.htm`.

Listing 2-11
`Scriptlet.htm.`

```
<HTML>

<HEAD>
<TITLE>
A Scriptlet Example
</TITLE>
</HEAD>

<BODY>

<OBJECT
width=200
height=100
NAME="Scriptlet1"
TYPE="text/x-scriptlet"
DATA="s.htm">
</OBJECT>

<SCRIPT LANGUAGE = JScript>

Scriptlet1.textString = "Hello from scriptlets!"

document.writeln(Scriptlet1.textString)

</SCRIPT>

<BR>
<BR>
<BR>

<CENTER>
<H1>
A Scriptlet Example.
</H1>
</CENTER>

</BODY>
</HTML>
```

Listing 2-12
S.htm.

```
                              <SCRIPT LANGUAGE = JScript>
public_textString = ""

function public_get_textString()
{
    return textString
}

</SCRIPT>
```

CONCLUSION

That's it for this chapter. We've covered a great deal in this chapter, from how to use loops like for, while, and do-while to using functions, passing arguments to functions, getting values back from functions, seeing how objects, methods, and properties work, how to use the built-in String and Array objects, how to work with objects using the for-in and with statements, how to create your own custom objects, and how to use Internet Explorer scriptlets. We've added a lot of JavaScript power to our arsenal in this chapter.

In the next chapter, we'll continue our exploration of JavaScript when we start seeing how to work with HTML controls in Web pages. This is the main attraction of JavaScript for many programmers.

Forms: Text Boxes and Buttons

In this chapter, we'll start working with HTML controls. For many programmers, this is the point of JavaScript—you embed scripts in your Web page so you can manipulate HTML controls and their behavior. In this chapter, we'll start learning how to do that.

We'll examine many central HTML controls: text boxes, buttons, text areas, submit buttons, reset buttons, file controls, and hidden controls. If you're familiar with Windows, you've seen some of these controls before, and in this chapter, we'll see how to work with them under JavaScript's control. This is our first real step in creating powerful Web pages that respond to the user the way we want them to—and that's what JavaScript is all about.

Text Boxes

A *text box*, also called a *text control*, is a rectangular control that lets the user enter text. We can set the text in a text box, as well as read what the user has typed.

The actual text in a text box is held in its value property. Other properties of text boxes include defaultValue, form, name, and type. Its methods are the following:

- **blur:** This method releases the input focus (the control with the focus is the control that's the target of mouse clicks and struck keys).

- **select:** Selects text.

- **focus:** This method restores the input focus to the check box.

Now we'll put together a text box example in which we simply display a text box in a Web page.

Using the <INPUT> Tag

This will be our first true HTML control example. You place HTML controls into a Web page with the <INPUT> tag; in Internet Explorer, that tag works like this:

```
<INPUT
ACCESSKEY=string
ALIGN=ABSBOTTOM | ABSMIDDLE | BASELINE | BOTTOM | LEFT |
     MIDDLE |
RIGHT | TEXTTOP | TOP
DATAFLD=string
DATASRC=string
DISABLED
ID=string
LANGUAGE=JAVASCRIPT | VBSCRIPT
MAXLENGTH=long
NAME=string
READONLY=string
SIZE=variant
STYLE=string
TABINDEX=integer
TITLE=string
TYPE=BUTTON | CHECKBOX | HIDDEN | IMAGE | PASSWORD | RADIO
     | RESET |
SELECT-MULTIPLE | SELECT-ONE | SELECT-ONE | SUBMIT | TEXT |
     TEXTAREA | FILE
```

```
VALUE=string
event = script
>
```

Here's the <INPUT> tag in Netscape Navigator:

```
<INPUT
ALIGN=ABSBOTTOM | ABSMIDDLE | BASELINE | BOTTOM | LEFT |
      MIDDLE |
RIGHT | TEXTTOP | TOP
ID=string
LANGUAGE=JAVASCRIPT
MAXLENGTH=long
NAME=string
SRC=string
SIZE=string
TITLE=string
TYPE=BUTTON | CHECKBOX | HIDDEN | IMAGE | PASSWORD | RADIO
      | RESET |
FILE | SUBMIT | TEXT | TEXTAREA
VALUE=string
event = script
>
```

We will start our text box example, `Textbox.htm`, by placing a header into the Web page to show what this example is about:

```
<HTML>
<HEAD>
<TITLE>Text Box Example</TITLE>
</HEAD>
<BODY>

<FORM>
<CENTER>
<BR>
<H1>
Type into the text box...
</H1>
     .
     .
     .
```

Next we add the text box itself, making it 20 characters wide:

```
<HTML>
<HEAD>
<TITLE>Text Box Example</TITLE>
</HEAD>
<BODY>
```

```
<FORM>
<CENTER>
<BR>
<H1>
Type into the text box...
</H1>
<BR>
<BR>
<BR>
<INPUT TYPE = TEXT SIZE = 20>
</CENTER>
</FORM>

</BODY>
</HTML>
```

TIP: *The default width for text boxes, if you don't specify a size, is 20 characters.*

That's all we need—open the page now, as shown in Figure 3-1. You can see our text box there; note that you can type into it. In this way, we've supported our first HTML control.

The code for this page, `Textbox.htm`, is shown in Listing 3-1.

Figure 3-1
Our text box
example.

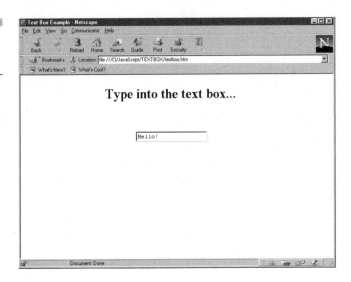

```
<HTML>
<HEAD>
<TITLE>Text Box Example</TITLE>
</HEAD>
<BODY>

<FORM>
<CENTER>
<BR>
<H1>
Type into the text box...
</H1>
<BR>
<BR>
<BR>
<INPUT TYPE = TEXT SIZE = 20>
</CENTER>
</FORM>

</BODY>
</HTML>
```

You might note that we used the <FORM> HTML tag in the preceding text box example:

```
<FORM>
<CENTER>
<BR>
<H1>
Type into the text box...
</H1>
<BR>
<BR>
<BR>
<INPUT TYPE = TEXT SIZE = 20>
</CENTER>
</FORM>
```

Technically, it's not necessary to use the <FORM> tag here, but we added it because when we start using JavaScript, it requires enclosing your controls in *forms* (forms are not visible HTML elements—they simply provide ways of grouping your controls in a page). It's not necessary here because we haven't used JavaScript with the text box, but it points out what's to come when we start working with other controls, such as buttons.

Buttons

We'll turn to HTML buttons now. These controls display a visual image of a button that the user can click (and depress) with the mouse. Buttons support a value property, which holds the button's caption; a name property, which holds the name of the button as used in code; and a form and a type property. The button methods are blur, click, and focus. The button event handlers—we'll see what event handlers are in a minute—are on-Blur, onClick, and onFocus.

We will put together a button example to show how to connect buttons to JavaScript. In this case, we'll show the user both a text box and a button, giving the button the caption "Display Message." When the user clicks the button, we'll display a message—"Hello from JavaScript"—in the text box.

Let's put this together in code. First, we set up a form for our controls:

```
<HTML>

<TITLE>A Button Example</TITLE>

<BODY>

<CENTER>
<FORM>
    .
    .
    .
</FORM>
</CENTER>
    .
    .
    .
```

Next, we add the text box we'll use:

```
<HTML>

<TITLE>A Button Example</TITLE>

<BODY>

<CENTER>
<FORM>
<INPUT TYPE = TEXT NAME = "Textbox" SIZE = 25>
    .
    .
    .
```

```
</FORM>
</CENTER>
     .
     .
     .
```

Next, we add the button itself, using the <INPUT> tag with the TYPE attribute set to BUTTON and setting the caption of the button to "Display Message" with the VALUE attribute:

```
<HTML>

<TITLE>A Button Example</TITLE>

<BODY>

<CENTER>
<FORM>
<INPUT TYPE = TEXT NAME = "Textbox" SIZE = 25>
<BR>
<BR>
<INPUT TYPE = BUTTON Value = "Display Message">
</FORM>
</CENTER>
```

The next step is to connect the button to JavaScript code, and to do that we'll need an understanding of HTML events.

Using HTML Events

When the user clicks the button in our Web page, we want to display the message "Hello from JavaScript" in the text box. To do that, we'll need to be notified when the user clicks the button, and the notification process depends on HTML *events*.

In graphical user environments, users direct what happens in the program. They are usually presented with many visual elements they can work with, and it's up to them to click or activate those elements as they choose—the programmer can't predict exactly what course the program will take. For that reason, programming in graphical user interfaces (GUIs) is *event-driven*.

For example, if the user clicks the mouse, a *click* event occurs. If he or she changes the text in a text box, a *change* event occurs. We can respond to those events by tying code to them in our programs.

When the user does click the button, a click event occurs that we can tie to a JavaScript function. In this case, we'll tie the button's click event to a JavaScript function named `DisplayMessage()`. We do that like this, using the onClick attribute:

```
<HTML>

<TITLE>A Button Example</TITLE>

<BODY>

<CENTER>
<FORM>
<INPUT TYPE = TEXT NAME = "Textbox" SIZE = 25>
<BR>
<BR>
<INPUT TYPE = BUTTON Value = "Display Message" onClick =
     "DisplayMessage()">
</FORM>
</CENTER>
```

In the `DisplayMessage()` function, we'll set the text in the text box to `"Hello from JavaScript"`. We need some way of referring to that text box; because that box is in our HTML form, we can pass that form to `DisplayMessage()` by passing an argument of `this.form` (the *this* keyword refers to the button control here, because "this" always refers to the current object; therefore, "this.form" refers to the form enclosing the button control):

```
<HTML>

<TITLE>A Button Example</TITLE>

<BODY>

<CENTER>
<FORM>
<INPUT TYPE = TEXT NAME = "Textbox" SIZE = 25>
<BR>
<BR>
<INPUT TYPE = BUTTON Value = "Display Message" onClick =
        "DisplayMessage(this.form)">
</FORM>
</CENTER>
```

Now we'll write the `DisplayMessage()` function:

```
<HTML>

<TITLE>A Button Example</TITLE>
```

```
<BODY>

<CENTER>
<FORM>
<INPUT TYPE = TEXT NAME = "Textbox" SIZE = 25>
<BR>
<BR>
<INPUT TYPE = BUTTON Value = "Display Message" onClick
        = "DisplayMessage(this.form)">
</FORM>
</CENTER>

</BODY>

<SCRIPT LANGUAGE = JavaScript>
    function DisplayMessage(form1)
    {
          .
          .
          .
    }
</SCRIPT>
```

In this function, all we need to do is to set the text box's value property to "Hello from JavaScript":

```
<HTML>

<TITLE>A Button Example</TITLE>

<BODY>

<CENTER>
<FORM>
<INPUT TYPE = TEXT NAME = "Textbox" SIZE = 25>
<BR>
<BR>
<INPUT TYPE = BUTTON Value = "Display Message" onClick
        = "DisplayMessage(this.form)">
</FORM>
</CENTER>

</BODY>

<SCRIPT LANGUAGE = JavaScript>
    function DisplayMessage(form1)
    {
            form1.Textbox.value = "Hello from JavaScript"
    }
</SCRIPT>

</HTML>
```

Now open the page, as shown in Figure 3-2. When you click the button in that page, the browser calls `DisplayMessage()` and the message appears in the text box. Now we're working with HTML controls in JavaScript.

Listing 3-2 shows the code for this page, `Buttons.htm`.

Figure 3-2
Connecting a button to JavaScript.

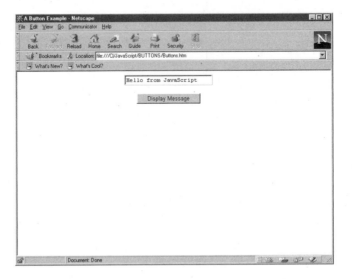

Listing 3-2
`Buttons.htm`.

```
<HTML>

<TITLE>A Button Example</TITLE>

<BODY>

<CENTER>
<FORM>
<INPUT TYPE = TEXT NAME = "Textbox" SIZE = 25>
<BR>
<BR>
<INPUT TYPE = BUTTON Value = "Display Message" onClick
        = "DisplayMessage(this.form)">
</FORM>
</CENTER>

</BODY>

<SCRIPT LANGUAGE = JavaScript>
    function DisplayMessage(form1)
    {
        form1.Textbox.value = "Hello from JavaScript"
    }
</SCRIPT>

</HTML>
```

In the preceding example, we passed the button's form to the
`DisplayMessage()` function, but it's not necessary to do so. We can name
the form by using the NAME attribute this way:

```
<FORM Name = form1>
<INPUT TYPE = TEXT NAME = "Textbox" SIZE = 25>
<BR>
<BR>
    .
    .
    .
```

Then we can call the `DisplayMessage()` function without any arguments:

```
<FORM Name = form1>
<INPUT TYPE = TEXT NAME = "Textbox" SIZE = 25>
<BR>
<BR>
<INPUT TYPE = BUTTON Value = "Display Message" onClick =
    "DisplayMessage()">
</FORM>
</CENTER>
    .
    .
    .
```

In `DisplayMessage()`, we need some way to refer to the button's form.
We can do that now by name: form1. That form is a member object of the
document object, so we refer to the value property of the text box this way:

```
<FORM Name = form1>
<INPUT TYPE = TEXT NAME = "Textbox" SIZE = 25>
<BR>
<BR>
<INPUT TYPE = BUTTON Value = "Display Message" onClick =
    "DisplayMessage()">
</FORM>
</CENTER>

</BODY>

<SCRIPT LANGUAGE = JavaScript>
    function DisplayMessage()
    {
        document.form1.Textbox.value = "Hello from
    JavaScript"
    }
</SCRIPT>

</HTML>
```

In this way, we don't have to pass the text box's form to the `DisplayMessage()` function to be able to use that text box.

Now we've seen how to work with text boxes and buttons, giving us an introduction to working with HTML controls with JavaScript. Besides HTML controls, we can work with scripting objects in the Web page. For example, we will take a quick look at changing the properties of the document object when the user clicks a button.

Using Controls to Set a Page's Background Color

One of the document properties we can change when the user clicks a button is the bgColor property, which holds the document's background color. For example, we can display a button with the caption "Make background red."

When the user clicks that button, we'll set the document's bgColor property to red (#ff0000). We'll start our new example, bgcolor.htm, with a prompt and a button, connecting the button to a function named colorBackground():

```
<HTML>

<HEAD>
<TITLE>bgColor Example</TITLE>
</HEAD>

<BODY>

<CENTER>
<FORM>
<BR>
<H1>
Set the document's bgColor property...
</H1>
<BR>
<BR>
<BR>
<INPUT TYPE = BUTTON Value = "Make background red" onClick
         = "colorBackground()">
</FORM>
</CENTER>
```

All that's left is to color the background by setting the document's bgColor property in the colorBackground() function:

```
<HTML>

<HEAD>
<TITLE>bgColor Example</TITLE>
</HEAD>

<BODY>

<CENTER>
<FORM>
<BR>
<H1>
Set the document's bgColor property...
</H1>
<BR>
<BR>
<BR>
<INPUT TYPE = BUTTON Value = "Make background red" onClick
        = "colorBackground()">
</FORM>
</CENTER>

</BODY>

<SCRIPT LANGUAGE = JavaScript>
  function colorBackground()
  {
      document.bgColor = 0xff0000
  }
</SCRIPT>

</HTML>
```

Open this page now, as shown in Figure 3-3. When you click the button, the program sets the background color to red, as you can see. Now we're manipulating the document scripting object's properties—not just HTML elements—when the user clicks a button.

The code for this page, bgColor.htm, is shown in Listing 3-3.

In this way, we can work with the document's properties in code. This example works with both Internet Explorer and Netscape Navigator. However, far more objects and properties are available in Internet Explorer that we can change on the fly and immediately see reflected in the Web page. In our next example, we'll see how to resize a text box by changing its size property, something you can't do in Netscape Navigator (the properties of objects you can change on the fly in Netscape Navigator are listed in Table 2-1).

Figure 3-3

We set a document
property to color a
Web page red.

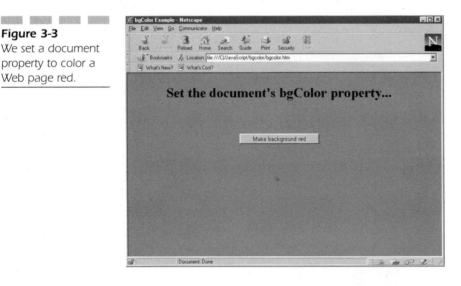

Listing 3-3
bgColor.htm.

```
<HTML>

<HEAD>
<TITLE>bgColor Example</TITLE>
</HEAD>

<BODY>

<CENTER>
<FORM>
<BR>
<H1>
Set the document's bgColor property...
</H1>
<BR>
<BR>
<BR>
<INPUT TYPE = BUTTON Value = "Make background red" onClick
        = "colorBackground()">
</FORM>
</CENTER>

</BODY>

<SCRIPT LANGUAGE = JavaScript>
  function colorBackground()
  {
      document.bgColor = 0xff0000
  }
</SCRIPT>

</HTML>
```

TIP: *In fact, all HTML tags are active now in Internet Explorer, so you can change their properties in a script and see the changes immediately onscreen. This remarkable feature of Internet Explorer is new in version 4.0.*

Using Controls to Set a Text Box's Size

In this next example, we'll again display a text box and a button in an Internet Explorer Web page. This time, however, when the user clicks the button, we'll change the text box's size property from 20 to 40, widening that control.

This example is simple to create. We just add the controls we need to a form, form1:

```
<HTML>

<HEAD>
<TITLE>Resize Text Box Example</TITLE>
</HEAD>

<BODY>

<CENTER>
<FORM NAME = form1>
<INPUT TYPE = TEXT NAME = Textbox SIZE = 20 VALUE = "You
     can resize this box.">
<BR>
<BR>
<INPUT TYPE = BUTTON Value = "Resize text box" onClick =
     "ResizeTextbox()">
</FORM>
</CENTER>
```

We've connected the button's click event to a function named `ResizeTextbox()`, which we add this way:

```
<HTML>

<HEAD>
<TITLE>Resize Text Box Example</TITLE>
</HEAD>

<BODY>

<CENTER>
```

```
<FORM NAME = form1>
<INPUT TYPE = TEXT NAME = Textbox SIZE = 20 VALUE = "You
     can resize this box.">
<BR>
<BR>
<INPUT TYPE = BUTTON Value = "Resize text box" onClick =
     "ResizeTextbox()">
</FORM>
</CENTER>

</BODY>

<SCRIPT LANGUAGE = JavaScript>
  function ResizeTextbox()
  {
     .
     .
     .

  }
</SCRIPT>

</HTML>
```

When the user clicks the button, we want to increase the text box's size to 40 characters. We can also place a message in the text box ("This text box was resized."), as follows:

```
<HTML>

<HEAD>
<TITLE>Resize Text Box Example</TITLE>
</HEAD>

<BODY>

<CENTER>
<FORM NAME = form1>
<INPUT TYPE = TEXT NAME = Textbox SIZE = 20 VALUE = "You
     can resize this box.">
<BR>
<BR>
<INPUT TYPE = BUTTON Value = "Resize text box" onClick =
     "ResizeTextbox()">
</FORM>
</CENTER>

</BODY>

<SCRIPT LANGUAGE = JavaScript>
  function ResizeTextbox()
  {
       document.form1.Textbox.size = 40
       document.form1.Textbox.value = "This text box was
       resized."
```

```
        }
   </SCRIPT>

   </HTML>
```

That's all we need. Now open the page in Internet Explorer, as shown in Figure 3-4. When you click the button, the text box is widened. In this way, we can use one of Internet Explorer's instantly updateable HTML control properties. We'll learn more about using this aspect of Internet Explorer throughout this book.

The code for this page, `Resize.htm`, is shown in Listing 3-4.

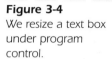

Figure 3-4
We resize a text box under program control.

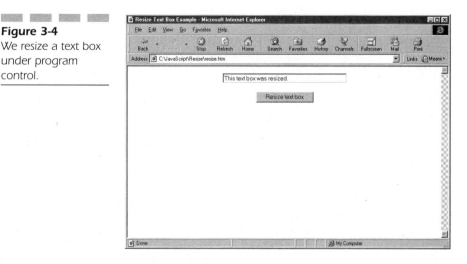

Listing 3-4
`Resize.htm`.

```
<HTML>

<HEAD>
<TITLE>Resize Text Box Example</TITLE>
</HEAD>

<BODY>

<CENTER>
<FORM NAME = form1>
<INPUT TYPE = TEXT NAME = Textbox SIZE = 20 VALUE = "You
      can resize this box.">
<BR>
<BR>
<INPUT TYPE = BUTTON Value = "Resize text box" onClick =
      "ResizeTextbox()">
</FORM>
</CENTER>
```

continues

Listing 3-4
Continued.

```
</BODY>

<SCRIPT LANGUAGE = JavaScript>
  function ResizeTextbox()
  {
      document.form1.Textbox.size = 40
      document.form1.Textbox.value = "This text box was
      resized."
  }
</SCRIPT>

</HTML>
```

Now we have some idea of how to work with scripting elements (the document object, for example) and HTML elements (like text boxes) in JavaScript. The rest of this book focuses working with the scripting elements available to us, so let's continue now with more HTML elements, starting with text areas.

Text Areas

You use text areas when you have multiple lines of text to display. Text areas are like multiline text boxes—you specify the number of rows and columns you want in your text area, and the text area is displayed with scrollbars so the user can scroll through your text if that text can't all be displayed at once.

Here are the properties, methods, and event handlers for text areas

Properties	Methods	Event Handlers
defaultValue	blur	onBlur
form	focus	onChange
name	select	onFocus
type		onSelect
value		

We'll put together a text area example that presents a text area and a button with the prompt "Display Message" to the user. When the user clicks the button, we can place a message—"Hello from JavaScript"—into the text area.

We start the text area example with the <TEXTAREA> tag, giving our text area 30 columns and 10 rows by using the COLS and ROWS attributes:

```
<HTML>

<TITLE>A Text Area Example</TITLE>

<BODY>

<CENTER>
<FORM>
<TEXTAREA NAME = "Textarea" COLS = 30 ROWS = 10></TEXTAREA>
      .
      .
      .
```

Next, we add a button that, when clicked, calls a function named `DisplayMessage()`:

```
<HTML>

<TITLE>A Text Area Example</TITLE>

<BODY>

<CENTER>
<FORM>
<TEXTAREA NAME = "Textarea" COLS = 30 ROWS = 10></TEXTAREA>
<BR>
<BR>
<INPUT TYPE = BUTTON Value = "Display Message" onClick
         = "DisplayMessage(this.form)">
</FORM>
</CENTER>

</BODY>
```

In that function, we simply set the text area's value property to `"Hello from JavaScript"`:

```
<HTML>

<TITLE>A Text Area Example</TITLE>

<BODY>

<CENTER>
<FORM>
<TEXTAREA NAME = "Textarea" COLS = 30 ROWS = 10></TEXTAREA>
<BR>
```

```
<BR>
<INPUT TYPE = BUTTON Value = "Display Message" onClick
        = "DisplayMessage(this.form)">
</FORM>
</CENTER>

</BODY>

<SCRIPT LANGUAGE = JavaScript>
    function DisplayMessage(form1)
    {
        form1.Textarea.value = "Hello from JavaScript"
    }
</SCRIPT>

</HTML>
```

That's it—now open this page, as shown in Figure 3-5. When you click the Display Message button, the program displays the `Hello from Java-Script` message.

NOTE: *As you can see, working with text areas is much like working with text boxes, except that now the user can scroll through multiple lines of text if we have a lot of text to display.*

The code for this page, **Textarea.htm**, is shown in Listing 3-5.

Figure 3-5
We support a text area control.

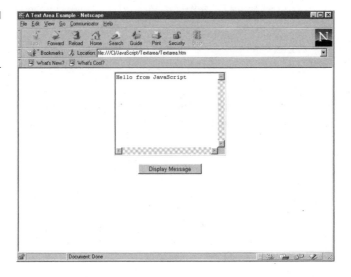

Listing 3-5
`Textarea.htm.`

```
<HTML>

<TITLE>A Text Area Example</TITLE>

<BODY>

<CENTER>
<FORM>
<TEXTAREA NAME = "Textarea" COLS = 30 ROWS = 10></TEXTAREA>
<BR>
<BR>
<INPUT TYPE = BUTTON Value = "Display Message" onClick
        = "DisplayMessage(this.form)">
</FORM>
</CENTER>

</BODY>

<SCRIPT LANGUAGE = JavaScript>
    function DisplayMessage(form1)
    {
        form1.Textarea.value = "Hello from JavaScript"
    }
</SCRIPT>

</HTML>
```

Text areas are one variation on the standard text box. There's another variation we'll take a look at now—the password control.

Password Controls

The *password control* is really just a text control that masks the characters you type into it, displaying each character as an asterisk (*). Because the text in the password control is masked, you can use it for low-security passwords because anyone looking over your shoulder won't be able to read the actual text you've typed.

The password control has these properties, methods, and event handlers:

Properties	**Methods**	**Event Handlers**
defaultValue	blur	onBlur
form	focus	onFocus
name	select	
type		
value		

We'll put together a quick password control example that displays a password control, a text box under that control, and a button. When you type a password into the top box, the password control, all characters are masked. However, when you click the Show Password button, we can read the text from the password control and display it in a standard text box.

We'll put this example, `Password.htm`, together now, starting with the password control itself, which uses the <INPUT> tag and requires the TYPE attribute set to PASSWORD:

```
<HTML>

<TITLE>A Password Example</TITLE>

<BODY>

<CENTER>

<H1>
Enter a password in the top box...
</H1>

<FORM NAME = form1>
<INPUT TYPE = PASSWORD NAME = "Password" SIZE = 25>
        .
        .
        .
```

Next, we add the text box we'll need:

```
<HTML>

<TITLE>A Password Example</TITLE>

<BODY>

<CENTER>

<H1>
Enter a password in the top box...
</H1>
```

```
<FORM NAME = form1>
<INPUT TYPE = PASSWORD NAME = "Password" SIZE = 25>
<BR>
<BR>
<INPUT TYPE = TEXT NAME = "Textbox" SIZE = 25>
          .
          .
          .
```

We also add the button the user clicks to display the password's unmasked text:

```
<HTML>

<TITLE>A Password Example</TITLE>

<BODY>

<CENTER>

<H1>
Enter a password in the top box...
</H1>

<FORM NAME = form1>
<INPUT TYPE = PASSWORD NAME = "Password" SIZE = 25>
<BR>
<BR>
<INPUT TYPE = TEXT NAME = "Textbox" SIZE = 25>
<BR>
<BR>
<INPUT TYPE = BUTTON Value = "Show Password" onClick =
      "ShowPassword()">
          .
          .
          .
```

In JavaScript, all we need to do is to copy the text from the password control and display it in the text box when the user clicks the button:

```
<HTML>

<TITLE>A Password Example</TITLE>

<BODY>

<CENTER>

<H1>
Enter a password in the top box...
</H1>
```

```
<FORM NAME = form1>
<INPUT TYPE = PASSWORD NAME = "Password" SIZE = 25>
<BR>
<BR>
<INPUT TYPE = TEXT NAME = "Textbox" SIZE = 25>
<BR>
<BR>
<INPUT TYPE = BUTTON Value = "Show Password" onClick =
     "ShowPassword()">
</FORM>
</CENTER>

</BODY>

<SCRIPT LANGUAGE = JavaScript>
    function ShowPassword()
    {
         document.form1.Textbox.value = document.form1.
    Password.value
    }
</SCRIPT>

</HTML>
```

That's all it takes. Now open this page as shown in Figure 3-6 and type a password into the top box, the password control. After doing so, click the Show Password button to see the password itself in the second box, the text box. As you can see, the text that was hidden in the password control is available to us in JavaScript.

NOTE: *Note that the password control really offers minimal security because the password is available to any script on the page. In fact, the password control should more properly be called a "masking control."*

Listing 3-6 shows the code for this page, `Password.htm`.

Now we've looked at two variations on the text box: text areas and password controls. We'll take a look some variations on the button control next —the submit and reset controls.

Figure 3-6
The password control
hides its text.

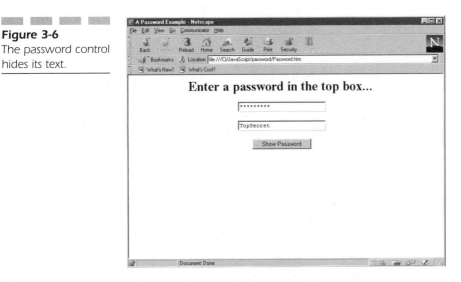

Figure 3-6
The password control
hides its text.

Listing 3-6
`Password.htm`.

```
<HTML>

<TITLE>A Password Example</TITLE>

<BODY>

<CENTER>

<H1>
Enter a password in the top box...
</H1>

<FORM NAME = form1>
<INPUT TYPE = PASSWORD NAME = "Password" SIZE = 25>
<BR>
<BR>
<INPUT TYPE = TEXT NAME = "Textbox" SIZE = 25>
<BR>
<BR>
<INPUT TYPE = BUTTON Value = "Show Password" onClick =
      "ShowPassword()">
</FORM>
</CENTER>

</BODY>
```

continues

Listing 3-6
Continued.

```
<SCRIPT LANGUAGE = JavaScript>
    function ShowPassword()
    {
        document.form1.Textbox.value = document.form1.
    Password.value
    }
</SCRIPT>
```

Submit and Reset Buttons

One of the reasons JavaScript uses controls organized into forms is that forms give us the capability of sending information back to the Web server. For example, you might have a guestbook in your Web page with a few text boxes and a text area, as shown here:

Sign the guestbook, include your comments
below, and see what others have said...

Name:

Email:

Submit   Reset

The user can type information into the controls in the page and click the buttom marked Submit to send all the information back to the Web server.

Back on the server, you must decode the information that's been sent, using *Common Gateway Interface* (CGI) programming techniques such as Perl programming (Perl is a server-side language for writing CGI scripts). In this case, the CGI program interprets the information sent by the user and enters that information into the guestbook. If the user clicks the Reset button, on the other hand, the controls in the form are cleared of all text, and the user can start over.

TIP: *Now you can run JavaScript on your server if you're running a Netscape server that includes Netscape LiveWire, which supports a set of server-side JavaScript extensions (in Netscape Enterprise Server 3.0 and later, the LiveWire JavaScript extensions are built into the server, instead of being considered a separate LiveWire addition). In this way, you can process the information sent from client-side Web pages back to the server using JavaScript.*

One common use of JavaScript is *form validation*—checking the information the user is trying to send before it has to travel back to the server. If there's an error of some kind, for example, you can display an error message before having to send the data back to the server and have the server send the error message back.

Let's see an example of this process. We'll consider it an error if the user hasn't put his or her name in the Name text box of our guest book. We can test the data with JavaScript before that data is sent and display an alert box if the user left the Name box blank.

In this example, `submit.htm`, we'll enclose our form in a table, giving it a colored background to set it off from the rest of the page. Here's how we start that table, coloring it cyan:

```
<HTML>

<HEAD>
<TITLE>
A Submit Button Example
</TITLE>

</HEAD>

<BODY>

<CENTER>
```

```
<H1>
A Submit Button Example
</H1>

<TABLE BORDER CELLPADDING = 6>
<font color = "#ffff00">
<TR ALIGN= CENTER><TD BGCOLOR = cyan>
        .
        .
        .
```

Next, we include a prompt to the user to enter the information and start our form. Here, we set the form's METHOD attribute to POST, which means this form's information can be sent back to the server, and its AC-TION attribute to the URL of the guestbook itself so the CGI file on the server knows where to find the guestbook (this is common for guestbook CGI scripts):

```
<HTML>

<HEAD>
<TITLE>
A Submit Button Example
</TITLE>

</HEAD>

<BODY>

<CENTER>
<H1>
A Submit Button Example
</H1>

<TABLE BORDER CELLPADDING = 6>
<font color = "#ffff00">
<TR ALIGN= CENTER><TD BGCOLOR = cyan>
Sign the guestbook, include your comments below, and see
        what others have said...

<BR>

<P>
<FORM NAME = form1 onSubmit = "return checkForm()"
        METHOD=POST

        ACTION="http://www.server.com/cgi/guestbook.cgi/guest-
        book.htm">
            .
            .
            .
```

Note also that we use the form's onSubmit event handler, the one that's called when the user clicks the Submit button. The function we'll use to check the user's name, `checkForm()`, will return a value of true if the form is acceptable and false otherwise. We then pass this value back to the browser; true means the browser should send the form, and false means it should not.

TIP: *If you want to actually implement a guestbook like this one, you'll need to install the appropriate CGI programs on your server. Many such CGI programs are available free on the Web.*

Now we add the first controls we'll need in the guestbook form—two text boxes and a text area:

```
<HTML>

<HEAD>
<TITLE>
A Submit Button Example
</TITLE>

</HEAD>

<BODY>

<CENTER>
<H1>
A Submit Button Example
</H1>

<TABLE BORDER CELLPADDING = 6>
<font color = "#ffff00">
<TR ALIGN= CENTER><TD BGCOLOR = cyan>
Sign the guestbook, include your comments below, and see
        what others have said...

<BR>

<P>
<FORM NAME = form1 onSubmit = "return checkForm()"
        METHOD=POST

        ACTION="http://www.server.com/cgi/guestbook.cgi/
        guestbook.htm">
Name: <INPUT TYPE="text" NAME="name" SIZE=30 MAXLENGTH=30>
</P>

<P>
Email: <INPUT TYPE="text" NAME="address" SIZE=30
        MAXLENGTH=30>
```

```
</P>

<BR>
<TEXTAREA ROWS=5 COLS=60 NAME="body"></TEXTAREA>
<BR>
<BR>
   .
   .
   .
```

Finally, we add the Submit and Reset buttons we'll use:

```
<HTML>

<HEAD>
<TITLE>
A Submit Button Example
</TITLE>

</HEAD>

<BODY>

<CENTER>
<H1>
A Submit Button Example
</H1>

<TABLE BORDER CELLPADDING = 6>
<font color = "#ffff00">
<TR ALIGN= CENTER><TD BGCOLOR = cyan>
Sign the guestbook, include your comments below, and see
     what others have said...

<BR>

<P>
<FORM NAME = form1 onSubmit = "return checkForm()"
     METHOD=POST

     ACTION="http://www.server.com/cgi/guestbook.cgi/
     guestbook.htm">
Name: <INPUT TYPE="text" NAME="name" SIZE=30 MAXLENGTH=30>
</P>

<P>
Email: <INPUT TYPE="text" NAME="address" SIZE=30
     MAXLENGTH=30>
</P>

<BR>
<TEXTAREA ROWS=5 COLS=60 NAME="body"></TEXTAREA>
<BR>
<BR>
```

```
<INPUT TYPE=submit VALUE="Submit">
<INPUT TYPE=reset VALUE="Reset">
</FORM>

</TD>
</TR>
</TABLE>

</CENTER>
```

That takes care of the controls in the form—the Submit and Reset buttons are active automatically. If the user clicks Submit, our `checkForm()` function is called to check the form; if it's OK, we'll send the form. If the user clicks Reset, the browser automatically clears all the controls in the form.

Now we'll write the `checkForm()` function. In this function, we want to check the text box we've called "Name" in the form because this text box holds the user's name. If this text box is empty, we will display an alert box with the text `"Please enter your name"` and return a value of false to the Web browser so it won't send the form. Here's how we test the data in the Name text box:

```
<SCRIPT LANGUAGE = JavaScript>

    function checkForm()
    {
        if (document.form1.name.value == ""){
            alert("Please enter your name")
            return false
        }

            .
            .
            .
```

If, on the other hand, the text box is not empty, we return a value of true so the browser will send the form:

```
<SCRIPT LANGUAGE = JavaScript>

    function checkForm()
    {
        if (document.form1.name.value == ""){
            alert("Please enter your name")
            return false
        }
        else{
            return true
        }
    }

</SCRIPT>
```

The Submit.htm example is ready to go, so try opening it. If you don't enter anything in the Name text box and click Submit, the program displays an alert box, as shown in Figure 3-7, and will not send the form back to the server. On the other hand, if you do include a name, the browser sends the form back to the server (although it won't get very far because the server name we've used in our form, www.server.com, is really just a placeholder for the name of your server). The Submit.htm example is working the way we want it to!

The code for this page, Submit.htm, is shown in Listing 3-7.

Figure 3-7
We check a form's data before sending it to the server.

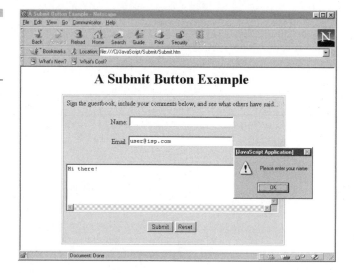

Listing 3-7
Submit.htm.

```
<HTML>

<HEAD>
<TITLE>
A Submit Button Example
</TITLE>

</HEAD>


<BODY>

<CENTER>
<H1>
A Submit Button Example
</H1>

<TABLE BORDER CELLPADDING = 6>
<font color = "#ffff00">
```

```
<TR ALIGN= CENTER><TD BGCOLOR = cyan>
Sign the guestbook, include your comments below, and see
     what others have said...

<BR>

<P>
<FORM NAME = form1 onSubmit = "return checkForm()"
     METHOD=POST

     ACTION="http://www.server.com/cgi/guestbook.cgi/
     guestbook.htm">
Name: <INPUT TYPE="text" NAME="name" SIZE=30 MAXLENGTH=30>
</P>

<P>
Email: <INPUT TYPE="text" NAME="address" SIZE=30
     MAXLENGTH=30>
</P>

<BR>
<TEXTAREA ROWS=5 COLS=60 NAME="body"></TEXTAREA>
<BR>
<BR>

<INPUT TYPE=submit VALUE="Submit">
<INPUT TYPE=reset VALUE="Reset">
</FORM>

</TD>
</TR>
</TABLE>

</CENTER>

<SCRIPT LANGUAGE = JavaScript>

    function checkForm()
    {
        if (document.form1.name.value == ""){
            alert("Please enter your name")
            return false
        }
        else{
            return true
        }
    }

</SCRIPT>

</BODY>
</HTML>
```

There's another control we should look at while discussing sending information back to Web servers—the file control.

File Controls

There's another way to upload information from a Web page in HTML—you can use a file control. This control uploads an entire file that the user selects.

The file control's properties are form, name, type, and value; its methods are blur and focus; and its events are onBlur, onChange, and onFocus. Visually, a file control consists of both a text box to hold the file's name and a button labeled Browse. The user can either enter a filename in the text box directly or click the Browse button to browse for a file (the brower opens a window with lists of files and drives for the user to look through).

Let's add a file control to our previous example, calling this new example `Filer.htm`. Adding a file control is easy. We just place a prompt into the Web page—"If you prefer, attach a file containing your comments..."—and label the file control with a string reading, "File name:", as shown here:

```
<HTML>

<HEAD>
<TITLE>
A Submit Button Example
</TITLE>

</HEAD>


<BODY>

<CENTER>
<H1>
A Submit Button Example
</H1>

<TABLE BORDER CELLPADDING = 6>
<font color = "#ffff00">
<TR ALIGN= CENTER><TD BGCOLOR = cyan>
```

```
Sign the guestbook, include your comments below, and see
    what others have said...

<BR>

<P>
<FORM NAME = form1 onSubmit = "return checkForm()"
    METHOD=POST

    ACTION="http://www.server.com/cgi/guestbook.cgi/
    guestbook.htm">
Name: <INPUT TYPE="text" NAME="name" SIZE=30 MAXLENGTH=30>
</P>

<P>
Email: <INPUT TYPE="text" NAME="address" SIZE=30
    MAXLENGTH=30>
</P>

<BR>
<TEXTAREA ROWS=5 COLS=60 NAME="body"></TEXTAREA>
<BR>
<BR>

<BR>
If you prefer, attach a file containing your comments...
<BR>
File name:<INPUT TYPE = FILE>
<BR>
<BR>

<INPUT TYPE=submit VALUE="Submit">
<INPUT TYPE=reset VALUE="Reset">
</FORM>

</TD>
</TR>
</TABLE>

</CENTER>
```

That's all it takes—open this page now, as shown in Figure 3-8. You can see the file control at the bottom of the form; the user can enter a filename there to automatically upload the file when he or she clicks the Submit button.

The code for this example, `Filer.htm`, is shown in Listing 3-8.

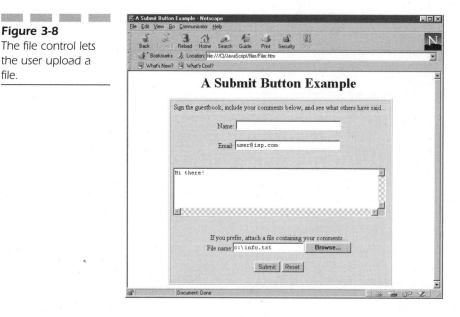

```
<HTML>

<HEAD>
<TITLE>
A Submit Button Example
</TITLE>

</HEAD>


<BODY>

<CENTER>
<H1>
A Submit Button Example
</H1>

<TABLE BORDER CELLPADDING = 6>
<font color = "#ffff00">
<TR ALIGN= CENTER><TD BGCOLOR = cyan>
Sign the guestbook, include your comments below, and see
        what others have said...

<BR>

<P>
<FORM NAME = form1 onSubmit = "return checkForm()"
        METHOD=POST
```

```
        ACTION="http://www.server.com/cgi/guestbook.cgi/
        guestbook.htm">
Name: <INPUT TYPE="text" NAME="name" SIZE=30 MAXLENGTH=30>
</P>

<P>
Email: <INPUT TYPE="text" NAME="address" SIZE=30
      MAXLENGTH=30>
</P>

<BR>
<TEXTAREA ROWS=5 COLS=60 NAME="body"></TEXTAREA>
<BR>
<BR>

<BR>
If you prefer, attach a file containing your comments...
<BR>
File name:<INPUT TYPE = FILE>
<BR>
<BR>

<INPUT TYPE=submit VALUE="Submit">
<INPUT TYPE=reset VALUE="Reset">
</FORM>

</TD>
</TR>
</TABLE>

</CENTER>

<SCRIPT LANGUAGE = JavaScript>

    function checkForm()
    {
        if (document.form1.name.value == ""){
            alert("Please enter your name")
            return false
        }
        else{
            return true
        }
    }

</SCRIPT>

</BODY>
</HTML>
```

The last control we'll examine in this chapter is the hidden control, which is very useful. All the data in the controls we've worked with so far has been visible to the user (even if it was masked, as with the password control), but sometimes you want to store data that the user can't see for some behind-the-scenes processing. You can do that with the hidden control.

Hidden Controls

The hidden control is really just a storage place for text data that you can use in a Web page. This data is hidden from the user, and you use it for internal processing in your program. For example, you can hold data in a hidden control as a backup and restore that data to other controls if needed. The hidden control has the properties name, type, and value, and it has no methods or event handlers.

We'll put together an example using the hidden control that display a text box with the text `Hello from JavaScript`. The user can change that text, altering it in some way. However, we will be able to restore that text if we have it stored as a backup in a hidden control, retrieving that data when the user clicks a button labeled `Restore default`.

We'll start this example, `Hidden.txt`, by placing the text box and the button into the Web page:

```
<HTML>

<HEAD>
<TITLE>A Hidden Control Example</TITLE>
</HEAD>

<BODY>

<CENTER>

<H1>
Change the text, then click the button to restore it...
</H1>

<BR>

<FORM NAME = form1>
<INPUT TYPE = TEXT NAME = "Textbox" SIZE = 25>
<BR>
<BR>
<INPUT TYPE = BUTTON Value = "Restore default" onClick =
     restoreData()>
```

.
.
.

Note that when the user clicks the Restore default button, the browser calls a function named restoreData(). In that function, we retrieve the original string—"Hello from JavaScript"—from a hidden control and restore it in the text box.

We add the hidden control, which we'll name "backup," to our Web page this way:

```
<HTML>

<HEAD>
<TITLE>A Hidden Control Example</TITLE>
</HEAD>

<BODY>

<CENTER>

<H1>
Change the text, then click the button to restore it...
</H1>

<BR>

<FORM NAME = form1>
<INPUT TYPE = TEXT NAME = "Textbox" SIZE = 25>
<BR>
<BR>
<INPUT TYPE = BUTTON Value = "Restore default" onClick =
        restoreData()>
<INPUT TYPE = HIDDEN NAME = backup VALUE = "Hello from
        JavaScript">          <-
</FORM>
</CENTER>

</BODY>
```

Note that we place the text "Hello from JavaScript" into the hidden control's value property to load our backup.

In the script portion of the page, then, we start by loading that same string into the page's text box:

```
<SCRIPT LANGUAGE = JavaScript>

    document.form1.Textbox.value =  "Hello from JavaScript"
         .
         .
```

Next, we write the function, `restoreData()`, that will be called when the user clicks the Restore default button:

```
<SCRIPT LANGUAGE = JavaScript>

    document.form1.Textbox.value =   "Hello from JavaScript"

    function restoreData()
    {
        .
        .
        .
    }
</SCRIPT>
```

When the browser calls this function, we are supposed to reload the text box with the string from the hiddencontrol. We can do that in one line of JavaScript:

```
<SCRIPT LANGUAGE = JavaScript>

    document.form1.Textbox.value =   "Hello from JavaScript"

    function restoreData()
    {
        document.form1.Textbox.value =
      document.form1.backup.value
    }
</SCRIPT>
```

That completes our `Hidden.htm` page, so try openin it now. The user can edit our `"Hello from JavaScript"` string, as shown in Figure 3-9.

Figure 3-9
The user changes the data in a text box, but we can restore that data.

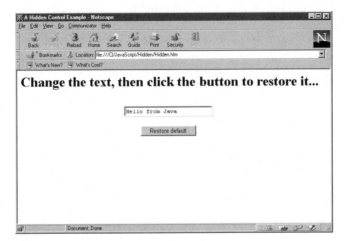

To restore the string to its original value when the user clicks the Restore default button, we simply reload the text box from the hidden control, as shown in Figure 3-10.

TIP: *Because we can store data in a JavaScript program as easily as we can in a hidden control, it usually makes sense to simply store our data in our code, not in hidden controls. Typically, hidden controls are used in forms to make sure some information not visible to the user is sent along with the rest of the form to the server when the user clicks the Submit button.*

The code for this page, `Hidden.htm`, is shown in Listing 3-9.

Figure 3-10
We restore data with
the hidden control.

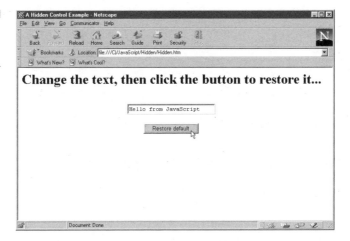

Listing 3-9
`Hidden.htm.`

```
<HTML>

<HEAD>
<TITLE>A Hidden Control Example</TITLE>
</HEAD>

<BODY>

<CENTER>

<H1>
Change the text, then click the button to restore it...
</H1>

<BR>

<FORM NAME = form1>
```
                                                                    continues

Listing 3-9
Continued.

```
<INPUT TYPE = TEXT NAME = "Textbox" SIZE = 25>
<BR>
<BR>
<INPUT TYPE = BUTTON Value = "Restore default" onClick =
    restoreData()>
<INPUT TYPE = HIDDEN NAME = backup VALUE = "Hello from
    JavaScript">
</FORM>
</CENTER>

</BODY>

<SCRIPT LANGUAGE = JavaScript>

    document.form1.Textbox.value =  "Hello from JavaScript"

    function restoreData()
    {
        document.form1.Textbox.value =
    document.form1.backup.value
    }
</SCRIPT>

</HTML>
```

CONCLUSION

That completes this chapter. We've covered a great deal here, from embedding controls like text boxes in Web pages to using active controls like buttons, text areas, password controls, and more. We've seen how to work with HTML elements in JavaScript and how to work with scripting objects such as the document object. We've also learned how to work with submit, reset, file, and hidden controls, adding more power to our Web pages. We've come a long way.

In the next chapter, we're going to work with even more powerful controls: check boxes, radio buttons, and select controls.

4

Forms: Check Boxes and Radio Buttons

In this chapter, we're going to continue the work we started in the previous chapter, exploring the form-based controls in JavaScript. We're going to learn about some truly powerful controls: check boxes, radio buttons, and select (scrolling list) controls.

These controls are familiar to Windows users. Check boxes display a checkmark when you click them, radio buttons display a black dot in their center, and select controls display a list of options the user can select from.

We'll start with check boxes, move on to radio buttons, and then use check boxes *with* radio buttons. After that, we'll work with select controls of two sorts: those for selecting one item and those for selecting multiple items.

Check Boxes

As mentioned, a check box appears as a small, labeled square box that, when clicked, toggles a checkmark on and off. Here are the properties, methods, and event handlers of the check box control:

Properties	Methods	Event Handlers
checked	blur	onBlur
defaultChecked	click	onClick
form	focus	onFocus
name		
type		
value		

In our first check box example, we'll show the user a number of check boxes, like this:

When the user clicks a check box, we'll use a text box to report which check box has been clicked.

We'll start this example, Checks.htm, with the form we'll need (form1) and a prompt to the user, as shown here:

```
<HTML>

<HEAD>
<TITLE>A Check Box Example</TITLE>
</HEAD>

<BODY>

<FORM NAME = form1>
<CENTER>
<H1>
Click one of the check boxes...
</H1>
    .
    .
    .
```

Creating Check Boxes

We'll create the check boxes we need with the <INPUT> tag, setting its TYPE attribute to CHECKBOX. Next, we'll name each of the check boxes we'll use and give each one its own click event handler. We'll connect the first check box to check1Clicked(), the second check box to check2Clicked(), and so on. To make the page look a little neater, we can place the check boxes in a table that has a cyan background. Here's how we add the check boxes and the text box:

```
<HTML>

<HEAD>
<TITLE>A Check Box Example</TITLE>
</HEAD>

<BODY>

<FORM NAME = form1>
<CENTER>
<H1>
Click one of the check boxes...
</H1>

<TABLE BORDER BGCOLOR = CYAN WIDTH = 200>
```

```
<TR><TD><INPUT TYPE = CHECKBOX NAME = Check1 onClick =
    check1Clicked()>Check 1</TD></TR>
    <TR><TD><INPUT TYPE = CHECKBOX NAME = Check2 onClick =
    check2Clicked()>Check 2</TD></TR>
    <TR><TD><INPUT TYPE = CHECKBOX NAME = Check3 onClick =
    check3Clicked()>Check 3</TD></TR>
    <TR><TD><INPUT TYPE = CHECKBOX NAME = Check4 onClick =
    check4Clicked()>Check 4</TD></TR>
    <TR><TD><INPUT TYPE = CHECKBOX NAME = Check5 onClick =
    check5Clicked()>Check 5</TD></TR>
</TABLE>
<BR>
<BR>
<INPUT TYPE  =  TEXT NAME  =  "Textbox" SIZE  =  25>     <-
</CENTER>
</FORM>
```

TIP: *If you want a check box to be checked when it's first displayed, place the attribute CHECKED in its <INPUT> tag. Nothing else is needed, such as "CHECKED = TRUE"—just use the keyword CHECKED.*

As we've set things up, when the user clicks the first check box, the browser calls the function check1Clicked(), when the user clicks the second check box, the browser calls check2Clicked(), and so on, so we'll add those functions now. In each of those functions, we indicate which check box the user clicked with a message in the text box:

```
<HTML>

<HEAD>
<TITLE>A Check Box Example</TITLE>
</HEAD>

<BODY>

<FORM NAME = form1>
<CENTER>
<H1>
Click one of the check boxes...
</H1>

<TABLE BORDER BGCOLOR = CYAN WIDTH = 200>
    <TR><TD><INPUT TYPE = CHECKBOX NAME = Check1 onClick =
    check1Clicked()>Check 1</TD></TR>
    <TR><TD><INPUT TYPE = CHECKBOX NAME = Check2 onClick =
    check2Clicked()>Check 2</TD></TR>
    <TR><TD><INPUT TYPE = CHECKBOX NAME = Check3 onClick =
    check3Clicked()>Check 3</TD></TR>
```

```
        <TR><TD><INPUT TYPE = CHECKBOX NAME = Check4 onClick =
            check4Clicked()>Check 4</TD></TR>
        <TR><TD><INPUT TYPE = CHECKBOX NAME = Check5 onClick =
            check5Clicked()>Check 5</TD></TR>
    </TABLE>
    <BR>
    <BR>
    <INPUT TYPE  =  TEXT NAME  =  "Textbox" SIZE  =  25>
    </CENTER>
    </FORM>

    </BODY>

    <SCRIPT LANGUAGE = JavaScript>

        function check1Clicked() {
            document.form1.Textbox.value = "Check box 1 was
        clicked."
        }

        function check2Clicked() {
            document.form1.Textbox.value = "Check box 2 was
        clicked."
        }

        function check3Clicked() {
            document.form1.Textbox.value = "Check box 3 was
        clicked."
        }

        function check4Clicked() {
            document.form1.Textbox.value = "Check box 4 was
        clicked."
        }

        function check5Clicked() {
            document.form1.Textbox.value = "Check box 5 was
        clicked."
        }

    </SCRIPT>

    </HTML>
```

The Checks.htm page is ready to go, so open it now. When you click one of the check boxes, the program indicates which one was clicked in the text box, as shown in Figure 4-1. Now we've added handling check boxes to our JavaScript capabilities.

Figure 4-1
We use check boxes
in a program.

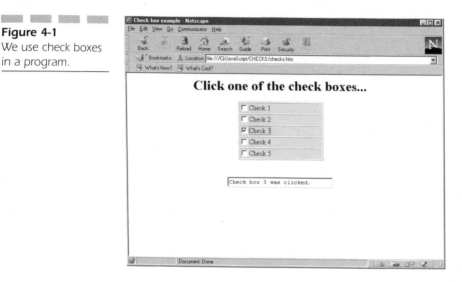

The code for this page, Checks.htm, is shown in Listing 4-1.

Listing 4-1
Checks.htm.

```
<HTML>

<HEAD>
<TITLE>A Check Box Example</TITLE>
</HEAD>

<BODY>

<FORM NAME = form1>
<CENTER>
<H1>
Click one of the check boxes...
</H1>

<TABLE BORDER BGCOLOR = CYAN WIDTH = 200>
    <TR><TD><INPUT TYPE = CHECKBOX NAME = Check1 onClick =
        check1Clicked()>Check 1</TD></TR>
    <TR><TD><INPUT TYPE = CHECKBOX NAME = Check2 onClick =
        check2Clicked()>Check 2</TD></TR>
    <TR><TD><INPUT TYPE = CHECKBOX NAME = Check3 onClick =
        check3Clicked()>Check 3</TD></TR>
    <TR><TD><INPUT TYPE = CHECKBOX NAME = Check4 onClick =
        check4Clicked()>Check 4</TD></TR>
    <TR><TD><INPUT TYPE = CHECKBOX NAME = Check5 onClick =
        check5Clicked()>Check 5</TD></TR>
</TABLE>
<BR>
<BR>
<INPUT TYPE  =   TEXT NAME  =   "Textbox" SIZE  =   25>
```

Listing 4-1
Coontinued

```
</CENTER>
</FORM>

</BODY>

<SCRIPT LANGUAGE = JavaScript>

    function check1Clicked() {
        document.form1.Textbox.value = "Check box 1 was
    clicked."
    }

    function check2Clicked() {
        document.form1.Textbox.value = "Check box 2 was
    clicked."
    }

    function check3Clicked() {
        document.form1.Textbox.value = "Check box 3 was
    clicked."
    }

    function check4Clicked() {
        document.form1.Textbox.value = "Check box 4 was
    clicked."
    }

    function check5Clicked() {
        document.form1.Textbox.value = "Check box 5 was
    clicked."
    }

</SCRIPT>

</HTML>
```

Radio buttons are very similar to check boxes; we'll take a look at them in the following section.

Radio Buttons

Radio buttons are like check boxes, except that they work in a group. Only one radio button in the group can be checked at once, making the options they present to the user exclusive ones. Check boxes let the user select a number of options at once—like condiments on a hamburger—but radio buttons let the user select only one option at a time, such as the current day of the week.

Radio buttons have the same properties, methods, and event handlers as check boxes:

Properties	Methods	Event Handlers
checked	blur	onBlur
defaultChecked	click	onClick
form	focus	onFocus
name		
type		
value		

To get experience with these new controls, we'll write a radio button example that displays several radio buttons to the user, as shown here:

When the user clicks one of the radio buttons, we'll indicate in the text box which radio button was clicked. Because these controls are radio buttons, only one can be selected (that is, display a black dot in its center) at a time; if you click a new radio button, the old one is automatically deselected.

Creating Radio Buttons

How do the radio buttons know to act in concert? We design them that way by giving the radio buttons we want to group together the same name. Here's how we do that in our new example, Radios.htm:

```
<HTML>

<HEAD>
<TITLE>A Radio Button Example</TITLE>
</HEAD>

<BODY>

<FORM NAME = "form1">

<CENTER>
<H1>
Click one of the radio buttons...
</H1>

<TABLE BORDER BGCOLOR = CYAN WIDTH = 200>
    <TR><TD><INPUT TYPE = RADIO NAME = RadioButtons
      onClick = radio1Clicked()>Radio 1</TD></TR>
    <TR><TD><INPUT TYPE = RADIO NAME = RadioButtons
      onClick = radio2Clicked()>Radio 2</TD></TR>
    <TR><TD><INPUT TYPE = RADIO NAME = RadioButtons
      onClick = radio3Clicked()>Radio 3</TD></TR>
    <TR><TD><INPUT TYPE = RADIO NAME = RadioButtons
      onClick = radio4Clicked()>Radio 4</TD></TR>
    <TR><TD><INPUT TYPE = RADIO NAME = RadioButtons
      onClick = radio5Clicked()>Radio 5</TD></TR>
</TABLE>
```

TIP: *As with check boxes, if you want a radio button to be checked when it's first displayed, place the attribute CHECKED in its <INPUT> tag.*

Giving each radio button the same name groups them together so they act together, as opposed to the check boxes, which we named individually:

```
<TABLE BORDER BGCOLOR = CYAN WIDTH = 200>
    <TR><TD><INPUT TYPE = CHECKBOX NAME = Check1 onClick =
      check1Clicked()>Check 1</TD></TR>
    <TR><TD><INPUT TYPE = CHECKBOX NAME = Check2 onClick =
      check2Clicked()>Check 2</TD></TR>
    <TR><TD><INPUT TYPE = CHECKBOX NAME = Check3 onClick =
      check3Clicked()>Check 3</TD></TR>
```

```
    <TR><TD><INPUT TYPE = CHECKBOX NAME = Check4 onClick =
    check4Clicked()>Check 4</TD></TR>
    <TR><TD><INPUT TYPE = CHECKBOX NAME = Check5 onClick =
    check5Clicked()>Check 5</TD></TR>
</TABLE>
```

We've connected the radio buttons to the functions radio1Clicked(), radio2Clicked(), and so on, so we add those functions now:

```
<HTML>

<HEAD>
<TITLE>A Radio Button Example</TITLE>
</HEAD>

<BODY>

<FORM NAME = "form1">

<CENTER>
<H1>
Click one of the radio buttons...
</H1>

<TABLE BORDER BGCOLOR = CYAN WIDTH = 200>
    <TR><TD><INPUT TYPE = RADIO NAME = RadioButtons onClick
    = radio1Clicked()>Radio 1</TD></TR>
    <TR><TD><INPUT TYPE = RADIO NAME = RadioButtons onClick
    = radio2Clicked()>Radio 2</TD></TR>
    <TR><TD><INPUT TYPE = RADIO NAME = RadioButtons onClick
    = radio3Clicked()>Radio 3</TD></TR>
    <TR><TD><INPUT TYPE = RADIO NAME = RadioButtons onClick
    = radio4Clicked()>Radio 4</TD></TR>
    <TR><TD><INPUT TYPE = RADIO NAME = RadioButtons onClick
    = radio5Clicked()>Radio 5</TD></TR>
</TABLE>
<BR>
<BR>
<INPUT TYPE  =  TEXT NAME  =  TextBox SIZE  =  35>
</CENTER>

</FORM>

</BODY>

<SCRIPT LANGUAGE = JavaScript>

    function radio1Clicked()
    {
        document.form1.TextBox.value = "Radio button 1
    was clicked."
    }

    function radio2Clicked()
```

```
        {
                document.form1.TextBox.value = "Radio button 2
        was clicked."
        }

        function radio3Clicked()
        {
                document.form1.TextBox.value = "Radio button 3
        was clicked."
        }

        function radio4Clicked()
        {
                document.form1.TextBox.value = "Radio button 4
        was clicked."
        }

        function radio5Clicked()
        {
                document.form1.TextBox.value = "Radio button 5
        was clicked."
        }

</SCRIPT>

</HTML>
```

Open the Radios.htm page now. When you click a radio button, the program reports which one you clicked, as shown in Figure 4-2. When you click another radio button, the first one is deselected automatically. The Radios.htm example works as we intended.

Figure 4-2
We support radio buttons in a program.

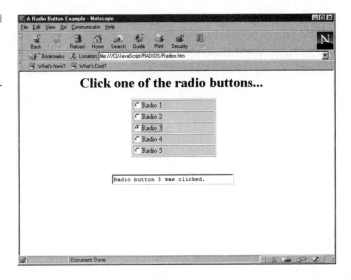

The code for this example, Radios.htm, is shown in Listing 4-2.

Listing 4-2
Radios.htm.

```
<HTML>

<HEAD>
<TITLE>A Radio Button Example</TITLE>
</HEAD>

<BODY>

<FORM NAME = "form1">
<CENTER>
<H1>
Click one of the radio buttons...
</H1>

<TABLE BORDER BGCOLOR = CYAN WIDTH = 200>
    <TR><TD><INPUT TYPE = RADIO NAME = RadioButtons onClick
      = radio1Clicked()>Radio 1</TD></TR>
    <TR><TD><INPUT TYPE = RADIO NAME = RadioButtons onClick
      = radio2Clicked()>Radio 2</TD></TR>
    <TR><TD><INPUT TYPE = RADIO NAME = RadioButtons onClick
      = radio3Clicked()>Radio 3</TD></TR>
    <TR><TD><INPUT TYPE = RADIO NAME = RadioButtons onClick
      = radio4Clicked()>Radio 4</TD></TR>
    <TR><TD><INPUT TYPE = RADIO NAME = RadioButtons onClick
      = radio5Clicked()>Radio 5</TD></TR>
</TABLE>
<BR>
<BR>
<INPUT TYPE  =  TEXT NAME  =  TextBox SIZE  =  35>
</CENTER>

</FORM>

</BODY>

<SCRIPT LANGUAGE = JavaScript>

    function radio1Clicked()
    {
        document.form1.TextBox.value = "Radio button 1 was
      clicked."
    }

    function radio2Clicked()
    {
        document.form1.TextBox.value = "Radio button 2 was
      clicked."
    }

    function radio3Clicked()
    {
        document.form1.TextBox.value = "Radio button 3 was
      clicked."
```

Listing 4-2
Continued.

```
    }

    function radio4Clicked()
    {
        document.form1.TextBox.value = "Radio button 4 was
    clicked."
    }

    function radio5Clicked()
    {
        document.form1.TextBox.value = "Radio button 5 was
    clicked."
    }

</SCRIPT>

</HTML>
```

Now that we've seen how to use check boxes and radio buttons, we will take a look at how to use these controls together.

Putting Check Boxes and Radio Buttons Together

It's common to use radio buttons and check boxes together. For example, we can create a Web page offering different types of donuts to buy—plain, chocolate, jelly, and so on—with options like sprinkles, powdered sugar, and frosting. When the user clicks a radio button to select a type of donut —only one type of donut can be selected because radio buttons have been used—the program checks different check boxes indicating which "options" come with that donut.

We'll display a price for the donut in the text box at the bottom (to keep it simple in this example, we'll just make each donut option worth fifty cents). When the user selects another type of donut, we can display that donut's options. In fact, we can even let users select their own options by clicking check boxes; when they click a check box, we'll compute and display the new cost.

Let's start this example, Donuts.htm, with a form (form1) and a prompt to the user:

```
<HTML>

<HEAD>
```

```
<TITLE>The Donut Example</TITLE>
</HEAD>

<BODY>

<FORM NAME = "form1">

<CENTER>
<H1>Select your donut!</H1>
</CENTER>
<BR>
<BR>
```

Next, we add the radio buttons we'll use. These buttons will go in a table on the left side of the page, so we use the ALIGN attribute here, setting it to LEFT:

```
<HTML>

<HEAD>
<TITLE>The Donut Example</TITLE>
</HEAD>

<BODY>

<FORM NAME = "form1">

<CENTER>
<H1>Select your donut!</H1>
</CENTER>
<BR>
<BR>

<TABLE BORDER BGCOLOR = CYAN WIDTH = 300 ALIGN = LEFT>
    <TR><TD><INPUT TYPE = RADIO NAME = RadioGroup onClick
    = radio1Clicked()>Plain</TD></TR>
    <TR><TD><INPUT TYPE = RADIO NAME = RadioGroup onClick
    = radio2Clicked()>Chocolate</TD></TR>
    <TR><TD><INPUT TYPE = RADIO NAME = RadioGroup onClick
    = radio3Clicked()>Jelly</TD></TR>
    <TR><TD><INPUT TYPE = RADIO NAME = RadioGroup onClick
    = radio4Clicked()>Cream-filled</TD></TR>
    <TR><TD><INPUT TYPE = RADIO NAME = RadioGroup onClick
    = radio5Clicked()>Strawberry</TD></TR>
</TABLE>
    .
    .
    .
```

Next, we add the check boxes on the right, using ALIGN = RIGHT:

```
<HTML>
```

```
<HEAD>
<TITLE>The Donut Example</TITLE>
</HEAD>

<BODY>

<FORM NAME = "form1">

<CENTER>
<H1>Select your donut!</H1>
</CENTER>
<BR>
<BR>

<TABLE BORDER BGCOLOR = CYAN WIDTH = 300 ALIGN = LEFT>
    <TR><TD><INPUT TYPE = RADIO NAME = RadioGroup onClick
    = radio1Clicked()>Plain</TD></TR>
    <TR><TD><INPUT TYPE = RADIO NAME = RadioGroup onClick
    = radio2Clicked()>Chocolate</TD></TR>
    <TR><TD><INPUT TYPE = RADIO NAME = RadioGroup onClick
    = radio3Clicked()>Jelly</TD></TR>
    <TR><TD><INPUT TYPE = RADIO NAME = RadioGroup onClick
    = radio4Clicked()>Cream-filled</TD></TR>
    <TR><TD><INPUT TYPE = RADIO NAME = RadioGroup onClick
    = radio5Clicked()>Strawberry</TD></TR>
</TABLE>

<TABLE BORDER BGCOLOR = CYAN WIDTH = 300 ALIGN = RIGHT>
    <TR><TD><INPUT TYPE = CHECKBOX NAME = Check1 onClick =
    check1Clicked()>Plain</TD></TR>
    <TR><TD><INPUT TYPE = CHECKBOX NAME = Check2 onClick =
    check2Clicked()>Sprinkles</TD></TR>
    <TR><TD><INPUT TYPE = CHECKBOX NAME = Check3 onClick =
    check3Clicked()>Powdered sugar</TD></TR>
    <TR><TD><INPUT TYPE = CHECKBOX NAME = Check4 onClick =
    check4Clicked()>Frosted</TD></TR>
    <TR><TD><INPUT TYPE = CHECKBOX NAME = Check5 onClick =
    check5Clicked()>Filled</TD></TR>
</TABLE>
```

Now that we've installed the radio buttons and the check boxes, we add the text box we'll use. To end the right and left alignment of page elements, we use a <BR CLEAR = ALL> tag:

```
<HTML>

<HEAD>
<TITLE>The Donut Example</TITLE>
</HEAD>

<BODY>
```

```
<FORM NAME = "form1">

<CENTER>
<H1>Select your donut!</H1>
</CENTER>
<BR>
<BR>

<TABLE BORDER BGCOLOR = CYAN WIDTH = 300 ALIGN = LEFT>
   <TR><TD><INPUT TYPE = RADIO NAME = RadioGroup onClick =
      radio1Clicked()>Plain</TD></TR>
   <TR><TD><INPUT TYPE = RADIO NAME = RadioGroup onClick =
      radio2Clicked()>Chocolate</TD></TR>
   <TR><TD><INPUT TYPE = RADIO NAME = RadioGroup onClick =
      radio3Clicked()>Jelly</TD></TR>
   <TR><TD><INPUT TYPE = RADIO NAME = RadioGroup onClick =
      radio4Clicked()>Cream-filled</TD></TR>
   <TR><TD><INPUT TYPE = RADIO NAME = RadioGroup onClick =
      radio5Clicked()>Strawberry</TD></TR>
</TABLE>

<TABLE BORDER BGCOLOR = CYAN WIDTH = 300 ALIGN = RIGHT>
   <TR><TD><INPUT TYPE = CHECKBOX NAME = Check1 onClick =
      check1Clicked()>Plain</TD></TR>
   <TR><TD><INPUT TYPE = CHECKBOX NAME = Check2 onClick =
      check2Clicked()>Sprinkles</TD></TR>
   <TR><TD><INPUT TYPE = CHECKBOX NAME = Check3 onClick =
      check3Clicked()>Powdered sugar</TD></TR>
   <TR><TD><INPUT TYPE = CHECKBOX NAME = Check4 onClick =
      check4Clicked()>Frosted</TD></TR>
   <TR><TD><INPUT TYPE = CHECKBOX NAME = Check5 onClick =
      check5Clicked()>Filled</TD></TR>
</TABLE>

<BR CLEAR = ALL>
<BR>

<CENTER>
<INPUT TYPE  =  TEXT NAME  =  TextBox SIZE  =  30 ALIGN =
      CENTER>
</CENTER>

</FORM>
```

Now we'll work on the code for this page. When the user clicks a radio button, we want to do three things—clear all the check boxes that might have already been clicked, check the check boxes that represent the correct options for the current type of donut, and calculate the cost of the donut. We'll handle each of these tasks in a function: clearCheckBoxes(), setCheckBox(), and calculateCost().

Writing these three functions will show us how to examine check boxes from code to see whether they've been clicked and how to select them ourselves if we need to.

The clearCheckBoxes() Function

The first function we'll write is clearCheckBoxes(), which clears the check boxes, Check1 to Check5, in our Web page:

```
function clearCheckBoxes()
{
    .
    .
    .
}
```

One way (and not the shortest way, as we'll see in a minute) to clear a check box is to use the check box method click() to make the program act as though we've clicked a check box. We can clear a check box by seeing if it's currently checked, and if so, execute its click() method. But how do we see whether a check box is currently selected?

We can use the check box's *checked* property to determine whether the check box is checked, like this for Check1:

```
function clearCheckBoxes()
{
    if(document.form1.Check1.checked){
        .
        .
        .
    }
}
```

If the check box is clicked, we want to click it again to clear it, which we do like this:

```
function clearCheckBoxes()
{
    if(document.form1.Check1.checked){
        document.form1.Check1.click()
    }
}
```

We can clear the other check boxes as well:

```
function clearCheckBoxes()
{
    if(document.form1.Check1.checked){
        document.form1.Check1.click()
    }
    if(document.form1.Check2.checked){
        document.form1.Check2.click()
```

```
        }
        if(document.form1.Check3.checked){
            document.form1.Check3.click()
        }
        if(document.form1.Check4.checked){
            document.form1.Check4.click()
        }
        if(document.form1.Check5.checked){
            document.form1.Check5.click()
        }
    }
```

This method for clearing all the check boxes introduces us to the checked property and the click() method. However, it's *not* the best way. There's a simpler way; the checked property turns out to be a read/write property, which means we can set the state of a check box by writing to this property—"checked = true" sets the check box and "checked = false" clears the check box. Using that method, here's what our clearCheck-Boxes() method will look like:

```
function clearCheckBoxes()
{
        document.form1.Check1.checked = false
        document.form1.Check2.checked = false
        document.form1.Check3.checked = false
        document.form1.Check4.checked = false
        document.form1.Check5.checked = false
}
```

That's all there is to it; next, we'll create the setCheckBox() function.

The setCheckBox(number) Function

We can pass the number of the check box to check to the setCheckBox() function. For example, if we pass 1 to setCheckBox(), we check the first check box; passing 2 sets check box 2, and so on.

We can use a switch statement to check the correct check box, as shown here:

```
function setCheckBox(number)
{
        switch(number){
            case 1:
                document.form1.Check1.checked = true
                break
            case 2:
                document.form1.Check2.checked = true
```

```
                              break
                   case 3:
                        document.form1.Check3.checked = true
                        break
                   case 4:
                        document.form1.Check4.checked = true
                        break
                   case 5:
                        document.form1.Check5.checked = true
                        break
              }
    }
```

The only function left to write is the calculateCost() function.

The calculateCost() Function

In the calculateCost() function, we will determine what check boxes are checked and calculate the cost of a donut that way, at fifty cents per checked option. At the end of the function, we display the total cost in the Web page's text box.

The calculateCost() function is easy to write—we just look at the check boxes and add up the cost:

```
function calculateCost()
{
     var cost = 0
     if(document.form1.Check1.checked){
         cost = cost + .50
     }
     if(document.form1.Check2.checked){
         cost = cost + .50
     }
     if(document.form1.Check3.checked){
         cost = cost + .50
     }
     if(document.form1.Check4.checked){
         cost = cost + .50
     }
     if(document.form1.Check5.checked){
         cost = cost + .50
     }
     document.form1.TextBox.value = "Total cost: $" + cost
}
```

Now our three functions, clearCheckBoxes(), setCheckBox(), and calculateCost(), are finished. Let's put them to work.

Responding to the Radio Buttons in Donuts.htm

When the user clicks the first radio button—the Plain donuts option—we should clear the check boxes and set the first check box, which corresponds to the Plain option. Then we calculate and display the cost of the donut with calculateCost() this way:

```
<SCRIPT LANGUAGE = JavaScript>

    function radio1Clicked()
    {
        clearCheckBoxes()
        setCheckBox(1)
        calculateCost()
    }    .
             .
             .
```

We can do the same for the other donut types, as follows:

```
<SCRIPT LANGUAGE = JavaScript>

    function radio1Clicked()
    {
        clearCheckBoxes()
        setCheckBox(1)
        calculateCost()
    }

    function radio2Clicked()
    {
        clearCheckBoxes()
        setCheckBox(4)
        calculateCost()
    }

    function radio3Clicked()
    {
        clearCheckBoxes()
        setCheckBox(3)
        setCheckBox(5)
        calculateCost()
    }

    function radio4Clicked()
    {
        clearCheckBoxes()
        setCheckBox(2)
        setCheckBox(3)
```

```
        setCheckBox(5)
        calculateCost()
}

function radio5Clicked()
{
        clearCheckBoxes()
        setCheckBox(4)
        setCheckBox(5)
        calculateCost()
}
```

In addition, if the user clicks a check box to change the options for the displayed donut, we should recalculate the cost, so we call calculateCost() each time a check box is clicked:

```
function check1Clicked()
{
        calculateCost()
}

function check2Clicked()
{
        calculateCost()
}

function check3Clicked()
{
        calculateCost()
}

function check4Clicked()
{
        calculateCost()
}

function check5Clicked()
{
        calculateCost()
}
```

That's it—now open this page, as shown in Figure 4-3. As you can see, when you click a radio button, the corresponding check boxes are automatically selected. In this way, we can integrate radio buttons and check boxes in our programs.

The code for this page, Donuts.htm, is shown in Listing 4-3.

The program we've just developed is a long one, and it's long because we have treated each check box as a separate control—Check1, Check2, and so on. However, JavaScript has provisions for working with many con-

Figure 4-3
We use check boxes
and radio buttons to
list donut options.

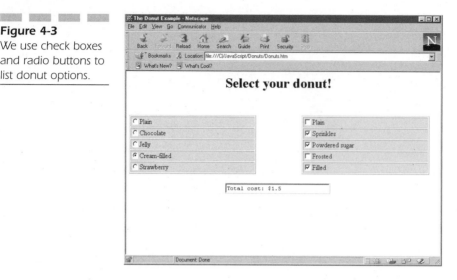

trols in a Web page; now that we're working with multiple controls, we'll
take a look at those provisions in the following section.

Listing 4-3
Dounts.htm.

```
<HTML>

<HEAD>
<TITLE>The Donut Example</TITLE>
</HEAD>

<BODY>

<FORM NAME = "form1">

<CENTER>
<H1>Select your donut!</H1>
</CENTER>
<BR>
<BR>

<TABLE BORDER BGCOLOR = CYAN WIDTH = 300 ALIGN = LEFT>
    <TR><TD><INPUT TYPE = RADIO NAME = RadioGroup onClick =
        radio1Clicked()>Plain</TD></TR>
    <TR><TD><INPUT TYPE = RADIO NAME = RadioGroup onClick =
        radio2Clicked()>Chocolate</TD></TR>
    <TR><TD><INPUT TYPE = RADIO NAME = RadioGroup onClick =
        radio3Clicked()>Jelly</TD></TR>
    <TR><TD><INPUT TYPE = RADIO NAME = RadioGroup onClick =
        radio4Clicked()>Cream-filled</TD></TR>
    <TR><TD><INPUT TYPE = RADIO NAME = RadioGroup onClick =
        radio5Clicked()>Strawberry</TD></TR>
</TABLE>
```

Listing 4-3
Continued.

```
<TABLE BORDER BGCOLOR = CYAN WIDTH = 300 ALIGN = RIGHT>
    <TR><TD><INPUT TYPE = CHECKBOX NAME = Check1 onClick =
        check1Clicked()>Plain</TD></TR>
    <TR><TD><INPUT TYPE = CHECKBOX NAME = Check2 onClick =
        check2Clicked()>Sprinkles</TD></TR>
    <TR><TD><INPUT TYPE = CHECKBOX NAME = Check3 onClick =
        check3Clicked()>Powdered sugar</TD></TR>
    <TR><TD><INPUT TYPE = CHECKBOX NAME = Check4 onClick =
        check4Clicked()>Frosted</TD></TR>
    <TR><TD><INPUT TYPE = CHECKBOX NAME = Check5 onClick =
        check5Clicked()>Filled</TD></TR>
</TABLE>

<BR CLEAR = ALL>
<BR>

<CENTER>
<INPUT TYPE =    TEXT NAME =   TextBox SIZE  =   30 ALIGN =
        CENTER>
</CENTER>

</FORM>

</BODY>

<SCRIPT LANGUAGE = JavaScript>

    function radio1Clicked()
    {
        clearCheckBoxes()
        setCheckBox(1)
        calculateCost()
    }

    function radio2Clicked()
    {
        clearCheckBoxes()
        setCheckBox(4)
        calculateCost()
    }

    function radio3Clicked()
    {
        clearCheckBoxes()
        setCheckBox(3)
        setCheckBox(5)
        calculateCost()
    }

    function radio4Clicked()
    {
        clearCheckBoxes()
        setCheckBox(2)
```

Listing 4-3
Continued.

```
        setCheckBox(3)
        setCheckBox(5)
        calculateCost()
}

function radio5Clicked()
{
        clearCheckBoxes()
        setCheckBox(4)
        setCheckBox(5)
        calculateCost()
}

function check1Clicked()
{
        calculateCost()
}

function check2Clicked()
{
        calculateCost()
}

function check3Clicked()
{
        calculateCost()
}

function check4Clicked()
{
        calculateCost()
}

function check5Clicked()
{
        calculateCost()
}

function clearCheckBoxes()
{
        document.form1.Check1.checked = false
        document.form1.Check2.checked = false
        document.form1.Check3.checked = false
        document.form1.Check4.checked = false
        document.form1.Check5.checked = false
}

function setCheckBox(number)
{
        switch(number){
            case 1:
                document.form1.Check1.checked = true
                break
```

Listing 4-3
Continued.

```
             case 2:
                   document.form1.Check2.checked = true
                   break
             case 3:
                   document.form1.Check3.checked = true
                   break
             case 4:
                   document.form1.Check4.checked = true
                   break
             case 5:
                   document.form1.Check5.checked = true
                   break
         }
     }

     function calculateCost()
     {
         var cost = 0
         if(document.form1.Check1.checked){
             cost = cost + .50
         }
         if(document.form1.Check2.checked){
             cost = cost + .50
         }
         if(document.form1.Check3.checked){
             cost = cost + .50
         }
         if(document.form1.Check4.checked){
             cost = cost + .50
         }
         if(document.form1.Check5.checked){
             cost = cost + .50
         }
         document.form1.TextBox.value = "Total cost: $" +
     cost
     }
</SCRIPT>

</HTML>
```

Using the elements[] Arrays

The controls in our Web page are already part of an array—the *elements[]* array—which means we don't have to refer to them by specific name like Check1, Check2, and so on. Instead, we can loop over those elements by using the elements[] array; that method makes our code much shorter.

For example, the clearCheckBoxes() function looks like this currently:

```
function clearCheckBoxes()
{
```

```
document.form1.Check1.checked = false
document.form1.Check2.checked = false
document.form1.Check3.checked = false
document.form1.Check4.checked = false
document.form1.Check5.checked = false
}
```

We can make this shorter by using the document.form1.elements[] array, which holds all the HTML elements in form1. Because we added the five radio buttons first, those elements are document.form1.elements[0] through document.form1.elements[4], and the check boxes are document.form1.elements[5] to document.form1.elements[9].

Using the elements[] array, then, we can rewrite the clearCheckBoxes() function this way:

```
function clearCheckBoxes()
{
    for(var loop_index = 0; loop_index <= 4; loop_in-
dex++){
        document.form1.elements[loop_index +
5].checked = false
    }
}
```

Similarly, the setCheckBox() function looks like this now:

```
function setCheckBox(number)
{
    switch(number){
        case 1:
            document.form1.Check1.checked = true
            break
        case 2:
            document.form1.Check2.checked = true
            break
        case 3:
            document.form1.Check3.checked = true
            break
        case 4:
            document.form1.Check4.checked = true
            break
        case 5:
            document.form1.Check5.checked = true
            break
    }
}
```

Now that we can refer to the check boxes by index in the elements[] array, we can change that function to one line of code:

```
function setCheckBox(number)
{
```

```
        document.form1.elements[number - 1 + 5].checked =
    true
}
```

We can even make the calculateCost() function shorter, as shown here:

```
function calculateCost()
{
    var cost = 0
    if(document.form1.Check1.checked){
        cost = cost + .50
    }
    if(document.form1.Check2.checked){
        cost = cost + .50
    }
    if(document.form1.Check3.checked){
        cost = cost + .50
    }
    if(document.form1.Check4.checked){
        cost = cost + .50
    }
    if(document.form1.Check5.checked){
        cost = cost + .50
    }
    document.form1.TextBox.value = "Total cost: $" +
    cost
}
```

Using the elements[] array, we can loop over the check boxes this way:

```
function calculateCost()
{
    var cost = 0

    for(var loop_index = 0; loop_index <= 4; loop_in-
    dex++){
        if(document.form1.elements[loop_index +
    5].checked){
            cost = cost + .50
        }
    }

    document.form1.TextBox.value = "Total cost: $" +
    cost
}
```

As you can see, looping over an indexed array makes our program much shorter.

There's one more shortcut we can take. Currently, each check box has its own click event handler—check1Clicked(), check2Clicked() and so on:

```
<TABLE BORDER BGCOLOR = CYAN WIDTH = 300 ALIGN = RIGHT>
    <TR><TD><INPUT TYPE = CHECKBOX NAME = Check1 onClick =
```

```
    check1Clicked()>Plain</TD></TR>
<TR><TD><INPUT TYPE = CHECKBOX NAME = Check2 onClick =
    check2Clicked()>Sprinkles</TD></TR>
<TR><TD><INPUT TYPE = CHECKBOX NAME = Check3 onClick =
    check3Clicked()>Powdered sugar</TD></TR>
<TR><TD><INPUT TYPE = CHECKBOX NAME = Check4 onClick =
    check4Clicked()>Frosted</TD></TR>
<TR><TD><INPUT TYPE = CHECKBOX NAME = Check5 onClick =
    check5Clicked()>Filled</TD></TR>
</TABLE>
```

However, those event handlers just call calculateCost() anyway:

```
function check1Clicked()
{
    calculateCost()
}

function check2Clicked()
{
    calculateCost()
}

function check3Clicked()
{
    calculateCost()
}

function check4Clicked()
{
    calculateCost()
}

function check5Clicked()
{
    calculateCost()
}
```

We can shorten our code by simply calling calculateCost() directly as the check boxes' click event handlers:

```
<TABLE BORDER BGCOLOR = CYAN WIDTH = 300 ALIGN = RIGHT>
    <TR><TD><INPUT TYPE = CHECKBOX NAME = Check onClick =
        calculateCost()>Plain</TD></TR>
    <TR><TD><INPUT TYPE = CHECKBOX NAME = Check onClick =
        calculateCost()>Sprinkles</TD></TR>
    <TR><TD><INPUT TYPE = CHECKBOX NAME = Check onClick =
        calculateCost()>Powdered sugar</TD></TR>
    <TR><TD><INPUT TYPE = CHECKBOX NAME = Check onClick =
        calculateCost()>Frosted</TD></TR>
    <TR><TD><INPUT TYPE = CHECKBOX NAME = Check onClick =
        calculateCost()>Filled</TD></TR>
</TABLE>
```

That's it—the new version of our page, Donuts2.htm, is shown in Listing 4-4. As you can see, that page is much shorter than the original, Donuts.htm in Listing 4-3. Using the elements[] array, we can loop over our check boxes as needed.

Listing 4-4
Donuts2.htm.

```
<HTML>

<HEAD>
<TITLE>The Donut Example</TITLE>
</HEAD>

<BODY>

<FORM NAME = "form1">

<CENTER>
<H1>Select your donut!</H1>
</CENTER>
<BR>
<BR>

<TABLE BORDER BGCOLOR = CYAN WIDTH = 300 ALIGN = LEFT>
    <TR><TD><INPUT TYPE = RADIO NAME = RadioGroup onClick =
        Radio1Clicked()>Plain</TD></TR>
    <TR><TD><INPUT TYPE = RADIO NAME = RadioGroup onClick =
        Radio2Clicked()>Chocolate</TD></TR>
    <TR><TD><INPUT TYPE = RADIO NAME = RadioGroup onClick =
        Radio3Clicked()>Jelly</TD></TR>
    <TR><TD><INPUT TYPE = RADIO NAME = RadioGroup onClick =
        Radio4Clicked()>Cream-filled</TD></TR>
    <TR><TD><INPUT TYPE = RADIO NAME = RadioGroup onClick =
        Radio5Clicked()>Strawberry</TD></TR>
</TABLE>

<TABLE BORDER BGCOLOR = CYAN WIDTH = 300 ALIGN = RIGHT>
    <TR><TD><INPUT TYPE = CHECKBOX NAME = Check onClick =
        calculateCost()>Plain</TD></TR>
    <TR><TD><INPUT TYPE = CHECKBOX NAME = Check onClick =
        calculateCost()>Sprinkles</TD></TR>
    <TR><TD><INPUT TYPE = CHECKBOX NAME = Check onClick =
        calculateCost()>Powdered sugar</TD></TR>
    <TR><TD><INPUT TYPE = CHECKBOX NAME = Check onClick =
        calculateCost()>Frosted</TD></TR>
    <TR><TD><INPUT TYPE = CHECKBOX NAME = Check onClick =
        calculateCost()>Filled</TD></TR>
</TABLE>

<BR CLEAR = ALL>
<BR>

<CENTER>
<INPUT TYPE  =  TEXT NAME  =  TextBox SIZE  =  30 ALIGN =
```

Listing 4-4
Continued.

```
     CENTER>
</CENTER>

</FORM>

</BODY>

<SCRIPT LANGUAGE = JavaScript>

    function Radio1Clicked()
    {
        clearCheckBoxes()
        setCheckBox(1)
        calculateCost()
    }

    function Radio2Clicked()
    {
        clearCheckBoxes()
        setCheckBox(4)
        calculateCost()
    }

    function Radio3Clicked()
    {
        clearCheckBoxes()
        setCheckBox(3)
        setCheckBox(5)
        calculateCost()
    }

    function Radio4Clicked()
    {
        clearCheckBoxes()
        setCheckBox(2)
        setCheckBox(3)
        setCheckBox(5)
        calculateCost()
    }

    function Radio5Clicked()
    {
        clearCheckBoxes()
        setCheckBox(4)
        setCheckBox(5)
        calculateCost()
    }

    function clearCheckBoxes()
    {
        for(var loop_index = 0; loop_index <= 4; loop_in-
    dex++){
            document.form1.elements[loop_index +
```

Listing 4-4
Continued.

```
          5].checked = false
          }
      }

  function setCheckBox(number)
  {
      document.form1.elements[number - 1 + 5].checked =
      true
  }

  function calculateCost()
  {
      var cost = 0

      for(var loop_index = 0; loop_index <= 4; loop_in-
  dex++){
              if(document.form1.elements[loop_index +
  5].checked){
                  cost = cost + .50
              }
      }

      document.form1.TextBox.value = "Total cost: $" +
      cost
  }
  </SCRIPT>

  </HTML>
```

That completes our discussion of check boxes and radio buttons for the moment. As you can see, those controls are powerful ways for the user to select from a set of options. The next control we'll look at also allows the user to select from a set of options: the select control.

Select Controls

A *select control* is a drop-down list box with the following properties, methods, and event handlers:

Properties	Methods	Event Handlers
form	blur	onBlur
length	focus	onChange
name		onFocus

continues

Properties	**Methods**	**Event Handlers**	*Continued*
options			
selectedIndex			
text			
type			

When the user makes a selection in the select control, its onChange event handler is called, so that's the event handler we will use in an example. In particular, we will construct one that displays a text box and a select control to the user, like this:

Click an item in the select control...

Selection 1 | v |

When the user clicks the downward-pointing arrow at the right of the select control, a drop-down list appears to display the control's possible selections:

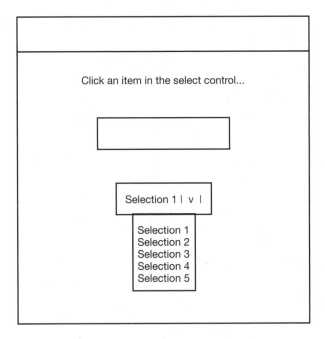

Using the mouse, the user can make a selection from that list, which we'll then display in the text box.

We'll start this new example, Select.htm, by using the <SELECT> tag to install our select control, select1:

```
<HTML>

<HEAD>
<TITLE>A Select Control Example</TITLE>
</HEAD>

<BODY>

<FORM NAME = form1>
<CENTER>
<H1>Click an item in the select control...</H1>
<BR>
<BR>
<INPUT NAME = TextBox TYPE = Text SIZE = 30>
<BR>
<BR>
<SELECT NAME = Select1>
          .
          .
          .
```

The next step is to install all the options in the select control that we want to appear when the user opens the select control.

Installing the Options in a Select Control

We can add options to a select control with the <OPTION> tag. To add the
strings "Selection 1", "Selection 2", and so on, we use the <OPTION> tag
this way:

```
<HTML>

<HEAD>
<TITLE>A Select Control Example</TITLE>
</HEAD>

<BODY>

<FORM NAME = form1>
<CENTER>
<H1>Click an item in the select control...</H1>
<BR>
<BR>
<INPUT NAME = TextBox TYPE = Text SIZE = 30>
<BR>
<BR>
<SELECT NAME = Select1>
<OPTION>Selection 1
<OPTION>Selection 2
<OPTION>Selection 3
<OPTION>Selection 4
<OPTION>Selection 5
</SELECT>
```

Our select control is almost ready. We still have to connect the on-
Change event handler to a JavaScript function, however. Here's how we
do that, calling the function selectionMade():

```
<HTML>

<HEAD>
<TITLE>A Select Control Example</TITLE>
</HEAD>

<BODY>

<FORM NAME = form1>
<CENTER>
<H1>Click an item in the select control...</H1>
<BR>
<BR>
<INPUT NAME = TextBox TYPE = Text SIZE = 30>
<BR>
<BR>
```

```
<SELECT NAME = Select1 onChange = selectionMade()>
<OPTION>Selection 1
<OPTION>Selection 2
<OPTION>Selection 3
<OPTION>Selection 4
<OPTION>Selection 5
</SELECT>

</CENTER>
</FORM>

</BODY>
```

Then we add that function to the <SCRIPT> section of our page:

```
<SCRIPT LANGUAGE = JavaScript>

function selectionMade()
{
    .
    .
    .
}

</SCRIPT>
```

This is the function that's called when the user makes a selection in the select control, and we want to report that selection in the page's text box. The index of the item chosen in the select control is stored in that control's selectedIndex property, so we report which selection the user made, as shown here:

```
<SCRIPT LANGUAGE = JavaScript>

function selectionMade()
{
    document.form1.TextBox.value = "You chose selection " +
    (document.form1.Select1.selectedIndex + 1)
}

</SCRIPT>
```

TIP: *If you want the text of the current selection in the select control, you can retrieve it from the select control's text property.*

The Select.htm example is ready to go, so open the select control with the mouse, making a selection, as shown in Figure 4-4.

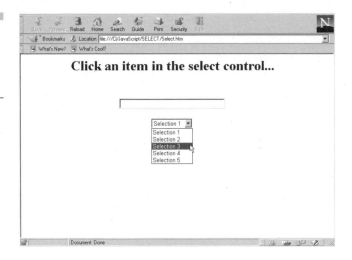

When you do make a selection in the select control, the program reports which selection you made, as shown in Figure 4-5. The Select.htm example is working!

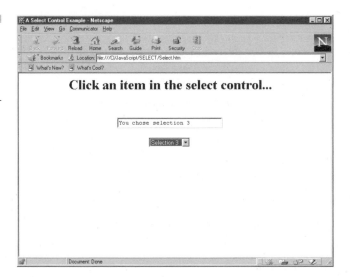

The code for this page, Select.htm, is shown in Listing 4-5.

So far, we've made only one selection in the select control, but select controls support multiple selections, too, as we'll see in the next section.

Listing 4-5
`Select.htm.`

```
<HTML>

<HEAD>
<TITLE>A Select Control Example</TITLE>
</HEAD>

<BODY>

<FORM NAME = form1>
<CENTER>
<H1>Click an item in the select control...</H1>
<BR>
<BR>
<INPUT NAME = TextBox TYPE = Text SIZE = 30>
<BR>
<BR>
<SELECT NAME = Select1 onChange = selectionMade()>
<OPTION>Selection 1
<OPTION>Selection 2
<OPTION>Selection 3
<OPTION>Selection 4
<OPTION>Selection 5
</SELECT>

</CENTER>
</FORM>

</BODY>

<SCRIPT LANGUAGE = JavaScript>

function selectionMade()
{
    document.form1.TextBox.value = "You chose selection " +
    (document.form1.Select1.selectedIndex + 1)
}

</SCRIPT>

</HTML>
```

Selecting Multiple Items in a Select Control

A select control supports multiple selections if you include the MULTIPLE attribute in the <SELECT> tag. To see how this works, we'll create a new example, Multiple.htm. This example will display a multiple-selection select control (unlike single-selection select controls, multiple-selection controls are not drop-down lists; they display a scrollable list to the user) and a text area (used to display the possibly multiple selections the user will make).

Using the mouse, the user can select a number of items in the select control, and we'll display which items they've selected. We'll start this Multiple.htm example by placing a text area in our Web page:

```
<HTML>

<HEAD>
<TITLE>Select Example</TITLE>
</HEAD>

<BODY>

<FORM NAME = form1>
<CENTER>
<H1>Select a number of items...</H1>
<BR>
<TEXTAREA NAME = Textarea COLS = 20 ROWS = 10></TEXTAREA>
        .
        .
        .
```

Next, we add the select control we'll need, making it a multiple-selection select control with the MULTIPLE attribute:

```
<HTML>

<HEAD>
<TITLE>Select Example</TITLE>
</HEAD>

<BODY>

<FORM NAME = form1>
<CENTER>
<H1>Select a number of items...</H1>
<BR>
<TEXTAREA NAME = Textarea COLS = 20 ROWS = 10></TEXTAREA>
<BR>
<BR>
<SELECT NAME = Select1 onChange = selectionMade() MULTIPLE>
<OPTION>Selection 1
<OPTION>Selection 2
<OPTION>Selection 3
<OPTION>Selection 4
<OPTION>Selection 5
</SELECT>

</CENTER>
```

```
</FORM>

</BODY>
```

Now when the user selects items in our select control, it's up to us to determine which items he or she has selected. The select control has an internal array named "options[]" that holds all the options the select control displays. If a particular option's selected property is true, the user has selected that option.

We can set up a loop over all the items in the select control if we use its *length* property, which holds the number of items in the select control. That loop looks like this:

```
<SCRIPT LANGUAGE = JavaScript>

function selectionMade()
{
    document.form1.Textarea.value = ""

    with(document.form1.Select1){
        for(var loop_index = 0; loop_index < length;
      loop_index++){
                    .
                    .
                    .

        }
    }
}
</SCRIPT>
```

Now if an item in the select control is selected, we can add it to the text area control in the Web page, as shown here:

```
<SCRIPT LANGUAGE = JavaScript>

function selectionMade()
{
    document.form1.Textarea.value = ""

    with(document.form1.Select1){
        for(var loop_index = 0; loop_index < length;
      loop_index++){
                if (options[loop_index].selected){
                        document.form1.Textarea.value +=
        options[loop_index].text + "\r"
                }
        }
    }
}
</SCRIPT>
```

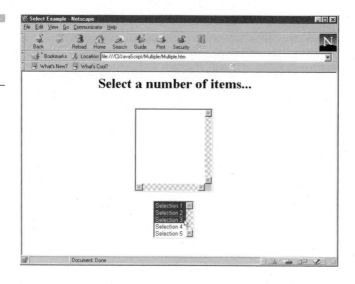

Open the Multiple.htm page now. Using the mouse, the user can select a number of items in the select control, as shown in Figure 4-6.

If the user does select an item or items in the select control, the program reports that action, as shown in Figure 4-7. The Multiple.htm page works as we designed it.

The code for this page, Multiple.htm, is shown in Listing 4-6.

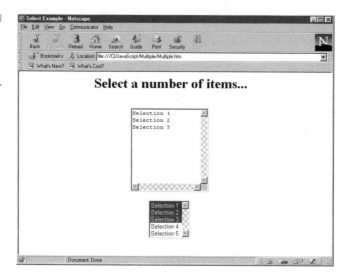

Listing 4-6
`Multiple.htm`.

```html
<HTML>

<HEAD>
<TITLE>Select Example</TITLE>
</HEAD>

<BODY>

<FORM NAME = form1>
<CENTER>
<H1>Select a number of items...</H1>
<BR>
<TEXTAREA NAME = Textarea COLS = 20 ROWS = 10></TEXTAREA>
<BR>
<BR>
<SELECT NAME = Select1 onChange = selectionMade() MULTIPLE>
<OPTION>Selection 1
<OPTION>Selection 2
<OPTION>Selection 3
<OPTION>Selection 4
<OPTION>Selection 5
</SELECT>

</CENTER>
</FORM>

</BODY>

<SCRIPT LANGUAGE = JavaScript>

function selectionMade()
{
    document.form1.Textarea.value = ""

    with(document.form1.Select1){
        for(var loop_index = 0; loop_index < length;
    loop_index++){
            if (options[loop_index].selected){
                document.form1.Textarea.value +=
    options[loop_index].text + "\r"
            }
        }
    }
}

</SCRIPT>

</HTML>
```

CONCLUSION

That completes this chapter. We've covered a great deal here—how to set up and use both radio buttons and check boxes in our programs, and when they're appropriate to use. We've seen how to use radio controls and check boxes together, too.

We've also learned how to treat the controls in a Web page as part of an array, the elements[] array. Using that array, we can loop over the HTML elements in a Web page, control by control, processing those controls as needed. In addition, we've seen how to use select controls (which can present single or multiple selections) to give the user several selections to choose from.

All in all, we've come far in this chapter. In the next chapter, we'll continue exploring HTML controls as we take a look at how to work with the keyboard and the mouse.

5

Keyboard and Mouse Handling

In this chapter, we're going to work in two powerful areas: mouse and keyboard handling. We'll see how to use the mouse in a Web page, keeping track of its location and writing code to respond to the user's mouse actions. We'll see how to react to mouse movements by swapping images in a Web page and how to let users get a preview of Web pages they can navigate to simply by letting the mouse move over the corresponding hyperlinks.

Then we'll turn to working with the keyboard. It's possible to read keys directly from the keyboard with JavaScript, and we'll see how to do that in this chapter. In addition, we'll learn how to use keystrokes to control window actions—for example, displaying a help screen the user can dismiss by pressing the Esc key.

Finally, we'll see how to bring together text and mouse handling in an example where we highlight and enlarge text as the user lets the mouse travel over it.

There's a lot of power in the techniques we'll develop in this chapter, so let's start now by working with the mouse. What will quickly become evident in this chapter is the incompatibilities between the two browsers we're using, which we'll see frequently in this book. As far as this chapter goes, it turns out that Internet Explorer handles both the mouse and the keyboard completely differently from Netscape Navigator (the two browsers used to be closer on this issue, but starting with Internet Explorer 4.0, they've completely diverged). However, we'll see how to create Web pages that use the keyboard and mouse that function in both Web browsers in the chapter—and allowing your Web pages to work with these two disparate browsers is itself a skill worth picking up.

Mouser

Our first page, called Mouser.htm, will let us explore what JavaScript has to offer for mouse support. When the user clicks the mouse in the Web page, we'll be able to report the mouse location, for example. When the user releases the mouse button, we'll report that the mouse button is up. If the user presses the mouse button while holding down the Shift key, we can report that the key has been pressed. We can also report on the Ctrl and Alt keys in the same way—and even a combination of the Shift and Ctrl keys.

NOTE: It's possible to determine which mouse button the user is holding down—left or right—but in practice, the right mouse button has been made useless for program control because Web browsers have preempted it for context-sensitive help, so we'll stick to the left mouse button in this chapter. If you click the right mouse button in a Web page, the browser will display a help menu that our program has no control over.

Before we start writing our Mouser.htm example, we need some knowledge of handling mouse events, so we'll cover that now, starting with handling mouse events in Netscape Navigator.

Using Mouse Events in Netscape Navigator

In our Web page, we want to use the document's mouseDown and mouseUp events, which, as their names indicate, handle mouse press and release events.

When you program for Netscape Navigator, you connect those events to event handler functions named mouseDownHandler() and mouse-UpHandler() in a script, as shown here:

```
<SCRIPT LANGUAGE= "JavaScript">
    document.onMouseDown = mouseDownHandler
    document.onMouseUp = mouseUpHandler
```

.
.
.

When the user presses the mouse button, the mouseDown event occurs and the browser calls our mouseDown event handler:

```
function mouseDownHandler(e)
{
    .
    .
    .
}
```

Our mouse event handling function is passed an object of Netscape's *event* type; we'll get the mouse location and key information we need from this object. The location of the mouse in the page is held in the pageX and pageY properties. All the Netscape Navigator event object properties are listed in Table 5–1.

Now let's turn to the other browser we support in this book—Internet Explorer.

Table 5–1

The Netscape Navigator event object properties.

Event Property	Means This
type	Event type
layerX	The cursor's horizontal position in relation to the layer in which the event occurred
layerY	The cursor's vertical position in pixels relative to the layer in which the event occurred
pageX	The cursor's horizontal position in pixels, relative to the page
pageY	The cursor's vertical position in pixels relative to the page
screenX	The cursor's horizontal position in pixels, relative to the screen
screenY	The cursor's vertical position in pixels, relative to the screen
which	The mouse button that was pressed or the ASCII value of a pressed key
modifiers	The modifier keys associated with a mouse or key event. Possible values are ALT_MASK, CONTROL_MASK, SHIFT_MASK, and META_MASK
data	An array of strings containing the URLs of the dropped objects, used with the dragdrop event

Using Mouse Events in Internet Explorer

Handling mouse events in Internet Explorer is completely different. Here, to catch mouse events in the document, you must connect the mouse handlers in the <BODY> element, not in the <SCRIPT> element:

```
<BODY onMouseDown = "mouseDownHandler()" onMouseUp =
    "mouseUpHandler()">
            .
            .
            .
```

These mouse event handlers are not passed any parameters:

```
function mouseDownHandler()
{
    .
    .
    .
}
```

Instead, you determine where the mouse was by taking a look at the event object, which is a member object of the window object. The Internet Explorer window.event object's properties are listed in Table 5–2. We'll get the mouse's x and y position from the x and y properties.

Table 5–2

The Internet Explorer window.event object properties.

Event Property	Means This
altKey	True if the Alt key was down
button	Specifies which mouse button, if any, is pressed
cancelBubble	Indicates if this event should move up the event hierarchy
clientX	x coordinate with respect to the client area
clientY	y coordinate with respect to the client area
ctrlKey	True if the Ctrl key was down
fromElement	Specifies element being moved
keyCode	Code of struck key
offsetX	Container relative x position
offsetY	Container relative y position
reason	Disposition of data transfer
returnValue	Specifies the return value from the event
screenX	x coordinate relative to physical screen size
screenY	y coordinate relative to physical screen size

shiftKey	True if the Shift key was down
srcElement	Element that caused the event
srcFilter	Filter event if this is a filterChange event
toElement	Specifies element being moved to
type	Returns event type as a string
x	x position of the event in context
y	y position of the event in context

Writing Mouser.htm

Now that we've gotten an introduction to handling mouse events, we can start writing the code for Mouser.htm. We start with the <BODY> tag and the connection to the mouse event handlers for Internet Explorer:

```
<HTML>
<HEAD>
<TITLE>A Mouse Handling Example</TITLE>
</HEAD>
<!-Event handlers added for Internet Explorer>
<BODY onMouseDown = "mouseDownHandler()" onMouseUp =
     "mouseUpHandler()">
          .
          .
          .
```

Next, we add the Web page's form (form1) and the text box:

```
<HTML>
<HEAD>
<TITLE>A Mouse Handling Example</TITLE>
</HEAD>
<!-Event handlers added for Internet Explorer>
<BODY onMouseDown = "mouseDownHandler()" onMouseUp =
     "mouseUpHandler()">
<CENTER>
<FORM name = "form1">
<H1>A Mouse Handling Example</H1>
<BR>
<H2>Click the mouse button and Shift, Ctrl, and Alt</H2>
<BR>
<INPUT TYPE = "text" name = "Textbox" SIZE = 60>
</FORM>
</CENTER>
</BODY>
```

Now we're ready to write the code for the page.

Working With the mouseDown and mouseUp Events

We start the code by connecting the document mouseDown and mouseUp events to event handlers for Netscape Navigator:

```
<SCRIPT LANGUAGE= "JavaScript">
    document.onMouseDown = mouseDownHandler
    document.onMouseUp = mouseUpHandler
        .
        .
        .
```

Next, we write the mouseDown event handler, which we've named mouseDownHandler():

```
<SCRIPT LANGUAGE= "JavaScript">
    document.onMouseDown = mouseDownHandler
    document.onMouseUp = mouseUpHandler
    function mouseDownHandler(e)
    {
        .
        .
        .
    }
```

Immediately, we run into problems here. Because the two browsers handle mouse events so differently, there's no way to write the same code for both.

TIP: *Netscape Navigator's mouse down handler gets one argument passed to it, and Internet Explorer's mouse down handler is passed no arguments; however, because JavaScript is flexible on the number of arguments passed to functions, we can use one function with one argument passed to it in our code: mouseDownHandler(e).*

The way to fix this problem is to write different code for the two browsers. First, however, we have to determine which browser the user has. This is a common problem, and solving it is useful for dozens of applications.

Determining Which Browser the User Has

Finding out which browser the page is in turns out to be easy: You just check the browser's *navigator* object (we'll learn more about this object in

Chapter 10, "The Navigator, Location, and History Objects"). This object has a property called *appName*, which is set to "Microsoft Internet Explorer" for Internet Explorer and "Netscape" for Netscape Navigator. That means we can write code for Internet Explorer—after making sure it's the browser we're dealing with—as follows:

```
<SCRIPT LANGUAGE= "JavaScript">
    document.onMouseDown = mouseDownHandler
    document.onMouseUp = mouseUpHandler
    function mouseDownHandler(e)
    {
    if (navigator.appName == "Microsoft Internet Explorer")
      {
            .
            .
            .
```

If this is Internet Explorer, we get the mouse position from the window.event object's x and y properties.

We also want to test whether the Shift, Ctrl, or Alt keys are being held down, so we'll use the window.event.shiftKey, window.event.ctrlKey, and window.event.altKey flags. We'll check for all these keys, as well as when the Shift and Ctrl keys are held down together.

Here's how we check for the Shift and Ctrl combination using the JavaScript logical AND operator (&&), which requires that both its operands are true before it returns a value of true:

```
<SCRIPT LANGUAGE= "JavaScript">
    document.onMouseDown = mouseDownHandler
    document.onMouseUp = mouseUpHandler
    function mouseDownHandler(e)
    {
        if (navigator.appName == "Microsoft Internet
      Explorer") {
                if(window.event.shiftKey &&
      window.event.ctrlKey){
                        .
                        .
                        .

        }
                        .
                        .
                        .
```

If both the Shift and Ctrl keys are down, we should report that fact, along with the mouse location. Here's how we do that:

```
<SCRIPT LANGUAGE= "JavaScript">
    document.onMouseDown = mouseDownHandler
```

```
document.onMouseUp = mouseUpHandler
function mouseDownHandler(e)
{
    if (navigator.appName == "Microsoft Internet
Explorer") {
        if(window.event.shiftKey &&
window.event.ctrlKey){
            document.form1.Textbox.value = "Shift and
Ctrl keys and mouse
                button down at: " + window.event.x +
", " + window.event.y
            return
        }

            .
            .
            .
```

Now we've handled the mouseDown event when both the Shift and Ctrl
keys are down. If both those keys are not being held down, we continue
to check for the Shift key, the Ctrl key, and so on, all the way to no key
being held down at all; that situation looks like this in code:

```
<SCRIPT LANGUAGE= "JavaScript">
    document.onMouseDown = mouseDownHandler
    document.onMouseUp = mouseUpHandler
    function mouseDownHandler(e)
    {
        if (navigator.appName == "Microsoft Internet
Explorer") {
            if(window.event.shiftKey &&
window.event.ctrlKey){
                document.form1.Textbox.value = "Shift and
Ctrl keys and mouse
                    button down at: " + window.event.x +
", " + window.event.y
                return
            }
            if(window.event.shiftKey)
            {
                document.form1.Textbox.value = "Shift key
and mouse button down
                    at: " + window.event.x + ", " +
window.event.y
                return
            }
            if(window.event.ctrlKey)
            {
                document.form1.Textbox.value = "Ctrl key
and mouse button down
                    at: " + window.event.x + ", " +
window.event.y
                return
            }
```

```
            if(window.event.altKey)
            {
                    document.form1.Textbox.value = "Alt key
and mouse button down
                            at: " + window.event.x + ", " +
window.event.y
                    return
            }
            document.form1.Textbox.value = "Mouse button
down at: " +
                    window.event.x + ", " + window.event.y
    }
```

Now we'll handle Netscape Navigator:

```
<SCRIPT LANGUAGE= "JavaScript">
    document.onMouseDown = mouseDownHandler
    document.onMouseUp = mouseUpHandler
    function mouseDownHandler(e)
    {
        if (navigator.appName == "Microsoft Internet
    Explorer") {
            .
            .
            .
        }
        if(navigator.appName == "Netscape") {
            .
            .
            .
        }
    }
```

If the browser is Netscape Navigator, we can get the mouse location
from the event object that's passed to us; that object's pageX and pageY
properties hold the mouse location. In addition, the event object's modifiers object holds information about which keys are down, so we can check
for the different keys and report the mouse position this way:

```
<SCRIPT LANGUAGE= "JavaScript">
    document.onMouseDown = mouseDownHandler
    document.onMouseUp = mouseUpHandler
    function mouseDownHandler(e)
    {
        if (navigator.appName == "Microsoft Internet
    Explorer") {
            .
            .
            .
        }
        if(navigator.appName == "Netscape") {
        switch(e.modifiers){
            case 0:
```

```
        document.form1.Textbox.value = "Mouse
button down at: "
                + e.pageX + ", " + e.pageY
        break
    case 2:
        document.form1.Textbox.value = "Ctrl key
and mouse button down
            at: " + e.pageX + ", " + e.pageY
        break
    case 4:
        document.form1.Textbox.value = "Shift key
and mouse button down
            at: " + e.pageX + ", " + e.pageY
        break
    case 6:
        document.form1.Textbox.value = "Shift and
Ctrl keys and mouse
            button down at: " + e.pageX + ", " +
e.pageY
        break
    case 1:
        document.form1.Textbox.value = "Alt key
and mouse button down
            at: " + e.pageX + ", " + e.pageY
        break
    }
  }
 }
```

Now we will handle the mouseUp event. In programming terms, this event is the same as the mouseDown event, except that the mouse is going up, not down; here's how we handle the mouseUp event in code:

```
function mouseUpHandler(e)
{
    if (navigator.appName == "Microsoft Internet
Explorer") {
        if(window.event.shiftKey &&
window.event.ctrlKey){
            document.form1.Textbox.value = "Shift and
Ctrl keys and mouse
                button up at: " + window.event.x + ",
" + window.event.y
            return
        }
        if(window.event.shiftKey)
        {
            document.form1.Textbox.value = "Shift key
and mouse button up
                at: " + window.event.x + ", " +
window.event.y
            return
        }
```

```
            if(window.event.ctrlKey)
            {
                 document.form1.Textbox.value = "Ctrl key
and mouse button up
                      at: " + window.event.x + ", " +
window.event.y
                 return
            }
            if(window.event.altKey)
            {
                 document.form1.Textbox.value = "Alt key
and mouse button up
                      at: " + window.event.x + ", " +
window.event.y
                 return
            }
            document.form1.Textbox.value = "Mouse button
up at: " +
                 window.event.x + ", " + window.event.y
       }
    if(navigator.appName == "Netscape") {
         switch(e.modifiers){
              case 0:
                 document.form1.Textbox.value = "Mouse
button up at: "
                       + e.pageX + ", " + e.pageY
                 break
              case 2:
                 document.form1.Textbox.value = "Ctrl
key down and mouse
                       button up at: " + e.pageX + ", "
+ e.pageY
                 break
              case 4:
                 document.form1.Textbox.value = "Shift
key down and mouse
                       button up at: " + e.pageX + ", "
+ e.pageY
                 break
              case 6:
                 document.form1.Textbox.value = "Shift
and Ctrl keys down and
                       mouse button up at: " + e.pageX
+ ", " + e.pageY
                 break
              case 1:
                 document.form1.Textbox.value = "Alt
key down and mouse
                       button up at: " + e.pageX + ", "
+ e.pageY
                 break
         }
    }
}
```

That's it; the Mouser.htm page is ready to go. When you press the mouse button, the program indicates your action, as shown in Figure 5–1, along with the location of the mouse. When you release the mouse button, the program reports that action, too.

When you hold down the Shift, Ctrl, or Alt keys when pressing the mouse button, the program reports that also, as shown in Figure 5–2. Now we're using the mouse directly in JavaScript.

The code for this page, Mouser.htm, is shown in Listing 5–1.

Figure 5–1
The Mouser.htm page reports the mouse position.

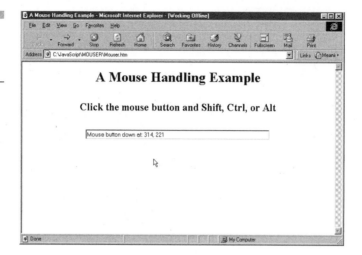

Figure 5–2
The Mouser.htm page reports the mouse position and the Shift key being held down.

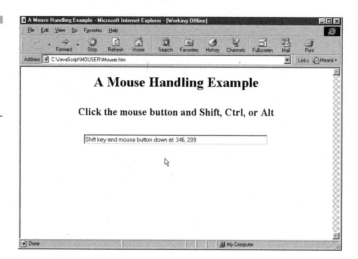

Listing 5–1
Mouser.htm.

```
<HTML>
<HEAD>
<TITLE>A Mouse Handling Example</TITLE>
</HEAD>
<!—Event handlers added for Internet Explorer>
<BODY onMouseDown = "mouseDownHandler()" onMouseUp =
     "mouseUpHandler()">
<CENTER>
<FORM name = "form1">
<H1>A Mouse Handling Example</H1>
<BR>
<H2>Click the mouse button and Shift, Ctrl, and Alt</H2>
<BR>
<A HREF = "mouser.htm" onMouseOver = "mouseOverHandler()"
    onMouseOut = "mouseOutHandler()">
    Move the mouse over this link!</A>
<BR>
<BR>
<INPUT TYPE = "text" name = "Textbox" SIZE = 60>
</FORM>
</CENTER>
</BODY>
<SCRIPT LANGUAGE= "JavaScript">
    document.onMouseDown = mouseDownHandler
    document.onMouseUp = mouseUpHandler
    function mouseDownHandler(e)
    {
        if (navigator.appName == "Microsoft Internet
    Explorer") {
            if(window.event.shiftKey &&
        window.event.ctrlKey){
                document.form1.Textbox.value = "Shift and
        Ctrl keys and mouse
                    button down at: " + window.event.x +
        ", " + window.event.y
                return
            }
            if(window.event.shiftKey)
            {
                document.form1.Textbox.value = "Shift key
        and mouse button down
                    at: " + window.event.x + ", " +
        window.event.y
                return
            }
            if(window.event.ctrlKey)
            {
                document.form1.Textbox.value = "Ctrl key
        and mouse button down
                    at: " + window.event.x + ", " +
        window.event.y
                return
            }
```

Listing 5–1
Continued.

```
            if(window.event.altKey)
            {
                    document.form1.Textbox.value = "Alt key
and mouse button down
                        at: " + window.event.x + ", " +
window.event.y
                    return
            }
            document.form1.Textbox.value = "Mouse button
down at: " +
                    window.event.x + ", " + window.event.y
        }
    if(navigator.appName == "Netscape") {
        switch(e.modifiers){
                case 0:
                    document.form1.Textbox.value = "Mouse
button down at: "
                            + e.pageX + ", " + e.pageY
                    break
                case 2:
                    document.form1.Textbox.value = "Ctrl
key and mouse button
                            down at: " + e.pageX + ", " +
e.pageY
                    break
                case 4:
                    document.form1.Textbox.value = "Shift
key and mouse button
                            down at: " + e.pageX + ", " +
e.pageY
                    break
                case 6:
                    document.form1.Textbox.value = "Shift
and Ctrl keys and
                            mouse button down at: " + e.pageX
+ ", " + e.pageY
                    break
                case 1:
                    document.form1.Textbox.value = "Alt
key and mouse button
                            down at: " + e.pageX + ", " +
e.pageY
                    break
            }
        }
}
function mouseUpHandler(e)
{
    if (navigator.appName == "Microsoft Internet
Explorer") {
        if(window.event.shiftKey &&
window.event.ctrlKey){
                document.form1.Textbox.value = "Shift and
```

```
Ctrl keys and mouse
                button up at: " + window.event.x + ",
" + window.event.y
            return
        }
        if(window.event.shiftKey)
        {
                document.form1.Textbox.value = "Shift key
and mouse button up
                at: " + window.event.x + ", " +
window.event.y
            return
        }
        if(window.event.ctrlKey)
        {
                document.form1.Textbox.value = "Ctrl key
and mouse button up
                at: " + window.event.x + ", " +
window.event.y
            return
        }
        if(window.event.altKey)
        {
                document.form1.Textbox.value = "Alt key
and mouse button up
                at: " + window.event.x + ", " +
window.event.y
            return
        }
        document.form1.Textbox.value = "Mouse button
up at: " +
                window.event.x + ", " + window.event.y
    }
  if(navigator.appName == "Netscape") {
      switch(e.modifiers){
            case 0:
                document.form1.Textbox.value = "Mouse
button up at: "
                        + e.pageX + ", " + e.pageY
                break
            case 2:
                document.form1.Textbox.value = "Ctrl
key down and mouse
                        button up at: " + e.pageX + ", "
+ e.pageY
                break
            case 4:
                document.form1.Textbox.value = "Shift
key down and mouse
                        button up at: " + e.pageX + ", "
+ e.pageY
                break
            case 6:
```

Listing 15-1.
A collection example.

```
                          document.form1.Textbox.value = "Shift
          and Ctrl keys down and
                              mouse button up at: " + e.pageX
          + ", " + e.pageY
                      break
                  case 1:
                          document.form1.Textbox.value = "Alt
          key down and mouse
                              button up at: " + e.pageX + ", "
          + e.pageY
                      break
              }
          }
      }
  </SCRIPT>
  </HTML>
```

We'll put the mouse to use in our Web pages now. In the next example, we'll use the mouse to give users a preview of the pages our page links to. When they let the mouse cursor move across a hyperlink, we'll automatically display a preview of the page being linked to, which provides some useful mouse functionality.

The Preview Page

In this next example, we'll give users a preview of what the pages we link to look like. To do that, when the mouse is over a hyperlink in our page, we can display a small preview image of the page being linked to; in this way, users can look before they leap. In the previous example, we used the mouseDown and mouseUp events; this example will use a new mouse event called *mouseOver*.

NOTE: *We're sticking to indicating when the mouse is placed over hyperlinks in the Web page to satisfy both browsers; in fact, Internet Explorer lets you know when the mouse is over practically every Web page element. Netscape Navigator does so only for hyperlinks and <AREA> tags. (You can easily modify the following techniques to other elements in Internet Explorer as you like.)*

In this example, Preview.htm, we will display five hyperlinks and an image to users. If they let the mouse move over one of the hyperlinks, we'll display a thumbnail image of the page being linked to. If they move the mouse to another hyperlink, we can display a thumbnail of the new link's page.

Working With the mouseOver Event

We'll begin this example by placing the hyperlinks we'll use in the Web page. Each of these hyperlinks has a mouseOver event (in both Netscape Navigator and Internet Explorer) that we can connect to an event handler. We accomplish that connection like this, adding the event handlers link1Over(),link2Over() and so on:

```
<HTML>
<HEAD>
<TITLE>Hyperlink Previews</TITLE>
</HEAD>
<BODY LINK = 0000>
<CENTER>
<FORM NAME = form1>
<H1>
Place the mouse over a link to get a preview of the
      linked-to page . . .
</H1>
<A HREF="http://www.server.com" name= link1 onMouseOver
        = "link1Over()">Here is link 1</A>
<BR>
<BR>
<A HREF="http://www.server.com" name= link2 onMouseOver
        = "link2Over()">Here is link 2</A>
<BR>
<BR>
<A HREF="http://www.server.com" name= link3 onMouseOver
        = "link3Over()">Here is link 3</A>
<BR>
<BR>
<A HREF="http://www.server.com" name= link4 onMouseOver
        = "link4Over()">Here is link 4</A>
<BR>
<BR>
<A HREF="http://www.server.com" name= link5 onMouseOver
        = "link5Over()">Here is link 5</A>
<BR>
<BR>
<IMG NAME = "IMG1" SRC = "gif/image1.gif" WIDTH = 236
      HEIGHT = 118>
</FORM>
</CENTER>
</BODY>
```

Next, we add the mouseOver event handlers in the <SCRIPT> element:

```
<SCRIPT LANGUAGE= JavaScript>
    function link1Over()
    {
         .
         .
         .
    }
    function link2Over()
    {
         .
         .
         .
    }
    function link3Over()
    {
         .
         .
         .
    }
    function link4Over()
    {
         .
         .
         .
    }
    function link5Over()
    {
         .
         .
         .
    }
</SCRIPT>
_H
```

In the mouseOver event handlers, all we have to do is reload the<IMG> element's image, and we do that like this:

```
_G
<SCRIPT LANGUAGE= JavaScript>
    function link1Over()
    {
        document.form1.IMG1.src = 'gif/image1.gif'
    }
    function link2Over()
    {
        document.form1.IMG1.src = 'gif/image2.gif'
    }
    function link3Over()
    {
```

```
                document.form1.IMG1.src = 'gif/image3.gif'
        }
        function link4Over()
        {
                document.form1.IMG1.src = 'gif/image4.gif'
        }
        function link5Over()
        {
                document.form1.IMG1.src = 'gif/image5.gif'
        }
</SCRIPT>
```

Open this page now, as shown in Figure 5–3. When the mouse is over a hyperlink, we display an image intended to be a thumbnail image of the linked-to. When the user moves the mouse to another hyperlink, the new thumbnail image appears. Our Preview page is working as we intended.

The code for this page, Preview.htm, is shown in Listing 5–2.

In our next example, we'll take a look at a new mouse event—the mouseOut event.

Figure 5–3
Our Preview page lets users look before they leap with previews of linked-to pages.

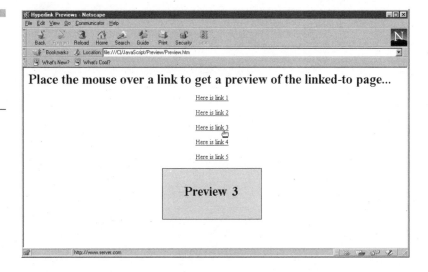

Listing 5–2
Preview.htm.

```
<HTML>
<HEAD>
<TITLE>Hyperlink Previews</TITLE>
</HEAD>
<BODY LINK = 0000>
<CENTER>
<FORM NAME = form1>
<H1>
Place the mouse over a link to get a preview of the
        linked-to page . . .
```

Listing 5–2

continued.

```
</H1>
<A HREF="http://www.server.com" name= link1 onMouseOver
        = "link1Over()">Here is link 1</A>
<BR>
<BR>
<A HREF="http://www.server.com" name= link2 onMouseOver
        = "link2Over()">Here is link 2</A>
<BR>
<BR>
<A HREF="http://www.server.com" name= link3 onMouseOver
        = "link3Over()">Here is link 3</A>
<BR>
<BR>
<A HREF="http://www.server.com" name= link4 onMouseOver
        = "link4Over()">Here is link 4</A>
<BR>
<BR>
<A HREF="http://www.server.com" name= link5 onMouseOver
        = "link5Over()">Here is link 5</A>
<BR>
<BR>
<IMG NAME = "IMG1" SRC = "gif/image1.gif" WIDTH = 236
     HEIGHT = 118>
</FORM>
</CENTER>
</BODY>
<SCRIPT LANGUAGE= JavaScript>
    function link1Over()
    {
        document.form1.IMG1.src = 'gif/image1.gif'
    }
    function link2Over()
    {
        document.form1.IMG1.src = 'gif/image2.gif'
    }
    function link3Over()
    {
        document.form1.IMG1.src = 'gif/image3.gif'
    }
    function link4Over()
    {
        document.form1.IMG1.src = 'gif/image4.gif'
    }
    function link5Over()
    {
        document.form1.IMG1.src = 'gif/image5.gif'
    }
</SCRIPT>
</HTML>
_H
```

SwapImage

Say we're displaying an image in a Web page. When the user moves the mouse over the image, we can swap that image for a new one. Then, when the user moves the mouse away, the original image is restored. In this way, we can respond to mouse movements, changing the image as the user moves the mouse over it (and possibly supplying more information by perhaps switching from a thumbnail image to a more complete image).

We can start this new example, SwapImage.htm, by adding the image itself to the Web page, giving it the mouseOver event handler ImgOver() and the mouseOut event handler (called when the user moves the mouse away from the image) ImgOut().

Netscape Navigator doesn't support the mouseOver or mouseOut events for images, although it does support those events for hyperlinks and <AREA> elements. In this case, we will make our image into a dummy hyperlink so our mouse handlers will be called:

```
<HTML>
<HEAD>
<TITLE>Responding to mouse movements</TITLE>
</HEAD>
<BODY LINK = 0000>
<CENTER>
<FORM NAME = form1>
<H1>
Move the mouse to swap the image . . .
</H1>
<A HREF="" name= link1 onMouseOver = "ImgOver()" onMouseOut
    = "ImgOut()">
    <IMG NAME = "IMG1" SRC = "gif/image1.gif" WIDTH = 236
    HEIGHT = 118> <—
</A>
</CENTER>
</BODY>
```

Now in the <SCRIPT> element, we add the two event handlers we want:

```
<SCRIPT LANGUAGE= JavaScript>
    function ImgOver()
    {
        .
        .
        .
    }
    function ImgOut()
```

```
    {
        .
        .
        .
    }
</SCRIPT>
```

When the mouse is over the image, we can display the second image, and when the mouse leaves the image, we restore the first image this way:

```
<SCRIPT LANGUAGE= JavaScript>
    function ImgOver()
    {
        document.form1.IMG1.src = 'gif/image2.gif'
    }
    function ImgOut()
    {
        document.form1.IMG1.src = 'gif/image1.gif'
    }
</SCRIPT>
```

That's it! Open the page now. When the mouse moves over the image, we swap images to the second image, as shown Figure 5–4.

The code for this page, SwapImage.htm, is shown in Listing 5–3.

This example completes our work with the mouse for the moment, although we'll come back to it at the end of the chapter. For now, however, we'll start working with the keyboard.

Figure 5–4

We swap images
when the mouse
moves over an
image.

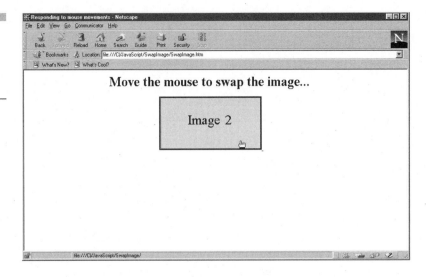

```
<HTML>
<HEAD>
<TITLE>Responding to mouse movements</TITLE>
</HEAD>
<BODY LINK = 0000>
<CENTER>
<FORM NAME = form1>
<H1>
Move the mouse to swap the image . . .
</H1>
<A HREF="" name= link1 onMouseOver = "ImgOver()" onMouseOut
    = "ImgOut()">
    <IMG NAME = "IMG1" SRC = "gif/image1.gif" WIDTH = 236
    HEIGHT = 118>
</A>
</CENTER>
</BODY>
<SCRIPT LANGUAGE= JavaScript>
    function ImgOver()
    {
        document.form1.IMG1.src = 'gif/image2.gif'
    }
    function ImgOut()
    {
        document.form1.IMG1.src = 'gif/image1.gif'
    }
</SCRIPT>
</HTML>
```

Reading Keys in JavaScript

Besides using the mouse through JavaScript, we can also use the keyboard. To see how this works, we will construct an example called "Keys.htm," which displays a prompt and a text box.

When the user types some text, the characters appear in the text box. The text box doesn't have the focus, so it's not reading the keys itself; instead, we'll read the keys directly, as soon as they are struck, and place them in the text box. To create this example, we'll use the keyPress event.

Using the keyPress Event

When the user presses a key, a keyPress event is generated; we'll read the key the user typed then. As you might expect, Netscape Navigator and Internet Explorer handle keystrokes in very different ways, so we'll divide our program into two sections for the two browsers.

TIP: *The keyPress event, which occurs when the user presses a key, has a companion event: keyUp, which takes place when the user releases the key.*

We'll start this new example, Keys.htm, by connecting the keyPress event to an event handler—which we'll call KeyPress()—in the <BODY> tag, which is where Internet Explorer needs that connection:

```
<HTML>
<HEAD>
<TITLE>Key reading example</TITLE>
</HEAD>
<BODY onKeyPress = "keyPress()">          <!—For Internet
      Explorer>
        .
        .
        .
```

Then we add the prompt and text box we'll display:

```
<HTML>
<HEAD>
<TITLE>Key reading example</TITLE>
</HEAD>
<BODY onKeyPress = "keyPress()">          <!—For Internet
      Explorer>
<CENTER>
<FORM NAME = form1>
<H1>Type something . . . </H1>
      <—
<BR>
<BR>
<INPUT NAME = Textbox TYPE = TEXT SIZE = 20>
      <—
</CENTER>
</FORM>
</BODY>
```

Now we'll read the keys the user types, starting by writing code for Netscape Navigator.

Reading Keys in Netscape Navigator

For Netscape Navigator, we connect the document's keyPress event to an event handler, like this:

```
<SCRIPT LANGUAGE = JavaScript>
document.onKeyPress = keyPress                    //For Netscape
      Navigator
          .
          .
          .
```

Now we're ready to write our key event handler. We start by making sure we're working with Netscape Navigator:

```
<SCRIPT LANGUAGE = JavaScript>
document.onKeyPress = keyPress                    //For Netscape
      Navigator
function keyPress(e)
{
    if(navigator.appName == "Netscape") {
          .
          .
          .
```

If so, we can read the ASCII code of the struck key, using the event object's *which* property, as shown here:

```
<SCRIPT LANGUAGE = JavaScript>
document.onKeyPress = keyPress                    //For Netscape
      Navigator
function keyPress(e)
{
    if(navigator.appName == "Netscape") {
        var keyCode = new Number(e.which)
          .
          .
          .
```

Note that we store this key code as a *Number* object; we'll see why we do so in a moment. The next step is to turn the key code into a character we can display in the text box; we'll use Netscape *unescape()* method to do that. That method takes an argument that's a string representing a hexadecimal ASCII code prefaced with "%" and turns it into the corresponding character. For example, the ASCII code in hexadecimal for a space is 0×20, so this call to unescape() returns a space character: unescape ("%20").

That means we have to represent our key's code as a hexadecimal value in string format. We can do that with the Number object's toString() method, passing a base of 16 so we get that value in hexadecimal. We add the new character to a string named "inString" so that we can store and display all the characters the user has typed:

```
<SCRIPT LANGUAGE = JavaScript>
document.onKeyPress = keyPress                    //For Netscape
      Navigator
var inString = ""
function keyPress(e)
{
   if(navigator.appName == "Netscape") {
      var keyCode = new Number(e.which)
      inString += unescape("%" + keyCode.toString(16))
            .
            .
            .
```

NOTE: *You might be surprised to see the operator += here. This operator is simply a contraction of the + and = operators in JavaScript. That is, the statement "a += b" is the same as "a = a + b." Most operators in JavaScript can be combined with the assignment operator, such as -=, *=, and so on.*

All that remains is to display the string in the text box, which we do like this:

```
<SCRIPT LANGUAGE = JavaScript>
document.onKeyPress = keyPress                    //For Netscape
      Navigator
var inString = ""
function keyPress(e)
{
   if(navigator.appName == "Netscape") {
      var keyCode = new Number(e.which)
      inString += unescape("%" + keyCode.toString(16))
      document.form1.Textbox.value = inString
   }
```

That completes the Netscape Navigator portion of the page. Now we'll deal with Internet Explorer.

Reading Keys in Internet Explorer

In Internet Explorer, we can read the struck key from the window.event object's keyCode property. As in Netscape Navigator, we get the struck character's key code and turn it into a string we can display. We turn the key code into a string by using Internet Explorer's String class's from-CharCode() method, adding the newly struck key to our inString string:

```
<SCRIPT LANGUAGE = JavaScript>
var inString = ""
```

```
function keyPress(e)
{
    if(navigator.appName == "Netscape") {
         .
         .
         .
    }
    if (navigator.appName == "Microsoft Internet Explorer")
       {
       inString += String.fromCharCode(window.event.keyCode)
         .
         .
         .
```

Then we display that string in the text box as before:

```
<SCRIPT LANGUAGE = JavaScript>
var inString = ""
function keyPress(e)
{
    if(navigator.appName == "Netscape") {
         .
         .
         .
    }
    if (navigator.appName == "Microsoft Internet Explorer")
       {
         inString += String.fromCharCode(window.event.keyCode)
         document.form1.Textbox.value = inString
    }
}
</SCRIPT>
```

Now open the page and click the document (not the text box, making sure the text box does *not* have the focus and its blinking cursor doesn't appear). Then type some characters; you'll see them appear in the text box, as shown in Figure 5–5. Now we're using the keyboard directly in JavaScript.

NOTE: *Because of the way Netscape Navigator passes keys to our program, uppercase letters don't appear in Netscape's version of this page when you type them. To check whether a letter is uppercase, you can add code to check the event object's modifiers property to see if the Shift key was active when the user typed the key.*

The code for this page, Keys.htm, is shown in Listing 5–4.

Figure 5–5
We read keys directly
from the keyboard.

Listing 5–4
Keys.htm.

```
<HTML>
<HEAD>
<TITLE>Key reading example</TITLE>
</HEAD>
<BODY onKeyPress = "keyPress()">          <!-For Internet
     Explorer>
<CENTER>
<FORM NAME = form1>
<H1>Type something . . . </H1>
<BR>
<BR>
<INPUT NAME = Textbox TYPE = TEXT SIZE = 20>
</CENTER>
</FORM>
</BODY>
<SCRIPT LANGUAGE = JavaScript>
document.onKeyPress = keyPress              //For Netscape
     Navigator
var inString = ""
function keyPress(e)
{
   if(navigator.appName == "Netscape") {
       var keyCode = new Number(e.which)
       inString += unescape("%" + keyCode.toString(16))
       document.form1.Textbox.value = inString
   }
   if (navigator.appName == "Microsoft Internet Explorer")
     {
       inString += String.fromCharCode(window.event.keyCode)
       document.form1.Textbox.value = inString
     }
}
</SCRIPT>
</HTML>
```

Now we're using the keyboard in JavaScript. In fact, using the keyboard, you can support user actions that the user can't normally perform in a Web browser, as we'll see in the next example.

Controlling a Window With Keystrokes

In this next example, we'll get a preview of Chapter 9, "JavaScript and the Window Object," where we work with the window object in depth, seeing how to open new browser windows. Here, we'll display a page with a button that the user can click to get help.

When the user does click the help button, we'll open a new window—the help window. This second window can be controlled by both the mouse and the keyboard. If you want to close the help window with the keyboard, you just press the Esc key (it's a Windows convention to close help windows when you press Esc).

We'll write this example, Helper.htm, now. Because Netscape Navigator suppresses keystrokes like the Esc key, the function keys F1 through F16, and so on, this example is an Internet Explorer example only.

We start Helper.htm by displaying the prompt and the help button to the user:

```
<HTML>
<TITLE>Controlling a window with keystrokes</TITLE>
<BODY>
<FORM>
<CENTER>
<BR>
<H1>Click the button to open the help window . . . </H1>
<BR>
<BR>
<INPUT TYPE = BUTTON Value = "Show help" onClick =
    "ShowHelp()">
</CENTER>
</FORM>
</BODY>
```

When the user clicks the help button, we open a new browser window, displaying a new Web page called "HelpWindow.htm." We use the window object's open() method to do this, as we'll see later in this book:

```
<SCRIPT LANGUAGE = JavaScript>
```

```
function ShowHelp()
{
     window.open("HelpWindow.htm")
}
</SCRIPT>
</HTML>
```

The next step is to design the help window.

Designing the Help Window

In the help window, we'll display a message saying that help hasn't been implemented yet and a prompt indicating that this window can be closed with the Esc key:

```
<HTML>
<HEAD>
<TITLE>Help Window</TITLE>
</HEAD>
<BODY onKeyPress = "keyPress()">
<CENTER>
<FORM NAME = form1>
<H1>Here's the help screen</H1>
<BR>
<BR>
<H2>(Help not yet implemented, sorry.)</H2>
<BR>
<BR>
This window controlled by keystrokes: press the Esc key to
     close this window.
</CENTER>
</FORM>
</BODY>
```

Note that we have connected the document's keyPress event to an event handler, keyPress(), in the <BODY> tag. We add that function like this:

```
<SCRIPT LANGUAGE = JavaScript>
function keyPress(e)
{
   .
   .
   .
}
</SCRIPT>
```

To check whether the Esc key was pressed, we can take a look at the ASCII key code passed to us; if it's the code for the Esc character, ASCII 27, the user did indeed press Esc:

```
<SCRIPT LANGUAGE = JavaScript>
function keyPress(e)
{
    if(window.event.keyCode == 27){
      .
      .
      .
    }
}
</SCRIPT>
```

If the user pressed the Esc key, we want to close the current window, which we do with its close() method:

```
<SCRIPT LANGUAGE = JavaScript>
function keyPress(e)
{
    if(window.event.keyCode == 27){
        window.close()
    }
}
</SCRIPT>
```

Open the Helper.htm page and press the help button to open the help window, as shown in that Figure 5–6. The user can close the help window simply by pressing the Esc key, adding some functionality to our program that didn't exist before—all because we can now read and interpret keystrokes.

The code for this page, Helper.htm, is shown in Listing 5–5, and Listing 5–6 shows the code for the help window, HelpWindow.htm.

Figure 5–6
This window is controlled with keystrokes.

```
<HTML>
<TITLE>Controlling a window with keystrokes</TITLE>
<BODY>
<FORM>
<CENTER>
<BR>
<H1>Click the button to open the help window . . . </H1>
<BR>
<BR>
<INPUT TYPE = BUTTON Value = "Show help" onClick =
     "ShowHelp()">
</CENTER>
</FORM>
</BODY>
<SCRIPT LANGUAGE = JavaScript>
    function ShowHelp()
    {
         window.open("HelpWindow.htm")
    }
</SCRIPT>
</HTML>
```

```
<HTML>
<HEAD>
<TITLE>Help Window</TITLE>
</HEAD>
<BODY onKeyPress = "keyPress()">
<CENTER>
<FORM NAME = form1>
<H1>Here's the help screen</H1>
<BR>
<BR>
<H2>(Help not yet implemented, sorry.)</H2>
<BR>
<BR>
This window controlled by keystrokes: press the Esc key to
     close this window.
</CENTER>
</FORM>
</BODY>
<SCRIPT LANGUAGE = JavaScript>
function keyPress(e)
{
    if(window.event.keyCode == 27){
        window.close()
    }
}
</SCRIPT>
</HTML>
```

We've covered a lot of techniques for keyboard and mouse handling in this chapter, but we'll take a look at one last example that brings these two topics together as we see how to use the mouse to highlight text in a Web page.

Highlighting Text with the Mouse

One of the flashy things that Microsoft does on its Web sites is emphasize hyperlinks when you run the mouse over them by enlarging the link's text and coloring it brightly. We'll see how to do that in this next example that has five hyperlinks on a Web page.

When the user moves the mouse over a hyperlink, we'll change its style, enlarging its text to 36 point (a point is 1/72 of an inch) and coloring it red (we'll see more about using styles in Chapter 12, "JavaScript and Cascading Stylesheest"). You can change styles on-the-fly in Internet Explorer only, so this example will be targeted at that browser.

We'll start this new page, Emphasize.htm, with the hyperlinks we'll use in this page. Note that we add a mouseOver and mouseOut event handler to each hyperlink:

```
<HTML>
<HEAD>
<TITLE>Emphasizing hyperlinks</TITLE>
</HEAD>
<BODY LINK = 0000>
<CENTER>
<FORM NAME = form1>
<H1>
Place the mouse over a link to emphasize it . . .
</H1>
<A HREF="http://www.server.com" name= link1 onMouseOver =
    "link1Over()"
    onMouseOut = "link1Out()">Here is link 1</A>
<BR>
<BR>
<A HREF="http://www.server.com" name= link2 onMouseOver =
    "link2Over()"
    onMouseOut = "link2Out()">Here is link 2</A>
<BR>
<BR>
<A HREF="http://www.server.com" name= link3 onMouseOver =
    "link3Over()"
    onMouseOut = "link3Out()">Here is link 3</A>
<BR>
<BR>
```

```
<A HREF="http://www.server.com" name= link4 onMouseOver =
    "link4Over()"
    onMouseOut = "link4Out()">Here is link 4</A>
<BR>
<BR>
<A HREF="http://www.server.com" name= link5 onMouseOver =
    "link5Over()"
    onMouseOut = "link5Out()">Here is link 5</A>
</FORM>
</CENTER>
</BODY>
```

When the user moves the mouse over the first hyperlink, we want to color that link red and set its font size to 36. We can do that by setting the color and fontSize properties of that link's *style* object:

```
<SCRIPT LANGUAGE= JavaScript>
    function link1Over()
    {
        link1.style.color="red"
        link1.style.fontSize=36
    }
```

When the user moves the mouse away from the hyperlink, we can restore its original size and color in the mouseOut handler, as shown here:

```
<SCRIPT LANGUAGE= JavaScript>
    function link1Over()
    {
        link1.style.color="red"
        link1.style.fontSize=36
    }
    function link1Out()
    {
        link1.style.color="black"
        link1.style.fontSize=16
    }
```

We can do the same for the other hyperlinks:

```
<SCRIPT LANGUAGE= JavaScript>
    function link1Over()
    {
        link1.style.color="red"
        link1.style.fontSize=36
    }
    function link1Out()
    {
        link1.style.color="black"
        link1.style.fontSize=16
    }
    function link2Over()
```

```
        {
            link2.style.color="red"
            link2.style.fontSize=36
        }
        function link2Out()
        {
            link2.style.color="black"
            link2.style.fontSize=16
        }

        function link3Over()
        {
            link3.style.color="red"
            link3.style.fontSize=36
        }
        function link3Out()
        {
            link3.style.color="black"
            link3.style.fontSize=16
        }
        function link4Over()
        {
            link4.style.color="red"
            link4.style.fontSize=36
        }
        function link4Out()
        {
            link4.style.color="black"
            link4.style.fontSize=16
        }
        function link5Over()
        {
            link5.style.color="red"
            link5.style.fontSize=36
        }
        function link5Out()
        {
            link5.style.color="black"
            link5.style.fontSize=16
        }
</SCRIPT>
</HTML>
```

The page is finished, so try opening it in Internet Explorer, as shown in Figure 5–7. When you run the mouse over a hyperlink, that hyperlink's text is enlarged and colored red; after the mouse passes over it, the hyperlink returns to normal. In this way, we can support a striking effect in Internet Explorer, making the page "come alive."

The code for this page, Emphasize.htm, is shown in Listing 5–8.

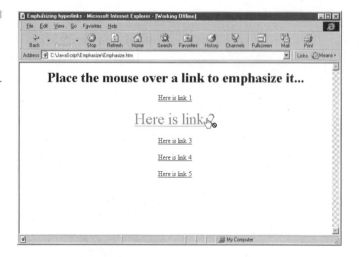

```
<HTML>
<HEAD>
<TITLE>Emphasizing hyperlinks</TITLE>
</HEAD>
<BODY LINK = 0000>
<CENTER>
<FORM NAME = form1>
<H1>
Place the mouse over a link to emphasize it . . .
</H1>
<A HREF="http://www.server.com" name= link1 onMouseOver =
     "link1Over()"
     onMouseOut = "link1Out()">Here is link 1</A>
<BR>
<BR>
<A HREF="http://www.server.com" name= link2 onMouseOver =
     "link2Over()"
     onMouseOut = "link2Out()">Here is link 2</A>
<BR>
<BR>
<A HREF="http://www.server.com" name= link3 onMouseOver =
     "link3Over()"
     onMouseOut = "link3Out()">Here is link 3</A>
<BR>
<BR>
<A HREF="http://www.server.com" name= link4 onMouseOver =
     "link4Over()"
     onMouseOut = "link4Out()">Here is link 4</A>
<BR>
<BR>
<A HREF="http://www.server.com" name= link5 onMouseOver =
     "link5Over()"
     onMouseOut = "link5Out()">Here is link 5</A>
</FORM>
```

Listing 5–8
Continued.

```
</CENTER>
</BODY>
<SCRIPT LANGUAGE= JavaScript>
    function link1Over()
    {
        link1.style.color="red"
        link1.style.fontSize=36
    }
    function link1Out()
    {
        link1.style.color="black"
        link1.style.fontSize=16
    }
    function link2Over()
    {
        link2.style.color="red"
        link2.style.fontSize=36
    }
    function link2Out()
    {
        link2.style.color="black"
        link2.style.fontSize=16
    }

    function link3Over()
    {
        link3.style.color="red"
        link3.style.fontSize=36
    }
    function link3Out()
    {
        link3.style.color="black"
        link3.style.fontSize=16
    }
    function link4Over()
    {
        link4.style.color="red"
        link4.style.fontSize=36
    }
    function link4Out()
    {
        link4.style.color="black"
        link4.style.fontSize=16
    }
    function link5Over()
    {
        link5.style.color="red"
        link5.style.fontSize=36
    }
    function link5Out()
    {
        link5.style.color="black"
        link5.style.fontSize=16
```

Listing 5–8
Continued.

```
        }
</SCRIPT>
</HTML>
```

CONCLUSION

That example finishes this chapter. We've covered a lot of material—how to work with the mouse when the user presses or releases the mouse button (with or without the Shift, Ctrl, or Alt keys); how to use the mouseOver and mouseOut events to produce some powerful visual effects in Web pages, including giving users a preview of Web pages when they let the mouse run over a hyperlink to that page; how to use the keyboard in JavaScript; and even how to control a window with the keyboard. We also combined keyboard and mouse handling in an example that emphasizes hyperlinks when the user runs the mouse over them. We've added a lot of power to our JavaScript programming.

In the next chapter, we'll explore a related topic that will also add power to Web pages—image handling.

6

Image Handling With JavaScript

In this chapter, we're going to explore what JavaScript has to offer for image handling. Images are a big part of the Web, so we'll learn about some powerful techniques to add to Web pages.

First, we'll see how to change an image with the click of a button, loading in a new image as required. Next, we'll discuss the JavaScript *image* object and the *images[]* array and see how to place images and text on top of each other in a Web page. We'll also see how to use Internet Explorer's Structured Graphics control, which lets you create your own graphics under program control. and cover how to let the user *drag* images around in a Web page with the mouse. (As you might expect, the two browsers handle this process entirely differently.)

Finally, we'll take a look at image maps, those clickable images with active "hotspots" that when clicked, cause the browser to navigate to a new location. We'll start working with image maps in this chapter and add more JavaScript power to them in Chapter 11, "Connecting JavaScript and Java."

As you can see, considerable programming power is coming up, so let's begin by loading images into a Web page on demand.

Changing Images With the Click of a Button

We got a preview of our image-loading example, Img.htm, in Chapter 1, "Welcome to JavaScript!" When that page first loads, it displays an image named "image1." When the user clicks the Change Image button, the program loads in a new image named "image2" to replace image1.

This program will introduce us to image handling in JavaScript. Start Img.htm with the image itself and the button the user clicks to change that image:

```
<HTML>

<TITLE>IMG example</TITLE>

<BODY>

<CENTER>

<FORM NAME = form1>

<IMG NAME = "IMG1" SRC = "gif/image1.gif" WIDTH = 236
    HEIGHT = 118>

<BR>

<BR>

<INPUT TYPE = BUTTON Value = "Change Image" onClick =
    "ChangeImage()">

</FORM>

</CENTER>
</BODY>
```

We've connected the button to a click event handler, ChangeImage(). Here's how we write that function:

```
<SCRIPT LANGUAGE = Javascript>
    function ChangeImage()
```

```
    {
        .
        .
        .
    }
</SCRIPT>
```

In that function, we reload the image with image2.gif, as shown here:

```
<SCRIPT LANGUAGE = Javascript>
    function ChangeImage()
    {
        document.form1.IMG1.src = "gif/image2.gif"
    }
</SCRIPT>
```

We've used the <IMG> element's src property, which points out something interesting we've mentioned before: Many of the HTML elements in Netscape Navigator, and all the HTML elements in Internet Explorer, can be treated as objects in your code. In this example, we've named the <IMG> element IMG1, so we can use it as an object in our program, changing its properties as we want.

Although all HTML elements can be treated as objects in Internet Explorer, that's not true in Netscape Navigator (the objects that browser supports are listed in Table 2–1).

Open the Img.htm page. When you click the Change Image button, the browser loads a new image into the page, as you can see in Figure 6–1. Now we can change our Web page graphics under program control.

The code for this page, Img.htm, is shown in Listing 6–1.

Figure 6–1
We load a new image when the user clicks a button.

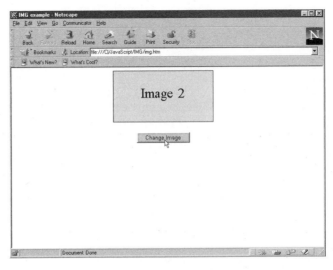

Listing 6–1
Img.htm.

```
<HTML>
<TITLE>IMG example</TITLE>
<BODY>
<CENTER>
<FORM NAME = form1>
<IMG NAME = "IMG1" SRC = "gif/image1.gif" WIDTH = 236
      HEIGHT = 118>
<BR>
<BR>
<INPUT TYPE = BUTTON Value = "Change Image" onClick =
      "ChangeImage()">
</FORM>
</CENTER>
</BODY>
<SCRIPT LANGUAGE = Javascript>
      function ChangeImage()
      {
            document.form1.IMG1.src = "gif/image2.gif"
      }
</SCRIPT>
</HTML>
```

TIP: *You can now load images into Submit and Reset buttons by using those buttons' src property.*

We've gotten an introduction to image handling with the preceding example. In the next one, we'll take a look at the JavaScript image object and what it can do for us.

The Colors Page

In this example, we'll get an overview of how to work with images when you have many to work with, and the techniques for making that task easier. This example introduces us to the images[] array, which holds all the images in a Web page, and the JavaScript image object, which lets you work with individual images as objects.

This example, Colors.htm, will display 50 images, each of which is white, black, red, green, or blue, randomly assorted. When the user clicks the button marked "New colors," the program places a new colored image, selected at random, into one of the images already displayed, also selected at random.

Start Colors.htm with all the <IMG> tags we'll need:

```
<HTML>
<HEAD>
<TITLE>The Colors Example</TITLE>
</HEAD>
<BODY>
<FORM>
<CENTER>
<BR>
<H1>
Click the button to see new colors . . .
</H1>
<BR>
<BR>
<IMG WIDTH = 50 HEIGHT = 50 SRC = "gif/blue.gif"></IMG>
<IMG WIDTH = 50 HEIGHT = 50 SRC = "gif/blue.gif"></IMG>
<IMG WIDTH = 50 HEIGHT = 50 SRC = "gif/blue.gif"></IMG>
<IMG WIDTH = 50 HEIGHT = 50 SRC = "gif/blue.gif"></IMG>
<IMG WIDTH = 50 HEIGHT = 50 SRC = "gif/blue.gif"></IMG>
<IMG WIDTH = 50 HEIGHT = 50 SRC = "gif/blue.gif"></IMG>
<IMG WIDTH = 50 HEIGHT = 50 SRC = "gif/blue.gif"></IMG>
<IMG WIDTH = 50 HEIGHT = 50 SRC = "gif/blue.gif"></IMG>
<IMG WIDTH = 50 HEIGHT = 50 SRC = "gif/blue.gif"></IMG>
<IMG WIDTH = 50 HEIGHT = 50 SRC = "gif/blue.gif"></IMG>
<IMG WIDTH = 50 HEIGHT = 50 SRC = "gif/blue.gif"></IMG>
<IMG WIDTH = 50 HEIGHT = 50 SRC = "gif/blue.gif"></IMG>
<IMG WIDTH = 50 HEIGHT = 50 SRC = "gif/blue.gif"></IMG>
<IMG WIDTH = 50 HEIGHT = 50 SRC = "gif/blue.gif"></IMG>
<IMG WIDTH = 50 HEIGHT = 50 SRC = "gif/blue.gif"></IMG>
<IMG WIDTH = 50 HEIGHT = 50 SRC = "gif/blue.gif"></IMG>
<IMG WIDTH = 50 HEIGHT = 50 SRC = "gif/blue.gif"></IMG>
<IMG WIDTH = 50 HEIGHT = 50 SRC = "gif/blue.gif"></IMG>
<IMG WIDTH = 50 HEIGHT = 50 SRC = "gif/blue.gif"></IMG>
<IMG WIDTH = 50 HEIGHT = 50 SRC = "gif/blue.gif"></IMG>
<IMG WIDTH = 50 HEIGHT = 50 SRC = "gif/blue.gif"></IMG>
<IMG WIDTH = 50 HEIGHT = 50 SRC = "gif/blue.gif"></IMG>
<IMG WIDTH = 50 HEIGHT = 50 SRC = "gif/blue.gif"></IMG>
<IMG WIDTH = 50 HEIGHT = 50 SRC = "gif/blue.gif"></IMG>
<IMG WIDTH = 50 HEIGHT = 50 SRC = "gif/blue.gif"></IMG>
<IMG WIDTH = 50 HEIGHT = 50 SRC = "gif/blue.gif"></IMG>
<IMG WIDTH = 50 HEIGHT = 50 SRC = "gif/blue.gif"></IMG>
<IMG WIDTH = 50 HEIGHT = 50 SRC = "gif/blue.gif"></IMG>
<IMG WIDTH = 50 HEIGHT = 50 SRC = "gif/blue.gif"></IMG>
<IMG WIDTH = 50 HEIGHT = 50 SRC = "gif/blue.gif"></IMG>
<IMG WIDTH = 50 HEIGHT = 50 SRC = "gif/blue.gif"></IMG>
<IMG WIDTH = 50 HEIGHT = 50 SRC = "gif/blue.gif"></IMG>
```

```
<IMG WIDTH = 50 HEIGHT = 50 SRC = "gif/blue.gif"></IMG>
<IMG WIDTH = 50 HEIGHT = 50 SRC = "gif/blue.gif"></IMG>
<IMG WIDTH = 50 HEIGHT = 50 SRC = "gif/blue.gif"></IMG>
<IMG WIDTH = 50 HEIGHT = 50 SRC = "gif/blue.gif"></IMG>
<IMG WIDTH = 50 HEIGHT = 50 SRC = "gif/blue.gif"></IMG>
<IMG WIDTH = 50 HEIGHT = 50 SRC = "gif/blue.gif"></IMG>
<IMG WIDTH = 50 HEIGHT = 50 SRC = "gif/blue.gif"></IMG>
<IMG WIDTH = 50 HEIGHT = 50 SRC = "gif/blue.gif"></IMG>
<IMG WIDTH = 50 HEIGHT = 50 SRC = "gif/blue.gif"></IMG>
<IMG WIDTH = 50 HEIGHT = 50 SRC = "gif/blue.gif"></IMG>
<IMG WIDTH = 50 HEIGHT = 50 SRC = "gif/blue.gif"></IMG>
<IMG WIDTH = 50 HEIGHT = 50 SRC = "gif/blue.gif"></IMG>
<BR>
<BR>
<INPUT TYPE = BUTTON VALUE = "New colors" onClick =
       newImage()>
</CENTER>
</FORM>
</BODY>
```

Note that we also added the button we'll use, and connected it to a function, newImage(). Now we'll turn to the JavaScript code for this page.

Using the Image Object

In this program, we want to place a randomly chosen image into a randomly chosen <IMG> element. Working with images this way is much easier if they are indexed—that is, can be addressed by index rather than name.

To index the five colored images we use in this program (the white, black, red, green, and blue images), we'll create an array of JavaScript *image* objects. That takes care of the source for the images, and it introduces us to the image object. That object has these properties: border, complete, height, hspace, lowsrc, name, prototype, src, vspace, and width; it has no methods, but it does have the event handlers onAbort, onError, and onLoad.

It turns out that the <IMG> elements in the Web page are already indexed in the document object's images[] array, so we'll use that array in this program, which takes care of the images' target locations.

First, we'll create the image object array, which we'll name "imageArray[]." We'll load five images into this array from the files white.gif, black.gif, red.gif, green.gif, and blue.gif. Begin by creating imageArray[]:

```
<SCRIPT LANGUAGE = JavaScript>
var imageArray = new Array(5)
       .
       .
       .
```

Next, create the first image object and store it in the first element of imageArray[]. You pass the dimensions of the image in the new image object to the image object's constructor. We'll make that image 50×50 pixels:

```
<SCRIPT LANGUAGE = JavaScript>
var imageArray = new Array(5)
imageArray[0] = new Image(50, 50)
        .
        .
        .
```

You load an image into an image object by assigning the name of an image file to the image object's src property, so load in the white.gif file this way:

```
<SCRIPT LANGUAGE = JavaScript>
var imageArray = new Array(5)
imageArray[0] = new Image(50, 50)
imageArray[0].src = "gif/white.gif"
        .
        .
        .
```

TIP: *Because images are loaded into an image object as soon as you assign an image to the object's src property, you can use the image object to cache images, loading them in off-screen and then flashing them into view immediately as needed. Caching images like this avoids long download times when the images are called for.*

In the same way, load the other colored images into imageArray[]:

```
<SCRIPT LANGUAGE = JavaScript>
var imageArray = new Array(5)
imageArray[0] = new Image(50, 50)
imageArray[0].src = "gif/white.gif"
imageArray[1] = new Image(50, 50)
imageArray[1].src = "gif/black.gif"
imageArray[2] = new Image(50, 50)
imageArray[2].src = "gif/red.gif"
imageArray[3] = new Image(50, 50)
imageArray[3].src = "gif/green.gif"
imageArray[4] = new Image(50, 50)
imageArray[4].src = "gif/blue.gif"
        .
        .
        .
```

Now we have our images in the imageArray[]. The next step is to place those images in the Web page <IMG> elements when called for, and we'll use the document object's images[] array for that.

Using the images[] Array

Because all the <IMG> elements in the Web page are indexed in the document.images[] array, we will use that array when we place an image in the Web page. To choose an <IMG> element at random, we need to create a random number that varies from 0 to 49 to use as an index into that array, and we'll use the JavaScript *math* object's random() method to create that random number.

NOTE: *The math object's methods are abs, acos, asin, atan, atan2, ceil, cos, exp, floor, log, max, min, pow, random, round, sin, sqrt, and tan.*

Here's how we select a colored image at random from the imageArray[] array and place it into an <IMG> element in the images[] array:

```
<SCRIPT LANGUAGE = JavaScript>
var imageArray = new Array(5)
imageArray[0] = new Image(50, 50)
imageArray[0].src = "gif/white.gif"
imageArray[1] = new Image(50, 50)
imageArray[1].src = "gif/black.gif"
imageArray[2] = new Image(50, 50)
imageArray[2].src = "gif/red.gif"
imageArray[3] = new Image(50, 50)
imageArray[3].src = "gif/green.gif"
imageArray[4] = new Image(50, 50)
imageArray[4].src = "gif/blue.gif"
function newImage()
{
    document.images[Math.round(49.5 * Math.random())].src
        = imageArray[Math.round(4.5 * Math.random())].src
}
</SCRIPT>
</HTML>
```

And that's it—we've stored our images as image objects in an array, then selected one image at random when the user clicks the button and placed that image into an <IMG> element at random.

Open the page and click the New colors button several times. As you can see in Figure 6–2, new colors (unfortunately, converted to shades of gray in this book!) appear in various locations throughout the page. Now we've gotten an introduction to the image object in JavaScript.

The code for this page, Colors.htm, is shown in Listing 6–2.

Figure 6–2

We use image objects to display colored tiles when the user clicks a button.

Listing 6–2

Colors.htm.

```
HTML>
<HEAD>
<TITLE>The Colors Example</TITLE>
</HEAD>
<BODY>
<FORM>
<CENTER>
<BR>
<H1>
Click the button to see new colors . . .
</H1>
<BR>
<BR>
<IMG WIDTH = 50 HEIGHT = 50 SRC = "gif/blue.gif"></IMG>
<IMG WIDTH = 50 HEIGHT = 50 SRC = "gif/blue.gif"></IMG>
<IMG WIDTH = 50 HEIGHT = 50 SRC = "gif/blue.gif"></IMG>
<IMG WIDTH = 50 HEIGHT = 50 SRC = "gif/blue.gif"></IMG>
<IMG WIDTH = 50 HEIGHT = 50 SRC = "gif/blue.gif"></IMG>
<IMG WIDTH = 50 HEIGHT = 50 SRC = "gif/blue.gif"></IMG>
<IMG WIDTH = 50 HEIGHT = 50 SRC = "gif/blue.gif"></IMG>
<IMG WIDTH = 50 HEIGHT = 50 SRC = "gif/blue.gif"></IMG>
<IMG WIDTH = 50 HEIGHT = 50 SRC = "gif/blue.gif"></IMG>
```

continues

Listing 6–2
Colors.htm.
(Continued)

```
<IMG WIDTH = 50 HEIGHT = 50 SRC = "gif/blue.gif"></IMG>
<IMG WIDTH = 50 HEIGHT = 50 SRC = "gif/blue.gif"></IMG>
<IMG WIDTH = 50 HEIGHT = 50 SRC = "gif/blue.gif"></IMG>
<IMG WIDTH = 50 HEIGHT = 50 SRC = "gif/blue.gif"></IMG>
<IMG WIDTH = 50 HEIGHT = 50 SRC = "gif/blue.gif"></IMG>
<IMG WIDTH = 50 HEIGHT = 50 SRC = "gif/blue.gif"></IMG>
<IMG WIDTH = 50 HEIGHT = 50 SRC = "gif/blue.gif"></IMG>
<IMG WIDTH = 50 HEIGHT = 50 SRC = "gif/blue.gif"></IMG>
<IMG WIDTH = 50 HEIGHT = 50 SRC = "gif/blue.gif"></IMG>
<IMG WIDTH = 50 HEIGHT = 50 SRC = "gif/blue.gif"></IMG>
<IMG WIDTH = 50 HEIGHT = 50 SRC = "gif/blue.gif"></IMG>
<IMG WIDTH = 50 HEIGHT = 50 SRC = "gif/blue.gif"></IMG>
<IMG WIDTH = 50 HEIGHT = 50 SRC = "gif/blue.gif"></IMG>
<IMG WIDTH = 50 HEIGHT = 50 SRC = "gif/blue.gif"></IMG>
<IMG WIDTH = 50 HEIGHT = 50 SRC = "gif/blue.gif"></IMG>
<IMG WIDTH = 50 HEIGHT = 50 SRC = "gif/blue.gif"></IMG>
<IMG WIDTH = 50 HEIGHT = 50 SRC = "gif/blue.gif"></IMG>
<IMG WIDTH = 50 HEIGHT = 50 SRC = "gif/blue.gif"></IMG>
<IMG WIDTH = 50 HEIGHT = 50 SRC = "gif/blue.gif"></IMG>
<IMG WIDTH = 50 HEIGHT = 50 SRC = "gif/blue.gif"></IMG>
<IMG WIDTH = 50 HEIGHT = 50 SRC = "gif/blue.gif"></IMG>
<IMG WIDTH = 50 HEIGHT = 50 SRC = "gif/blue.gif"></IMG>
<IMG WIDTH = 50 HEIGHT = 50 SRC = "gif/blue.gif"></IMG>
<IMG WIDTH = 50 HEIGHT = 50 SRC = "gif/blue.gif"></IMG>
<IMG WIDTH = 50 HEIGHT = 50 SRC = "gif/blue.gif"></IMG>
<IMG WIDTH = 50 HEIGHT = 50 SRC = "gif/blue.gif"></IMG>
<IMG WIDTH = 50 HEIGHT = 50 SRC = "gif/blue.gif"></IMG>
<IMG WIDTH = 50 HEIGHT = 50 SRC = "gif/blue.gif"></IMG>
<IMG WIDTH = 50 HEIGHT = 50 SRC = "gif/blue.gif"></IMG>
<IMG WIDTH = 50 HEIGHT = 50 SRC = "gif/blue.gif"></IMG>
<IMG WIDTH = 50 HEIGHT = 50 SRC = "gif/blue.gif"></IMG>
<IMG WIDTH = 50 HEIGHT = 50 SRC = "gif/blue.gif"></IMG>
<IMG WIDTH = 50 HEIGHT = 50 SRC = "gif/blue.gif"></IMG>
<IMG WIDTH = 50 HEIGHT = 50 SRC = "gif/blue.gif"></IMG>
<IMG WIDTH = 50 HEIGHT = 50 SRC = "gif/blue.gif"></IMG>
<IMG WIDTH = 50 HEIGHT = 50 SRC = "gif/blue.gif"></IMG>
<IMG WIDTH = 50 HEIGHT = 50 SRC = "gif/blue.gif"></IMG>
<IMG WIDTH = 50 HEIGHT = 50 SRC = "gif/blue.gif"></IMG>
<BR>
<BR>
<INPUT TYPE = BUTTON VALUE = "New colors" onClick = newIm-
     age()>
</CENTER>
</FORM>
</BODY>
<SCRIPT LANGUAGE = JavaScript>
var imageArray = new Array(5)
```

```
imageArray[0] = new Image(50, 50)
imageArray[0].src = "gif/white.gif"
imageArray[1] = new Image(50, 50)
imageArray[1].src = "gif/black.gif"
imageArray[2] = new Image(50, 50)
imageArray[2].src = "gif/red.gif"
imageArray[3] = new Image(50, 50)
imageArray[3].src = "gif/green.gif"
imageArray[4] = new Image(50, 50)
imageArray[4].src = "gif/blue.gif"
function newImage()
{
    document.images[Math.round(49.5 * Math.random())].src
        = imageArray[Math.round(4.5 * Math.random())].src
}
</SCRIPT>
</HTML>
```

In the previous example, we loaded graphics images into image objects from files on disk: white.gif, black.gif and so on. As it turns out, however, there's a way to generate graphics in code—at least in Internet Explorer. We'll examine that browser's *Structured Graphics control* next.

The Internet Explorer Structured Graphics Control

The Structured Graphics control is a Microsoft ActiveX control that comes with Internet Explorer 4.0 (and is installed automatically when you install that browser). You set this control up with the <OBJECT> tag, as you do for all ActiveX controls. This control has both properties and methods; to use its properties, place a <PARAM> tag in the <OBJECT> element, as shown in the following code. Note that you must specify the control's class ID value, 369303C2-D7AC−11d0–89D5–00A0C90833E6, which Windows uses to keep track of the control in the Windows registry:

```
<OBJECT ID=object
    STYLE="WIDTH:width; HEIGHT:height: Z-INDEX:z-index"
    CLASSID="CLSID:369303C2-D7AC-11d0-89D5-00A0C90833E6" >
    <PARAM NAME="PropertyName" VALUE="Value">
</OBJECT>
```

Here's what the values in this element do:

object   String identifying the Structured Graphics control.

width   Desired width for the Structured Graphics drawing area

height   Desired height for the Structured Graphics drawing area

z-index   Desired z-index value for the Structured Graphics drawing area

Property   One of the Structured Graphics properties in Table 6–1.

Value   Valid value for that property.

You can find a list of this control's properties in Table 6–1.

Table 6–1

The Structured
Graphics control's
properties.

Property	Means
CoordinateSystem	Sets the coordinate system to use for the world.
DrawingSurface	Sets or returns the DirectAnimation drawing surface, the visible rendering of the control's contents for use (script only).
ExtentHeight, ExtentWidth, ExtentLeft, ExtentTop properties	Sets the height, width, left and top values of the shape (in pixels).
HighQuality	Turns anti-aliasing on or off.
Image	Fills the structured graphic shape with a DirectAnimation IDAImage (script only).
Library	Returns the DirectAnimation Library reference (script only).
MouseEventsEnabled	Sets or returns whether Mouse events should be processed against the Structured Graphics object.
PreserveAspectRatio	Sets or returns a value indicating whether aspect ratio should be preserved when extents are set.
SourceURL	Enables the Structured Graphic control to use an external file as the shape primitive description.
Transform	Transforms the object using a DirectAnimation IDATransform2 behavior (script only).

To use the structured graphics control's methods, you set up the <OBJECT> tag this way:

```
<OBJECT ID=object
    STYLE="WIDTH:width; HEIGHT:height: Z-INDEX:z-index"
    CLASSID="CLSID:369303C2-D7AC-11d0-89D5-00A0C90833E6">
    <PARAM NAME="LINEnnnn" VALUE="method">
</OBJECT>
```

Here's what the values in this element do:

object	String identifying the object.
width	Desired width for the Structured graphics drawing area.
height	Desired height for the Structured graphics drawing area
z-index	z-index value for the Structured graphics drawing area.
nnnn	A sequence number for the method execution order. Must be in order starting with 0001.
method	One of the elements in Table 6–2.

You can find a list of this control's methods in Table 6–2.

Table 6–2

The Structured Graphics control's methods.

Method	Means
Arc	Creates a single circular or elliptical arc.
FillSpline	Creates a closed spline shape, defined by a series of points.
Oval	Creates an ellipse.
Pie	Creates an elliptical arc closed at the center of the bounding rectangle to form a wedge (pie) shape.
Polygon	Creates a closed polygon.
PolyLine	Creates a segmented line.
PolySpline	Creates an open spline shape, defined by a series of points.
Rect	Creates a rectangle.
RoundRect	Creates a rounded rectangle.
SetFillColor	Sets the foreground and background colors for graphic fills.
SetFillStyle	Sets the type of fill.
SetFont	Sets the font for the control.
SetGradientFill	Specifies the start and end points for a gradient fill.
SetHatchFill	Specifies whether the hatch fill is transparent.
SetLineColor	Sets the line color for drawing graphics.
SetLineStyle	Changes the line style for the current shape.
SetGradientShape	Sets the shape of a gradient to be an outline of a polygon shape.
SetTextureFill	Sets the texture source to be used for filling a Structured Graphics shape.
Text	Creates a string with the current font and color.

The control's events are listed in Table 6–3.

Event	Means
onclick	Occurs when the user has clicked the left mouse button on the structured graphic.
ondblclick	Occurs when the user has double-clicked on the structured graphic.
onmousedown	Occurs when the left button is pressed.
onmousemove	Occurs when the user moves the mouse pointer across the structured graphic.
onmouseout	Occurs when the cursor leaves the structured graphic.
onmouseover	Occurs when the mouse pointer has entered the structured graphic.
onmouseup	Occurs when the user releases the mouse button.

We can make all this clearer with an example, Struct.htm, where we'll use the Structured Graphics control to display a green square. Then we'll place a circle in this square, dividing that circle up into eight pie-like sections of alternating light and dark blue. Start Struct.htm by creating a Structured Graphics control in that Web page:

```
<HTML>
<HEAD>
<TITLE>Internet Explorer Structured Graphics Control Exam-
     ple</TITLE>
</HEAD>
<BODY>
<CENTER>
<H1>Internet Explorer Structured Graphics Control Exam-
     ple</H1>
<OBJECT
    STYLE="HEIGHT:250; WIDTH:250"
    CLASSID="CLSID:369303C2-D7AC-11D0-89D5-00A0C90833E6">
      <—

        .


        .
        .
```

We'll use this control's methods to draw our figure, so the name we give to each <PARAM> element will be Line0001, Line0002, Line0003, as this control requires.

TIP: *If you skip a number in the Linexxxx sequence, or get that sequence out of order, the Structured Graphics control will stop execution.*

Setting Drawing Colors

We can set the color of the lines we'll draw to red with the SetLineColor() method, passing it red, green, and blue color values, as shown here:

```
<HTML>
<HEAD>
<TITLE>Internet Explorer Structured Graphics Control
    Example</TITLE>
</HEAD>
<BODY>
<CENTER>
<H1>Internet Explorer Structured Graphics Control
    Example</H1>
<OBJECT
    STYLE="HEIGHT:250; WIDTH:250"
    CLASSID="CLSID:369303C2-D7AC-11D0-89D5-00A0C90833E6">
    <PARAM NAME="Line0001" VALUE="SetLineColor(255, 0, 0)">
          .
          .
          .
```

In this example, we will start by drawing a green square, so set the *fill color* (the color figures will be filled with) to green with SetFillColor():

```
<HTML>
<HEAD>
<TITLE>Internet Explorer Structured Graphics Control
    Example</TITLE>
</HEAD>
<BODY>
<CENTER>
<H1>Internet Explorer Structured Graphics Control
    Example</H1>
<OBJECT
    STYLE="HEIGHT:250; WIDTH:250"
    CLASSID="CLSID:369303C2-D7AC-11D0-89D5-00A0C90833E6">
    <PARAM NAME="Line0001" VALUE="SetLineColor(255, 0, 0)">
->  <PARAM NAME="Line0002" VALUE="SetFillColor(0, 255, 0)">
          .
          .
          .
```

Then set the *fill style* to 1, which means our figures will be filled in with solid color:

```
<HTML>
<HEAD>
<TITLE>Internet Explorer Structured Graphics Control
    Example</TITLE>
</HEAD>
<BODY>
<CENTER>
<H1>Internet Explorer Structured Graphics Control
    Example</H1>
<OBJECT
    STYLE="HEIGHT:250; WIDTH:250"
    CLASSID="CLSID:369303C2-D7AC-11D0-89D5-00A0C90833E6">
    <PARAM NAME="Line0001" VALUE="SetLineColor(255, 0, 0)">
    <PARAM NAME="Line0002" VALUE="SetFillColor(0, 255, 0)">
    <PARAM NAME="Line0003" VALUE="SetFillStyle(1)">
        .
        .
        .
```

Now we're ready to draw the green square.

Drawing Rectangles

We draw the square with the Rect() method. Pass the origin of the rectangle as (x, y) to Rect(), its width and height, as well as its rotation (in degrees—we'll use 0 here) this way:

```
<HTML>
<HEAD>
<TITLE>Internet Explorer Structured Graphics Control
    Example</TITLE>
</HEAD>
<BODY>
<CENTER>
<H1>Internet Explorer Structured Graphics Control
    Example</H1>
<OBJECT
    STYLE="HEIGHT:250; WIDTH:250"
    CLASSID="CLSID:369303C2-D7AC-11D0-89D5-00A0C90833E6">
    <PARAM NAME="Line0001" VALUE="SetLineColor(255, 0, 0)">
    <PARAM NAME="Line0002" VALUE="SetFillColor(0, 255, 0)">
    <PARAM NAME="Line0003" VALUE="SetFillStyle(1)">
    <PARAM NAME="Line0004" VALUE="Rect(-80, -80, 180, 180,
    0)">
        .
        .
        .
```

The green square appears at this point. The next operation is to place a circle in the square with alternating light and dark blue pie sections. We'll do that by drawing a blue circle and then adding lighter pie sections.

Drawing Ovals

To draw the blue circle, we'll use the Oval() method. You pass the origin of the oval, as well as its width and height (which are the same for our circle) and a rotation angle to the Oval() method. Note that we also set the fill color to blue:

```
<HTML>
<HEAD>
<TITLE>Internet Explorer Structured Graphics Control Exam-
    ple</TITLE>
</HEAD>
<BODY>
<CENTER>
<H1>Internet Explorer Structured Graphics Control Exam-
    ple</H1>
<OBJECT
    STYLE="HEIGHT:250; WIDTH:250"
    CLASSID="CLSID:369303C2-D7AC-11D0-89D5-00A0C90833E6">
    <PARAM NAME="Line0001" VALUE="SetLineColor(255, 0, 0)">
    <PARAM NAME="Line0002" VALUE="SetFillColor(0, 255, 0)">
    <PARAM NAME="Line0003" VALUE="SetFillStyle(1)">
    <PARAM NAME="Line0004" VALUE="Rect(-80, -80, 180, 180,
    0)">
    <PARAM NAME="Line0005" VALUE="SetFillColor(0, 0, 255)">
    <PARAM NAME="Line0006" VALUE="Oval(-80, -80, 180, 180,
    0)">
        .
        .
        .
```

Finally, we will add the lighter pie sections to the circle.

Drawing Pie Sections

To draw a pie section, use the Pie() method, passing the origin of the pie slice, the width and height of an enclosing oval, the start and end angle of the pie, and a rotation angle. Here's how we draw our pie sections after changing the fill color to light blue:

```
<HTML>
<HEAD>
<TITLE>Internet Explorer Structured Graphics Control Exam-
     ple</TITLE>
</HEAD>
<BODY>
<CENTER>
<H1>Internet Explorer Structured Graphics Control Exam-
     ple</H1>
<OBJECT
     STYLE="HEIGHT:250; WIDTH:250"
     CLASSID="CLSID:369303C2-D7AC-11D0-89D5-00A0C90833E6">
     <PARAM NAME="Line0001" VALUE="SetLineColor(255, 0, 0)">
     <PARAM NAME="Line0002" VALUE="SetFillColor(0, 255, 0)">
     <PARAM NAME="Line0003" VALUE="SetFillStyle(1)">
     <PARAM NAME="Line0004" VALUE="Rect(-80, -80, 180, 180,
     0)">
     <PARAM NAME="Line0005" VALUE="SetFillColor(0, 0, 255)">
     <PARAM NAME="Line0006" VALUE="Oval(-80, -80, 180, 180,
     0)">
     <PARAM NAME="Line0007" VALUE="SetFillColor(0, 200,
     200)">
     <PARAM NAME="Line0008" VALUE="Pie(-80, -80, 180, 180,
     0, 40, 0)">
     <PARAM NAME="Line0009" VALUE="Pie(-80, -80, 180, 180,
     0, 40, 90)">
     <PARAM NAME="Line0010" VALUE="Pie(-80, -80, 180, 180,
     0, 40, 180)">
     <PARAM NAME="Line0011" VALUE="Pie(-80, -80, 180, 180,
     0, 40, 270)">
</OBJECT>
</CENTER>
</BODY>
</HTML>
```

That's it—open this page in Internet Explorer. As you can see in Figure 6–3, the Structured Graphics control has drawn the figure we wanted in that page. Our example is working—we're drawing our own graphics figures.

The code for this page, Struct.htm, is shown in Listing 6–3.

The next topic we'll cover in image handling is how to *position* your images in a Web page, even how to have one image overlap another.

Figure 6–3
Internet Explorer's
Structured Graphics
control at work.

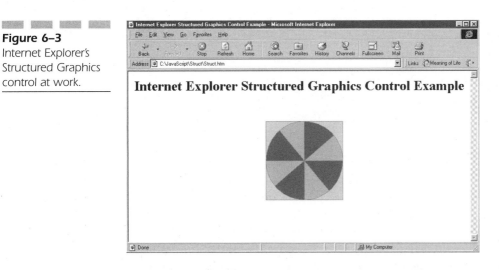

Listing 6–3
Struct.htm.

```
<HTML>
<HEAD>
<TITLE>Internet Explorer Structured Graphics Control Exam-
    ple</TITLE>
</HEAD>
<BODY>
<CENTER>
<H1>Internet Explorer Structured Graphics Control Exam-
    ple</H1>
<OBJECT
    STYLE="HEIGHT:250; WIDTH:250"
    CLASSID="CLSID:369303C2-D7AC-11D0-89D5-00A0C90833E6">
    <PARAM NAME="Line0001" VALUE="SetLineColor(255, 0, 0)">
    <PARAM NAME="Line0002" VALUE="SetFillColor(0, 255, 0)">
    <PARAM NAME="Line0003" VALUE="SetFillStyle(1)">
    <PARAM NAME="Line0004" VALUE="Rect(-80, -80, 180, 180,
    0)">
    <PARAM NAME="Line0005" VALUE="SetFillColor(0, 0, 255)">
    <PARAM NAME="Line0006" VALUE="Oval(-80, -80, 180, 180,
    0)">
    <PARAM NAME="Line0007" VALUE="SetFillColor(0, 200,
    200)">
    <PARAM NAME="Line0008" VALUE="Pie(-80, -80, 180, 180,
    0, 40, 0)">
    <PARAM NAME="Line0009" VALUE="Pie(-80, -80, 180, 180,
    0, 40, 90)">
    <PARAM NAME="Line0010" VALUE="Pie(-80, -80, 180, 180,
    0, 40, 180)">
    <PARAM NAME="Line0011" VALUE="Pie(-80, -80, 180, 180,
    0, 40, 270)">
</OBJECT>
</CENTER>
</BODY>
</HTML>
```

Positioning Your Images in a Web Page

Part of handling images is placing them where you want them, and that task has gotten easier in HTML. We'll take a look at the new HTML support for positioning images, and then see how to move images *dynamically* under user control when they drag images around the screen.

In this first example, ImagePile.htm, we'll see how to draw two images, one on top of the other. This is relatively easy to do in HTML by using the <DIV> tag, which lets you set up divisions in your Web page that you can name and use as objects. We'll use two <DIV>s in this example, one for each image. You can position a <DIV> by using its STYLE attribute, and we'll do that to place one image on top of another.

Start with the first <DIV>, placing its upper-left corner at (150, 150) in our Web page and giving it a width and height this way (notice we indicate that we're giving its position in absolute terms):

```
<HTML>
<HEAD>
<TITLE>Overlapping Image Example</TITLE>
</HEAD>
<BODY>
<CENTER>
<H1>
Overlapping Images . . .
</H1>
</CENTER>
<HTML>
<HEAD>
<TITLE>Putting images on top of each other</TITLE>
</HEAD>
<DIV STYLE="POSITION:ABSOLUTE; LEFT:150; TOP:150;
    WIDTH:240; HEIGHT:300">
    .
    .
    .
```

Next we add the first image to this <DIV>, using the <IMG> tag:

```
<HTML>
<HEAD>
<TITLE>Overlapping Image Example</TITLE>
</HEAD>
<BODY>
<CENTER>
```

```
<H1>
Overlapping Images . . .
</H1>
</CENTER>
<HTML>
<HEAD>
<TITLE>Putting images on top of each other</TITLE>
</HEAD>
<DIV STYLE="POSITION:ABSOLUTE; LEFT:150; TOP:150;
    WIDTH:240; HEIGHT:300">
    <IMG ID = "image2" WIDTH = 236 HEIGHT = 118  SRC="im-
    ages/image1.gif">
</DIV>
    .
    .
    .
```

We set up the second <DIV> and image in almost the same way, just offsetting it a little from the first image:

```
<HTML>
<HEAD>
<TITLE>Overlapping Image Example</TITLE>
</HEAD>
<BODY>
<CENTER>
<H1>
Overlapping Images . . .
</H1>
</CENTER>
<HTML>
<HEAD>
<TITLE>Putting images on top of each other</TITLE>
</HEAD>
<DIV STYLE="POSITION:ABSOLUTE; LEFT:150; TOP:150;
    WIDTH:240; HEIGHT:300">
    <IMG ID = "image2" WIDTH = 236 HEIGHT = 118  SRC="im-
    ages/image1.gif">
</DIV>
<DIV STYLE="POSITION:ABSOLUTE; LEFT:120; TOP:60; WIDTH:240;
    HEIGHT:250">
    <IMG HEIGHT = 118px SRC="images/image2.gif">
</DIV>
</BODY>
</HTML>
```

Now open this page. As you can see in Figure 6–4, Image 2 overlaps Image 1—a relatively new feature in Web pages.

The code for this page, ImagePile,htm, is shown in Listing 6–4.

Figure 6–4
Supporting
overlapping images.

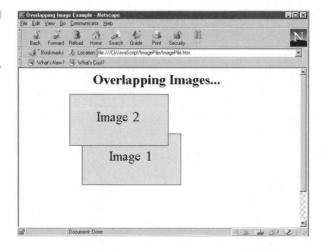

Listing 6–4
ImagePile.htm.

```
<HTML>
<HEAD>
<TITLE>Overlapping Image Example</TITLE>
</HEAD>
<BODY>
<CENTER>
<H1>
Overlapping Images . . .
</H1>
</CENTER>
<HTML>
<HEAD>
<TITLE>Putting text on top of text</TITLE>
</HEAD>
<DIV STYLE="POSITION:ABSOLUTE; LEFT:150; TOP:150;
    WIDTH:240; HEIGHT:300">
        <IMG ID = "image2" WIDTH = 236 HEIGHT = 118
    SRC="images/image1.gif">
</DIV>
<DIV STYLE="POSITION:ABSOLUTE; LEFT:120; TOP:60; WIDTH:240;
    HEIGHT:250">
  <IMG HEIGHT = 118px SRC="images/image2.gif">
</DIV>
</BODY>
</HTML>
```

Now that we've seen how to position images in HTML, let's take a look at how to work with that position in JavaScript. In particular, we'll let the user drag an image around the Web page using the mouse. Internet Explorer and Netscape Navigator really diverge on how to drag images, however—so much so that it hardly makes sense to write one Web page for this task. Therefore, we'll write two pages: one for Internet Explorer and one for Netscape Navigator.

To move an image around in Internet Explorer, you can simply set the style position properties of one of the images, following the user's mouse movements. However, you can't dynamically update style position properties in Netscape Navigator, so our approach must be different there. In Navigator, we'll use *layers*, new in JavaScript 1.2 (and not available in Internet Explorer), placing each image in its own layer. We can then move an image around by moving its layer in response to mouse movements.

TIP: *You could, if you really wanted to, write one page for both browsers, using the Navigator's <NOLAYER> and </NOLAYER> tags. You use these tags to hide HTML (and code in <SCRIPT> elements) from browsers that don't support layers. By checking the appName property to see what browser the page is running in, and using the <NOLAYER> tag, you could combine the image-dragging examples we're about to write into one multibrowser page.*

Dragging and Dropping in Internet Explorer

In this next example, we'll display two images to users: one they can drag with the mouse, and one they can't. To move an image, the user just presses the mouse button when the mouse cursor is on an image and then drags that image to a new location, releasing the mouse button to complete the operation.

We'll begin this new page, Move.htm, with two <DIV>s, one for each image, and then include the two images we'll need:

```
<HTML>
<HEAD>
<TITLE>Dragging and Dropping in Internet Explorer</TITLE>
</HEAD>
<BODY>
<CENTER>
<H1>
Dragging and Dropping in Internet Explorer
</H1>
</CENTER>
<DIV STYLE = "position:relative" ID = ImageDiv>
```

```
    <IMG ID = "image2" STYLE = "CONTAINER:POSITIONED; POSI-
        TION:ABSOLUTE;
            TOP:150px; LEFT:150px; WIDTH: 236px; HEIGHT =
        118PX;"
            SRC="images/move1.gif">
    <IMG STYLE = "CONTAINER:POSITIONED; POSITION:ABSOLUTE;
            TOP = 60px; LEFT = 60px; WIDTH:236px;
        HEIGHT:118px;"
            SRC="images/move2.gif" onMouseMove = moveImage()>
</DIV>
    .
    .
    .
```

Notice that we have connected a new mouse event to the second image
—the *mouseMove* event.

The mouseMove Event

As you might expect, the mouseMove event occurs when the user moves
the mouse. Here's how we create our mouseMove event handler in
Move.htm:

```
<HTML>
<HEAD>
<TITLE>Dragging and Dropping in Internet Explorer</TITLE>
</HEAD>
<BODY>
<CENTER>
<H1>
Dragging and Dropping in Internet Explorer
</H1>
</CENTER>
<DIV STYLE = "position:relative" ID = ImageDiv>
  <IMG ID = "image2" STYLE = "CONTAINER:POSITIONED; POSI-
      TION:ABSOLUTE;
          TOP:150px; LEFT:150px; WIDTH: 236px; HEIGHT =
      118PX;"
          SRC="images/move1.gif">
  <IMG STYLE = "CONTAINER:POSITIONED; POSITION:ABSOLUTE;
          TOP = 60px; LEFT = 60px; WIDTH:236px;
      HEIGHT:118px;"
          SRC="images/move2.gif" onMouseMove = moveImage()>
</DIV>
<SCRIPT LANGUAGE = "JavaScript">
function moveImage()
{
    .
```

```
        .
        .
}
</SCRIPT>
</BODY>
</HTML>
```

In that event handler, we first check to make sure the left mouse button is down; if not, the user is moving the mouse but not dragging anything, so we should quit:

```
<SCRIPT LANGUAGE = "JavaScript">
function moveImage()
{
    if(window.event.button != 1){
        return
    }
        .
        .
        .
}
</SCRIPT>
```

If the left mouse button is down, the user is dragging the mouse. In that case, we want to move the image accordingly. We can refer to the object the user is dragging with the *srcElement* member of the window.event object—that's the object that caused the mouseMove event. We will change the srcElement's style properties, so we start by using a *with* statement:

```
<SCRIPT LANGUAGE = "JavaScript">
function moveImage()
{
    if(window.event.button != 1){
        return
    }
    with(window.event.srcElement.style){
        .
        .
        .
    }
}
</SCRIPT>
```

The actual location of the image is set with its pixelLeft and pixelTop style properties. Here's how we set pixelLeft, using the mouse's x location from window.event.x, adjusting our position in the image to be halfway across its width (the image is 236 pixels wide), and allowing for the <DIV> element to be offset from the window's origin at the upper-left corner:

```
<SCRIPT LANGUAGE = "JavaScript">
function moveImage()
{
    if(window.event.button != 1){
        return
    }
    with(window.event.srcElement.style){
->      pixelLeft = window.event.x - 236 / 2 -
        document.all.ImageDiv.offsetLeft
                    .
                    .
                    .

    }
}
</SCRIPT>
```

We set the y location of the image with its pixelTop property in the same way:

```
<SCRIPT LANGUAGE = "JavaScript">
function moveImage()
{
    if(window.event.button != 1){
        return
    }
    with(window.event.srcElement.style){
        pixelLeft = window.event.x - 236 / 2 -
    document.all.ImageDiv.offsetLeft
->      pixelTop = window.event.y - 118 / 2 -
        document.all.ImageDiv.offsetTop
    }
}
</SCRIPT>
```

There's one very important consideration. Both Internet Explorer and Netscape Navigator support drag-and-drop Windows 95 operations, so if users just drag the mouse, each browser assumes they're trying to drag and drop a standard object (like a file) into the browser to open that object. Because there's no such object in reality, the browser blocks the operation and stops the dragging, so we have to cancel the system drag-and-drop operation ourselves to allow the user to continue.

Cancelling System Drag and Drop

We can cancel the standard Windows 95 drag-and-drop operation by returning a value of false from the mouseMove event handler. We do that by placing a false value in the window.event object's *returnValue* (retval in earlier versions of Internet Explorer) property:

```
<SCRIPT LANGUAGE = "JavaScript">
function moveImage()
{
    if(window.event.button != 1){
        return
    }
    with(window.event.srcElement.style){
        pixelLeft = window.event.x - 236 / 2 -
    document.all.ImageDiv.offsetLeft
        pixelTop = window.event.y - 118 / 2 -
    document.all.ImageDiv.offsetTop
    }
-> window.event.returnValue = false
}
</SCRIPT>
```

That's it—now we've set up our own dragging and dropping of images in Internet Explorer.

TIP: *Although we're dragging and dropping images in this example, you can use the same code to drag and drop any HTML element in Internet Explorer. Just replace the <IMG> element with the element(s) you want to use.*

Open this page in Internet Explorer, as shown in Figure 6–5. You can drag the "Move me with the mouse!" image around at will. Our Move.htm example is a success!

The code for this page, Move.htm, is shown in Listing 6–5.

Figure 6–5
We drag and drop images in Internet Explorer.

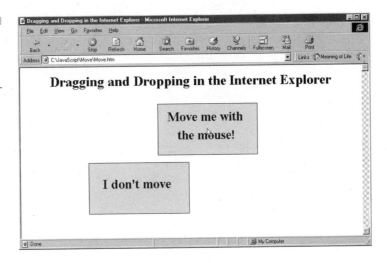

```
<HTML>
<HEAD>
<TITLE>Dragging and Dropping in Internet Explorer</TITLE>
</HEAD>
<BODY>
<CENTER>
<H1>
Dragging and Dropping in Internet Explorer
</H1>
</CENTER>
<DIV STYLE = "position:relative" ID = ImageDiv>
   <IMG ID = "image2" STYLE = "CONTAINER:POSITIONED; POSI-
      TION:ABSOLUTE;
         TOP:150px; LEFT:150px; WIDTH: 236px; HEIGHT =
      118PX;"
         SRC="images/move1.gif">
   <IMG STYLE = "CONTAINER:POSITIONED; POSITION:ABSOLUTE;
         TOP = 60px; LEFT = 60px; WIDTH:236px;
      HEIGHT:118px;"
         SRC="images/move2.gif" onMouseMove = moveImage()>
</DIV>
<SCRIPT LANGUAGE = "JavaScript">
function moveImage()
{
    if(window.event.button != 1){
        return
    }
    with(window.event.srcElement.style){
        pixelLeft = window.event.x - 236 / 2 -
    document.all.ImageDiv.offsetLeft
        pixelTop = window.event.y - 118 / 2 -
    document.all.ImageDiv.offsetTop
    }
    window.event.returnValue = false
}
</SCRIPT>
</BODY>
</HTML>
```

TIP: *You can disable the pop-up help menu that appears in a browser when the user clicks the right mouse button by returning false from the onMouse-Down event handler.*

Now we'll do the same thing in Netscape Navigator—but we'll do it a whole different way.

Dragging and Dropping in Netscape Navigator

Unlike Internet Explorer, you can't dynamically update the style position properties of objects in Netscape Navigator. Instead, we'll use Netscape Navigator *layers* to let the user move images around with the mouse.

Just as in the previous example, we will display two images in our Web page—one the user can move and the other one they can't.

Using the mouse, they can drag the first image around as they like.

To perform this operation, we'll use Netscape layers, which work just as you might expect—by letting you place elements in layers, one on top of another. The properties of the layer object are shown in Table 6–4, and its methods are listed in Table 6–5.

Table 6–4

The layer object's properties.

Property	Can be Modified	Means
document	No	Each layer object contains its own document object, which can be used to access the images, applets, embeds, links, anchors, and layers contained within the layer. Methods of the document object can be invoked only to change the contents of the layer.
name	No	The name assigned to the layer through the NAME or ID attribute.
left	Yes	The horizontal position of the layer's left edge, relative to the origin of its parent layer (for layers with absolute positions) or relative to the natural flow position (for layers with relative positions).
top	Yes	The vertical position of the layer's top edge relative to the origin of its parent layer.
pageX	Yes	The horizontal position of the layer relative to the page.
pageY	Yes	The vertical position of the layer relative to the page.
zIndex	Yes	The relative z-order of this layer with respect to siblings.
visibility	Yes	Determines whether the layer is visible.

continues

Table 6–4

The layer object's properties.

(Continued)

clip.top clip. left clip.right clip.bottom clip.height clip. width	Yes	These properties define the clipping rectangle, which specifies the part of the layer that's visible.
background	Yes	The image to use as the background for the layer.
bgColor	Yes	The color to use as a solid background color for the layer.
siblingAbove	No	The layer object above this one in the stacking order, among all layers that share the same parent layer or null if the layer has no sibling above.
siblingBelow	No	The layer object below this one in z-order, among all layers that share the same parent layer or null if the layer is at the very bottom.
above	No	The layer object above this one in z-order, among all layers in the document or the enclosing window object if this layer is topmost.
below	No	The layer object below this one in z-order, among all layers in the document or null if this layer is at the very bottom.
parentLayer	No	The layer object that contains this layer, or the enclosing window object if this layer is not nested in another layer.
src	Yes	Source of the content for the layer, specified as a URL.

Table 6–5

The layer object's methods.

Method	Does This
moveBy(dx, dy)	Moves this layer by dx pixels to the left, and dy pixels down, from its current position.
moveTo(x, y)	For layers with absolute positions, this method changes the layer's position to the specified pixel coordinates within the containing layer or document.
moveToAbsolute(x, y)	Changes the layer position to the specified pixel coordinates within the page.
resizeBy(dwidth, dheight)	Resizes the layer by the specified height and width values (in pixels).

resizeTo(width, height)	Resizes the layer to have the specified height and width values (in pixels).
moveAbove(layer)	Stacks this layer (in z-order) above the layer specified in the argument, without changing either layer's horizontal or vertical position.
moveBelow(layer)	Stacks this layer (in z-order) below the specified layer, without changing the layer's horizontal or vertical position.
load(sourcestring, width)	Changes the source of a layer to the contents of the file indicated.

We start this new page, Move2.htm, by setting up two layers, layer1 and layer2, each of which holds an <IMG> element (much like the <DIV> elements in the previous example each held an <IMG> element):

```
<HTML>
<HEAD>
<TITLE>Dragging and Dropping in Netscape Navigator</TITLE>
</HEAD>
<BODY>
<CENTER>
<H1>Dragging and Dropping in Netscape Navigator</H1>
</CENTER>
<LAYER NAME="layer1" LEFT = 100; TOP = 200;>
   <IMG NAME = IMG1 SRC = "move1.gif" WIDTH = 236 HEIGHT =
      118>
</LAYER>
<LAYER NAME="layer2">
   <IMG NAME = IMG1 SRC = "move2.gif" WIDTH = 236 HEIGHT =
      118>
</LAYER>
</BODY>
```

Note that we name each layer and give its position by using the LEFT and TOP attributes to position it in our Web page. Next, we'll add the code we need for this page in the <SCRIPT> element:

```
<HTML>
<HEAD>
<TITLE>Dragging and Dropping in Netscape Navigator</TITLE>
</HEAD>
<BODY>
<CENTER>
<H1>Dragging and Dropping in Netscape Navigator</H1>
</CENTER>
<LAYER NAME="layer1" LEFT = 100; TOP = 200;>
   <IMG NAME = IMG1 SRC = "move1.gif" WIDTH = 236 HEIGHT =
      118>
```

```
</LAYER>
<LAYER NAME="layer2">
  <IMG NAME = IMG1 SRC = "move2.gif" WIDTH = 236 HEIGHT =
     118>
</LAYER>
</BODY>
<SCRIPT LANGUAGE = JavaScript>
  .
  .
  .

</SCRIPT>
</HTML>
```

Our first step will be to use Netscape Navigator's mouseMove event.

The mouseMove Event

To catch any mouseMove events in Netscape Navigator, you must capture those events specifically with the *captureEvents()* method. This method captures mouse events and lets you send those events to an event handler.

Although you don't normally need to use captureEvents() with mouse-Down and mouseUp events, we'll use that method here because we support layers in our page that will have their own mouse events. By capturing all mouse events, we can send them to the event handlers we connect to the document. In OCE, that process looks like this, where we send all mouseDown events to the document's event handler, mouse-DownHandler():

```
<SCRIPT LANGUAGE = JavaScript>
document.captureEvents(Event.MOUSEDOWN)
  .
  .
  .

</SCRIPT>
<SCRIPT LANGUAGE = JavaScript>
document.captureEvents(Event.MOUSEDOWN)
document.onMouseDown = mouseDownHandler
  .
  .
  .

</SCRIPT>
```

In the same way, we can capture all mouseUp and mouseMove events for all layers and the document itself, as shown here:

```
<SCRIPT LANGUAGE = JavaScript>
document.captureEvents(Event.MOUSEDOWN)
document.onMouseDown = mouseDownHandler
document.captureEvents(Event.MOUSEUP)
document.onMouseUp = mouseUpHandler
document.captureEvents(Event.MOUSEMOVE)
document.onMouseMove = mouseMoveHandler
        .
        .
        .
```

Now our mouse event handlers will be called no matter where the mouse event originated. We'll keep track of the state of the mouse button —up or down—in a Boolean flag named "downFlag," which we set to true when the mouse button goes down (and we should start dragging the image):

```
<SCRIPT LANGUAGE = JavaScript>
var downFlag = false
document.captureEvents(Event.MOUSEDOWN)
document.onMouseDown = mouseDownHandler
document.captureEvents(Event.MOUSEUP)
document.onMouseUp = mouseUpHandler
document.captureEvents(Event.MOUSEMOVE)
document.onMouseMove = mouseMoveHandler
function mouseDownHandler()
{
    downFlag = true
}
```

Also, we set downFlag to false when the button goes up (and we should end the dragging procedure):

```
<SCRIPT LANGUAGE = JavaScript>
var downFlag = false
document.captureEvents(Event.MOUSEDOWN)
document.onMouseDown = mouseDownHandler
document.captureEvents(Event.MOUSEUP)
document.onMouseUp = mouseUpHandler
document.captureEvents(Event.MOUSEMOVE)
document.onMouseMove = mouseMoveHandler
function mouseDownHandler()
{
    downFlag = true
}
function mouseUpHandler()
{
    downFlag = false
}
</SCRIPT>
```

In the mouseMovehandler() event handler, first check to see whether the mouse button is down by examining downFlag:

```
<SCRIPT LANGUAGE = JavaScript>
var downFlag = false
document.captureEvents(Event.MOUSEDOWN)
document.onMouseDown = mouseDownHandler
document.captureEvents(Event.MOUSEUP)
document.onMouseUp = mouseUpHandler
document.captureEvents(Event.MOUSEMOVE)
document.onMouseMove = mouseMoveHandler
function mouseDownHandler()
{
    downFlag = true
}
function mouseUpHandler()
{
    downFlag = false
}
function mouseMoveHandler(e)
{
    if(downFlag){
        .
        .
        .
    }
}
</SCRIPT>
```

If the button is down and the mouse is moving, the user is dragging the mouse, so we should move the movable image to match. To do that, first get a layer object corresponding to the layer with that image:

```
<SCRIPT LANGUAGE = JavaScript>
var downFlag = false
document.captureEvents(Event.MOUSEDOWN)
document.onMouseDown = mouseDownHandler
document.captureEvents(Event.MOUSEUP)
document.onMouseUp = mouseUpHandler
document.captureEvents(Event.MOUSEMOVE)
document.onMouseMove = mouseMoveHandler
function mouseDownHandler()
{
    downFlag = true
}
function mouseUpHandler()
{
    downFlag = false
}
function mouseMoveHandler(e)
{
    if(downFlag){
        Image1 = document.layers['layer2'];
```

```
            .
            .
            .
        }
    }
    </SCRIPT>
```

Now we move the layer to correspond to the mouse location, using the Layer object's moveTo() method:

```
<SCRIPT LANGUAGE = JavaScript>
var downFlag = false
document.captureEvents(Event.MOUSEDOWN)
document.onMouseDown = mouseDownHandler
document.captureEvents(Event.MOUSEUP)
document.onMouseUp = mouseUpHandler
document.captureEvents(Event.MOUSEMOVE)
document.onMouseMove = mouseMoveHandler
function mouseDownHandler()
{
    downFlag = true
}
function mouseUpHandler()
{
    downFlag = false
}
function mouseMoveHandler(e)
{
    if(downFlag){
        Image1 = document.layers['layer2'];
        Image1.moveTo(e.pageX - 236 / 2, e.pageY - 118 /2);
    }
}
</SCRIPT>
```

Just as in Internet Explorer, we need to cancel system drag and drop. We do that by returning a value of false from the mouseMove handler:

```
<SCRIPT LANGUAGE = JavaScript>
var downFlag = false
document.captureEvents(Event.MOUSEDOWN)
document.onMouseDown = mouseDownHandler
document.captureEvents(Event.MOUSEUP)
document.onMouseUp = mouseUpHandler
document.captureEvents(Event.MOUSEMOVE)
document.onMouseMove = mouseMoveHandler
function mouseDownHandler()
{
    downFlag = true
}
function mouseUpHandler()
{
```

```
        downFlag = false
    }
    function mouseMoveHandler(e)
    {
        if(downFlag){
            Image1 = document.layers['layer2'];
            Image1.moveTo(e.pageX - 236 / 2, e.pageY - 118 /2);
        }
        return(false)
    }
    </SCRIPT>
```

That's it—open the page now in Netscape Navigator, as shown in Figure 6–6. Using the mouse, users can drag the movable image around. Now we're dragging and dropping images in Netscape Navigator by using layers!

The code for this page, Move2.htm, is shown in Listing 6–6.

Figure 6–6
We let the user drag
images in Netscape
Navigator.

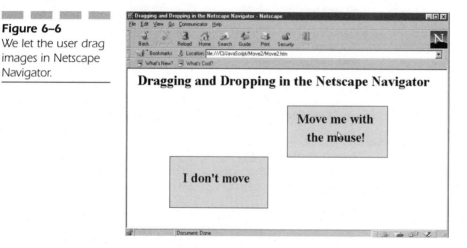

Listing 6–6
Move2.htm.

```
<HTML>
<HEAD>
<TITLE>Dragging and Dropping in Netscape Navigator</TITLE>
</HEAD>
<BODY>
<CENTER>
<H1>Dragging and Dropping in Netscape Navigator</H1>
</CENTER>
<LAYER NAME="layer1" LEFT = 100; TOP = 200;>
    <IMG NAME = IMG1 SRC = "move1.gif" WIDTH = 236 HEIGHT =
        118>
```

```
</LAYER>
<LAYER NAME="layer2">
   <IMG NAME = IMG1 SRC = "move2.gif" WIDTH = 236 HEIGHT =
      118>
</LAYER>
</BODY>
<SCRIPT LANGUAGE = JavaScript>
var downFlag = false
document.captureEvents(Event.MOUSEDOWN)
document.onMouseDown = mouseDownHandler
document.captureEvents(Event.MOUSEUP)
document.onMouseUp = mouseUpHandler
document.captureEvents(Event.MOUSEMOVE)
document.onMouseMove = mouseMoveHandler
function mouseDownHandler()
{
   downFlag = true
}
function mouseUpHandler()
{
   downFlag = false
}
function mouseMoveHandler(e)
{
   if(downFlag){
       Image1 = document.layers['layer2'];
       Image1.moveTo(e.pageX - 236 / 2, e.pageY - 118 /2);
   }
   return(false)
}
</SCRIPT>
</HTML>
```

The last topic we'll cover on image handling is how to create an *image map*.

Image Maps

As our final topic for this chapter, we'll take a look at how to create client-side image maps using HTML. At first, this might not seem to be a Java-Script topic, but later in this book we'll see how to modify our image map so that when the user clicks a *hotspot* in our map, we can execute lines of JavaScript instead of having the browser navigate to a new URL.

What's a hotspot? A *hotspot* is an active location in the image that makes up an image map; when clicked, it makes the browser navigate to a new location. In our image map example, we'll include two hotspots: one that will send us to Netscape's Web site and one for Microsoft's Web site. To navigate to these Web sites, the user simply clicks one of the hotspots.

Let's put this example together now. Use the HTML <MAP> tag, giving this map the name "IMAP":

```
<HTML>
<HEAD>
<TITLE>
An Image Map Example
</TITLE>
</HEAD>
<BODY>
<H1>
An Image Map Example
</H1>
<MAP NAME = "IMAP">
    .
    .
    .
```

Next, use the <AREA> tag to set up the Microsoft hotspot, giving the coordinates (in pixels) of the hotspot and the URL we want to link it to:

```
<HTML>
<HEAD>
<TITLE>
An Image Map Example
</TITLE>
</HEAD>
<BODY>
<H1>
An Image Map Example
</H1>
<MAP NAME = "IMAP">
<AREA NAME = "link1" COORDS = "54,105,118,125"
        HREF = "http://www.microsoft.com">
    .
    .
    .
```

Add the second hotspot for Netscape, as shown here:

```
<HTML>
<HEAD>
```

```
<TITLE>
An Image Map Example
</TITLE>
</HEAD>
<BODY>
<H1>
An Image Map Example
</H1>
<MAP NAME = "IMAP">
<AREA NAME = "link1" COORDS = "54,105,118,125"
        HREF = "http://www.microsoft.com">
<AREA NAME = "link2" COORDS = "104,53,171,75"
        HREF = "http://www.netscape.com">
    <—
</MAP>
```

Finally, display the image map itself, imap.gif, with the <IMG> tag:

```
<HTML>
<HEAD>
<TITLE>
An Image Map Example
</TITLE>
</HEAD>
<BODY>
<H1>
An Image Map Example
</H1>
<MAP NAME = "IMAP">
<AREA NAME = "link1" COORDS = "54,105,118,125"
        HREF = "http://www.microsoft.com">
<AREA NAME = "link2" COORDS = "104,53,171,75"
        HREF = "http://www.netscape.com">
</MAP>
<IMG SRC = "imap.gif" WIDTH = 240 HEIGHT = 155 USEMAP =
    "#IMAP"> <—
</BODY>
</HTML>
```

Note that we've used the USEMAP attribute to connect the <MAP> element we've already set up to the <IMG> element. Now open the page and click one of the hotspots, as shown in Figure 6–7. When you do, the browser will navigate to the URL you've selected.

The code for this page, Imap.htm, is shown in Listing 6–7.

Figure 6–7
We support an
image map with
hotspots.

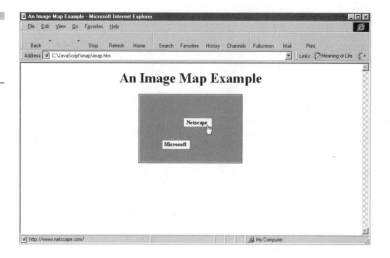

Listing 6–7
Imap.htm.

```
<HTML>
<HEAD>
<TITLE>
An Image Map Example
</TITLE>
</HEAD>
<BODY>
<CENTER>
<H1>
An Image Map Example
</H1>
<MAP NAME = "IMAP">
<AREA NAME = "link1" COORDS = "54,105,118,125" HREF
        = "http://www.microsoft.com">
<AREA NAME = "link2" COORDS = "104,53,171,75" HREF
        = "http://www.netscape.com">
</MAP>
<IMG SRC = "imap.gif" WIDTH = 240 HEIGHT = 155 USEMAP =
    "#IMAP">
</CENTER>
</BODY>
</HTML>
```

That example completes our image handling for the moment. In this
chapter, we've seen how to work with images, loading them into a Web
page on demand, how to use the images[] array and the image object, how
to use Internet Explorer's Structured Graphics control, and how to position images in Web pages. We've also learned how to reposition images in

a Web page under program control by using style properties in Internet Explorer and layers in Netscape Navigator. Finally, we've taken a quick look at image maps.

All this image handling has prepared us for the next chapter because we'll cover a popular topic there: graphics animation.

7

Graphics Animation With JavaScript

In this chapter, we're going to explore graphics animation, one of the most popular aspects of Web programming. As we'll see, the traditional JavaScript methods of supporting animation have been augmented by built-in methods in the browsers.

In this chapter, we'll cover the traditional method of supporting animation in JavaScript—changing images on-screen to animate them. Next, we'll work with the DirectAnimation controls, starting with the DirectAnimation viewer control, in Internet Explorer to get an overview of the animation support available in that browser.

Next, we'll turn to Netscape Navigator, seeing how to use layers to support animation in that browser. To end the chapter, we'll take a look at two of Internet Explorer's DirectAnimation multimedia controls: the Sequencer control, which can direct other controls in a timed sequence, and the Path control, which moves HTML objects along a path in a Web page.

There's a lot to cover in this chapter, so we'll get started at once with the simplest form of JavaScript animation as we take a look at our first example, the Randomizer.

JavaScript Animation: The Randomizer Example

In the previous chapter, we created an example named "Colors" that displayed 50 colored images. When the user clicked the New colors button, we picked a colored image at random and placed it into an <IMG> element (also chosen at random) on the page. We can animate that process now. In this new page, Random.htm, we'll display the same 50 images, but this time we'll fill them under program control—no button necessary.

The program automatically loads in the five images and places them at random into the 50 <IMG> elements, creating a pleasing display. Creating this example will acquaint us with one way of creating animation in JavaScript—the rapid introduction of cached images into a Web page. The technique is to cache your images in image objects and then flash them onscreen as needed. Your image sequence could depict any sort of animation as figures in that image appear to move around.

We'll start this new example, Random.htm, with the 50 <IMG> elements in the Web page where we'll display our colored images:

```
<HTML>
<HEAD>
<TITLE>Randomizer!</TITLE>
</HEAD>
<BODY>
<FORM>
<CENTER>
<BR>
<H1>
The Randomizer
</H1>
<BR>
<BR>
<IMG WIDTH = 50 HEIGHT = 50 SRC = "gif/blue.gif"></IMG>
<IMG WIDTH = 50 HEIGHT = 50 SRC = "gif/blue.gif"></IMG>
<IMG WIDTH = 50 HEIGHT = 50 SRC = "gif/blue.gif"></IMG>
<IMG WIDTH = 50 HEIGHT = 50 SRC = "gif/blue.gif"></IMG>
<IMG WIDTH = 50 HEIGHT = 50 SRC = "gif/blue.gif"></IMG>
<IMG WIDTH = 50 HEIGHT = 50 SRC = "gif/blue.gif"></IMG>
```

```
<IMG WIDTH = 50 HEIGHT = 50 SRC = "gif/blue.gif"></IMG>
<IMG WIDTH = 50 HEIGHT = 50 SRC = "gif/blue.gif"></IMG>
<IMG WIDTH = 50 HEIGHT = 50 SRC = "gif/blue.gif"></IMG>
<IMG WIDTH = 50 HEIGHT = 50 SRC = "gif/blue.gif"></IMG>
<IMG WIDTH = 50 HEIGHT = 50 SRC = "gif/blue.gif"></IMG>
<IMG WIDTH = 50 HEIGHT = 50 SRC = "gif/blue.gif"></IMG>
<IMG WIDTH = 50 HEIGHT = 50 SRC = "gif/blue.gif"></IMG>
<IMG WIDTH = 50 HEIGHT = 50 SRC = "gif/blue.gif"></IMG>
<IMG WIDTH = 50 HEIGHT = 50 SRC = "gif/blue.gif"></IMG>
<IMG WIDTH = 50 HEIGHT = 50 SRC = "gif/blue.gif"></IMG>
<IMG WIDTH = 50 HEIGHT = 50 SRC = "gif/blue.gif"></IMG>
<IMG WIDTH = 50 HEIGHT = 50 SRC = "gif/blue.gif"></IMG>
<IMG WIDTH = 50 HEIGHT = 50 SRC = "gif/blue.gif"></IMG>
<IMG WIDTH = 50 HEIGHT = 50 SRC = "gif/blue.gif"></IMG>
<IMG WIDTH = 50 HEIGHT = 50 SRC = "gif/blue.gif"></IMG>
<IMG WIDTH = 50 HEIGHT = 50 SRC = "gif/blue.gif"></IMG>
<IMG WIDTH = 50 HEIGHT = 50 SRC = "gif/blue.gif"></IMG>
<IMG WIDTH = 50 HEIGHT = 50 SRC = "gif/blue.gif"></IMG>
<IMG WIDTH = 50 HEIGHT = 50 SRC = "gif/blue.gif"></IMG>
<IMG WIDTH = 50 HEIGHT = 50 SRC = "gif/blue.gif"></IMG>
<IMG WIDTH = 50 HEIGHT = 50 SRC = "gif/blue.gif"></IMG>
<IMG WIDTH = 50 HEIGHT = 50 SRC = "gif/blue.gif"></IMG>
<IMG WIDTH = 50 HEIGHT = 50 SRC = "gif/blue.gif"></IMG>
<IMG WIDTH = 50 HEIGHT = 50 SRC = "gif/blue.gif"></IMG>
<IMG WIDTH = 50 HEIGHT = 50 SRC = "gif/blue.gif"></IMG>
<IMG WIDTH = 50 HEIGHT = 50 SRC = "gif/blue.gif"></IMG>
<IMG WIDTH = 50 HEIGHT = 50 SRC = "gif/blue.gif"></IMG>
<IMG WIDTH = 50 HEIGHT = 50 SRC = "gif/blue.gif"></IMG>
<IMG WIDTH = 50 HEIGHT = 50 SRC = "gif/blue.gif"></IMG>
<IMG WIDTH = 50 HEIGHT = 50 SRC = "gif/blue.gif"></IMG>
<IMG WIDTH = 50 HEIGHT = 50 SRC = "gif/blue.gif"></IMG>
<IMG WIDTH = 50 HEIGHT = 50 SRC = "gif/blue.gif"></IMG>
<IMG WIDTH = 50 HEIGHT = 50 SRC = "gif/blue.gif"></IMG>
<IMG WIDTH = 50 HEIGHT = 50 SRC = "gif/blue.gif"></IMG>
<IMG WIDTH = 50 HEIGHT = 50 SRC = "gif/blue.gif"></IMG>
<IMG WIDTH = 50 HEIGHT = 50 SRC = "gif/blue.gif"></IMG>
<IMG WIDTH = 50 HEIGHT = 50 SRC = "gif/blue.gif"></IMG>
<IMG WIDTH = 50 HEIGHT = 50 SRC = "gif/blue.gif"></IMG>
</CENTER>
</FORM>
</BODY>
```

Next, we load in the five images from their respective files—white.gif, black.gif, red.gif, and so on—placing those images into an array of image objects named "imageArray[]":

```
<SCRIPT LANGUAGE = JavaScript>
var imageArray = new Array(5)
imageArray[0] = new Image(50, 50)
imageArray[0].src = "gif/white.gif"
imageArray[1] = new Image(50, 50)
imageArray[1].src = "gif/black.gif"
imageArray[2] = new Image(50, 50)
imageArray[2].src = "gif/red.gif"
imageArray[3] = new Image(50, 50)
imageArray[3].src = "gif/green.gif"
imageArray[4] = new Image(50, 50)
imageArray[4].src = "gif/blue.gif"
           .
           .
           .
```

Now we're ready to support animation in our Web page.

Supporting Basic Animation

We'll start our exploration of animation with the simplest possible technique—using the setTimeout() method to introduce a delay in a repeated operation. You use setTimeout() this way:

```
timeoutID = setTimeout(expression, msec)
```

Here, *expression* is the JavaScript expression you want the program to evaluate after a delay of *msec* milliseconds (1/1000 of a second).

TIP: *The timeoutID* value above is an identifier you can use to cancel the evaluation of *expression* by using the clearTimeout() method.

In this example, we'll use setTimeout() to create a delay of 25 milliseconds; after the delay is over, we'll have the program call a new function, animateImage():

```
<SCRIPT LANGUAGE = JavaScript>
var imageArray = new Array(5)
imageArray[0] = new Image(50, 50)
imageArray[0].src = "gif/white.gif"
imageArray[1] = new Image(50, 50)
imageArray[1].src = "gif/black.gif"
imageArray[2] = new Image(50, 50)
imageArray[2].src = "gif/red.gif"
imageArray[3] = new Image(50, 50)
imageArray[3].src = "gif/green.gif"
```

```
imageArray[4] = new Image(50, 50)
imageArray[4].src = "gif/blue.gif"
animateInterval = setTimeout("animateImage()", 5);
        .
        .
        .
```

All that's left is to write the animateImage() method:

```
<SCRIPT LANGUAGE = JavaScript>
var imageArray = new Array(5)
imageArray[0] = new Image(50, 50)
imageArray[0].src = "gif/white.gif"
imageArray[1] = new Image(50, 50)
imageArray[1].src = "gif/black.gif"
imageArray[2] = new Image(50, 50)
imageArray[2].src = "gif/red.gif"
imageArray[3] = new Image(50, 50)
imageArray[3].src = "gif/green.gif"
imageArray[4] = new Image(50, 50)
imageArray[4].src = "gif/blue.gif"
animateInterval = setTimeout("animateImage()", 5);

function animateImage()
{
     .
     .
     .
}
</SCRIPT>
```

In this new function, we select an image at random and place it in a random <IMG> element:

```
<SCRIPT LANGUAGE = JavaScript>
var imageArray = new Array(5)
imageArray[0] = new Image(50, 50)
imageArray[0].src = "gif/white.gif"
imageArray[1] = new Image(50, 50)
imageArray[1].src = "gif/black.gif"
imageArray[2] = new Image(50, 50)
imageArray[2].src = "gif/red.gif"
imageArray[3] = new Image(50, 50)
imageArray[3].src = "gif/green.gif"
imageArray[4] = new Image(50, 50)
imageArray[4].src = "gif/blue.gif"
animateInterval = setTimeout("animateImage()", 5);

function animateImage()
{
```

```
document.images[Math.round(49.5 * Math.random())].src
    = imageArray[Math.round(4.5 * Math.random())].src
                    .
                    .
                    .

}
</SCRIPT>
```

That completes one iteration of the animation. To keep the animation going, we call setTimeout() again, calling the same function, animateImage(), again and again:

```
<SCRIPT LANGUAGE = JavaScript>
var imageArray = new Array(5)
imageArray[0] = new Image(50, 50)
imageArray[0].src = "gif/white.gif"
imageArray[1] = new Image(50, 50)
imageArray[1].src = "gif/black.gif"
imageArray[2] = new Image(50, 50)
imageArray[2].src = "gif/red.gif"
imageArray[3] = new Image(50, 50)
imageArray[3].src = "gif/green.gif"
imageArray[4] = new Image(50, 50)
imageArray[4].src = "gif/blue.gif"
animateInterval = setTimeout("animateImage()", 5);

function animateImage()
{
    document.images[Math.round(49.5 * Math.random())].src
        = imageArray[Math.round(4.5 * Math.random())].src
    animateInterval = setTimeout("animateImage()", 5);
}
</SCRIPT>
```

In this way, our animation keeps going forever. Of course, it's best to allow some way of ending such an animation; you can do so by adding a button that sets a flag to end the process and checking that flag each time through animateImage().

Open the page now, as shown in Figure 7–1. As you can see, the program selects images automatically, placing them at random in our Web page. We've completed our first, short JavaScript animation example.

TIP: *Of course, there's no reason to fill many different images if you want to animate a single image. In that case, you'd display a sequence of images in the same <IMG> element.*

The code for this page, Random.htm, is shown in Listing 7–1.

Figure 7–1
The Randomizer
illustrates simple
animation.

Listing 7–1
Random.htm.

```
<HTML>
<HEAD>
<TITLE>Randomizer!</TITLE>
</HEAD>
<BODY>
<FORM>
<CENTER>
<BR>
<H1>
The Randomizer
</H1>
<BR>
<BR>
<IMG WIDTH = 50 HEIGHT = 50 SRC = "gif/blue.gif"></IMG>
<IMG WIDTH = 50 HEIGHT = 50 SRC = "gif/blue.gif"></IMG>
<IMG WIDTH = 50 HEIGHT = 50 SRC = "gif/blue.gif"></IMG>
<IMG WIDTH = 50 HEIGHT = 50 SRC = "gif/blue.gif"></IMG>
<IMG WIDTH = 50 HEIGHT = 50 SRC = "gif/blue.gif"></IMG>
<IMG WIDTH = 50 HEIGHT = 50 SRC = "gif/blue.gif"></IMG>
<IMG WIDTH = 50 HEIGHT = 50 SRC = "gif/blue.gif"></IMG>
<IMG WIDTH = 50 HEIGHT = 50 SRC = "gif/blue.gif"></IMG>
<IMG WIDTH = 50 HEIGHT = 50 SRC = "gif/blue.gif"></IMG>
<IMG WIDTH = 50 HEIGHT = 50 SRC = "gif/blue.gif"></IMG>
<IMG WIDTH = 50 HEIGHT = 50 SRC = "gif/blue.gif"></IMG>
<IMG WIDTH = 50 HEIGHT = 50 SRC = "gif/blue.gif"></IMG>
<IMG WIDTH = 50 HEIGHT = 50 SRC = "gif/blue.gif"></IMG>
<IMG WIDTH = 50 HEIGHT = 50 SRC = "gif/blue.gif"></IMG>
<IMG WIDTH = 50 HEIGHT = 50 SRC = "gif/blue.gif"></IMG>
<IMG WIDTH = 50 HEIGHT = 50 SRC = "gif/blue.gif"></IMG>
<IMG WIDTH = 50 HEIGHT = 50 SRC = "gif/blue.gif"></IMG>
```

continues

Listing 7–1
(Continued)

```
<IMG WIDTH = 50 HEIGHT = 50 SRC = "gif/blue.gif"></IMG>
<IMG WIDTH = 50 HEIGHT = 50 SRC = "gif/blue.gif"></IMG>
<IMG WIDTH = 50 HEIGHT = 50 SRC = "gif/blue.gif"></IMG>
<IMG WIDTH = 50 HEIGHT = 50 SRC = "gif/blue.gif"></IMG>
<IMG WIDTH = 50 HEIGHT = 50 SRC = "gif/blue.gif"></IMG>
<IMG WIDTH = 50 HEIGHT = 50 SRC = "gif/blue.gif"></IMG>
<IMG WIDTH = 50 HEIGHT = 50 SRC = "gif/blue.gif"></IMG>
<IMG WIDTH = 50 HEIGHT = 50 SRC = "gif/blue.gif"></IMG>
<IMG WIDTH = 50 HEIGHT = 50 SRC = "gif/blue.gif"></IMG>
<IMG WIDTH = 50 HEIGHT = 50 SRC = "gif/blue.gif"></IMG>
<IMG WIDTH = 50 HEIGHT = 50 SRC = "gif/blue.gif"></IMG>
<IMG WIDTH = 50 HEIGHT = 50 SRC = "gif/blue.gif"></IMG>
<IMG WIDTH = 50 HEIGHT = 50 SRC = "gif/blue.gif"></IMG>
<IMG WIDTH = 50 HEIGHT = 50 SRC = "gif/blue.gif"></IMG>
<IMG WIDTH = 50 HEIGHT = 50 SRC = "gif/blue.gif"></IMG>
<IMG WIDTH = 50 HEIGHT = 50 SRC = "gif/blue.gif"></IMG>
<IMG WIDTH = 50 HEIGHT = 50 SRC = "gif/blue.gif"></IMG>
<IMG WIDTH = 50 HEIGHT = 50 SRC = "gif/blue.gif"></IMG>
<IMG WIDTH = 50 HEIGHT = 50 SRC = "gif/blue.gif"></IMG>
<IMG WIDTH = 50 HEIGHT = 50 SRC = "gif/blue.gif"></IMG>
<IMG WIDTH = 50 HEIGHT = 50 SRC = "gif/blue.gif"></IMG>
<IMG WIDTH = 50 HEIGHT = 50 SRC = "gif/blue.gif"></IMG>
<IMG WIDTH = 50 HEIGHT = 50 SRC = "gif/blue.gif"></IMG>
<IMG WIDTH = 50 HEIGHT = 50 SRC = "gif/blue.gif"></IMG>
<IMG WIDTH = 50 HEIGHT = 50 SRC = "gif/blue.gif"></IMG>
<IMG WIDTH = 50 HEIGHT = 50 SRC = "gif/blue.gif"></IMG>
<IMG WIDTH = 50 HEIGHT = 50 SRC = "gif/blue.gif"></IMG>
<IMG WIDTH = 50 HEIGHT = 50 SRC = "gif/blue.gif"></IMG>
<IMG WIDTH = 50 HEIGHT = 50 SRC = "gif/blue.gif"></IMG>
<IMG WIDTH = 50 HEIGHT = 50 SRC = "gif/blue.gif"></IMG>
</CENTER>
</FORM>
</BODY>
<SCRIPT LANGUAGE = JavaScript>
var imageArray = new Array(5)
imageArray[0] = new Image(50, 50)
imageArray[0].src = "gif/white.gif"
imageArray[1] = new Image(50, 50)
imageArray[1].src = "gif/black.gif"
imageArray[2] = new Image(50, 50)
imageArray[2].src = "gif/red.gif"
imageArray[3] = new Image(50, 50)
imageArray[3].src = "gif/green.gif"
imageArray[4] = new Image(50, 50)
imageArray[4].src = "gif/blue.gif"
animateInterval = setTimeout("animateImage()", 5);
```

```
function animateImage()
{
    document.images[Math.round(49.5 * Math.random())].src
        = imageArray[Math.round(4.5 * Math.random())].src
    animateInterval = setTimeout("animateImage()", 5);
}
</SCRIPT>
</HTML>
```

After having written our relatively simple first animation example, we'll plunge into the depths of Internet Explorer's DirectAnimation next.

Using Internet Explorer's DirectAnimation

Internet Explorer 4.0 supports an immense library of routines and methods for animation and multimedia collectively called "DirectAnimation." It would take several books to cover this complex topic adequately, so we'll just supply an overview of DirectAnimation here.

TIP: *You can get the documentation and samples for Microsoft DirectAnimation in the InetSDK at*
http://www.microsoft.com/msdn/sdk/inetsdk/asetup/first.asp. Note, however, that you'll need 60M free on your hard disk just for the DirectAnimation documentation and samples.

The Microsoft DirectAnimation Multimedia controls include the DAViewerControl control, the Path control, the Sequencer control, the Sprite control, and the Structured Graphics control. We used the Structured Graphics control in the previous chapter; in this chapter, we'll explore the DAViewerControl, Sequencer, and Path controls.

Our first DirectAnimation example uses the DAViewerControl, which you embed in a Web page this way:

```
<DIV ID=controlDiv>
<OBJECT ID="DAViewer"
    STYLE="position:absolute; left:10;
    top:10;width:450;height:450"
    CLASSID="CLSID:B6FFC24C-7E13-11D0-9B47-00C04FC2F51D">
</OBJECT>
</DIV>
```

We can use this control to display DirectAnimation objects, thus supporting animation. The methods of this control are listed in Table 7–1, and its properties are in Table 7–2.

Table 7-1. *The DAViewerControl methods.*	AddBvrToRun
	Drag
	Move
	SetFocus
	ShowWhatsThis
	Start
	ZOrder

Table 7–2 *The DAViewerControl properties.*	BackgroundImage	Object
	Container	Parent
	DragIcon	PixelLibrary
	DragMode	Sound
	Height	TabStop
	HelpContextID	Tag
	Image	ToolTipText
	Index	Top
	InputImage	UpdateInterval
	Left	Visible
	MeterLibrary	WhatsThisHelpID
	Name	Width

In this example, Animation.htm, we'll create a figure of colored triangles and boxes. After creating the figure, we'll animate it, sweeping it across the Web page from lower left to upper right, and twisting it in three dimensions as it moves.

We'll start this new page, Animation.htm, by adding a DAViewerControl object:

```
<HTML>
<HEAD>
<TITLE>
DirectAnimation in Internet Explorer
</TITLE>
</HEAD>
<BODY>
<CENTER>
<H1>
DirectAnimation in Internet Explorer
</H1>
<OBJECT ID="DirectAnimationControl"
    STYLE = "POSITION:ABSOLUTE; LEFT:10%; TOP:100;
       WIDTH:90%; HEIGHT:80%"
    CLASSID="CLSID:B6FFC24C-7E13-11D0-9B47-00C04FC2F51D">
</OBJECT>
</CENTER>
    .
    .
    .
```

TIP: *Note that you can specify the Left, Top, Width, and Height properties in terms of browser window percentanges, not just in terms of pixel measurements. In fact, it's often a good idea to do so because screen resolutions and running conditions can vary among your program's users.*

The DAViewerControl object is the only Web page object we'll need here, so we add our <SCRIPT> section next:

```
<HTML>
<HEAD>
<TITLE>
DirectAnimation in Internet Explorer
</TITLE>
</HEAD>
<BODY>
<CENTER>
<H1>
DirectAnimation in Internet Explorer
</H1>
<OBJECT ID="DirectAnimationControl"
    STYLE = "POSITION:ABSOLUTE; LEFT:10%; TOP:100;
       WIDTH:90%; HEIGHT:80%"
    CLASSID="CLSID:B6FFC24C-7E13-11D0-9B47-00C04FC2F51D">
</OBJECT>
</CENTER>
<SCRIPT LANGUAGE = JavaScript>
    .
    .
    .
```

Now we can pick a library of DirectAnimation routines to work with.

The PixelLibrary and the MeterLibrary

DirectAnimation has two extensive libraries of routines you can use: the PixelLibrary, where all measurements are in pixels, and the MeterLibrary, where all measurements are in meters. We'll use the MeterLibrary routines here:

```
<SCRIPT LANGUAGE = JavaScript>
var MeterLibrary = DirectAnimationControl.MeterLibrary
       .
       .
       .
```

Now that we've selected a library of routines, the next step is to create the figure we'll animate. We create that figure by drawing it on a *drawing surface*.

Using Drawing Surfaces

You draw graphics figures on drawing surfaces in DirectAnimation, so we'll use the MeterLibrary method NewDrawingSurface() to create such a surface, as shown here:

```
<SCRIPT LANGUAGE = JavaScript>
var MeterLibrary = DirectAnimationControl.MeterLibrary
var surface = MeterLibrary.NewDrawingSurface()
       .
       .
       .
```

The drawing surface methods are listed in Table 7–3.

Table 7–3

The DirectAnimation drawing surface methods.

ArcDegrees	LineColor
ArcRadians	LineDashStyle
AutoSizeFillScale	LineEndStyle
BorderColor	LineJoinStyle
BorderDashStyle	LinePoints
BorderJoinStyle	LineWidth
BorderWidth	Opacity

Clear	OpacityAnim
Crop	Oval
CropPoints	OverlayImage
DrawPath	PieDegrees
FillColor	PieRadians
FillImage	Polygon
FillPath	Polyline
FillStyle	Rect
FillTexture	Reset
FixedFillScale	RestoreGraphicsState
Font	RoundRect
GradientExtent	SaveGraphicsState
GradientExtentPoints	SecondaryFillColor
GradientRolloffPower	Text
GradientRolloffPowerAnim	TextPoint
GradientShape	Transform
HorizontalFillScale	VerticalFillScale
Line	

In this example, we want to create a figure composed of boxes and triangles and then animate it. We'll create this figure with the drawing surface Polyline() method, which lets you draw figures composed of line segments. We can fill in those figures as well, using the FillPath() method.

To start, set the *fill color* (the color we want our figures to use), using the drawing surface FillColor() method. We set colors with the MeterLibrary's ColorRgb() method, passing red, green, and blue color values that range from 0 to 1. Here's how we set the fill color to yellow:

```
<SCRIPT LANGUAGE = JavaScript>
var MeterLibrary = DirectAnimationControl.MeterLibrary
var surface = MeterLibrary.NewDrawingSurface()
surface.FillColor(MeterLibrary.ColorRgb(1, 1, 0))
          .
          .
          .
```

Now we use the MeterLibrary method Polyline() to draw a yellow rectangle. To do that, we create an array of the points (given as (x, y) coordinates) to the Polyline() method. We then pass the resulting figure to the drawing surface's FillPath() method to fill in the figure created by Polyline:

```
<SCRIPT LANGUAGE = JavaScript>
var MeterLibrary = DirectAnimationControl.MeterLibrary
var surface = MeterLibrary.NewDrawingSurface()
surface.FillColor(MeterLibrary.ColorRgb(1, 1, 0))
surface.FillPath(MeterLibrary.Polyline(Array(0, 0, 400, 0,
     400, 400, 0, 400,
         0, 0)))
                  .
                  .
                  .
```

In the same way, we can draw the rest of the figure, composed of colored triangles and boxes:

```
<SCRIPT LANGUAGE = JavaScript>

var MeterLibrary = DirectAnimationControl.MeterLibrary
var surface = MeterLibrary.NewDrawingSurface()
surface.FillColor(MeterLibrary.ColorRgb(1, 1, 0))
surface.FillPath(MeterLibrary.Polyline(Array(0, 0, 400, 0,
     400, 400, 0, 400,
         0, 0)))
surface.FillColor(MeterLibrary.ColorRgb(0, 1, 0))
surface.FillPath(MeterLibrary.Polyline(Array(200, 0, 0,
     400, 400, 400, 200,
         0)))
surface.FillColor(MeterLibrary.ColorRgb(0, 0, 1))
surface.FillPath(MeterLibrary.Polyline(Array(0, 0, -400, 0,
     -400, -400, 0,
         -400, 0, 0)))
surface.FillColor(MeterLibrary.ColorRgb(1, 0, 0))
surface.FillPath(MeterLibrary.Polyline(Array(-200, -400, -
     400, 0, 0, 0, -200,
         -400)))
                  .
                  .
                  .
```

That completes the graphics figure we'll animate; the next step is to animate it.

Creating a Translation

Our animation will have two parts. In the first part, we'll move the figure from lower left to upper right in our Web page; in the second, we'll rotate it in three dimensions as it moves.

We start the animation process by defining the *translation* (linear movement) of the figure, sweeping it up and across our Web page. To create that translation, define two points, the start and end points of the figure's path, with the MeterLibrary Point2() method:

```
<SCRIPT LANGUAGE = JavaScript>
var MeterLibrary = DirectAnimationControl.MeterLibrary
var surface = MeterLibrary.NewDrawingSurface()
surface.FillColor(MeterLibrary.ColorRgb(1, 1, 0))
surface.FillPath(MeterLibrary.Polyline(Array(0, 0, 400, 0,
    400, 400, 0, 400,
        0, 0)))
surface.FillColor(MeterLibrary.ColorRgb(0, 1, 0))
surface.FillPath(MeterLibrary.Polyline(Array(200, 0, 0,
    400, 400, 400, 200,
        0)))
surface.FillColor(MeterLibrary.ColorRgb(0, 0, 1))
surface.FillPath(MeterLibrary.Polyline(Array(0, 0, -400, 0,
    -400, -400, 0,
        -400, 0, 0)))
surface.FillColor(MeterLibrary.ColorRgb(1, 0, 0))
surface.FillPath(MeterLibrary.Polyline(Array(-200, -400, -
    400, 0, 0, 0, -200,
        -400)))
var start = MeterLibrary.Point2(-2000, -1000)
var end = MeterLibrary.Point2(2000, 1000)
            .
            .
            .
```

TIP: *The PixelLibrary and MeterLibrary routines have the same names. The only difference is that measurements in those routines are in either pixels or meters. Routines that end with a 2 are two-dimensional graphics routines, and routines that end with a 3 are three-dimensional.*

Next, we create the translation itself, which we'll name "Sweep." Use the MeterLibrary's FollowLine() method, creating a line from the two points with the Line() method:

```
<SCRIPT LANGUAGE = JavaScript>
var MeterLibrary = DirectAnimationControl.MeterLibrary
var surface = MeterLibrary.NewDrawingSurface()
surface.FillColor(MeterLibrary.ColorRgb(1, 1, 0))
surface.FillPath(MeterLibrary.Polyline(Array(0, 0, 400, 0,
    400, 400, 0, 400,
        0, 0)))
surface.FillColor(MeterLibrary.ColorRgb(0, 1, 0))
surface.FillPath(MeterLibrary.Polyline(Array(200, 0, 0,
    400, 400, 400, 200,
        0)))
surface.FillColor(MeterLibrary.ColorRgb(0, 0, 1))
surface.FillPath(MeterLibrary.Polyline(Array(0, 0, -400, 0,
    -400, -400, 0,
        -400, 0, 0)))
surface.FillColor(MeterLibrary.ColorRgb(1, 0, 0))
surface.FillPath(MeterLibrary.Polyline(Array(-200, -400, -
    400, 0, 0, 0, -200,
        -400)))
var start = MeterLibrary.Point2(-2000, -1000)
var end = MeterLibrary.Point2(2000, 1000)
var Sweep =
    MeterLibrary.FollowPath(MeterLibrary.Line(start, end),
    10)
        .
        .
        .
```

That creates our translation action. Before applying it to our graphics figure, however, we'll create the rotation action.

Creating a Rotation

To rotate our figure as it moves, we must define a three-dimensional axis our figure rotates around by using the MeterLibrary Vector() method, which gives the (x, y, z) orientation of a vector:

```
<SCRIPT LANGUAGE = JavaScript>
var MeterLibrary = DirectAnimationControl.MeterLibrary
var surface = MeterLibrary.NewDrawingSurface()
surface.FillColor(MeterLibrary.ColorRgb(1, 1, 0))
surface.FillPath(MeterLibrary.Polyline(Array(0, 0, 400, 0,
    400, 400, 0, 400,
        0, 0)))
surface.FillColor(MeterLibrary.ColorRgb(0, 1, 0))
surface.FillPath(MeterLibrary.Polyline(Array(200, 0, 0,
    400, 400, 400, 200,
        0)))
surface.FillColor(MeterLibrary.ColorRgb(0, 0, 1))
```

```
surface.FillPath(MeterLibrary.Polyline(Array(0, 0, -400, 0,
    -400, -400, 0,
        -400, 0, 0)))
surface.FillColor(MeterLibrary.ColorRgb(1, 0, 0))
surface.FillPath(MeterLibrary.Polyline(Array(-200, -400, -
    400, 0, 0, 0, -200,
        -400)))
var axis = MeterLibrary.Vector3(20, 20, 20)
var start = MeterLibrary.Point2(-2000, -1000)
var end = MeterLibrary.Point2(2000, 1000)
var Sweep =
    MeterLibrary.FollowPath(MeterLibrary.Line(start, end),
    10)
                        .
                        .
                        .
```

To create our figure's 3-D rotation, which we'll name "Twist," we use MeterLibrary's Rotate3RateDegrees() andParallelTransform2() methods, giving the complete rotation a period of 10 seconds:

```
<SCRIPT LANGUAGE = JavaScript>
var MeterLibrary = DirectAnimationControl.MeterLibrary
var surface = MeterLibrary.NewDrawingSurface()
surface.FillColor(MeterLibrary.ColorRgb(1, 1, 0))
surface.FillPath(MeterLibrary.Polyline(Array(0, 0, 400, 0,
    400, 400, 0, 400,
        0, 0)))
surface.FillColor(MeterLibrary.ColorRgb(0, 1, 0))
surface.FillPath(MeterLibrary.Polyline(Array(200, 0, 0,
    400, 400, 400, 200,
        0)))
surface.FillColor(MeterLibrary.ColorRgb(0, 0, 1))
surface.FillPath(MeterLibrary.Polyline(Array(0, 0, -400, 0,
    -400, -400, 0,
        -400, 0, 0)))
surface.FillColor(MeterLibrary.ColorRgb(1, 0, 0))
surface.FillPath(MeterLibrary.Polyline(Array(-200, -400, -
    400, 0, 0, 0, -200,
        -400)))
var axis = MeterLibrary.Vector3(20, 20, 20)
var start = MeterLibrary.Point2(-2000, -1000)
var end = MeterLibrary.Point2(2000, 1000)
var Sweep =
    MeterLibrary.FollowPath(MeterLibrary.Line(start, end),
    10)
var Twist = MeterLibrary.Rotate3RateDegrees(axis,
        180).Duration(10).ParallelTransform2()
                        .
                        .
                        .
```

Now our *transformations*, Twist and Sweep, are ready. Here's how we apply them to the figure we've created:

```
<SCRIPT LANGUAGE = JavaScript>
var MeterLibrary = DirectAnimationControl.MeterLibrary
var surface = MeterLibrary.NewDrawingSurface()
        .
        .
        .

var Twist = MeterLibrary.Rotate3RateDegrees(axis,
        180).Duration(10).ParallelTransform2()
DirectAnimationControl.Image
        = surface.Image.Transform(Twist).Transform(Sweep)
        .Transform(MeterLibrary.Scale2(1./12000.,
    1./12000.))   <-
        .
        .
        .
```

Notice that we also *scale* the figure in two dimensions; we do that because the measurements of MeterLibrary routines are in meters, so we scale the figure we've created down to screen size.

Finally, we start the animation with the DAViewerControl's Start() method:

```
<SCRIPT LANGUAGE = JavaScript>
var MeterLibrary = DirectAnimationControl.MeterLibrary
var surface = MeterLibrary.NewDrawingSurface()
surface.FillColor(MeterLibrary.ColorRgb(1, 1, 0))
surface.FillPath(MeterLibrary.Polyline(Array(0, 0, 400, 0,
        400, 400, 0, 400,
            0, 0)))
surface.FillColor(MeterLibrary.ColorRgb(0, 1, 0))
surface.FillPath(MeterLibrary.Polyline(Array(200, 0, 0,
        400, 400, 400, 200,
            0)))
surface.FillColor(MeterLibrary.ColorRgb(0, 0, 1))
surface.FillPath(MeterLibrary.Polyline(Array(0, 0, -400, 0,
        -400, -400, 0,
            -400, 0, 0)))
surface.FillColor(MeterLibrary.ColorRgb(1, 0, 0))
surface.FillPath(MeterLibrary.Polyline(Array(-200, -400, -
        400, 0, 0, 0, -200,
            -400)))
var axis = MeterLibrary.Vector3(20, 20, 20)
var start = MeterLibrary.Point2(-2000, -1000)
var end = MeterLibrary.Point2(2000, 1000)
var Sweep =
        MeterLibrary.FollowPath(MeterLibrary.Line(start, end),
        10)
var Twist = MeterLibrary.Rotate3RateDegrees(axis,
```

```
                         180).Duration(10).ParallelTransform2()
DirectAnimationControl.Image
        = surface.Image.Transform(Twist).Transform(Sweep)
        .Transform(MeterLibrary.Scale2(1./12000.,
    1./12000.))
DirectAnimationControl.Start()
</SCRIPT>
</BODY>
</HTML>
```

Open the Animation.htm page in Internet Explorer, as shown in Figure 7–2. When you do, the figure we've created appears from the lower-left area and twists its way across the screen to the upper-right area. Our DirectAnimation DAViewerControl example is working!

The code for this page, Animation.htm, is shown in Listing 7–2.

Figure 7–2
Using Internet Explorer's DirectAnimation, you can create a huge variety of effects.

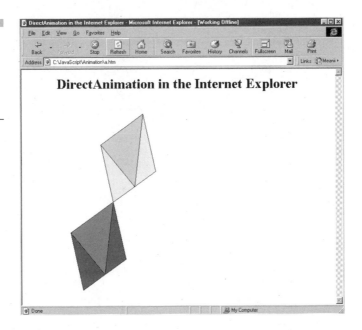

Listing 7–2
Animation.htm.

```
<HTML>
<HEAD>
<TITLE>
DirectAnimation in Internet Explorer
</TITLE>
</HEAD>
<BODY>
<CENTER>
<H1>
```

continues

Listing 7–2
(Continued.)

```
DirectAnimation in Internet Explorer
</H1>
<OBJECT ID="DirectAnimationControl"
    STYLE = "POSITION:ABSOLUTE; LEFT:10%; TOP:100;
        WIDTH:90%; HEIGHT:80%"
    CLASSID="CLSID:B6FFC24C-7E13-11D0-9B47-00C04FC2F51D">
</OBJECT>
</CENTER>
<SCRIPT LANGUAGE = JavaScript>
var MeterLibrary = DirectAnimationControl.MeterLibrary
var surface = MeterLibrary.NewDrawingSurface()
surface.FillColor(MeterLibrary.ColorRgb(1, 1, 0))
surface.FillPath(MeterLibrary.Polyline(Array(0, 0, 400, 0,
    400, 400, 0, 400,
        0, 0)))
surface.FillColor(MeterLibrary.ColorRgb(0, 1, 0))
surface.FillPath(MeterLibrary.Polyline(Array(200, 0, 0,
    400, 400, 400, 200,
        0)))
surface.FillColor(MeterLibrary.ColorRgb(0, 0, 1))
surface.FillPath(MeterLibrary.Polyline(Array(0, 0, -400, 0,
    -400, -400, 0,
        -400, 0, 0)))
surface.FillColor(MeterLibrary.ColorRgb(1, 0, 0))
surface.FillPath(MeterLibrary.Polyline(Array(-200, -400, -
    400, 0, 0, 0, -200,
        -400)))
var axis = MeterLibrary.Vector3(20, 20, 20)
var start = MeterLibrary.Point2(-2000, -1000)
var end = MeterLibrary.Point2(2000, 1000)
var Sweep =
    MeterLibrary.FollowPath(MeterLibrary.Line(start, end),
        10)
var Twist = MeterLibrary.Rotate3RateDegrees(axis,
        180).Duration(10).ParallelTransform2()
DirectAnimationControl.Image
        = surface.Image.Transform(Twist).Transform(Sweep)
        .Transform(MeterLibrary.Scale2(1./12000.,
    1./12000.))
DirectAnimationControl.Start()
</SCRIPT>
</BODY>
</HTML>
```

That's a taste of how you can create animation in Internet Explorer. Netscape Navigator doesn't support the DirectAnimation controls, but it does support something Internet Explorer does not—layers. We'll use layers in the following section to create animation in Netscape Navigator.

Animation Using Layers in Netscape

In our first example, Random.htm, we saw how to animate images in Netscape Navigator by replacing those images, one after another, with other images. However, we can also translate an image across the screen by moving the layer that holds an image.

In this example, Animation2.htm, we'll place an image in a layer and move it from left to right when the page opens. We'll also let the user restart the animation by clicked a button labeled "Click to restart."

Start Animation2.htm with the button and an image in a layer:

```
<HTML>
<HEAD>
<TITLE>
Layer-based Animation
</TITLE>
</HEAD>
<BODY>
<CENTER>
<H1>Layer-based Animation!</H1>
</CENTER>
<BR>
<BR>
<BR>
<BR>
<BR>
<BR>
<BR>
<BR>
<BR>
<CENTER>
<FORM NAME = form1>
<INPUT TYPE = BUTTON VALUE = "Click to restart" onClick =
    "startAnimation()">
</FORM>
</CENTER>
<LAYER NAME="Image1">
<IMG SRC="image1.gif" WIDTH=236 HEIGHT=118>
</LAYER>
```

Now we can write the JavaScript we'll use to start the animation. We will create a function—startAnimation()—for this purpose, and we begin that function by getting the layer that holds the image.

Because we'll move the image by moving the layer, it's easier to think of the image and the layer as the same object, so we refer to this layer simply as "Image1":

```
<SCRIPT LANGUAGE="JavaScript">
    var Image1
    function startAnimation()
    {
        Image1 = document.layers['Image1']
            .
            .
            .

    }
```

Begin by moving Image1 to its starting position in the browser window with the moveTo() method:

```
<SCRIPT LANGUAGE="JavaScript">
    var Image1
    function startAnimation()
    {
        Image1 = document.layers['Image1']
        Image1.moveTo(20, 90)
            .
            .
            .

    }
```

We'll need to keep track of how far we've moved our image to the left because it doesn't make sense to move it far past the edge of the window. We'll use a loop index for that purpose:

```
<SCRIPT LANGUAGE="JavaScript">
    var Image1
    var layerInterval
    function startAnimation()
    {
        Image1 = document.layers['Image1']
        Image1.moveTo(20, 90)
        loop_index = 1
            .
            .
            .

    }
```

Now we're ready to start the animation, and we'll do that with the set-Interval() method.

Animating With setInterval()

In the beginning of this chapter, we saw how to create animation using the setTimeout() method, but another method is frequently used for animation: setInterval(), which is actually a method of the window object. You use setInterval() to perform an action repeatedly, which is perfect for animation. In this case, we'll have the program call a new function, animateImage(), every 25 milliseconds:

```
<SCRIPT LANGUAGE="JavaScript">
    var Image1
    var layerInterval
    function startAnimation()
    {
        Image1 = document.layers['Image1']
        Image1.moveTo(20, 90)
        loop_index = 1
        layerInterval = setInterval(animateImage, 25)    <-
    }
```

The setInterval() method returns an identifier that we'll use to terminate the animation in the animateImage() function. In that function, we'll keep moving the image to the left until we've looped 100 times. We could move the image with the moveTo() method, but there's another way to move layers. If we move the layer to the left, for example, we simply have to increment its *left* property, as shown here:

```
<SCRIPT LANGUAGE="JavaScript">
    var Image1
    var layerInterval
    function startAnimation()
    {
        Image1 = document.layers['Image1']
        Image1.moveTo(20, 90)
        loop_index = 1
        layerInterval = setInterval(animateImage, 25)
    }
    function animateImage()
    {
        if (loop_index < 100){
            loop_index++;
            Image1.left += 5
        }
            .
            .
            .
    }
}
```

When we've looped 100 times, we end the animation with the clearInterval() method, passing it the identifier we got from setInterval():

```
<SCRIPT LANGUAGE="JavaScript">
    var Image1
    var layerInterval
    function startAnimation()
    {
        Image1 = document.layers['Image1']
        Image1.moveTo(20, 90)
        loop_index = 1
        layerInterval = setInterval(animateImage, 25)
    }
    function animateImage()
    {
        if (loop_index < 100){
            loop_index++;
            Image1.left += 5
        }
        else{
            clearInterval(layerInterval)
        }
    }
}
</SCRIPT>
```

We've allowed the user to start the animation by clicking the button in the page, which calls the startAnimation() function. However, we can also start the animation as soon as the page loads by using the document's *Load* event, which occurs when the document is first loaded into the Web browser:

```
<SCRIPT LANGUAGE="JavaScript">
    document.onLoad = startAnimation()
    var Image1
    var layerInterval
    function startAnimation()
    {
        Image1 = document.layers['Image1']
        Image1.moveTo(20, 90)
        loop_index = 1
        layerInterval = setInterval(animateImage, 25)
    }
    function animateImage()
    {
        if (loop_index < 100){
            loop_index++;
            Image1.left += 5
        }
        else{
            clearInterval(layerInterval)
        }
    }
}
</SCRIPT>
```

TIP: *The Load event, occurring when a page is first loaded, is a useful one for page initialization. Its counterpart is the Unload event, which takes place when the page is unloaded.*

Open the Animate2.htm page in Netscape Navigator now, as shown in Figure 7–3. When you do, the image glides across the screen from left to right. Now we're supporting animation in Netscape Navigator!

The code for this page, Animation2.htm, is shown in Listing 7–3.

Figure 7–3
We use layers in Netscape to support animation.

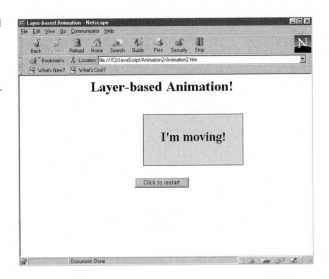

Listing 7–3
Animation2.htm.

```
<HTML>
<HEAD>
<TITLE>
Layer-based Animation
</TITLE>
</HEAD>
<BODY>
<CENTER>
<H1>Layer-based Animation!</H1>
</CENTER>
<BR>
<BR>
<BR>
<BR>
<BR>
<BR>
<BR>
```

continues

Listing 7–3
Continued.

```
<BR>
<BR>
<CENTER>
<FORM NAME = form1>
<INPUT TYPE = BUTTON VALUE = "Click to restart" onClick =
    "startAnimation()">
</FORM>
</CENTER>
<LAYER NAME="Image1">
<IMG SRC="image1.gif" WIDTH=236 HEIGHT=118>
</LAYER>
<SCRIPT LANGUAGE="JavaScript">
    document.onLoad = startAnimation()
    var Image1
    var layerInterval
    function animateImage()
    {
        if (loop_index < 100){
            loop_index++;
            Image1.left += 5
        }
        else{
            clearInterval(layerInterval)
        }
    }
    function startAnimation()
    {
        Image1 = document.layers['Image1']
        Image1.moveTo(20, 90)
        loop_index = 1
        layerInterval = setInterval(animateImage, 25)
    }
</SCRIPT>
</BODY>
</HTML>
```

There are two more Internet Explorer DirectAnimation multimedia controls to cover in this chapter: the Sequencer control and the Path control.

Animation Using the Sequencer Control: The Rotate Example

Internet Explorer's Sequencer control is the built-in timer of the DirectAnimation controls. It's the control that the rest of the DirectAnimation controls use internally to create action sequences. You can use the Sequencer control yourself to direct other controls; in this example, we'll use it to direct the actions of a Structured Graphics control, thus creating animation.

Here's how you embed a Sequencer control in a Web page by using the <OBJECT> tag:

```
<OBJECT ID=OBJECT
    CLASSID=clsid:B0A6BAE2-AAF0-11d0-A152-
00A0C908DB96>
    </OBJECT>
```

The Sequencer control's methods are listed in Table 7–4, and its events are in Table 7–5 (this control has no properties).

Table 7–4

DirectAnimation's Sequencer control's methods.

Method	Description
At	Specifies a new action in the action set.
Pause	Stops action set playback at current position.
Play	Starts the action set (if stopped).
Seek	Changes the current playback position of the action set to a new, specified time.
Stop	Stops action set playback, resets its playback position to the beginning.

Table 7–5

DirectAnimation's Sequencer control's events.

Event	Means
OnInit	Occurs when sequencer is first completely loaded into memory.
OnPause	Occurs when action set playback has been paused.
OnPlay	Occurs when the action set has started playback.
OnSeek	Occurs after the Seek method call has been completed.
OnStop	Occurs when the action set playback ends or is stopped.

You might recall that in the previous chapter we used the Structured Graphics control to produce a graphics image. The Structured Graphics control has a rotate() method, which we'll use with the Sequencer control to make that image rotate in the Web page.

We'll start this new example, Rotate.htm, by creating the same graphic image we created in the previous chapter, using the Structured Graphics control:

```
<HTML>
<HEAD>
<TITLE>
A Sequencer Control Example
</TITLE>
</HEAD>
<BODY onLoad = "startRotation()">
<FORM NAME = form1>
<CENTER>
<H1>Animation using the sequencer control . . . </H1>
</CENTER>
<OBJECT ID=Image
STYLE="POSITION: ABSOLUTE;
HEIGHT:300; WIDTH:300; TOP:100; LEFT:180"
CLASSID="CLSID:369303C2-D7AC-11d0-89D5-00A0C90833E6">
     <PARAM NAME="Line0001" VALUE="SetLineColor(255, 0, 0)">
     <PARAM NAME="Line0002" VALUE="SetFillColor(0, 255, 0)">
     <PARAM NAME="Line0003" VALUE="SetFillStyle(1)">
     <PARAM NAME="Line0004" VALUE="Rect(-80, -80, 180, 180,
       0)">
     <PARAM NAME="Line0005" VALUE="SetFillColor(0, 0, 255)">
     <PARAM NAME="Line0006" VALUE="Oval(-80, -80, 180, 180,
       0)">
     <PARAM NAME="Line0007" VALUE="SetFillColor(0, 200,
       200)">
     <PARAM NAME="Line0008" VALUE="Pie(-80, -80, 180, 180,
       0, 40, 0)">
     <PARAM NAME="Line0009" VALUE="Pie(-80, -80, 180, 180,
       0, 40, 90)">
     <PARAM NAME="Line0010" VALUE="Pie(-80, -80, 180, 180,
       0, 40, 180)">
     <PARAM NAME="Line0011" VALUE="Pie(-80, -80, 180, 180,
       0, 40, 270)">
</OBJECT>
     .
     .
     .
```

Next we add the Sequencer control we'll use:

```
<HTML>
<HEAD>
<TITLE>
A Sequencer Control Example
</TITLE>
```

```
</HEAD>
<BODY onLoad = "startRotation()">
<FORM NAME = form1>
<CENTER>
<H1>Animation using the sequencer control . . . </H1>
</CENTER>
<OBJECT ID=Image
STYLE="POSITION: ABSOLUTE;
HEIGHT:300; WIDTH:300; TOP:100; LEFT:180"
CLASSID="CLSID:369303C2-D7AC-11d0-89D5-00A0C90833E6">
     <PARAM NAME="Line0001" VALUE="SetLineColor(255, 0, 0)">
     <PARAM NAME="Line0002" VALUE="SetFillColor(0, 255, 0)">
     <PARAM NAME="Line0003" VALUE="SetFillStyle(1)">
     <PARAM NAME="Line0004" VALUE="Rect(-80, -80, 180, 180,
         0)">
     <PARAM NAME="Line0005" VALUE="SetFillColor(0, 0, 255)">
     <PARAM NAME="Line0006" VALUE="Oval(-80, -80, 180, 180,
         0)">
     <PARAM NAME="Line0007" VALUE="SetFillColor(0, 200,
         200)">
     <PARAM NAME="Line0008" VALUE="Pie(-80, -80, 180, 180,
         0, 40, 0)">
     <PARAM NAME="Line0009" VALUE="Pie(-80, -80, 180, 180,
         0, 40, 90)">
     <PARAM NAME="Line0010" VALUE="Pie(-80, -80, 180, 180,
         0, 40, 180)">
     <PARAM NAME="Line0011" VALUE="Pie(-80, -80, 180, 180,
         0, 40, 270)">
</OBJECT>
<OBJECT ID="sequencerControl"
        CLASSID="CLSID:B0A6BAE2-AAF0-11d0-A152-
     00A0C908DB96"
        STYLE= "WIDTH:1; HEIGHT:1">
</OBJECT>
</FORM>
```

All that's left is writing the JavaScript that will make the Sequencer control come alive.

Activating a Sequencer Control

To use a Sequencer control, you have to define an *action set*; you do that with the at() method:

object.item(*"actionsetname"*).At(*time*, "script", [*loop,
          interval, tiebreak, drop threshold*]);

The meaning of these parameters is shown in Table 7–6.

Table 7–6

The Sequencer control's at() method parameters.

Parameter	Means
object	Name of sequencer.
actionsetname	Name of the action set.
time	Sets the start time for the specified action. Double-value format: seconds.milliseconds (SS.MSS).
script	Text string identifying the named procedure to be called.
loop	Optional.Sets the loop count for this action. The default is 1. If set to −1, looping is infinite.
interval	Optional. Double-value format: seconds.milliseconds (SS.MSS). Sets the delay between iterations of this action.
tie break	Optional. Integer, −1(default), 0-n. Sets the priority for the action. If two actions happen at the same time, the action with the lower tie break number is performed first.
drop threshold	Optional. Double-value format: seconds.milliseconds (SS.MSS). Sets the time by which the action must be performed before it's dropped from the queue.

We'll set up our Sequencer control to call a function named rotateImage() every 15 milliseconds:

```
<SCRIPT LANGUAGE = JavaScript>
function startRotation()
{
    document.form1.sequencerControl("ActionSet1").At(0.000,
        "rotateImage()", -1, 0.150, 1)
        .
        .
        .

}
```

Now that our action set is initialized, we start the Sequencer control with its play() method, as shown here:

```
<SCRIPT LANGUAGE = JavaScript>
function startRotation()
{
    document.form1.sequencerControl("ActionSet1").At(0.000,
        "rotateImage()", -1, 0.150, 1)
    document.form1.sequencerControl("ActionSet1").Play()
}
```

All that's left is to rotate the image a little in three dimensions when we call the rotateImage() method. We do that with the Structured Graphics control's rotate() method, passing it the number of degrees to rotate the image in the x, y, and z directions:

```
<SCRIPT LANGUAGE = JavaScript>
function startRotation()
{
    document.form1.sequencerControl("ActionSet1").At(0.000,
        "rotateImage()", -1, 0.150, 1)
    document.form1.sequencerControl("ActionSet1").Play()
}
function rotateImage()
{
    document.form1.Image.Rotate(0, 20, 10)
}
</SCRIPT>
```

Now open the page in Internet Explorer, as shown in Figure 7–4. The image we created in the previous chapter now spins around in 3-D; we're successfully using the Sequencer control to animate graphics figures.

The code for this page, Rotate.htm, is shown in Listing 7–4.

Figure 7–4
We use Internet Explorer's Sequencer control to create animation.

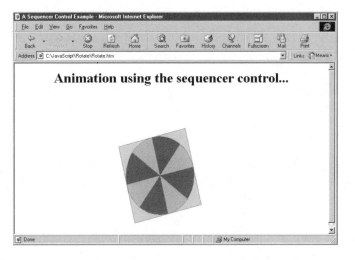

Listing 7–4
Rotate.htm.

```
<HTML>
<HEAD>
<TITLE>
A Sequencer Control Example
</TITLE>
</HEAD>
<BODY onLoad = "startRotation()">
<FORM NAME = form1>
```

continues

Listing 7–4
Continued.

```
<CENTER>
<H1>Animation using the sequencer control . . . </H1>
</CENTER>
<OBJECT ID=Image
STYLE="POSITION: ABSOLUTE;
HEIGHT:300; WIDTH:300; TOP:100; LEFT:180"
CLASSID="CLSID:369303C2-D7AC-11d0-89D5-00A0C90833E6">
    <PARAM NAME="Line0001" VALUE="SetLineColor(255, 0, 0)">
    <PARAM NAME="Line0002" VALUE="SetFillColor(0, 255, 0)">
    <PARAM NAME="Line0003" VALUE="SetFillStyle(1)">
    <PARAM NAME="Line0004" VALUE="Rect(-80, -80, 180, 180,
      0)">
    <PARAM NAME="Line0005" VALUE="SetFillColor(0, 0, 255)">
    <PARAM NAME="Line0006" VALUE="Oval(-80, -80, 180, 180,
      0)">
    <PARAM NAME="Line0007" VALUE="SetFillColor(0, 200,
      200)">
    <PARAM NAME="Line0008" VALUE="Pie(-80, -80, 180, 180,
      0, 40, 0)">
    <PARAM NAME="Line0009" VALUE="Pie(-80, -80, 180, 180,
      0, 40, 90)">
    <PARAM NAME="Line0010" VALUE="Pie(-80, -80, 180, 180,
      0, 40, 180)">
    <PARAM NAME="Line0011" VALUE="Pie(-80, -80, 180, 180,
      0, 40, 270)">
</OBJECT>
<OBJECT ID="sequencerControl"
      CLASSID="CLSID:B0A6BAE2-AAF0-11d0-A152-
    00A0C908DB96"
      STYLE= "WIDTH:1; HEIGHT:1">
</OBJECT>
</FORM>
<SCRIPT LANGUAGE = JavaScript>
function startRotation()
{
    document.form1.sequencerControl("ActionSet1").At(0.000,
      "rotateImage()", -1, 0.150, 1)
    document.form1.sequencerControl("ActionSet1").Play()
}
function rotateImage()
{
    document.form1.Image.Rotate(0, 20, 10)
}
</SCRIPT>
</BODY>
</HTML>
```

We'll take a look at one more DirectAnimation multimedia control in the following section—the Path control.

The Path Control

Internet Explorer's Path control lets you specify a path on which to move an HTML element. Its play() method moves the element along that path. We'll use the Path control to move an image around on the screen.

Here's how you use the Path control in a Web page:

```
<OBJECT ID=object
    CLASSID="CLSID:D7A7D7C3-D47F-11d0-89D3-00A0C90833E6">
    [<PARAM NAME="property" VALUE="setting">]
</OBJECT>
```

The properties of this control are listed in Table 7–7, its methods in Table 7–8, and its events in Table 7–9.

Table 7–7

The Path control's properties.

Property	Means
AutoStart	Determines whether the path starts playback upon loading.
Bounce	Sets the path behavior to either reverse direction and return to the beginning, or stop at the end of its playback.
Direction	Sets the direction of the path playback.
Duration	Sets the duration of the path playback.
Library	Returns the DirectAnimation Library reference.
PlayState	Returns the path's current playback state.
Relative	Determines whether the Path control starts playing from its current position or from the absolute position in the target object's coordinate space.
Repeat	Sets the number of times the path loops during playback.
Target	Sets the object that should follow the path.
Time	Returns the elapsed playback time from the start of the path.
TimerInterval	Sets or returns the length of time, in seconds.milliseconds, between the path updates.

Table 7–8

The Path control's methods.

Method	Does This
AddTimeMarker	Sets a marker to fire an event when playback reaches the marker position.
Oval	Specifies an oval Structured Graphics primitive to be used as the path, with the starting point at top center.

continues

Table 7–8

Continued.

Method	Does This
KeyFrame	Specifies points along the path in x, y coordinates and a designated time to reach each point.
Pause	Stops playback and maintains current elapsed time.
Play	Begins playback from the current elapsed time.
Polygon	Specifies a closed series of line segments to use a path.
PolyLine	Specifies an open set of line segments to be used as the path.
Rect	Specifies a rectangular Structured Graphics primitive to be used as the path, with starting point at top left.
Seek	Resets the current playback position to a new, specified position.
Spline	Specifies a spline to be used as the path.
Stop	Stops playback at current elapsed time and returns path to the beginning.

Table 7–9

The Path control's
events.

Event	Means
OnMarker	Occurs when a time marker has been reached either during path playback or when stopped.
OnPause	Occurs when path playback is paused.
OnPlay	Occurs when path playback is played.
OnPlayMarker	Occurs when a time marker is reached during path playback.
OnSeek	Occurs when a seek call has been completed.
OnStop	Occurs when path playback is stopped.

In this example, Path.htm, we'll display a button with the caption "Start animation." When the user clicks that button, we can display a previously hidden image and move it around the screen (we'll move the image on a horseshoe-like path, arcing up and then down).

Let's start with the button and image we'll use—note that we give the image the visibility type "hidden" to initially hide it:

```
<HTML>
<HEAD>
<TITLE>
An Internet Explorer Path Control Example
```

```
</TITLE>
</HEAD>
<CENTER>
<H1>
Using Internet Explorer Path Control . . .
</H1>
</CENTER>
</HEAD>
<BODY>
<CENTER>
<FORM NAME = form1>
<INPUT TYPE = BUTTON Value = "Start animation" onClick =
     "startAnimation()">
</FORM>
</CENTER>
<CENTER>
<IMG ID=pathImage SRC="Image1.gif" STYLE="position:ab-
     solute; visibility:hidden">
</CENTER>
          .
          .
          .
```

Next, we add the Path control itself, which we name "pathControl":

```
<HTML>
<HEAD>
<TITLE>
An Internet Explorer Path Control Example
</TITLE>
</HEAD>
<CENTER>
<H1>
Using Internet Explorer Path Control . . .
</H1>
</CENTER>
</HEAD>
<BODY>
<CENTER>
<FORM NAME = form1>
<INPUT TYPE = BUTTON Value = "Start animation" onClick =
     "startAnimation()">
</FORM>
</CENTER>
<CENTER>
<IMG ID=pathImage SRC="Image1.gif" STYLE="position:ab-
     solute; visibility:hidden">
</CENTER>
<OBJECT ID="pathControl"
CLASSID = "CLSID:D7A7D7C3-D47F-11D0-89D3-00A0C90833E6">
</OBJECT>
```

Next, specify a path with the Shape parameter. Using the PolyLine() method, you pass the number of points you want to use to define the path to PolyLine(), and then the coordinates of each point:

```
<OBJECT ID="pathControl"
CLASSID = "CLSID:D7A7D7C3-D47F-11D0-89D3-00A0C90833E6">
    <PARAM NAME="Shape" VALUE="PolyLine(10,
        305,190, 280,155, 255,130, 230,100, 205,75,
        185,95, 165,130, 135,160, 110,200, 100, 220)">
              .
              .
              .

</OBJECT>
```

To indicate the traversal speed of the image on the path, we use the Duration parameter, setting its value to 15 seconds:

```
<OBJECT ID="pathControl"
CLASSID = "CLSID:D7A7D7C3-D47F-11D0-89D3-00A0C90833E6">
    <PARAM NAME="Shape" VALUE="PolyLine(10,
        305,190, 280,155, 255,130, 230,100, 205,75,
        185,95, 165,130, 135,160, 110,200, 100, 220)">
    <PARAM NAME="Duration" VALUE="15">
              .
              .
              .

</OBJECT>
```

We also need to give the Path control a *target*—that is, an object to move around on the screen. We've named our image "pathImage," so we pass that as the Target parameter's value:

```
<OBJECT ID="pathControl"
CLASSID = "CLSID:D7A7D7C3-D47F-11D0-89D3-00A0C90833E6">
    <PARAM NAME="Shape" VALUE="PolyLine(10,
        305,190, 280,155, 255,130, 230,100, 205,75,
        185,95, 165,130, 135,160, 110,200, 100, 220)">
    <PARAM NAME="Duration" VALUE="15">
    <PARAM NAME="Target" VALUE="pathImage">
</OBJECT>
```

All that's left is to start the animation, and we do that in the function we've connected to the button, startAnimation().First make the image we'll move visible by setting its visibility style to "visible":

```
<SCRIPT LANGUAGE = JavaScript>
function startAnimation()
{
```

```
-> document.all.pathImage.style.visibility = "visible"
       .
       .
       .

}
</SCRIPT>
```

Here we use the document's *all* object to reach the image. (We'll see a lot more about the all object in the next chapter.) Finally, we use the Path control's play() method to make the image move on the screen:

```
<SCRIPT LANGUAGE = JavaScript>
function startAnimation()
{
    document.all.pathImage.style.visibility = "visible"
    pathControl.Play()
}
</SCRIPT>
```

The Path.htm example is ready to go, so open that page, as shown in Figure 7–5. When you click the button, the image appears and moves along the path.

The code for this page, Path.htm, is shown in Listing 7–5.

Figure 7–5
We create animation with Internet Explorer's Path control.

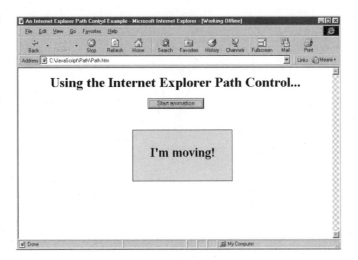

Listing 7–5
Path.htm.

```
<HTML>
<HEAD>
<TITLE>
An Internet Explorer Path Control Example
</TITLE>
```

continues

Listing 7–5
(Continued.)

```
</HEAD>
<CENTER>
<H1>
Using Internet Explorer Path Control . . .
</H1>
</CENTER>
</HEAD>
<BODY>
<CENTER>
<FORM NAME = form1>
<INPUT TYPE = BUTTON Value = "Start animation" onClick =
    "startAnimation()">
</FORM>
</CENTER>
<CENTER>
<IMG ID=pathImage SRC="Image1.gif" STYLE="position:ab-
    solute; visibility:hidden">
</CENTER>
<OBJECT ID="pathControl"
CLASSID = "CLSID:D7A7D7C3-D47F-11D0-89D3-00A0C90833E6">
    <PARAM NAME="Shape" VALUE="PolyLine(10,
        305,190, 280,155, 255,130, 230,100, 205,75,
        185,95, 165,130, 135,160, 110,200, 100, 220)">
    <PARAM NAME="Duration" VALUE="15">
    <PARAM NAME="Target" VALUE="pathImage">
</OBJECT>
<SCRIPT LANGUAGE = JavaScript>
function startAnimation()
{
    document.all.pathImage.style.visibility = "visible"
    pathControl.Play()
}
</SCRIPT>
</BODY>
</HTML>
```

That finishes our chapter on animation. We've covered a great deal in this chapter, from creating simple animation with the setTimeout() method to using the DirectAnimation multimedia DAViewerControl, from creating animation in Netscape Navigator with the setInterval() method and layers to using DirectAnimation's Sequencer and Path controls. We've added a lot of power to what we can do with JavaScript and Web pages.

In the next chapter, we'll turn to another important topic in JavaScript programming—working with the document object.

8

Using the Document Object in JavaScript

In the next three chapters, we're going to work in depth with the scripting objects—such as the navigator object, the document object, and the window object—available to us in JavaScript. These objects provide the interface we'll use to connect to the Web browser, and it's hard to over-estimate their importance for JavaScript programming. This chapter is about one of the most popular of those objects—the document object.

We've already used the document throughout this book—in fact, the first JavaScript example in the book used the document object's writeln() method to write HTML to a Web page:

```
<HTML>
<HEAD>
<TITLE>Our first JavaScript Example</TITLE>
<SCRIPT LANGUAGE = JavaScript>
document.writeln("Hello and welcome to JavaScript!")
</SCRIPT>
</HEAD>
```

We're going to take a look at what more you can do with the document object in this chapter, and there's a lot to explore. We'll see how to work with the document object's properties, collections (a *collection* is an array of HTML elements), events, and methods in this chapter. With the skills we gain here, we'll be able to change a Web page on the fly, changing the document's color, its HTML—even targeted sections of the HTML—and other aspects. In particular, we'll see how to change a Web page based on the time of day, how to let the user click a hyperlink and rewrite a page in another frame, how to let the user decide whether a Web page should be graphics-intensive, how to reset the target of hyperlinks, and much more.

It's wise to remember that the document object is only one of many scripting objects in JavaScript, so we'll begin this chapter by getting some perspective with a quick overview of the available scripting objects in JavaScript.

Scripting Object Overview

The "topmost" JavaScript scripting object is the *window* object, which we'll cover in the next chapter, that represents the browser itself. Just below that object in the hierarchy is the document object. These objects are called *scripting objects* (as opposed to JavaScript objects like the math or string objects), and many such objects are available to the JavaScript programmer.

Here's an overview of the object hierarchy in Internet Explorer 4.0 (not all objects are listed because there are so many of them):

```
window
            |
            +--location
            |
            +--frames
            |
            +--history
```

```
|
+--navigator
|
+--event
|
+--visual
|
+--document
        |
        +--links
        |
        +--anchors
        |
        +--images
        |
        +--forms
        |
        +--applets
        |
        +--embeds
        |
        +--plugins
        |
        +--frames
        |
        +--scripts
        |
        +--all
        |
        +--selection
        |
        +--body
        |
        +--anchor
        |
        +--applet
        |
        +--area
        |
        +--image
        |
        +--link
        |
        +--plugin
        |
        +--form
                |
                +--elements
                |
                +--button
                |
                +--checkbox
```

```
                    |
                    +--fileUpload
                    |
                    +--hidden
                    |
                    +--option
                    |
                    +--password
                    |
                    +--radio
                    |
                    +--select
                    |
                    +--submit
                    |
                    +--text
                    |
                    +--textarea
```

Here's the object hierachy in Netscape Navigator 4.0:

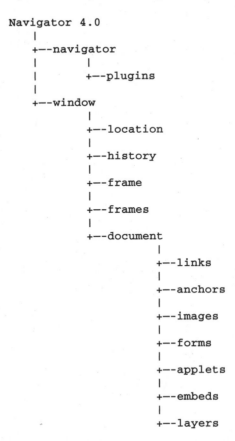

```
Navigator 4.0
    |
    +--navigator
    |         |
    |         +--plugins
    |
    +--window
            |
            +--location
            |
            +--history
            |
            +--frame
            |
            +--frames
            |
            +--document
                    |
                    +--links
                    |
                    +--anchors
                    |
                    +--images
                    |
                    +--forms
                    |
                    +--applets
                    |
                    +--embeds
                    |
                    +--layers
```

```
       |
       +--anchor
       |
       +--applet
       |
       +--area
       |
       +--image
       |
       +--link
       |
       +--plugin
       |
       +--form
              |
              +--button
              |
              +--checkbox
              |
              +--fileUpload
              |
              +--hidden
              |
              +--option
              |
              +--password
              |
              +--radio
              |
              +--select
              |
              +--submit
              |
              +--text
              |
              +--textarea
```

You can see there are many objects available to us, so let's start working on them. This chapter focuses on one of the most important scripting objects—the document object, which we'll cover in the following section.

Document Object Overview

The document object is already familiar to us. One of its most powerful aspects is *organizational* because you can treat the elements of a Web page as member objects of the document object if you've named those elements.

For example, if you have a text box named "Textbox" in a form named "form1," you can refer to the text in that text box this way:

document.form1.Textbox.value, as we did in the Checks.htm example in Chapter 3 ("Forms: Text Boxes and Buttons"):

```
<HTML>
<FORM NAME = form1>
<CENTER>
<H1>
Click one of the check boxes . . .
</H1>
<TABLE BORDER BGCOLOR = CYAN WIDTH = 200>
    <TR><TD><INPUT TYPE = CHECKBOX NAME = Check1 onClick
        = check1Clicked()>Check 1</TD></TR>
            .
            .
            .
    <TR><TD><INPUT TYPE = CHECKBOX NAME = Check5 onClick
        = check5Clicked()>Check 5</TD></TR>
</TABLE>
<BR>
<BR>
<INPUT TYPE  =  TEXT NAME  =  "Textbox" SIZE  =  25>
</CENTER>
</FORM>
</BODY>
<SCRIPT LANGUAGE = JavaScript>
    function check1Clicked() {
        document.form1.Textbox.value = "Check box 1 was
      clicked."
    }
    function check2Clicked() {
        document.form1.Textbox.value = "Check box 2 was
      clicked."
    }
    function check3Clicked() {
        document.form1.Textbox.value = "Check box 3 was
      clicked."
    }
    function check4Clicked() {
        document.form1.Textbox.value = "Check box 4 was
      clicked."
    }
    function check5Clicked() {
        document.form1.Textbox.value = "Check box 5 was
      clicked."
    }
</SCRIPT>
</HTML>
```

This use of the document object, already familiar to us, gives us an indication of its power. Besides organizing our HTML objects by name, the document object has properties, collections, events, and methods that we can use to extend our programs' power considerably. This chapter explores those items, too.

You'll find the properties, collection, events, and methods of Netscape Navigator's document object listed in Table 8–1, and those of Internet Explorer's document object in Table 8–2. As you can see, there are many items available to us,and we'll put them to work.

We'll work through the aspects of the document object in this chapter, starting with its properties.

Table 8–1

The Netscape Navigator document object's properties, collections, events, and methods.

Properties	alinkColor, Anchor, anchors, Applet, applets, Area, bgColor, cookie, domain, embeds, fgColor, Form, forms, Image, images, lastModified, linkColor, Link, links, referrer, title, URL, vlinkColor
Collections	anchors, applets, forms, layers, links, images, frames, embeds, plugins
Events	onBlur, onChange, onFocus, onClick, onMouseDown, onMouseUp, onMouseMove, onMouseOver, onKeyDown, onKeyUp, onMouseOut
Methods	close, open, write, writeln, getSelection

Table 8–2

The Internet Explorer document object's properties, collections, events, and methods.

Properties	alinkColor, linkColor, vlinkColor, mimeType, title, bgColor, link, vLink, aLink, cookie, lastModified, charset, location, referrer, fgColor, activeElement, strReadyState, domain, URL, fileSize, fileCreatedDate, fileModifiedDate, fileUpdatedDate
Collections gins	anchors, forms, links, all, scripts, images, applets, frames, embeds, plu-
Events	onclick, onmouseover, ondblclick, onkeypress, onmousedown, onmousemove, onmouseup, onkeydown, onkeyup, onmouseout, onreadystatechange, onhelp, onbeforeupdate, onafterupdate
Methods	close, open, clear, write, writeln, rangeFromText, rangeFromElement, execCommand, queryCommandEnabled, queryCommandText, elementFromPoint, queryCommandSupported, queryCommandState, queryCommandIndeterm, createElement

Document Properties

The document object's *properties* let you set aspects of your Web page such as its foreground (that is, text) color, background color, links color, title, and more, as shown in Tables 8–1 and 8–2.

In fact, we've already seen an example that changed the bgColor (background color) property of the document—the bgColor example in Chapter 3:

```
<HTML>
<HEAD>
<TITLE>bgColor Example</TITLE>
</HEAD>
<BODY>
<CENTER>
<FORM>
<BR>
<H1>
Set the document's bgColor property . . .
</H1>
<BR>
<BR>
<BR>
<INPUT TYPE = BUTTON Value = "Make background red" onClick
        = "colorBackground()">
</FORM>
</CENTER>
</BODY>
<SCRIPT LANGUAGE = JavaScript>
   function colorBackground()
   {
       document.bgColor = 0xff0000
   }
</SCRIPT>
</HTML>
```

In that example, we set the bgColor property of a document to black when the user clicked a button.

TIP: *Don't get the <BODY> element's attributes and the document object's properties confused. Many of them are the same, but you can change the document object's properties interactively only in JavaScript—if no document property corresponds to a <BODY> element attribute, you can't reach that attribute from code (unless you rewrite the <BODY> tag itself, as we'll learn how to do later in this chapter).*

The document's properties set display aspects of the document, but there's much more power coming up, so let's move on. Next, we will take a look at the document's collections.

Document Collections

A *collection* is an array of elements that you can refer to by index. The document object has several collections, such as anchors[], applets[], forms[], links[], images[], frames[], embeds[], and plugins[], as listed in Tables 8–1 and 8–2.

The collections contain the elements of your Web page arranged for easy reference. For example, here's how we used the document object's images[] array in the Colors.htm example in Chapter 6 ("Image Handling with JavaScript"):

```
<HTML>
<HEAD>
<TITLE>The Colors Example</TITLE>
</HEAD>
<BODY>
<FORM>
<CENTER>
<BR>
<H1>
Click the button to see new colors . . .
</H1>
<BR>
<BR>
<IMG WIDTH = 50 HEIGHT = 50 SRC = "gif/blue.gif"></IMG>
<IMG WIDTH = 50 HEIGHT = 50 SRC = "gif/blue.gif"></IMG>
<IMG WIDTH = 50 HEIGHT = 50 SRC = "gif/blue.gif"></IMG>
            .
            .
            .
<IMG WIDTH = 50 HEIGHT = 50 SRC = "gif/blue.gif"></IMG>
<IMG WIDTH = 50 HEIGHT = 50 SRC = "gif/blue.gif"></IMG>
<IMG WIDTH = 50 HEIGHT = 50 SRC = "gif/blue.gif"></IMG>
<BR>
<BR>
<INPUT TYPE = BUTTON VALUE = "New colors" onClick = newIm-
    age()>
</CENTER>
</FORM>
</BODY>
<SCRIPT LANGUAGE = JavaScript>
var imageArray = new Array(5)
imageArray[0] = new Image(50, 50)
imageArray[0].src = "gif/white.gif"
imageArray[1] = new Image(50, 50)
imageArray[1].src = "gif/black.gif"
imageArray[2] = new Image(50, 50)
imageArray[2].src = "gif/red.gif"
imageArray[3] = new Image(50, 50)
imageArray[3].src = "gif/green.gif"
imageArray[4] = new Image(50, 50)
imageArray[4].src = "gif/blue.gif"
function newImage()
{
    document.images[Math.round(49.5 * Math.random())].src
        = imageArray[Math.round(4.5 * Math.random())].src
```

```
}
</SCRIPT>
</HTML>
```

In this case, we could refer to all the images in a Web page by using the document images[] array.

The Internet Explorer document object has a special collection called *all[]* that holds all the elements in a Web page. For example, document.all[0] refers to the very first element in a Web page, the <HTML> element. If you gave that element an ID value, you could reach it this way in Internet Explorer:

```
document.form1.Textbox.value = "The HTML tag's ID
    = " + document.all[0].id
```

We'll take a quick look at an example that uses a document collection —the links[] collection—in the following section.

Document Collections: The ReLink Example

In this next example, we'll display two buttons and a hyperlink. The buttons will select either Internet Explorer or Netscape Navigator. If the user clicks the "I like Internet Explorer" button, we'll set the hyperlink to http://www.microsoft.com; if the user clicks the "I like Netscape Navigator" button, we'll set the hyperlink to http://www.netscape.com. We'll reach the link from JavaScript by using the document object's links[] array.

Start this page with the buttons and the hyperlink we'll need:

```
<HTML>
<HEAD>
<TITLE>
Set the link to your favorite browser!
</TITLE>
</HEAD>
<BODY>
<CENTER>
<FORM NAME = form1>
<H1>Set the link to your favorite browser!</H1>
<BR>
<INPUT TYPE = BUTTON Value = "I like Internet Explorer"
    onClick
        = "IE()">
```

```
<INPUT TYPE = BUTTON Value = "I like Netscape Navigator"
    onClick
        = "NS(this.form)">
<BR>
<BR>
<A HREF = "">My favorite browser</A>
<BR>
</FORM>
</CENTER>
</BODY>
```

Note that we set the hyperlink's HREF attribute to "" to begin with. We'll set that attribute to actual URLS in the functions we've tied the buttons to—IE() and NS(), as shown here:

```
<SCRIPT LANGUAGE = JavaScript>
    function IE()
    {
        .
        .
        .
    }
    function NS()
    {
        .
        .
        .
    }
</SCRIPT>
```

There's only one hyperlink in the page, so we can reach that link by referring to it with the document's links[] array as document.links[0]. To change that link's href property, we just reload it this way:

```
<SCRIPT LANGUAGE = JavaScript>
    function IE()
    {
        document.links[0].href = "http://www.microsoft.com"
    }
    function NS()
    {
        document.links[0].href = "http://www.netscape.com"
    }
</SCRIPT>
```

TIP: *If you want to find out how many elements are in a scripting element collection, just check that collection's length property.*

Open the Web page now, as shown in Figure 8–1. When the user clicks a button, the program resets the hyperlink accordingly (as you can see in the browser's status bar). Our ReLink example is successfully using a new document collection: the links[] collection.

The code for this page, ReLink.htm, is shown in Listing 8–1.

Figure 8–1
We reset a hyperlink's target under program control.

Listing 8–1
ReLink.htm.

```
<HTML>
<HEAD>
<TITLE>
Set the link to your favorite browser!
</TITLE>
</HEAD>
<BODY>
<CENTER>
<FORM NAME = form1>
<H1>Set the link to your favorite browser!</H1>
<BR>
<INPUT TYPE = BUTTON Value = "I like Internet Explorer"
     onClick
        = "IE()">
<INPUT TYPE = BUTTON Value = "I like Netscape Navigator"
     onClick
        = "NS(this.form)">
<BR>
<BR>
<A HREF = "">My favorite browser</A>
```

```
<BR>
</FORM>
</CENTER>
</BODY>
<SCRIPT LANGUAGE = JavaScript>
    function IE()
    {
        document.links[0].href = "http://www.microsoft.com"
    }
    function NS()
    {
        document.links[0].href = "http://www.netscape.com"
    }
</SCRIPT>
</HTML>
```

We'll turn to the document object's events next.

Document Events

We've seen most of the document's events already, such as onMouseDown, onKeyDown, and so forth. We made use of the mouse events in Chapter 5, "Keyboard and Mouse Handling," when we put together our Mouser.htm page:

```
<HTML>
<HEAD>
<TITLE>A Mouse Handling Example</TITLE>
</HEAD>
<BODY onMouseDown = "mouseDownHandler()" onMouseUp
        = "mouseUpHandler()">
<CENTER>
<FORM name = "form1">
<H1>A Mouse Handling Example</H1>
<BR>
<H2>Click the mouse button and Shift, Ctrl, and Alt</H2>
<BR>
<BR>
<INPUT TYPE = "text" name = "Textbox" SIZE = 60>
</FORM>
</CENTER>
</BODY>
<SCRIPT LANGUAGE= "JavaScript">
    document.onMouseDown = mouseDownHandler
    document.onMouseUp = mouseUpHandler
```

```
function mouseDownHandler(e)
{
        .
        .
        .
}
function mouseUpHandler(e)
{
        .
        .
        .
}
</SCRIPT>
</HTML>
```

Note that we connected the document events to the document in the script for Netscape Navigator (for example, document.onMouseDown = mouseDownHandler) and in the <BODY> tag for Internet Explorer (such as <BODY onMouseDown = "mouseDownHandler()">).

We've already gotten a good look at document events in this book, so we'll press on now to what, from a programming point of view, is the most interesting part of the document object—its methods.

Document Methods

We've already made some use of the document's most popular methods—write() and writeln()—in this book. Here's the first example we wrote, which uses writeln() to write text to a Web page:

```
<HTML>
<HEAD>
<TITLE>Our first JavaScript Example</TITLE>
<SCRIPT LANGUAGE = JavaScript>
document.writeln("Hello and welcome to JavaScript!")
</SCRIPT>
</HEAD>
```

In fact, we'll spend most of the rest of this chapter exploring the power of the write() and writeln() methods because by using them, you can create *self-modifying* Web pages. That's undoubtedly one of the most powerful aspects of JavaScript programming.

A Self-modifying Web Page: The Rewrite Example

In our first self-modifying Web page, we'll display a page with a button in it, prompting the user to click the button and rewrite the Web page.

When the user does click the button, we'll rewrite the Web page, getting rid of the button and displaying the message "This page is newly written" as an <H1> header. We'll start this page, Rewrite.htm, with the button we'll use:

```
<HTML>
<TITLE>Rewrite the Web page example</TITLE>
<BODY>
<CENTER>
<FORM>
<INPUT TYPE = BUTTON Value = "Rewrite this page!" onClick =
    Rewrite()>
</FORM>
</CENTER>
</BODY>
```

We've connected that button to a function named Rewrite():

```
<SCRIPT LANGUAGE = "JavaScript">
    function Rewrite()
    {
        .
        .
        .
    }
</SCRIPT>
```

In this function, we can rewrite the HTML of the page, including a new head and body—even a new <HTML> tag—this way:

```
<SCRIPT LANGUAGE = "JavaScript">
    function Rewrite()
    {
        document.write("<HTML>")
        document.write("<HEAD>")
        document.write("<TITLE>This page is newly writ-
    ten.</TITLE>")
        document.write("</HEAD>")
        document.write("<CENTER>")
```

```
        document.write("<H1>This page is newly
written.</H1>")
        document.write("We rewrote this page . . . ")
        document.write("<BR>")
        document.write("Using the document.write() method,
we ")
        document.write("were able to rewrite this page on
the fly. ")
        document.write("<BR>")
        document.write("The entire page has been rewrit-
ten.")
        document.write("<CENTER>")
        document.write("</HTML>")
    }
</SCRIPT>
```

That's all we need. Open the page now, as shown in Figure 8–2, and click the button.

When you click the button, the JavaScript code rewrites that page, as shown in Figure 8–3. Our first self-modifying Web page is a success.

The code for this page, Rewrite.htm, is shown in Listing 8–2.

This example has introduced us to self-modifying Web pages. Let's move on now to a new example that uses this aspect of JavaScript programming for something really useful.

Figure 8–2

The user can rewrite this Web page's HTML by clicking the button.

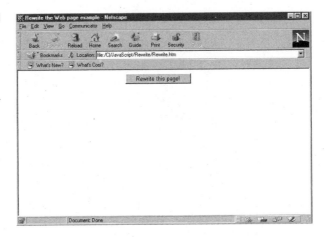

Figure 8–3
We've rewritten this
Web page on the fly.

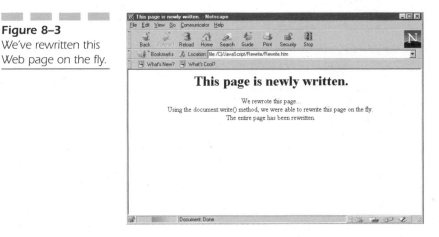

Listing 8–2
Rewrite.htm.

```
<HTML>
<TITLE>Rewrite the Web page example</TITLE>
<BODY>
<CENTER>
<FORM>
<INPUT TYPE = BUTTON Value = "Rewrite this page!" onClick =
    Rewrite()>
</FORM>
</CENTER>
</BODY>
<SCRIPT LANGUAGE = "JavaScript">
        function Rewrite()
        {
                document.write("<HTML>")
                document.write("<HEAD>")
                document.write("<TITLE>This page is newly
    written.</TITLE>")
                document.write("</HEAD>")
                document.write("<CENTER>")
                document.write("<H1>This page is newly
    written.</H1>")
                document.write("We rewrote this page . . .
    ")
                document.write("<BR>")
                document.write("Using the document.write()
    method, we ")
                document.write("were able to rewrite this
    page on the fly. ")
                document.write("<BR>")
                document.write("The entire page has been
    rewritten.")
                document.write("<CENTER>")
                document.write("</HTML>")
        }
</SCRIPT>
</HTML>
```

A Self-modifying Web Page: The Download Example

In our second self-modifying Web page, we'll display a JavaScript confirm box as the page is loading, indicating that we're going to download a large graphics file, and ask the user if that's OK.

If the user clicks the OK button, we'll rewrite the Web page to download a large image. If the user clicks the Cancel button, we'll download a smaller image.

This page, Download.htm, is easy to write. We just display the confirm box first in the <SCRIPT> element:

```
<HTML>
<HEAD>
<TITLE>Downloading customized graphics files . . . </TITLE>
</HEAD>
<BODY>
<CENTER>
<H1>Downloading customized graphics files . . . </H1>
<SCRIPT LANGUAGE = JavaScript>
    if(confirm("Starting download of big graphics file
    . . . "))
        .
        .
        .
```

As we'll see in the next chapter, the confirm() method returns a value of true if the user clicked the OK button. In that case, we'll write the HTML of our Web page to display the larger image, image1.gif:

```
<HTML>
<HEAD>
<TITLE>Downloading customized graphics files . . . </TITLE>
</HEAD>
<BODY>
<CENTER>
<H1>Downloading customized graphics files . . . </H1>
<SCRIPT LANGUAGE = JavaScript>
    if(confirm("Starting download of big graphics file
    . . . "))
        document.write("<BR><IMG WIDTH=236 HEIGHT=118
            SRC='gif/image1.gif'></IMG>")
        .
        .
        .
```

Otherwise, if the user clicked the Cancel button, we'll write the HTML of the page to display a smaller image, image2.gif:

```
<HTML>
<HEAD>
<TITLE>Downloading customized graphics files . . . </TITLE>
</HEAD>
<BODY>
<CENTER>
<H1>Downloading customized graphics files . . . </H1>
<SCRIPT LANGUAGE = JavaScript>
    if(confirm("Starting download of big graphics file
    . . . "))
        document.write("<BR><IMG WIDTH=236 HEIGHT=118
            SRC='gif/image1.gif'></IMG>")
    else
        document.write("<BR><IMG WIDTH=150 HEIGHT=75
            SRC='gif/image2.gif'></IMG>")
</SCRIPT>
</CENTER>
</BODY>
</HTML>
```

When you open this page, it displays a confirm box, as shown in Figure 8–4.

If you click OK, the program rewrites the page's HTML to download the large image, as shown in Figure 8–5. Now we're rewriting HTML on the fly!

The code for this page, Download.htm, is shown in Listing 8–3.

Figure 8–4

We ask the user if it's OK to download a large graphics file.

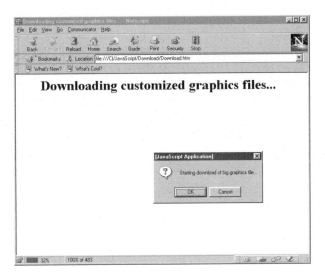

Figure 8–5
We rewrite a Web page's HTML to download a large image.

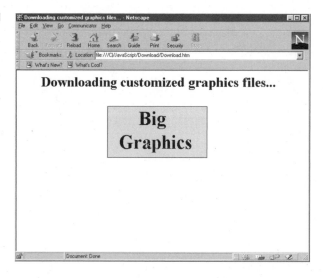

Listing 8–3
Download.htm.

```
<HTML>
<HEAD>
<TITLE>Downloading customized graphics files . . . </TITLE>
</HEAD>
<BODY>
<CENTER>
<H1>Downloading customized graphics files . . . </H1>
<SCRIPT LANGUAGE = JavaScript>
    if(confirm("Starting download of big graphics file
    . . . "))
        document.write("<BR><IMG WIDTH=236 HEIGHT=118
    SRC='gif/image1.gif'></IMG>")
    else
        document.write("<BR><IMG WIDTH=150 HEIGHT=75
    SRC='gif/image2.gif'></IMG>")
</SCRIPT>
</CENTER>
</BODY>
</HTML>
```

Another benefit of self-modifying Web pages is that they let you respond to the browser environment, such as the time of day. We'll examine such techniques in the following section.

Responding to the Time of Day: The Schedule Example

In this next example, we'll write a Web page that rewrites itself based on the time of day; in particular, we'll list a train schedule that has three versions: morning, afternoon, and evening. When the page is loaded into a browser, it'll check the current time and rewrite itself to display the appropriate schedule.

We'll start this page, Schedule.htm, by creating a JavaScript *date* object that holds the date and time:

```
<HTML>
<BODY>
<SCRIPT LANGUAGE = JavaScript>
var currentDate = new Date()
        .
        .
        .
```

Netscape Navigator's date object has these methods (Internet Explorer's date object has these and many more): getDate, getDay, getHours, getMinutes, getMonth, getSeconds, getTime, getTimezoneOffset, getYear, parse, setDate, setHours, setMinutes, setMonth, setSeconds, setTime, setYear, toGMTString, toLocaleString, toString, UTC, and valueOf.

We can get the current hour with the date method getHours():

```
<HTML>
<BODY>
<SCRIPT LANGUAGE = JavaScript>
var currentDate = new Date()
var currentHour = currentDate.getHours()
        .
        .
        .
```

In addition, we can display the current date and time with the date object's toLocaleString() method, along with a message welcoming the user to the train station:

```
<HTML>
<BODY>
<SCRIPT LANGUAGE = JavaScript>
var currentDate = new Date()
```

```
var currentHour = currentDate.getHours()
document.write( "<CENTER>")
document.write( "<H1>")
document.write( "Welcome to the Train Station")
document.write( "</H1>")
document.write( "<H2>")
document.write( "Date and time:")
document.write( currentDate.toLocaleString() )
document.write( "</H2>")
document.write( "</CENTER>")
              .
              .
              .
```

Now we can check the current hour and write the page's HTML accordingly. For example, if it's too late and the train station is closed, we indicate that this way:

```
<HTML>
<BODY>
<SCRIPT LANGUAGE = JavaScript>
var currentDate = new Date()
var currentHour = currentDate.getHours()
document.write( "<CENTER>")
document.write( "<H1>")
document.write( "Welcome to the Train Station")
document.write( "</H1>")
document.write( "<H2>")
document.write( "Date and time:")
document.write( currentDate.toLocaleString() )
document.write( "</H2>")
document.write( "</CENTER>")
if (currentHour < 5 || currentHour > 23){
    document.write( "<CENTER>")
    document.write( "<H1>")
    document.write( "The Train Station is closed." )
    document.write( "</H1>")
    document.write( "</CENTER>")
}
```

TIP: *Here we use the JavaScript OR logical operator, ||. This operator returns a value of true if either or both of its operands are true.*

In the same way, we can write the page to display the morning schedule if the current time is morning:

```
<HTML>
<BODY>
```

```
<SCRIPT LANGUAGE = JavaScript>
var currentDate = new Date()
var currentHour = currentDate.getHours()
document.write( "<CENTER>")
document.write( "<H1>")
document.write( "Welcome to the Train Station")
document.write( "</H1>")
document.write( "<H2>")
document.write( "Date and time:")
document.write( currentDate.toLocaleString() )
document.write( "</H2>")
document.write( "</CENTER>")
if (currentHour < 5 || currentHour > 23){
    .
    .
    .
}
if (currentHour > 6 && currentHour < 12 ) {
    document.write( "<CENTER>")
    document.write( "<TABLE BORDER BGCOLOR = '#ffff00'>")
    document.write(
        "<TR><TH COLSPAN = 2>Morning Trains</TH></TR>")
    document.write(
        "<TR><TD>Boston</TD><TD>6:30 AM</TD></TR>")
    document.write(
        "<TR><TD>San Francisco</TD><TD>7:00 AM</TD></TR>")
    document.write(
        "<TR><TD>Las Vegas</TD><TD>7:30 AM</TD></TR>")
    document.write(
        "<TR><TD>Toronto</TD><TD>8:00 AM</TD></TR>")
    document.write(
        "<TR><TD>Denver</TD><TD>8:30 AM</TD></TR>")
    document.write(
        "<TR><TD>Chicago</TD><TD>9:00 AM</TD></TR>")
    document.write(
        "<TR><TD>San Diego</TD><TD>9:30 AM</TD></TR>")
    document.write( "</TABLE>")
    document.write( "</CENTER>")
    document.write( "</TABLE>")
    document.write( "</CENTER>")
}
</SCRIPT>
</HTML>
```

If it's the afternoon, we display the afternoon schedule in a table like this:

```
<HTML>
<BODY>
<SCRIPT LANGUAGE = JavaScript>
var currentDate = new Date()
var currentHour = currentDate.getHours()
```

```
document.write( "<CENTER>")
document.write( "<H1>")
document.write( "Welcome to the Train Station")
document.write( "</H1>")
document.write( "<H2>")
document.write( "Date and time:")
document.write( currentDate.toLocaleString() )
document.write( "</H2>")
document.write( "</CENTER>")
if (currentHour < 5 || currentHour > 23){
    .
    .
    .

}
if (currentHour > 6 && currentHour < 12 ) {
    .
    .
    .

}
if ( currentHour >= 12 && currentHour < 17 ) {
    document.write( "<CENTER>")
    document.write( "<TABLE BORDER BGCOLOR = '#ffff00'>")
    document.write(
        "<TR><TH COLSPAN = 2>Afternoon Trains</TH></TR>")
    document.write(
        "<TR><TD>Boston</TD><TD>12:00 PM</TD></TR>")
    document.write(
        "<TR><TD>San Francisco</TD><TD>12:30 PM</TD></TR>")
    document.write(
        "<TR><TD>Las Vegas</TD><TD>1:30 PM</TD></TR>")
    document.write(
        "<TR><TD>Toronto</TD><TD>3:30 PM</TD></TR>")
    document.write(
        "<TR><TD>Denver</TD><TD>4:00 AM</TD></TR>")
    document.write(
        "<TR><TD>Chicago</TD><TD>4:30 PM</TD></TR>")
    document.write(
        "<TR><TD>San Diego</TD><TD>5:00 PM</TD></TR>")
    document.write( "</TABLE>")
    document.write( "</CENTER>")
}
</SCRIPT>
</HTML>
```

Finally, we can display the evening schedule if it's evening:

```
<HTML>
<BODY>
<SCRIPT LANGUAGE = JavaScript>
var currentDate = new Date()
var currentHour = currentDate.getHours()
```

```
document.write( "<CENTER>")
document.write( "<H1>")
document.write( "Welcome to the Train Station")
document.write( "</H1>")
document.write( "<H2>")
document.write( "Date and time:")
document.write( currentDate.toLocaleString() )
document.write( "</H2>")
document.write( "</CENTER>")
if (currentHour < 5 || currentHour > 23){
    .
    .
    .
}
if (currentHour > 6 && currentHour < 12 ) {
    .
    .
    .
}
if ( currentHour >= 12 && currentHour < 17 ) {
    .
    .
    .
}
if ( currentHour >= 17 && currentHour < 22 ) {
    document.write( "<CENTER>")
    document.write( "<TABLE BORDER BGCOLOR = '#ffff00'>")
    document.write(
        "<TR><TH COLSPAN = 2>Evening Trains</TH></TR>")
    document.write(
        "<TR><TD>Boston</TD><TD>6:30 PM</TD></TR>")
    document.write(
        "<TR><TD>San Francisco</TD><TD>7:00 PM</TD></TR>")
    document.write(
        "<TR><TD>Las Vegas</TD><TD>7:30 PM</TD></TR>")
    document.write(
        "<TR><TD>Toronto</TD><TD>8:00 PM</TD></TR>")
    document.write(
        "<TR><TD>Denver</TD><TD>8:30 PM</TD></TR>")
    document.write(
        "<TR><TD>Chicago</TD><TD>9:00 PM</TD></TR>")
    document.write(
        "<TR><TD>San Diego</TD><TD>9:30 PM</TD></TR>")
    document.write( "</TABLE>")
    document.write( "</CENTER>")
}
</SCRIPT>
</HTML>
```

That's it—now open this page, as shown in Figure 8–6. As you can see, the page has responded to the time of day, displaying the correct schedule. The code for this page, Schedule.htm, is shown in Listing 8–4.

Figure 8–6
This Web page responds to the time of day by rewriting itself accordingly.

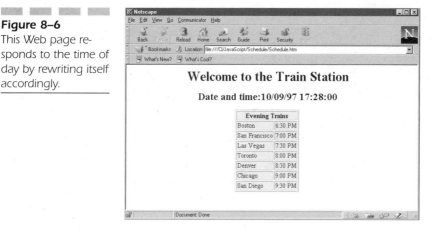

Listing 8–4
Schedule.htm.

```
<HTML>
<BODY>
<SCRIPT LANGUAGE = JavaScript>
var currentDate = new Date()
var currentHour = currentDate.getHours()
document.write( "<CENTER>")
document.write( "<H1>")
document.write( "Welcome to the Train Station")
document.write( "</H1>")
document.write( "<H2>")
document.write( "Date and time:")
document.write( currentDate.toLocaleString() )
document.write( "</H2>")
document.write( "</CENTER>")
if (currentHour < 5 || currentHour > 23){
    document.write( "<CENTER>")
    document.write( "<H1>")
    document.write( "The Train Station is closed." )
    document.write( "</H1>")
    document.write( "</CENTER>")
}
if (currentHour > 6 && currentHour < 12 ) {
    document.write( "<CENTER>")
    document.write( "<TABLE BORDER BGCOLOR = '#ffff00'>")
    document.write(
        "<TR><TH COLSPAN = 2>Morning Trains</TH></TR>")
    document.write(
        "<TR><TD>Boston</TD><TD>6:30 AM</TD></TR>")
    document.write(
        "<TR><TD>San Francisco</TD><TD>7:00 AM</TD></TR>")
    document.write(
        "<TR><TD>Las Vegas</TD><TD>7:30 AM</TD></TR>")
    document.write(
```

```
            "<TR><TD>Toronto</TD><TD>8:00 AM</TD></TR>")
    document.write(
        "<TR><TD>Denver</TD><TD>8:30 AM</TD></TR>")
    document.write(
        "<TR><TD>Chicago</TD><TD>9:00 AM</TD></TR>")
    document.write(
        "<TR><TD>San Diego</TD><TD>9:30 AM</TD></TR>")
    document.write( "</TABLE>")
    document.write( "</CENTER>")
    document.write( "</TABLE>")
    document.write( "</CENTER>")
}
if ( currentHour >= 12 && currentHour < 17 ) {
    document.write( "<CENTER>")
    document.write( "<TABLE BORDER BGCOLOR = '#ffff00'>")
    document.write(
        "<TR><TH COLSPAN = 2>Afternoon Trains</TH></TR>")
    document.write(
        "<TR><TD>Boston</TD><TD>12:00 PM</TD></TR>")
    document.write(
        "<TR><TD>San Francisco</TD><TD>12:30 PM</TD></TR>")
    document.write(
        "<TR><TD>Las Vegas</TD><TD>1:30 PM</TD></TR>")
    document.write(
        "<TR><TD>Toronto</TD><TD>3:30 PM</TD></TR>")
    document.write(
        "<TR><TD>Denver</TD><TD>4:00 AM</TD></TR>")
    document.write(
        "<TR><TD>Chicago</TD><TD>4:30 PM</TD></TR>")
    document.write(
        "<TR><TD>San Diego</TD><TD>5:00 PM</TD></TR>")
    document.write( "</TABLE>")
    document.write( "</CENTER>")
}
if ( currentHour >= 17 && currentHour < 22 ) {
    document.write( "<CENTER>")
    document.write( "<TABLE BORDER BGCOLOR = '#ffff00'>")
    document.write(
        "<TR><TH COLSPAN = 2>Evening Trains</TH></TR>")
    document.write(
        "<TR><TD>Boston</TD><TD>6:30 PM</TD></TR>")
    document.write(
        "<TR><TD>San Francisco</TD><TD>7:00 PM</TD></TR>")
    document.write(
        "<TR><TD>Las Vegas</TD><TD>7:30 PM</TD></TR>")
    document.write(
        "<TR><TD>Toronto</TD><TD>8:00 PM</TD></TR>")
    document.write(
        "<TR><TD>Denver</TD><TD>8:30 PM</TD></TR>")
    document.write(
        "<TR><TD>Chicago</TD><TD>9:00 PM</TD></TR>")
```

continues

Listing 8–4
Continued.

```
    document.write(
        "<TR><TD>San Diego</TD><TD>9:30 PM</TD></TR>")
    document.write( "</TABLE>")
    document.write( "</CENTER>")
}
</SCRIPT>
</HTML>
```

We can do more using the write() method. For example, we can rewrite a page in another frame.

Rewriting Another Frame: The Railroad Example

In the next self-modifying example, we'll write HTML in another frame. Here, we'll display a set of hyperlinks in one frame and a train schedule in another. When the user clicks a hyperlink, such as Morning Trains, in the left frame, we'll display the corresponding train schedule in the right frame.

This example will consist of several Web pages. The main Web page, called "Railroad.htm," just sets up the frames, placing two other pages—menu.htm and intro.htm—into those frames. Note that we name the right-hand frame, calling it "display" because we'll use that frame as the target of hyperlinks:

```
Railroad.htm
<HTML>
<HEAD>
<TITLE>Rewriting frames . . . </TITLE>
</HEAD>
<FRAMESET COLS = "30%, 70%">
<FRAME SRC = menu.htm >
<FRAME SRC = intro.htm NAME = "display">
</FRAMESET>
</HTML>
```

The intro page, Intro.htm, just welcomes the user to the train station:

```
<HTML>
<HEAD>
<TITLE>Welcome to the Train Station</TITLE>
</HEAD>
<BODY>
```

```
<CENTER>
<H1>Welcome to the Train Station</H1>
</CENTER>
</BODY>
</HTML>
```

The real action takes place in the menu page, which is displayed in the frame on the left and holds the links the user can click. We'll list the links in an unordered (that is, bulleted) list, starting with a page that shows the times the station is open:

```
<HTML>
<BODY LINK = 0000>
<FORM>
<UL>
<LI><A HREF = "hours.htm" TARGET = "display">
    Train Station Hours
</A>
       .
       .
       .
```

This is just a standard hyperlink that, when clicked, will load the page named "Hours.htm" into the right-hand frame, which we've named "display." Here's what the Hours.htm page looks like:

```
<HTML>
<HEAD>
<TITLE>Train Station Hours</TITLE>
</HEAD>
<BODY>
<CENTER>
<H1>Train Station Hours</H1>
<BR>
<BR>
The train station is open from 5 AM to 2 AM daily.
<BR>
<BR>
Please come back when the station is open.
</CENTER>
</BODY>
</HTML>
```

We'll connect the other hyperlinks to JavaScript functions like this:

```
<HTML>
<BODY LINK = 0000>
<FORM>
<UL>
<LI><A HREF = "hours.htm" TARGET = "display">
    Train Station Hours
</A>
```

```
</LI>
<LI><A HREF = "menu.htm" onClick = "MorningTrains()">
    <U>Morning Trains</U>
</A>
<LI><A HREF = "menu.htm" onClick = "AfternoonTrains()">
    <U>Afternoon Trains</U>
</A>
<LI><A HREF = "menu.htm" onClick = "EveningTrains()">
    <U>Evening Trains</U>
</A>
</UL>
</FORM>
```

In those functions, we'll rewrite the page in the right-hand frame to display the appropriate train schedule.

Writing to Documents in Other Frames

When the user clicks the hyperlink labeled Morning Trains, the program calls the MorningTrains() function. In that function, we will rewrite the Web page now in the right-hand frame to display the table of morning train departures.

That raises a question—how do we refer to the page in the right-hand frame from code in the left-hand frame? We do that with the *parent* keyword, which refers to a window's parent window. Our parent window is the Railroad.htm window itself, so we can refer to the other frame as "parent.frames[1]" and the document in that frame as "parent.frames[1].document." To write to that document, we first have to open it with the open() method:

```
function MorningTrains()
{
    parent.frames[1].document.open()
        .
        .
        .
```

Now we can write the morning schedule of trains to the document in the second frame; note that we use that document's close() method at the end to close the document:

```
function MorningTrains()
{
    parent.frames[1].document.open()
    parent.frames[1].document.write( "<CENTER>")
    parent.frames[1].document.write(
        "<TABLE BORDER BGCOLOR = '#ffff00'>")
```

```
        parent.frames[1].document.write(
            "<TR><TH COLSPAN = 2>Morning
    Trains</TH></TR>")
        parent.frames[1].document.write(
            "<TR><TD>Boston</TD><TD>6:30 AM</TD></TR>")
        parent.frames[1].document.write(
            "<TR><TD>San Francisco</TD><TD>7:00
    AM</TD></TR>")
        parent.frames[1].document.write(
            "<TR><TD>Las Vegas</TD><TD>7:30 AM</TD></TR>")
        parent.frames[1].document.write(
            "<TR><TD>Toronto</TD><TD>8:00 AM</TD></TR>")
        parent.frames[1].document.write(
            "<TR><TD>Denver</TD><TD>8:30 AM</TD></TR>")
        parent.frames[1].document.write(
            "<TR><TD>Chicago</TD><TD>9:00 AM</TD></TR>")
        parent.frames[1].document.write(
            "<TR><TD>San Diego</TD><TD>9:30 AM</TD></TR>")
        parent.frames[1].document.write( "</TABLE>")
        parent.frames[1].document.write( "</CENTER>")
        parent.frames[1].document.close()
    }
```

Similarly, we can display the afternoon train schedule, as shown here:

```
    function AfternoonTrains()
    {
        parent.frames[1].document.open()
        parent.frames[1].document.write( "<CENTER>")
        parent.frames[1].document.write(
            "<TABLE BORDER BGCOLOR = '#ffff00'>")
        parent.frames[1].document.write(
            "<TR><TH COLSPAN = 2>Afternoon
    Trains</TH></TR>")
        parent.frames[1].document.write(
            "<TR><TD>Boston</TD><TD>12:00 PM</TD></TR>")
        parent.frames[1].document.write(
            "<TR><TD>San Francisco</TD><TD>12:30
    PM</TD></TR>")
        parent.frames[1].document.write(
            "<TR><TD>Las Vegas</TD><TD>1:30 PM</TD></TR>")
        parent.frames[1].document.write(
            "<TR><TD>Toronto</TD><TD>3:30 PM</TD></TR>")
        parent.frames[1].document.write(
            "<TR><TD>Denver</TD><TD>4:00 AM</TD></TR>")
        parent.frames[1].document.write(
            "<TR><TD>Chicago</TD><TD>4:30 PM</TD></TR>")
        parent.frames[1].document.write(
            "<TR><TD>San Diego</TD><TD>5:00 PM</TD></TR>")
        parent.frames[1].document.write( "</TABLE>")
        parent.frames[1].document.write( "</CENTER>")
        parent.frames[1].document.close()
    }
```

And we can display the evening train schedule this way:

```
function EveningTrains()
{
    parent.frames[1].document.open()
    parent.frames[1].document.write( "<CENTER>")
    parent.frames[1].document.write( "<TABLE BORDER
BGCOLOR = '#ffff00'>")
    parent.frames[1].document.write(
        "<TR><TH COLSPAN = 2>Evening
Trains</TH></TR>")
    parent.frames[1].document.write(
        "<TR><TD>Boston</TD><TD>6:30 PM</TD></TR>")
    parent.frames[1].document.write(
        "<TR><TD>San Francisco</TD><TD>7:00
PM</TD></TR>")
    parent.frames[1].document.write(
        "<TR><TD>Las Vegas</TD><TD>7:30 PM</TD></TR>")
    parent.frames[1].document.write(
        "<TR><TD>Toronto</TD><TD>8:00 PM</TD></TR>")
    parent.frames[1].document.write(
        "<TR><TD>Denver</TD><TD>8:30 PM</TD></TR>")
    parent.frames[1].document.write(
        "<TR><TD>Chicago</TD><TD>9:00 PM</TD></TR>")
    parent.frames[1].document.write(
        "<TR><TD>San Diego</TD><TD>9:30 PM</TD></TR>")
    parent.frames[1].document.write( "</TABLE>")
    parent.frames[1].document.write( "</CENTER>")
    parent.frames[1].document.close()
}
```

Now open this page, as shown in Figure 8–7. When you click a hyperlink, the corresponding train schedule is written to the document in the other frame. Now we're modifying documents in other frames.

Figure 8–7

The user can rewrite the page in the right-hand frame with the links in the left.

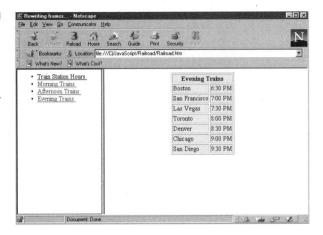

The code for this page is shown in these listings:

Railroad.htm   Listing 8–5

Hours.htm   Listing 8–6

Intro.htm   Listing 8–7

Menu.htm   Listing 8–8

Listing 8–5
Railroad.htm.

```
<HTML>
<HEAD>
<TITLE>Rewriting frames . . . </TITLE>
</HEAD>
<FRAMESET COLS = "30%, 70%">
<FRAME SRC = menu.htm >
<FRAME SRC = intro.htm NAME = "display">
</FRAMESET>
</HTML>
```

Listing 8–6
Hours.htm.

```
<HTML>
<HEAD>
<TITLE>Train Station Hours</TITLE>
</HEAD>
<BODY>
<CENTER>
<H1>Train Station Hours</H1>
<BR>
<BR>
The train station is open from 5 AM to 2 AM daily.
<BR>
<BR>
Please come back when the station is open.
</CENTER>
</BODY>
</HTML>
```

Listing 8–7
Intro.htm.

```
<HTML>
<HEAD>
<TITLE>Welcome to the Train Station</TITLE>
</HEAD>
<BODY>
<CENTER>
<H1>Welcome to the Train Station</H1>
</CENTER>
</BODY>
</HTML>
```

Listing 8–8

Menu.htm.

```html
<HTML>
<BODY LINK = 0000>
<FORM>
<UL>
<LI><A HREF = "hours.htm" TARGET = "display">
    Train Station Hours
</A>
</LI>
<LI><A HREF = "menu.htm" onClick = "MorningTrains()">
    <U>Morning Trains</U>
</A>
<LI><A HREF = "menu.htm" onClick = "AfternoonTrains()">
    <U>Afternoon Trains</U>
</A>
<LI><A HREF = "menu.htm" onClick = "EveningTrains()">
    <U>Evening Trains</U>
</A>
</UL>
</FORM>
</BODY>
<SCRIPT LANGUAGE = JavaScript>
    function MorningTrains()
    {
        parent.frames[1].document.open()
        parent.frames[1].document.write( "<CENTER>")
        parent.frames[1].document.write(
            "<TABLE BORDER BGCOLOR = '#ffff00'>")
        parent.frames[1].document.write(
            "<TR><TH COLSPAN = 2>Morning
    Trains</TH></TR>")
        parent.frames[1].document.write(
            "<TR><TD>Boston</TD><TD>6:30 AM</TD></TR>")
        parent.frames[1].document.write(
            "<TR><TD>San Francisco</TD><TD>7:00
    AM</TD></TR>")
        parent.frames[1].document.write(
            "<TR><TD>Las Vegas</TD><TD>7:30 AM</TD></TR>")
        parent.frames[1].document.write(
            "<TR><TD>Toronto</TD><TD>8:00 AM</TD></TR>")
        parent.frames[1].document.write(
            "<TR><TD>Denver</TD><TD>8:30 AM</TD></TR>")
        parent.frames[1].document.write(
            "<TR><TD>Chicago</TD><TD>9:00 AM</TD></TR>")
        parent.frames[1].document.write(
            "<TR><TD>San Diego</TD><TD>9:30 AM</TD></TR>")
        parent.frames[1].document.write( "</TABLE>")
        parent.frames[1].document.write( "</CENTER>")
        parent.frames[1].document.close()
    }

    function AfternoonTrains()
    {
        parent.frames[1].document.open()
        parent.frames[1].document.write( "<CENTER>")
```

```
        parent.frames[1].document.write(
            "<TABLE BORDER BGCOLOR = '#ffff00'>")
        parent.frames[1].document.write(
            "<TR><TH COLSPAN = 2>Afternoon
    Trains</TH></TR>")
        parent.frames[1].document.write(
            "<TR><TD>Boston</TD><TD>12:00 PM</TD></TR>")
        parent.frames[1].document.write(
            "<TR><TD>San Francisco</TD><TD>12:30
    PM</TD></TR>")
        parent.frames[1].document.write(
            "<TR><TD>Las Vegas</TD><TD>1:30 PM</TD></TR>")
        parent.frames[1].document.write(
            "<TR><TD>Toronto</TD><TD>3:30 PM</TD></TR>")
        parent.frames[1].document.write(
            "<TR><TD>Denver</TD><TD>4:00 AM</TD></TR>")
        parent.frames[1].document.write(
            "<TR><TD>Chicago</TD><TD>4:30 PM</TD></TR>")
        parent.frames[1].document.write(
            "<TR><TD>San Diego</TD><TD>5:00 PM</TD></TR>")
        parent.frames[1].document.write( "</TABLE>")
        parent.frames[1].document.write( "</CENTER>")
        parent.frames[1].document.close()
    }

    function EveningTrains()
    {
        parent.frames[1].document.open()
        parent.frames[1].document.write( "<CENTER>")
        parent.frames[1].document.write( "<TABLE BORDER
    BGCOLOR = '#ffff00'>")
        parent.frames[1].document.write(
            "<TR><TH COLSPAN = 2>Evening
    Trains</TH></TR>")
        parent.frames[1].document.write(
            "<TR><TD>Boston</TD><TD>6:30 PM</TD></TR>")
        parent.frames[1].document.write(
            "<TR><TD>San Francisco</TD><TD>7:00
    PM</TD></TR>")
        parent.frames[1].document.write(
            "<TR><TD>Las Vegas</TD><TD>7:30 PM</TD></TR>")
        parent.frames[1].document.write(
            "<TR><TD>Toronto</TD><TD>8:00 PM</TD></TR>")
        parent.frames[1].document.write(
            "<TR><TD>Denver</TD><TD>8:30 PM</TD></TR>")
        parent.frames[1].document.write(
            "<TR><TD>Chicago</TD><TD>9:00 PM</TD></TR>")
        parent.frames[1].document.write(
            "<TR><TD>San Diego</TD><TD>9:30 PM</TD></TR>")
        parent.frames[1].document.write( "</TABLE>")
        parent.frames[1].document.write( "</CENTER>")
        parent.frames[1].document.close()
    }
</SCRIPT>
</HTML>
```

So far, we've rewritten whole pages with the write() method, but another technique is available in Internet Explorer that allows you to rewrite single HTML elements. We'll take a look at that process in the following section.

Targeting HTML: The ReHead Example

Internet Explorer gives each HTML tag two properties that are worth taking a look at: innerHTML and outerHTML. Using these properties, we can refer to the HTML of specific tags and rewrite just that HTML, leaving the rest of the page alone. For example, we might display a header in a Web page. When the user clicks that header, we can rewrite that header —and *only* that header.

We'll start this example, ReHead.htm, with the header we're rewriting, giving it the ID "Header":

```
<HTML>
<HEAD>
<TITLE>
Rewriting a header on the fly
</TITLE>
</HEAD>
<BODY>
<CENTER>
<H1 ID = "Header" onClick = "rewriteHeader()">A Header</H1>
<BR>
Click the header once to rewrite it.
</CENTER>
</BODY>
```

In Internet Explorer, all HTML tags are active, so we connect the header's onClick event to a function named "rewriteHeader()":

```
<SCRIPT LANGUAGE = JavaScript>
function rewriteHeader()
{
```

```
        .
        .
        .
}
</SCRIPT>
```

When the user clicks the header, we will change its text to "This header has been changed!" by using the header's innerHTML property. This property refers to the text inside an element, and the outerHTML tag refers to the whole element, HTML and text together. In this case, we'll just replace the text in this element:

```
<SCRIPT LANGUAGE = JavaScript>
function rewriteHeader()
{
    document.all.Header.innerHTML = "This header has been
        changed!"
}
</SCRIPT>
```

That's all it takes—now open the page in Internet Explorer, as shown in Figure 8–8.

When you click the header in the Web page, the program rewrites the header—and only the header—as shown in Figure 8–9.

The code for this page, Rehead.htm, is shown in Listing 8–9.

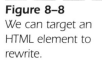

Figure 8–8
We can target an
HTML element to
rewrite.

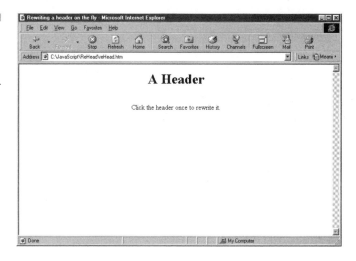

Figure 8–9
We rewrite just the
header of the page.

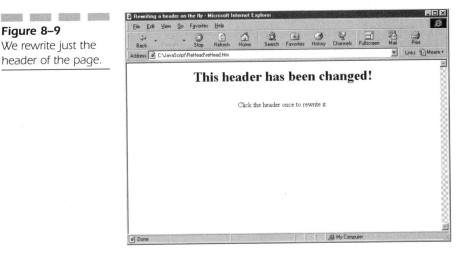

Listing 8–9
ReHead.htm.

```
<HTML>
<HEAD>
<TITLE>
Rewriting a header on the fly
</TITLE>
</HEAD>
<BODY>
<CENTER>
<H1 ID = "Header" onClick = "rewriteHeader()">A Header</H1>
<BR>
Click the header once to rewrite it.
</CENTER>
</BODY>
<SCRIPT LANGUAGE = JavaScript>
function rewriteHeader()
{
    document.all.Header.innerHTML = "This header has been
    changed!"
}
</SCRIPT>
</HTML>
```

That completes our chapter on the document object. We've covered a lot in this chapter, from getting an overview of scripting objects in general to an overview of the document object, including its properties, collections, events, and methods; from rewriting a Web page to loading in large or small images on demand; from designing a Web page to respond to the time of day to rewriting pages in other frames with the frames[] collection. We've also learned how to rewrite only specific parts of specific HTML elements in Internet Explorer. We've made a lot of progress in this chapter.

In the next chapter, we'll examine some other popular scripting objects: the window and dialog objects.

CHAPTER 9

JavaScript and the Window Object

In the previous chapter, we explored the document object; in this chapter, we'll take a look at that object's parent—the *window* object. This object refers to the browser window itself, and it includes many new and powerful methods that we'll examine in this chapter.

We'll see how to use window methods to open new windows, tailoring them as we want, and how to display alert boxes, prompt boxes, and confirm boxes. Internet Explorer also has a special *dialog* object based on the window object that we'll cover, too.

Let's start now with the window object.

Working with the Window Object

In JavaScript, a document is displayed inside a window, and both the document and the window are considered objects. We saw how rich the document object is in properties, methods, and events in the previous chapter; now we're going to see what the window object has to offer us.

There are many ways to refer to a window—you can use the identifier *window* or the identifier *self*. The topmost window (the browser window) is called *top*. A window's parent window is called *parent*. You can also create variables of the window object type. Here are the ways to refer to the properties and methods of windows:

```
window.propertyName
window.methodName(parameters)
self.propertyName
self.methodName(parameters)
top.propertyName
top.methodName(parameters)
parent.propertyName
parent.methodName(parameters)
windowVariable.propertyName
windowVariable.methodName(parameters)
propertyName
methodName(parameters)
```

We've already seen how to refer to members of the window object in this book—for example, in Chapter 5, "Keyboard and Mouse Handling," we referred to Internet Explorer's x and y members of the window.event object (that is, the event member object of the window object) as window.event.x and window.event.y.

Internet Explorer's window object's properties, methods, and events are listed in Table 9–1, and those for Netscape Navigator are in Table 9–2.

Table 9–1

The Internet Explorer window object.

Properties	name, length, parent, self, top, status, defaultStatus, opener, closed
Collections	frames
Methods	item, navigate, blur, focus, alert, confirm, prompt, setTimeout, clearTimeout, close, open, scroll, showModalDialog
Events	onfocus, onload, onunload, onblur, onhelp,

Table 9–2

The Netscape Navigator window object.

Properties	closed, defaultStatus, document, Frame, frames, history, length, location, name, opener, parent, self, status, top, window
Methods	alert, blur, clearTimeOut, close, confirm, focus, open, prompt, setTimeOut
Events	onBlur, onError, onFocus, onLoad, onUnload

In this chapter, we'll mainly cover the most popular part of the window object—its methods—starting with the open() method.

Using the open() Method

You use the window object's open() method to open a new browser window and display a document. In fact, we've already seen the open() method at work in the Helper.htm example in Chapter 5, where we opened a window that was controlled by keystrokes:

```
<HTML>
<TITLE>Controlling a window with keystrokes</TITLE>
<BODY>
<FORM>
<CENTER>
<BR>
<H1>Click the button to open the help window . . . </H1>
<BR>
<BR>
<INPUT TYPE = BUTTON Value = "Show help" onClick =
     "ShowHelp()">
</CENTER>
</FORM>
</BODY>
<SCRIPT LANGUAGE = JavaScript>
    function ShowHelp()
    {
        window.open("HelpWindow.htm")
    }
</SCRIPT>
</HTML>
```

That's a simple way of using window.open()—simply passing the URL of a document you want to open in a new browser window.

Let's make better use of the window open() method in this next example. We'll see how to open a new window, give it a certain size, add a status bar at the bottom of the window, and other options. We start by displaying a window with a button. When the user clicks the button, we display a new, free-floating window, loading a new document into that new window.

To construct this new example, Open.htm, we'll need to take a close look at the window.open() method; in general, here's how you use that method:

```
Window = object.open(URL [, name [, features]])
```

This method returns a window variable that represents your new window. *URL* is the URL of the document you want to open (if any), *name* is the name of the window, and *features* is a string that holds one or more options; Internet Explorer options are listed in Table 9–3, and the Netscape Navigator options are in Table 9–4.

TIP: *To close the newly opened window, you can save the window object returned by the open() method and then use that object's close() method.*

Table 9–3

Netscape Navigator's window.open() fea-

Feature	Values	Means
toolbar	yes/no/1/0	The browser toolbar
location	yes/no/1/0	The input field for entering URLs
directories	yes/no/1/0	Directory buttons
status	yes/no/1/0	Status line at bottom of window
menubar	yes/no/1/0	Menu bar
scrollbars	yes/no/1/0	Enables horizontal and vertical scrollbars
resizable	yes/no/1/0	Whether resize handles appear at the edge
width	pixels	Width of window in pixels
height	pixels	Height of window in pixels

Table 9–4 Internet Explorer's window.open() features.

Feature	Values	IE3/IE4	Means	Open	Dialog	Help
toolbar	yes/no/1/0	IE3/IE4	The browser toolbar (back and forward buttons, etc.)	yes	no	no
location	yes/no/1/0	IE3/IE4	The input field for entering URLs directly into the browser	yes		
font-size font-weight font-style		IE4	Syntax should look like CSS. For example, font:3;font-size:4. To define multiple font values, use multiple font attributes.	yes	yes	yes
edgeStyle	raised/ sunken	IE4	Style for the window border	yes	yes	yes
borderSize	thick/thin	IE4	Size of the border around the window	yes	yes	yes
helpIcon	yes/no/1/0	IE4	Whether the help icon appears in the title bar	yes	yes	yes
minimize	yes/no/1/0	IE4	Whether the minimize button appears in the title bar	yes	yes	yes
maximize	yes/no/1/0	IE4	Whether the maximize button appears in the title bar	yes	yes	yes
systemMenu	yes/no/1/0	IE4	Whether the system menu is available from the border icon	yes	yes	yes
directories	yes/no/1/0	IE3/IE4	Directory buttons	yes	no	no
status	yes/no/1/0	IE3/IE4	Status line at bottom of window	yes	yes	yes
menubar	yes/no/1/0	IE3/IE4	Menu bar	yes	no	no
scrollbars	yes/no/1/0	IE3/IE4	Enables horizontal and vertical scrollbars	yes	yes	yes
resizeable	yes/no/1/0	IE3/IE4	Whether resize handles appear at the edge	yes	yes	yes
width	pixel	IE3/IE4	Width of window (defaults to pixels)	yes	yes	yes
height	pixel	IE3/IE4	Height of window in pixels	yes	yes	yes
top	pixel	IE3/IE4	Top position in pixels wrt desktop	yes	yes	yes
left	pixel	IE3/IE4	Left position in pixels wrt desktop	yes	yes	yes
center	yes/no/1/0	IE4	Centered wrt desktop	yes	yes	yes

This example, Open.htm, is easy to write. We just place the prompt to the user and the button we'll need in a window:

```
<HTML>
<TITLE>
New window example
</TITLE>
<BODY>
<FORM>
<CENTER>
<BR>
<H1>Opening a new window example . . . </H1>
<BR>
<BR>
<INPUT TYPE = BUTTON Value = "Open window" onClick = "Open-
      Window()">
</CENTER>
</FORM>
</BODY>
```

When the user does click the button, we'll execute the code in the function we've called OpenWindow():

```
<SCRIPT LANGUAGE = JavaScript>
   function OpenWindow()
   {
         .
         .
         .

   }
</SCRIPT>
```

Here's how we'll set the features of the browser window we're going to open in our call to window.open():

```
<SCRIPT LANGUAGE = JavaScript>
   function OpenWindow()
   {

        window.open("wnd.htm", null,

       "height=200,width=400,status=yes,toolbar=no,menubar=no
       '
                  location=no")
   }
</SCRIPT>
```

Here's the document we'll display in the new browser window, Wnd.htm; note that for the user's convenience, we include a button for closing the new window, using the window.close() method:

```
<HTML>
<HEAD>
<TITLE>New Window</TITLE>
</HEAD>
<BODY>
<CENTER>
<H1>This is a newly opened window</H1>
</CENTER>
<FORM>
<CENTER>
<INPUT TYPE = BUTTON VALUE = "Close me" onClick =
    "Closer()">
</CENTER>
</FORM>
</BODY>
<SCRIPT LANGUAGE = JavaScript>
    function Closer()
    {
        window.close()
    }
</SCRIPT>
</HTML>
```

That's it—open this page now, as shown in Figure 9–1.

When you click the "Open window" button, a new browser window opens, as shown in Figure 9–2, displaying the second page, Wnd.htm, sized the way we want it and with the options we've specified. Now we can tailor new windows to meet our requirements.

The code for this page, Open.htm, is shown in Listing 9–1, and the code for the second page we opened, Wnd.htm, is shown in Listing 9–2.

Figure 9–1
We let the user open a new browser window.

Figure 9–2
We open and size a
new window.

Listing 9–1
Open.htm.

```
<HTML>
<TITLE>
New window example
</TITLE>
<BODY>
<FORM>
<CENTER>
<BR>
<H1>Opening a new window example . . . </H1>
<BR>
<BR>
<INPUT TYPE = BUTTON Value = "Open window" onClick = "Open-
    Window()">
</CENTER>
</FORM>
</BODY>
<SCRIPT LANGUAGE = JavaScript>
    function OpenWindow()
    {

        window.open("wnd.htm", null,

    "height=200,width=400,status=yes,toolbar=no,menubar=no
    ,location=no")
    }
</SCRIPT>
</HTML>
```

Listing 9–2
Wnd.htm.

```
<HTML>
<HEAD>
<TITLE>New Window</TITLE>
</HEAD>
<BODY>
```

```
<CENTER>
<H1>This is a newly opened window</H1>
</CENTER>
<FORM>
<CENTER>
<INPUT TYPE = BUTTON VALUE = "Close me" onClick =
     "Closer()">
</CENTER>
</FORM>
</BODY>
<SCRIPT LANGUAGE = JavaScript>
    function Closer()
    {
        window.close()
    }
</SCRIPT>
</HTML>
```

When you open a new window, you don't need to load an already existing page into it. You can create the new page on the fly, as we'll see in the following section.

Writing to a Newly Opened Window

Our new example will look much like the previous one. When the user clicks the button, we display a new window. This time, however, we'll create and write that new document on the fly; this document doesn't exist as a file on disk anywhere.

In this example, we'll fill the new document with HTML written from JavaScript. This example, Filler.htm, is much like the previous example. We place the prompt and button we'll use in the page first:

```
<HTML>
<TITLE>
New window example
</TITLE>
<BODY>
<FORM>
<CENTER>
<BR>
<H1>Opening a new window example . . . </H1>
<BR>
<BR>
<INPUT TYPE = BUTTON Value = "Open window" onClick = "Open-
     Window()">
```

```
</CENTER>
</FORM>
</BODY>
```

When the user clicks the button, we'll open a new window, but note that we don't give any document URL to open, which means that a blank document is created:

```
<SCRIPT LANGUAGE = JavaScript>
    function OpenWindow()
    {

        var newWindow = window.open("wnd.htm", null,

    "height=200,width=400,status=yes,toolbar=no,menubar=no
    ,location=no")
                            .
                            .
                            .

    }
</SCRIPT>
```

All that's left is to write the HTML for the new document, and we do that with that document's write() method:

```
<SCRIPT LANGUAGE = JavaScript>
    function OpenWindow()
    {

        var newWindow = window.open("wnd.htm", null,

    "height=200,width=400,status=yes,toolbar=no,menubar=no
    ,location=no")
        newWindow.document.write("<BR><BR><CENTER><H1>This
    is a newly opened and written window!</H1></CENTER>")
    }
</SCRIPT>
```

Open this page now. When you click the button in that page, the program opens and creates an entirely new document on the fly, as shown in Figure 9–3.

The code for this page, Filler.htm, is shown in Listing 9–3.

Now that we've taken a look at the open() method, we'll move on to other window methods. There are more ways to display windows than just using the open() method, and we'll take a look at one of them now—the alert() method.

Figure 9–3
We create and open a new window, writing to that window after opening it.

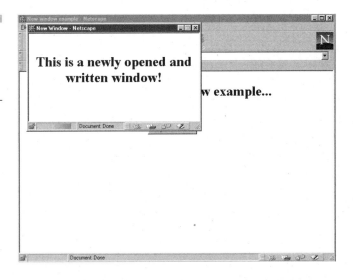

Listing 9–3
Filler.htm.

```
<HTML>
<TITLE>
New window example
</TITLE>
<BODY>
<FORM>
<CENTER>
<BR>
<H1>Opening a new window example . . . </H1>
<BR>
<BR>
<INPUT TYPE = BUTTON Value = "Open window" onClick = "Open-
    Window()">
</CENTER>
</FORM>
</BODY>
<SCRIPT LANGUAGE = JavaScript>
    function OpenWindow()
    {

        var newWindow = window.open("wnd.htm", null,

    "height=200,width=400,status=yes,toolbar=no,menubar=no
    ,location=no")
        newWindow.document.write("<BR><BR><CENTER><H1>This
    is a newly
            opened and written window!</H1></CENTER>")
    }
</SCRIPT>
</HTML>
```

Window Alert Boxes

Using the window object's alert() method, you can place alert boxes on-screen. These boxes indicate some condition to the user with a short message, but the user can dismiss the alert by clicking an OK button.

For example, we can create a page with a button marked Alert! When the user clicks the button, we can use an alert box to inform them of some important fact. Then, when the user clicks the OK button, the alert box disappears. This example, Alerter.htm, is simple to write; we just place the controls we'll need in the Web page like this:

```
<HTML>
<HEAD>
<TITLE>
An Alert example
</TITLE>
</HEAD>
<BODY>
<FORM>
<CENTER>
<H1>Click the button . . . </H1>
<BR>
<BR>
<INPUT TYPE=BUTTON VALUE="Alert!" onClick = "Alerter()">
</CENTER>
</FORM>
</BODY>
```

When the user clicks the button, we will display an alert box using the window.alert() method; here's how you pass the text you want to display to that method:

```
<SCRIPT LANGUAGE = JavaScript>
    function Alerter()
    {
        window.alert("You're running a Web browser!")
    }
</SCRIPT>
```

Open this page and click the button in that page. When you do, an alert box appears with our message in it, as shown in Figure 9–4. Our Alerter example is a success!

The code for this page, Alerter.htm, is shown in Listing 9–4.

The next step up from alert boxes is to use the window confirm() method, which we'll use in the following section.

Figure 9–4

Using a window alert box.

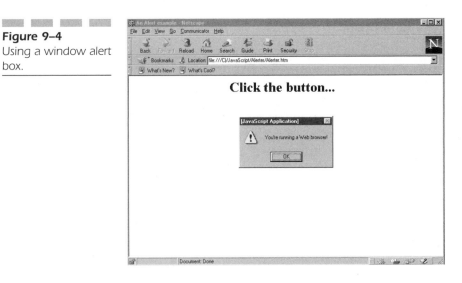

Listing 9–4

Alerter.htm.

```
<HTML>
<HEAD>
<TITLE>
An Alert example
</TITLE>
</HEAD>
<BODY>
<FORM>
<CENTER>
<H1>Click the button . . . </H1>
<BR>
<BR>
<INPUT TYPE=BUTTON VALUE="Alert!" onClick = "Alerter()">
</CENTER>
</FORM>
</BODY>
<SCRIPT LANGUAGE = JavaScript>
    function Alerter()
    {
        window.alert("You're running a Web browser!")
    }
</SCRIPT>
</BODY>
</HTML>
```

Window Confirm Boxes

The window object's confirm() method displays a confirm box that can accept user input—that is, when users click an OK or Cancel button, we can determine which action they've taken.

For example, we can display a button and a text box in a page. When users click the button, we can open a confirm box with a message in it. Then, when users click OK or Cancel, the confirm box closes, and we'll let them know which selection they made by displaying a message in the original page.

Start this new example, Confirmer.htm, with the controls needed in the Web page:

```
<HTML>
<HEAD>
<TITLE>
A Window Confirm box example
</TITLE>
</HEAD>
<BODY>
<FORM name = "form1">
<CENTER>
<H1>Click the button . . . </H1>
<BR>
<INPUT TYPE = BUTTON VALUE = "Click Me" onClick = "Con-
     firmer()">
<BR>
<BR>
<INPUT TYPE = TEXT NAME = Textbox SIZE = 30>
</CENTER>
</FORM>
</BODY>
```

When the user clicks the button, we display a confirm box using the window.confirm() method; this method returns true if the user clicked the OK button, and false otherwise. Here's how we indicate that the user clicked OK if confirm() returns true:

```
<SCRIPT LANGUAGE = JavaScript>
function Confirmer()
{
    if (confirm("Click the OK or Cancel button . . . ")) {
        document.form1.Textbox.value = "OK button was
    clicked!"
```

```
}
    .
    .
    .
```

Otherwise, we indicate that the user clicked the Cancel button:

```
<SCRIPT LANGUAGE = JavaScript>
function Confirmer()
{
    if (confirm("Click the OK or Cancel button . . . ")) {
        document.form1.Textbox.value = "OK button was
     clicked!"
    }
    else{
        document.form1.Textbox.value = "Cancel button was
     clicked!"
    }
}
</SCRIPT>
```

Open this page now, as shown in Figure 9–5, and click the button.

Clicking the button displays the confirm box. When the user clicks the OK or Cancel button, we report that fact, as shown in Figure 9–6. Now we're using the window object's confirm() method to get information from the user.

The code for this page, Confirmer.htm, is shown in Listing 9–5.

Figure 9–5
We let the user open a confirm box.

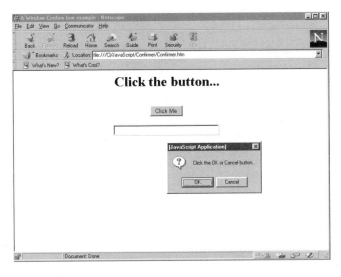

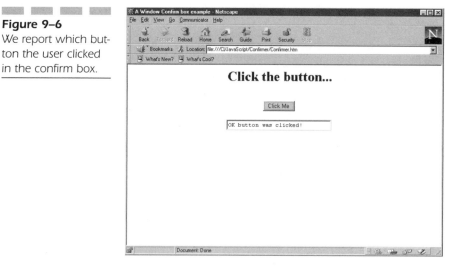

Listing 9–5
Confirmer.htm.

```
<HTML>
<HEAD>
<TITLE>
A Window Confirm box example
</TITLE>
</HEAD>
<BODY>
<FORM name = "form1">
<CENTER>
<H1>Click the button . . . </H1>
<BR>
<INPUT TYPE = BUTTON VALUE = "Click Me" onClick = "Con-
     firmer()">
<BR>
<BR>
<INPUT TYPE = TEXT NAME = Textbox SIZE = 30>
</CENTER>
</FORM>
</BODY>
<SCRIPT LANGUAGE = JavaScript>
function Confirmer()
{
    if (confirm("Click the OK or Cancel button . . . ")) {
        document.form1.Textbox.value = "OK button was
    clicked!"
    }
    else{
        document.form1.Textbox.value = "Cancel button was
    clicked!"
    }
}
</SCRIPT>
</HTML>
```

The last window object method we'll take a look at here is the prompt() method.

Window Prompt Boxes

The window object's prompt() method lets users enter a string. For example, we can display a button and a text box. When users click the button, we can display a prompt box that will accept text, and we can even place some default text into that box. When users click the OK button, we can report back what they've entered.

In this example, Prompter.htm, we start with the controls we'll need:

```
<HTML>
<HEAD>
<TITLE>
A Window Prompt example
</TITLE>
</HEAD>
<BODY>
<CENTER>
<FORM NAME = form1>
<BR>
<H1>Click the button . . . </H1>
<BR>
<INPUT TYPE = BUTTON Value = "Click Me" onClick =
     "Prompter()">
<BR>
<BR>
<INPUT TYPE = TEXT NAME = Textbox SIZE = 25>
</FROM>
</CENTER>
</BODY>
```

Now we turn to the JavaScript section of the page. Here, we place the prompt box onscreen and pass a default string for the prompt's text box:

```
<SCRIPT LANGUAGE = JavaScript>
    function Prompter()
    {
        var text = new String()
        text = window.prompt("Do you program in Java-
    Script?", "Yes, I do")
        .
        .
        .
```

If the prompt() method returns an empty string, the user didn't enter any text, so we indicate that in the main page's text box:

```
<SCRIPT LANGUAGE = JavaScript>
    function Prompter()
    {
        var text = new String()
        text = window.prompt("Do you program in Java-
    Script?", "Yes, I do")
        if (text == "")
            document.form1.Textbox.value = "You didn't en-
    ter anything."
                       .
                       .
                       .
```

Otherwise, we display the text the user has entered:

```
<SCRIPT LANGUAGE = JavaScript>
    function Prompter()
    {
        var text = new String()
        text = window.prompt("Do you program in Java-
    Script?", "Yes, I do")
        if (text == "")
            document.form1.Textbox.value = "You didn't en-
    ter anything."
        else
            document.form1.Textbox.value = "You entered: "
    + text
    }
</SCRIPT>
</HTML>
```

Open this page and click the button to open the prompt box, as shown in Figure 9–7.

When the user enters some text or accepts the default, and then clicks the OK button, the prompt box closes. We then display the text in a text box, as shown in Figure 9–8. Our Prompter.htm example works as intended—now we can get input from the user with the prompt() method.

The code for this page, Prompter.htm, is shown in Listing 9–6.

Figure 9–7
We support the
window prompt()
method.

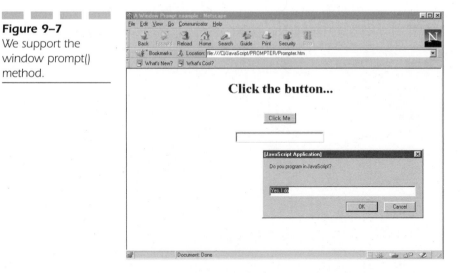

Figure 9–8
We report the string
the user entered.

There's a new object in Internet Explorer based on the window object
—the *dialog* object. Using this object, we can support dialog boxes in Internet Explorer, as we'll see in the following section.

```
<HTML>
<HEAD>
<TITLE>
A Window Prompt example
</TITLE>
</HEAD>
<BODY>
<CENTER>
<FORM NAME = form1>
<BR>
<H1>Click the button . . . </H1>
<BR>
<INPUT TYPE = BUTTON Value = "Click Me" onClick =
     "Prompter()">
<BR>
<BR>
<INPUT TYPE = TEXT NAME = Textbox SIZE = 25>
</FROM>
</CENTER>
</BODY>
<SCRIPT LANGUAGE = JavaScript>
    function Prompter()
    {
        var text = new String()
        text = window.prompt("Do you program in Java-
    Script?", "Yes, I do")
        if (text == "")
```

Dialog Boxes: the Day Example

You can create dialog boxes in Internet Explorer with the window object's showModalDialog() method. It creates a new window constructed from the *dialog* object (which is based on the window object). The properties of Internet Explorer's dialog object are width, height, dialogArgs, and returnValue; its single method is close().

We'll put together an example using Internet Explorer's dialog object, showing how to support dialog boxes in that browser. In this example, we'll display a button and a text box and let the user use a dialog box to select the day of the week.

When the user clicks the button, we'll display a dialog box with seven radio buttons, one for each day of the week. If the user clicks a radio button followed by the OK button, we close the dialog box and display his or her selection in the main window.

Start this new example, Day.htm, with the controls we'll need in the main window:

```
<HTML>
<TITLE>Dialog example</TITLE>
<BODY>
<CENTER>
<FORM NAME = form1>
<BR>
<H1>Click the button to select the day of the week . . .
     </H1>
<BR>
<INPUT TYPE = BUTTON Value = "Select day of the week"
     onClick
        = "SelectDay()">
<BR>
<BR>
<INPUT TYPE = TEXT NAME = "Textbox" SIZE = 30>
<BR>
</FORM>
</CENTER>
</BODY>
```

When the user clicks the button, we will display our dialog box.

Displaying a Dialog Box

To create a dialog box, use the window object's showModalDialog()
method, loading in a new document—Dlg.htm—as our dialog box:

```
<SCRIPT LANGUAGE = JavaScript>
   function SelectDay()
   {
        document.form1.Textbox.value = window.showModalDia-
      log("dlg.htm")
   }
</SCRIPT>
</HTML>
```

This displays the new document in a dialog box, where the user can
work with it. Next, we'll read a return value from showModalDialog(); this
return value will be the day of the week the user has selected, and we'll
display that result in a text box.

Creating a Dialog Box

In the actual dialog box, Dlg.htm, we place all the radio buttons we'll use,
one for each day of the week:

```
<HTML>
<BODY>
<CENTER>
<FORM NAME = "form1">
<BR>
<BR>
<H1>Select the day of the week . . . </H1>
<BR>
<TABLE BORDER BGCOLOR = CYAN WIDTH = 200>
<TABLE BORDER BGCOLOR = CYAN WIDTH = 200>
    <TR><TD><INPUT TYPE = RADIO NAME = RadioButtons
        onClick = radio1Clicked()>Sunday</TD></TR>
    <TR><TD><INPUT TYPE = RADIO NAME = RadioButtons
        onClick = radio2Clicked()>Monday</TD></TR>
    <TR><TD><INPUT TYPE = RADIO NAME = RadioButtons
        onClick = radio3Clicked()>Tuesday</TD></TR>
    <TR><TD><INPUT TYPE = RADIO NAME = RadioButtons
        onClick = radio4Clicked()>Wednesday</TD></TR>
    <TR><TD><INPUT TYPE = RADIO NAME = RadioButtons
        onClick = radio5Clicked()>Thursday</TD></TR>
    <TR><TD><INPUT TYPE = RADIO NAME = RadioButtons
        onClick = radio6Clicked()>Friday</TD></TR>
    <TR><TD><INPUT TYPE = RADIO NAME = RadioButtons
        onClick = radio7Clicked()>Saturday</TD></TR>
</TABLE>
<BR>
<INPUT TYPE = BUTTON Value = "  OK  "
        onClick = "OKButton()">
<INPUT TYPE = BUTTON Value = "Cancel"
        onClick = "CancelButton()">
</FORM>
</CENTER>
</BODY>
```

We'll set up a new variable, weekday, that will hold the selection the user makes. We start that variable off with the string "No selection":

```
<SCRIPT LANGUAGE = JavaScript>
    var weekday = "No selection"
        .
        .
        .
```

If the user clicks the OK button without making a selection, we'll return this "No selection" string.

Next, we add a click handler for each of the radio buttons, setting the weekday variable to the appropriate day of the week for that button:

```
<SCRIPT LANGUAGE = JavaScript>
    var weekday = "No selection"
```

```
function radio1Clicked() {
    weekday = "Sunday"
}
function radio2Clicked() {
    weekday = "Monday"
}
function radio3Clicked() {
    weekday = "Tuesday"
}
function radio4Clicked() {
    weekday = "Wednesday"
}
function radio5Clicked() {
    weekday = "Thursday"
}
function radio6Clicked() {
    weekday = "Friday"
}
function radio7Clicked() {
    weekday = "Saturday"
}
```

If the user clicks the OK button, we will return their selection to the main window as the return value from the showModalDialog() method. We do that simply by setting the window object's *returnValue* property to the string we want to return and closing the dialog box:

```
function OKButton()
{
    window.returnValue = "Day of the week: " + weekday
    window.close()
}
```

On the other hand, if the user clicks the Cancel button, we return a string that reads "No selection":

```
function CancelButton()
{
    window.returnValue = "No selection"
    window.close()
}
```

That's it—open Day.htm in Internet Explorer and click the button, opening the dialog box as shown in Figure 9–9.

If you click a radio button in the dialog box and click the OK button, the dialog box closes and the main page reports what selection you've made, as shown in Figure 9–10. Now we're using dialog boxes in Internet Explorer.

The code for this page, Day.htm, is shown in Listing 9–7, and the code for the dialog box, Dlg.htm, is shown in Listing 9–8.

Figure 9–9
We support dialog
boxes.

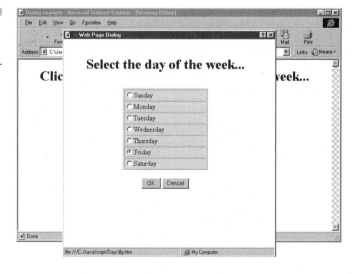

Figure 9–9
We support dialog
boxes.

Figure 9–10
We read a value re-
turned by a dialog
box.

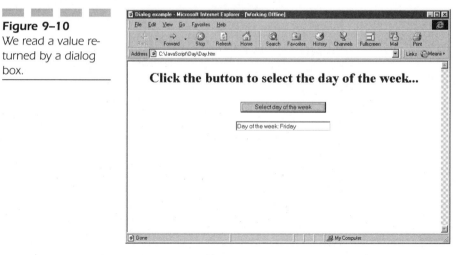

Listing 9–7
Day.htm.

```
<HTML>
<TITLE>Dialog example</TITLE>
<BODY>
<CENTER>
<FORM NAME = form1>
<BR>
<H1>Click the button to select the day of the week . . .
    </H1>
<BR>
<INPUT TYPE = BUTTON Value = "Select day of the week"
    onClick
        = "SelectDay()">
```

```
<BR>
<BR>
<INPUT TYPE = TEXT NAME = "Textbox" SIZE = 30>
<BR>
</FORM>
</CENTER>
</BODY>
<SCRIPT LANGUAGE = JavaScript>
    function SelectDay()
    {
        document.form1.Textbox.value = window.showModalDia-
    log("dlg.htm")
    }
</SCRIPT>
</HTML>
```

Listing 9–8

Dlg.htm.

```
<HTML>
<BODY>
<CENTER>
<FORM NAME = "form1">
<BR>
<BR>
<H1>Select the day of the week . . . </H1>
<BR>
<TABLE BORDER BGCOLOR = CYAN WIDTH = 200>
<TABLE BORDER BGCOLOR = CYAN WIDTH = 200>
    <TR><TD><INPUT TYPE = RADIO NAME = RadioButtons
         onClick = radio1Clicked()>Sunday</TD></TR>
    <TR><TD><INPUT TYPE = RADIO NAME = RadioButtons
         onClick = radio2Clicked()>Monday</TD></TR>
    <TR><TD><INPUT TYPE = RADIO NAME = RadioButtons
         onClick = radio3Clicked()>Tuesday</TD></TR>
    <TR><TD><INPUT TYPE = RADIO NAME = RadioButtons
         onClick = radio4Clicked()>Wednesday</TD></TR>
    <TR><TD><INPUT TYPE = RADIO NAME = RadioButtons
         onClick = radio5Clicked()>Thursday</TD></TR>
    <TR><TD><INPUT TYPE = RADIO NAME = RadioButtons
         onClick = radio6Clicked()>Friday</TD></TR>
    <TR><TD><INPUT TYPE = RADIO NAME = RadioButtons
         onClick = radio7Clicked()>Saturday</TD></TR>
</TABLE>
<BR>
<INPUT TYPE = BUTTON Value = "  OK  "
         onClick = "OKButton()">
<INPUT TYPE = BUTTON Value = "Cancel"
         onClick = "CancelButton()">
</FORM>
</CENTER>
</BODY>
```

continues

Listing 9–8
Continued.

```
<SCRIPT LANGUAGE = JavaScript>
    var weekday = "No selection"
    function radio1Clicked() {
        weekday = "Sunday"
    }
    function radio2Clicked() {
        weekday = "Monday"
    }
    function radio3Clicked() {
        weekday = "Tuesday"
    }
    function radio4Clicked() {
        weekday = "Wednesday"
    }
    function radio5Clicked() {
        weekday = "Thursday"
    }
    function radio6Clicked() {
        weekday = "Friday"
    }
    function radio7Clicked() {
        weekday = "Saturday"
    }
    function OKButton()
    {
        window.returnValue = "Day of the week: " + weekday
        window.close()
    }
    function CancelButton()
    {
        window.returnValue = "No selection"
        window.close()
    }
</SCRIPT>
</HTML>
```

So far, we've just read values returned from a dialog box, but we can send values to a dialog box, too, as we'll see in the following section.

Using Dialog Box Arguments

Our next example shows how to send arguments to an Internet Explorer dialog box. In this example, the user will select the hour of the day in a dialog box. We start with a page displaying a button and a text box.

When the user clicks the button, we'll display a dialog box with 12 radio buttons, one for each of the 12 clock hours of the day. We'll pass the current hour of the day from the main window to the dialog box so that one radio button will appear clicked as the default.

The user can accept the default or click a radio button, followed by the OK button, in which case we close the dialog box and display the selection in the main window. Passing the hour of the day to the dialog box in this way will show us how to pass arguments to dialog boxes.

Start this new Web page, Hour.htm, with the controls we'll need—the text box and button:

```
<HTML>
<TITLE>Dialog arguments example</TITLE>
<BODY>
<CENTER>
<FORM NAME = form1>
<BR>
<H1>Click the button to select the hour of the day . . .
    </H1>
<BR>
<INPUT TYPE = BUTTON Value = "Select the hour of the day"
    onClick
        = "SelectHour()">
<BR>
<BR>
<INPUT TYPE = TEXT NAME = "Textbox" SIZE = 30>
<BR>
</FORM>
</CENTER>
</BODY>
```

When the user clicks the button, we will determine the current hour of the day and send that to the dialog box when we open it. We determine the hour of the day with the JavaScript date object:

```
<SCRIPT LANGUAGE = JavaScript>
    function SelectHour()
    {
        var currentDate = new Date()
        var currentHour = currentDate.getHours()
        .
        .
        .
```

Now we have to pass this value to the dialog box.

Passing an Argument to a Dialog Box

When we open the dialog box, Dlg.htm, we pass the current hour to it by including currentHour as an argument in the call to showModalDialog():

```
<SCRIPT LANGUAGE = JavaScript>
    function SelectHour()
    {
        var currentDate = new Date()
        var currentHour = currentDate.getHours()
        document.form1.Textbox.value
            = window.showModalDialog("dlg.htm", curren-
    tHour)
    }
</SCRIPT>
</HTML>
```

That's all it takes; now we've sent the current hour of the day to the dialog box.

We're ready to create the dialog box document, Dlg.htm, and we do that by setting up the radio buttons we'll use for the hours of the day, 1–12, as well as the OK and Cancel buttons:

```
<HTML>
<BODY>
<CENTER>
<FORM NAME = "form1">
<BR>
<BR>
<H1>Select the hour of the day . . . </H1>
<BR>
<TABLE BORDER BGCOLOR = CYAN WIDTH = 200>
<TABLE BORDER BGCOLOR = CYAN WIDTH = 200>
    <TR><TD><INPUT TYPE = RADIO NAME = RadioButtons
        onClick = radio1Clicked()>1</TD></TR>
    <TR><TD><INPUT TYPE = RADIO NAME = RadioButtons
        onClick = radio2Clicked()>2</TD></TR>
    <TR><TD><INPUT TYPE = RADIO NAME = RadioButtons
        onClick = radio3Clicked()>3</TD></TR>
    <TR><TD><INPUT TYPE = RADIO NAME = RadioButtons
        onClick = radio4Clicked()>4</TD></TR>
    <TR><TD><INPUT TYPE = RADIO NAME = RadioButtons
        onClick = radio5Clicked()>5</TD></TR>
    <TR><TD><INPUT TYPE = RADIO NAME = RadioButtons
        onClick = radio6Clicked()>6</TD></TR>
    <TR><TD><INPUT TYPE = RADIO NAME = RadioButtons
        onClick = radio7Clicked()>7</TD></TR>
    <TR><TD><INPUT TYPE = RADIO NAME = RadioButtons
        onClick = radio8Clicked()>8</TD></TR>
    <TR><TD><INPUT TYPE = RADIO NAME = RadioButtons
```

```
               onClick = radio9Clicked()>9</TD></TR>
    <TR><TD><INPUT TYPE = RADIO NAME = RadioButtons
               onClick = radio10Clicked()>10</TD></TR>
    <TR><TD><INPUT TYPE = RADIO NAME = RadioButtons
               onClick = radio11Clicked()>11</TD></TR>
    <TR><TD><INPUT TYPE = RADIO NAME = RadioButtons
               onClick = radio12Clicked()>12</TD></TR>
</TABLE>
<BR>
<INPUT TYPE = BUTTON Value = "  OK  "
          onClick = "OKButton()">
<INPUT TYPE = BUTTON Value = "Cancel"
          onClick = "CancelButton()">
</FORM>
</CENTER>
</BODY>
```

Now we're ready to read the argument passed to us by the main window so we can initialize the dialog box's radio buttons accordingly.

Reading an Argument Passed to a Dialog Box

The value passed to us in the showModalDialog() method is available in the dialog box's code as the *dialogArguments* property. In our case, this argument holds the current hour of the day in string form. We can convert a string to an integer with the JavaScript parseInt() method:

```
<SCRIPT LANGUAGE = JavaScript>
    hour = parseInt(dialogArguments)
           .
           .
           .
```

TIP: _Besides parseInt(), which converts a string representation of a number to an integer, JavaScript also includes parseFloat(), which parses a string into a floating point number._

Because the date object works in 24-hour intervals, and we have only 12 radio buttons, we convert the current hour to a 12-hour scale, as shown here:

```
<SCRIPT LANGUAGE = JavaScript>
    hour = parseInt(dialogArguments)
    if(hour > 12){
        hour -= 12
```

```
    }
    if(hour == 0){
        hour = 12
    }
        .
        .
        .
```

To initialize the dialog box by setting the correct radio button, then, we just select the radio button corresponding to the hour of the day:

```
<SCRIPT LANGUAGE = JavaScript>
    hour = parseInt(dialogArguments)
    if(hour > 12){
        hour -= 12
    }
    if(hour == 0){
        hour = 12
    }
    document.form1.RadioButtons[hour - 1].checked = true
        .
        .
        .
```

Now we've initialized a dialog box with arguments sent from the main window.

The rest of the program is easy to write. We simply handle the radio button clicks as shown in the following code, setting the value of the hour variable to the hour the user has selected:

```
<SCRIPT LANGUAGE = JavaScript>
    hour = parseInt(dialogArguments)
    if(hour > 12){
        hour -= 12
    }
    if(hour == 0){
        hour = 12
    }
    document.form1.RadioButtons[hour - 1].checked = true
    function radio1Clicked() {
        hour = "1"
    }
    function radio2Clicked() {
        hour = "2"
    }
    function radio3Clicked() {
        hour = "3"
    }
    function radio4Clicked() {
        hour = "4"
```

```
    }
    function radio5Clicked() {
        hour = "5"
    }
    function radio6Clicked() {
        hour = "6"
    }
    function radio7Clicked() {
        hour = "7"
    }
    function radio8Clicked() {
        hour = "8"
    }
    function radio9Clicked() {
        hour = "9"
    }
    function radio10Clicked() {
        hour = "10"
    }
    function radio11Clicked() {
        hour = "11"
    }
    function radio12Clicked() {
        hour = "12"
    }
```

Now when the user clicks the OK button, we can return the hour of the day to the main window:

```
    function OKButton()
    {
        window.returnValue = "Hour of the day: " + hour
        window.close()
    }
```

If the user clicks the Cancel button, we return a string reading "No selection":

```
    function CancelButton()
    {
        window.returnValue = "No selection"
        window.close()
    }
</SCRIPT>
```

Now open the Hour.htm page and click the button in that page, opening the dialog box, as shown in Figure 9–11. As you can see, we've passed the current hour to that dialog box, and the radio button corresponding to the current hour was initialized.

When you click the OK button, the hour you've selected is displayed in the main page, as shown in Figure 9–12. Now we can pass arguments to dialog boxes.

The code for this page, Hour.htm, is shown in Listing 9–9, and the dialog box itself, Dlg.htm, is shown in Listing 9–10.

Figure 9–11
We pass values to a dialog box.

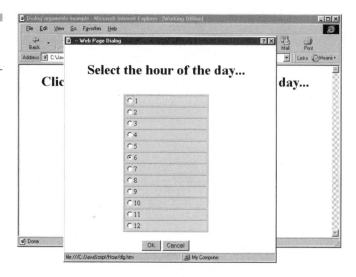

Figure 9–12
We read a value from a dialog box.

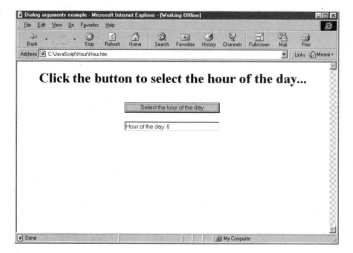

```
<HTML>
<TITLE>Dialog arguments example</TITLE>
<BODY>
<CENTER>
<FORM NAME = form1>
<BR>
<H1>Click the button to select the hour of the day . . .
    </H1>
<BR>
<INPUT TYPE = BUTTON Value = "Select the hour of the day"
    onClick
        = "SelectHour()">
<BR>
<BR>
<INPUT TYPE = TEXT NAME = "Textbox" SIZE = 30>
<BR>
</FORM>
</CENTER>
</BODY>
<SCRIPT LANGUAGE = JavaScript>
    function SelectHour()
    {
        var currentDate = new Date()
        var currentHour = currentDate.getHours()
        document.form1.Textbox.value
            = window.showModalDialog("dlg.htm", curren-
    tHour)
    }
</SCRIPT>
</HTML>
```

```
<HTML>
<BODY>
<CENTER>
<FORM NAME = "form1">
<BR>
<BR>
<H1>Select the hour of the day . . . </H1>
<BR>
<TABLE BORDER BGCOLOR = CYAN WIDTH = 200>
<TABLE BORDER BGCOLOR = CYAN WIDTH = 200>
    <TR><TD><INPUT TYPE = RADIO NAME = RadioButtons
        onClick = radio1Clicked()>1</TD></TR>
    <TR><TD><INPUT TYPE = RADIO NAME = RadioButtons
        onClick = radio2Clicked()>2</TD></TR>
    <TR><TD><INPUT TYPE = RADIO NAME = RadioButtons
        onClick = radio3Clicked()>3</TD></TR>
    <TR><TD><INPUT TYPE = RADIO NAME = RadioButtons
        onClick = radio4Clicked()>4</TD></TR>
```

continues

Listing 9–10
Continued.

```
   <TR><TD><INPUT TYPE = RADIO NAME = RadioButtons
        onClick = radio5Clicked()>5</TD></TR>
   <TR><TD><INPUT TYPE = RADIO NAME = RadioButtons
        onClick = radio6Clicked()>6</TD></TR>
   <TR><TD><INPUT TYPE = RADIO NAME = RadioButtons
        onClick = radio7Clicked()>7</TD></TR>
   <TR><TD><INPUT TYPE = RADIO NAME = RadioButtons
        onClick = radio8Clicked()>8</TD></TR>
   <TR><TD><INPUT TYPE = RADIO NAME = RadioButtons
        onClick = radio9Clicked()>9</TD></TR>
   <TR><TD><INPUT TYPE = RADIO NAME = RadioButtons
        onClick = radio10Clicked()>10</TD></TR>
   <TR><TD><INPUT TYPE = RADIO NAME = RadioButtons
        onClick = radio11Clicked()>11</TD></TR>
   <TR><TD><INPUT TYPE = RADIO NAME = RadioButtons
        onClick = radio12Clicked()>12</TD></TR>
</TABLE>
<BR>
<INPUT TYPE = BUTTON Value = "  OK  "
        onClick = "OKButton()">
<INPUT TYPE = BUTTON Value = "Cancel"
        onClick = "CancelButton()">
</FORM>
</CENTER>
</BODY>
<SCRIPT LANGUAGE = JavaScript>
   hour = parseInt(dialogArguments)
   if(hour > 12){
       hour -= 12
   }
   if(hour == 0){
       hour = 12
   }
   document.form1.RadioButtons[hour - 1].checked = true
   function radio1Clicked() {
       hour = "1"
   }
   function radio2Clicked() {
       hour = "2"
   }
   function radio3Clicked() {
       hour = "3"
   }
   function radio4Clicked() {
       hour = "4"
   }
   function radio5Clicked() {
       hour = "5"
   }
   function radio6Clicked() {
       hour = "6"
   }
```

```
    function radio7Clicked() {
        hour = "7"
    }
    function radio8Clicked() {
        hour = "8"
    }
    function radio9Clicked() {
        hour = "9"
    }
    function radio10Clicked() {
        hour = "10"
    }
    function radio11Clicked() {
        hour = "11"
    }
    function radio12Clicked() {
        hour = "12"
    }
    function OKButton()
    {
        window.returnValue = "Hour of the day: " + hour
        window.close()
    }
    function CancelButton()
    {
        window.returnValue = "No selection"
        window.close()
    }
</SCRIPT>
</HTML>
```

CONCLUSION

That's it for our chapter on the window object. We've learned how to use it to open new windows and create alert boxes, confirm boxes, and prompt boxes. We've also seen how to use Internet Explorer's dialog object to create dialog objects that we can pass arguments to and that can pass arguments back to us. We've covered a lot in this chapter, and we've added to our JavaScript coding skills.

In the next chapter, we'll explore some other powerful scripting objects available in JavaScript: the navigator, location, and history objects.

10

The Navigator, Location, and History Objects

In this chapter, we're going to learn about the built-in scripting objects that allow you to navigate the Web: the navigator, location, and history objects. These objects let you move around the Web from JavaScript, and we'll put them to work for us here.

We'll also see a few other ways of moving around the Web in this chapter, including how to use *JavaScript URLs* (a URL that actually points to JavaScript statements), how to retrieve information passed to the browser in a URL string (that is, those strings you see at the end of a URL that start with a question mark, such as http://www.server.com?app=15"), and how to use *cookies*, those text strings a server can store on your computer and read later to customize the information that server shows you. We'll see how to set and use cookies in this chapter.

Using cookies has become a sensitive subject these days. Some people resent the ability of nameless Web entities writing information to their personal computers without their knowledge. There have been abuses, such as Web sites that write over 15 cookies to a person's computer without his or her knowledge (approaching the cookie limit of most browsers, which is 20). Perhaps the best policy currently is to explain to users what cookies are all about, and exactly what yours does before writing one to their machine.

TIP: *Both Internet Explorer and Netscape Navigator have ways to warn users before accepting cookies.*

Cookies are just one of the topics we'll cover in this chapter. We'll start with an object we've seen before—the *navigator* object.

The navigator Object

The navigator object gives us information about the browser, something that can be very useful with such big differences between browsers these days. For example, Netscape Navigator's navigator object's properties are appCodeName, appName, appVersion, mimeTypes, plugins, userAgent, javaEnabled, and taintEnabled.

TIP: *Notice the taintEnabled() method in Netscape Navigator's navigator object. Tainting prevents scripts from passing information that should be private, such as directory structures or the session history. JavaScript can't pass tainted values on to any server without the end user's permission. You use taint() to mark data that otherwise isn't tainted.*

Internet Explorer's navigator object's properties are appName, appVersion, appCodeName, userAgent, cookieEnabled, and javaEnabled.

As mentioned before, the navigator object helps determine what browser your page is running, and that's what most JavaScript programmers use it for.

Using the Navigator Object: The AppType Example

We briefly reviewed the navigator object in Chapter 5, "Keyboard and Mouse Handling," when we needed to write different code for the two browsers in our Mouser.htm page. However, the navigator object supplies more information than just the browser name; for example, you can determine the browser's version number and operating platform, as we'll see in our next example, AppType.htm.

In this example, we'll determine the browser's type with the navigator object's appName property:

```
<HTML>
<HEAD>
<TITLE>
Determining your browser type . . .
</TITLE>
</HEAD>
<BODY>
<CENTER>
<H1>Determining your browser type . . . </H1>
</CENTER>
<SCRIPT LANGUAGE = JavaScript>
    if(navigator.appName == "Netscape") {

        .
        .
        .

    }
    if (navigator.appName == "Microsoft Internet Explorer")
      {

        .
        .
        .

    }
</SCRIPT>
</BODY>
</HTML>
```

We can also get a string holding the browser's version number and supported platform by using the navigator object's appVersion property:

```
<HTML>
<HEAD>
<TITLE>
Determining your browser type . . .
</TITLE>
</HEAD>
```

```
<BODY>
<CENTER>
<H1>Determining your browser type . . . </H1>
</CENTER>
<SCRIPT LANGUAGE = JavaScript>
    if(navigator.appName == "Netscape") {
        document.write("<H2><CENTER>")
        document.write("Netscape Navigator " +
    navigator.appVersion)
        document.write("</H2></CENTER>")
    }
    if (navigator.appName == "Microsoft Internet Explorer")
    {
        document.write("<H2><CENTER>")
        document.write("Microsoft Internet Explorer " +
    navigator.appVersion)
        document.write("</H2></CENTER>")
    }
</SCRIPT>
</BODY>
</HTML>
```

That's all it takes. Now open this page, as shown in Figure 10–1. As you can see, the program has determined the browser's name, version, and supported platform and displays that information.

The code for this page, AppType.htm, is shown in Listing 10–1.

Next, we'll turn to another powerful object—the *location* object.

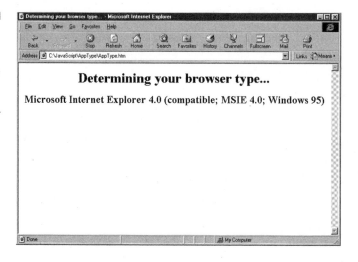

Figure 10–1
We determine a browser's name, version, and platform by using the navigator object.

Listing 10–1
AppType.htm.

```
<HTML>
<HEAD>
<TITLE>
Determining your browser type . . .
</TITLE>
</HEAD>
<BODY>
<CENTER>
<H1>Determining your browser type . . . </H1>
</CENTER>
<SCRIPT LANGUAGE = JavaScript>
    if(navigator.appName == "Netscape") {
        document.write("<H2><CENTER>")
        document.write("Netscape Navigator " +
    navigator.appVersion)
        document.write("</H2></CENTER>")
    }
    if (navigator.appName == "Microsoft Internet Explorer")
    {
        document.write("<H2><CENTER>")
        document.write("Microsoft Internet Explorer " +
    navigator.appVersion)
        document.write("</H2></CENTER>")
    }
</SCRIPT>
</BODY>
</HTML>
```

Using the Location Object

You can control where the browser navigates to by using its location object in JavaScript. Netscape Navigator's location object has these properties: hash, host, hostname, href, pathname, port, protocol, and search. Its methods are reload and replace.

Internet Explorer's location object has these properties: hash, host, hostname, href, pathname, port, protocol, and search. Its methods are reload and replace.

We will put the location object to work in an example, Jumper.htm, that lets users jump to a new URL with the click of a button. All they have to do is to place a URL into a text box and click a button; then the browser will navigate to the given URL.

Start this page, Jumper.htm, with the controls we'll need, the button and text box:

```
<HTML>
<HEAD>
<TITLE>
A location Object Example
</TITLE>
</HEAD>
</HEAD>
<BODY>
<CENTER>
<H1>
Enter a URL . . .
</H1>
<FORM NAME = form1>
<BR>
<INPUT TYPE = TEXT NAME = "Textbox" SIZE = 60>
<BR>
<BR>
<INPUT TYPE = BUTTON Value = "Jump to URL" onClick =
       "Jump()">
</FORM>
</CENTER>
</BODY>
```

When the user clicks the button, we just have to set the location object to the new URL the user has placed in the text box:

```
<SCRIPT LANGUAGE = JavaScript>
    function Jump()
    {
        window.location = document.form1.Textbox.value
    }
</SCRIPT>
</HTML>
```

Now open this page, enter a URL, as shown in Figure 10–2, and click the button.

When you do, the browser navigates to the Netscape home page, as shown in Figure 10–3.

TIP: *One curious fact is that referring to the location object is the same as referring to the location.href property. That is, the statement window.location = document.form1.Textbox.value; is the same as window.location.href = document.form1.Textbox.value.*

The code for this page, Jumper.htm, is shown in Listing 10–2.

Figure 10–2
We let the user navigate to a URL with the location object.

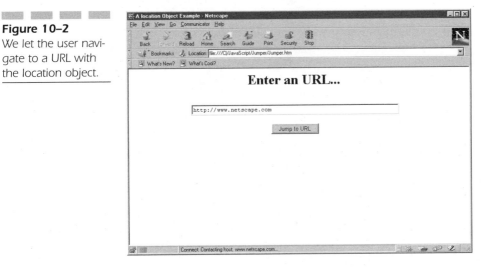

Figure 10–3
We navigate to Netscape's page by using the location object.

Listing 10–2
Jumper.htm.

```
<HTML>
<HEAD>
<TITLE>
A location Object Example
</TITLE>
</HEAD>
</HEAD>
<BODY>
<CENTER>
<H1>
```

Listing 10–2
Continued.

```
Enter a URL . . .
</H1>
<FORM NAME = form1>
<BR>
<INPUT TYPE = TEXT NAME = "Textbox" SIZE = 60>
<BR>
<BR>
<INPUT TYPE = BUTTON Value = "Jump to URL" onClick =
    "Jump()">
</FORM>
</CENTER>
</BODY>
<SCRIPT LANGUAGE = JavaScript>
    function Jump()
    {
        window.location = document.form1.Textbox.value
    }
</SCRIPT>
</HTML>
```

We can use the location object for another popular type of program—a slideshow page.

Sequence

In this next example, we'll let the user navigate from URL to URL by clicking buttons, displaying the new URLs in another frame. In this way, we'll support what's called a *slideshow*; we'll use the documents Target1.htm, Target2.htm, and Target3.htm as our "slides." When the user clicks the Next button, we navigate to the next slide, Target2.htm, placing that page in the upper frame. If the user clicks the Previous button, we move back to the previous page.

We'll write this new page, Sequence.htm, to set up two frames and display our first slide, Target1.htm, in the first frame, and the page with the Next and Previous buttons, Controls.htm, in the other frame:

```
<HTML>
<HEAD>
<TITLE>
Page Sequence Example
</TITLE>
</HEAD>
<FRAMESET ROWS = "70%,30%">
```

```
        <FRAME SRC = "target1.htm">
        <FRAME SRC = "controls.htm">
    </FRAMESET>
    </HTML>
```

To keep track of our location in the slideshow, we can place two variables, *next* and *previous*, in each of the slides, Target1.htm, Target2.htm, and Target3.htm. For example, here is Target2.htm:

```
<HTML>
<HEAD>
<TITLE>
Target 1
</TITLE>
<SCRIPT LANGUAGE = JavaScript>
var next = "target3.htm"
var previous = "target1.htm"
</SCRIPT>
</HEAD>
<BODY>
<H1>
Here is Target 2.
</H1>
</BODY>
</HTML>
```

Now we'll write the control panel, Controls.htm. First, we'll place the navigation buttons we'll need in this page:

```
<HTML>
<HEAD>
</HEAD>
<BODY>
<CENTER>
<FORM>
<BR>
<INPUT TYPE = BUTTON VALUE = "< Previous" onClick = "previ-
    ous()">
<INPUT TYPE = BUTTON VALUE = "Next >" onClick = "next()">
<BR>
<BR>
</FORM>
<H1>
Click a button to move through the page sequence . . .
</H1>
</CENTER>
</BODY>
```

Next, we write the JavaScript portion of the page. We've connected two functions, previous() and next(), to the Previous and Next buttons:

```
<SCRIPT LANGUAGE = JavaScript>

function previous()
{
    .
    .
    .
}
function next()
{
    .
    .
    .
}
</SCRIPT>
```

In these functions, we read the next slide's URL from the current slide's next property or the previous slide's URL from the current slide's previous property. We then set the top frame's location object to that URL to read that slide in; note that we use the top property to refer to the topmost window, Sequence.htm:

```
<SCRIPT LANGUAGE = JavaScript>
function previous()
{
    top.frames[0].location = top.frames[0].previous
}
function next()
{
    top.frames[0].location = top.frames[0].next
}
</SCRIPT>
```

That's it—open this page now, as shown in Figure 10–4. You can see the first slide displayed there.

When you use the Next and Previous buttons, you can navigate through the slide pages. For example, clicking the Next button causes the program to display Target2.htm, as shown in Figure 10–5.

The code for this page, Sequence.htm, is shown in Listing 10–3, Controls.htm is shown in Listing 10–4, Target1.htm is shown in Listing 10–5, Target2.htm in Listing 10–6, and Target3.htm in Listing 10–7.

Figure 10–4
Our Sequence page lets the user move through a sequence of URLs.

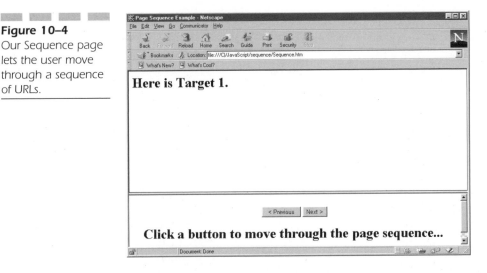

Figure 10–5
We display a new document in the Sequence page.

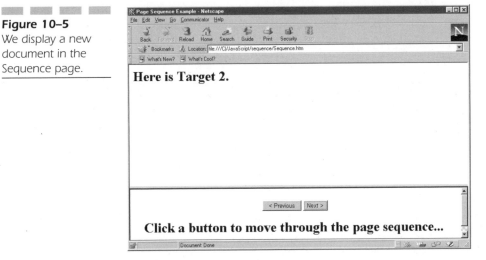

Listing 10–3
Sequence.htm.

```
<HTML>
<HEAD>
<TITLE>
Page Sequence Example
</TITLE>
</HEAD>
<FRAMESET ROWS = "70%,30%">
    <FRAME SRC = "target1.htm">
    <FRAME SRC = "controls.htm">
</FRAMESET>
</HTML>
```

Listing 10–4
Controls.htm.

```
<HTML>
<HEAD>
</HEAD>
<BODY>
<CENTER>
<FORM>
<BR>
<INPUT TYPE = BUTTON VALUE = "< Previous" onClick = "previ-
    ous()">
<INPUT TYPE = BUTTON VALUE = "Next >" onClick = "next()">
<BR>
<BR>
</FORM>
<H1>
Click a button to move through the page sequence . . .
</H1>
</CENTER>
</BODY>
<SCRIPT LANGUAGE = JavaScript>
function previous()
{
    top.frames[0].location = top.frames[0].previous
}
function next()
{
    top.frames[0].location = top.frames[0].next
}
</SCRIPT>
</HTML>
```

Listing 10–5
Target1.htm.

```
<HTML>
<HEAD>
<TITLE>
Target 1
</TITLE>
<SCRIPT LANGUAGE = JavaScript>
var next = "target2.htm"
var previous = "target3.htm"
</SCRIPT>
</HEAD>
<BODY>
<H1>
Here is Target 1.
</H1>
</BODY>
</HTML>
```

Listing 10–6
Target2.htm.

```
<HTML>
<HEAD>
<TITLE>
Target 1
</TITLE>
<SCRIPT LANGUAGE = JavaScript>
var next = "target3.htm"
var previous = "target1.htm"
</SCRIPT>
</HEAD>
<BODY>
<H1>
Here is Target 2.
</H1>
</BODY>
</HTML>
```

Listing 10–7
Target3.htm.

```
<HTML>
<HEAD>
<TITLE>
Target 1
</TITLE>
<SCRIPT LANGUAGE = JavaScript>
var next = "target1.htm"
var previous = "target2.htm"
</SCRIPT>
</HEAD>
<BODY>
<H1>
Here is Target 3.
</H1>
</BODY>
</HTML>
```

We'll move on now to the history object.

Using the History Object

You can keep track of where the browser has been with the *history* object, which lets you move to already visited pages. Netscape Navigator's history object has these properties: current, length, next, and previous. Its methods are back, forward, and go.

TIP: You can also use the history object as an array in Netscape Navigator, indexed by the previous pages the browser has displayed.

Internet Explorer's history object has one property, the length property. Its methods are back, forward, and go, just as for Netscape Navigator.

Let's see the history object in action. In this next example, History.htm, we give users the option of moving back one or two pages, or moving forward one or two pages, by using the history object. For example, if they click the Previous button, we move back to the page requested and display that page.

Start this page, History.htm, with the two buttons we'll use to move forward and back one page:

```
<HTML>
<HEAD>
<TITLE>
A history Object Example
</TITLE>
</HEAD>
<BODY>
<CENTER>
<H1>
A history Object Example.
</H1>
</CENTER>
<CENTER>
<FORM>
<BR>
Click a button to go forward or back . . .
<BR>
<INPUT TYPE = BUTTON Value = "< Back" onClick = "back()">
<INPUT TYPE = BUTTON Value = "Forward >" onClick = "for-
     ward()">
          .
          .
          .
```

Then we add the two buttons for moving two pages at a time:

```
<HTML>
<HEAD>
<TITLE>
A history Object Example
</TITLE>
</HEAD>
<BODY>
<CENTER>
<H1>
A history Object Example.
</H1>
```

```
</CENTER>
<CENTER>
<FORM>
<BR>
Click a button to go forward or back . . .
<BR>
<INPUT TYPE = BUTTON Value = "< Back" onClick = "back()">
<INPUT TYPE = BUTTON Value = "Forward >" onClick = "for-
    ward()">
<BR>
<BR>
Click a button to go forward or back two pages . . .
<BR>
<INPUT TYPE = BUTTON Value = "<< Back" onClick = "back2()">
<INPUT TYPE = BUTTON Value = "Forward >>" onClick = "for-
    ward2()">
</FORM>
</CENTER>
</BODY>
```

The Back button is tied to the function named back() and the Forward button to the function forward(), so add those functions now:

```
<SCRIPT LANGUAGE = JavaScript>
    function back()
    {
        .
        .
        .
    }
    function forward()
    {
        .
        .
        .
    }
```

Now it's time to use the history object.

Navigating with the History Object

We'll use the history object's forward() and back() methods to move though the recent pages the browser has visited. Here's how we implement our page's navigation buttons:

```
<SCRIPT LANGUAGE = JavaScript>
    function back()
    {
        window.history.back()
    }
    function forward()
```

```
        {
                window.history.forward()
        }
```

We will use these methods to move forward and back by two pages in the functions back2() and forward2():

```
<SCRIPT LANGUAGE = JavaScript>
    function back()
    {
            window.history.back()
    }
    function forward()
    {
            window.history.forward()
    }
    function back2()
    {
        .
        .
        .
    }
    function forward2()
    {
        .
        .
        .
    }
</SCRIPT>
```

In these two new functions, we just pass the number of pages to move to the history object's back() or forward() methods:

```
<SCRIPT LANGUAGE = JavaScript>
    function back()
    {
            window.history.back()
    }
    function forward()
    {
            window.history.forward()
    }
    function back2()
    {
            window.history.go(-2)
    }
    function forward2()
    {
            window.history.go(2)
    }
</SCRIPT>
```

That's all it takes—open this page now, as shown in Figure 10–6.

When we click the Back button, we move back to the previous page the browser displayed—that is, the previous example, Sequence.htm, as shown in Figure 10–7. We can move around using the buttons in the History.htm page—our history example is working!

The code for this page, History.htm, is shown in Listing 10–8.

Figure 10–6
We let the user move backward or forward with the history object.

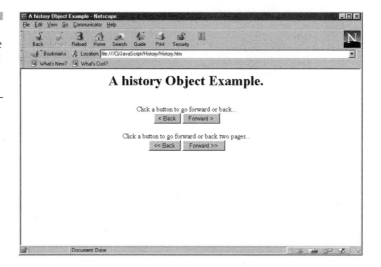

Figure 10–7
We move back a page to the previous example.

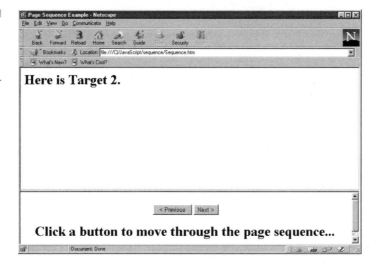

```
<HTML>
<HEAD>
<TITLE>
A history Object Example
</TITLE>
</HEAD>
<BODY>
<CENTER>
<H1>
A history Object Example.
</H1>
</CENTER>
<CENTER>
<FORM>
<BR>
Click a button to go forward or back . . .
<BR>
<INPUT TYPE = BUTTON Value = "< Back" onClick = "back()">
<INPUT TYPE = BUTTON Value = "Forward >" onClick = "for-
      ward()">
<BR>
<BR>
Click a button to go forward or back two pages . . .
<BR>
<INPUT TYPE = BUTTON Value = "<< Back" onClick = "back2()">
<INPUT TYPE = BUTTON Value = "Forward >>" onClick = "for-
      ward2()">
</FORM>
</CENTER>
</BODY>
<SCRIPT LANGUAGE = JavaScript>
    function back()
    {
         window.history.back()
    }
    function forward()
    {
         window.history.forward()
    }
    function back2()
    {
         window.history.go(-2)
    }
    function forward2()
    {
         window.history.go(2)
    }
</SCRIPT>
</HTML>
```

There's more we can do when navigating around with JavaScript. For
example, we can read information sent to us from another page, and we'll
see how to do that in the following section.

Retrieving Information from URL Strings

In this next example, we'll see how to determine where the user was before he or she navigated to our page. We start at a page named "Last-Loc.htm." When the user clicks the hyperlink in this page, we navigate to a new page, NewLoc.htm, which will display the name of the page we came from, LastLoc.htm.

We display the previous location by sending the browser to the URL "NewLoc.htm?LastLoc.htm" when the user clicks the hyperlink. The browser will ignore the text after the question mark—note that we place the name of the source page there, LastLoc.htm—but we can read that information in the target page and display it.

Let's see how this works. We simply place the hyperlink to "NewLoc.htm?LastLoc.htm" in the LastLoc.htm page, as shown here:

```
<HTML>
<HEAD>
<TITLE>
Tracking your location . . .
</TITLE>
</HEAD>
<BODY>
<CENTER>
<H1>
This link will send tracking information . . .
</H1>
<A HREF = "NewLoc.htm?LastLoc.htm">Go to the new location
    . . . </A> <—
</CENTER>
</BODY>
</HTML>
```

In the target page, NewLoc.htm, we start by indicating to the user that we will determine the page he or she came from:

```
<HTML>
<HEAD>
<TITLE>
Determining your last location . . .
</TITLE>
</HEAD>
<BODY>
<CENTER>
<H1>
Determining your last location . . .
</H1>
</CENTER>
```

.
.
.

We're ready to read the information passed to us by the previous page.

Reading Text Sent in a URL

The text that appears after the question mark in the URL string—
"NewLoc.htm?LastLoc.htm"—will be stored in the location object's *search*
property. In the target page, NewLoc.htm, we start by creating a string
from that property:

```
<HTML>
<HEAD>
<TITLE>
Determining your last location . . .
</TITLE>
</HEAD>
<BODY>
<CENTER>
<H1>
Determining your last location . . . .
</H1>
</CENTER>
<SCRIPT>
    var oldURL = new String()
    oldURL = location.search
        .
        .
        .
```

That string actually includes the leading question mark, so we cut off
that character with the String method substring(), getting the browser's
last location from that string and displaying it, as shown here:

```
<HTML>
<HEAD>
<TITLE>
Determining your last location . . .
</TITLE>
</HEAD>
<BODY>
<CENTER>
<H1>
Determining your last location . . .
</H1>
</CENTER>
<SCRIPT>
    var oldURL = new String()
```

```
        oldURL = location.search
        document.write("<CENTER><H2>")
        document.write("Your last location: " + oldURL.sub-
            string(1, oldURL.length))
        document.write("</CENTER></H2>")
    </SCRIPT>
    </BODY>
    </HTML>
```

That's all we need—now open LastLoc.htm ,as shown in Figure 10–8.

When you click the hyperlink, we move to the new page, NewLoc.htm, passing the URL "NewLoc.htm?LastLoc.htm" to the browser. The code in that page strips the name of the previous page out of that URL and displays it, as shown in Figure 10–9. Our LastLoc example is a success—now we're reading information passed to us in a URL.

The code for this page, LastLoc.htm, is shown in Listing 10–9, and the NewLoc.htm page is shown in Listing 10–10.

Figure 10–8
We will track information sent from this page.

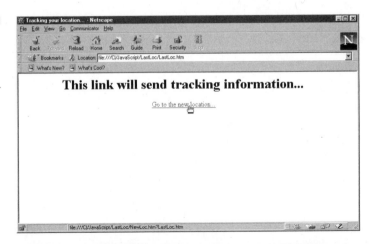

Figure 10–9
We determine where the browser navigated from.

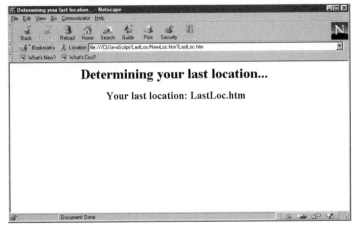

Listing 10–9
LastLoc.htm.

```
<HTML>
<HEAD>
<TITLE>
Tracking your location . . .
</TITLE>
</HEAD>
<BODY>
<CENTER>
<H1>
This link will send tracking information . . .
</H1>
<A HREF = "NewLoc.htm?LastLoc.htm">Go to the new location
    . . . </A>
</CENTER>
</BODY>
</HTML>
```

Listing 10–10
NewLoc.htm.

```
<HTML>
<HEAD>
<TITLE>
Determining your last location . . .
</TITLE>
</HEAD>
<BODY>
<CENTER>
<H1>
Determining your last location . . .
</H1>
</CENTER>
<SCRIPT>
    var oldURL = new String()
    oldURL = location.search
    document.write("<CENTER><H2>")
    document.write("Your last location: " + oldURL.sub-
      string(1, oldURL.length))
    document.write("</CENTER></H2>")
</SCRIPT>
</BODY>
</HTML>
```

To continue our exploration of navigating in JavaScript, we'll take a new look at image maps next.

The Next Step in Image Maps: JavaScript URLs

We constructed an image map in Chapter 6, "Image Handling with Java-Script"; there, the user could click a hotspot in the image map and the browser would navigate to the associated URL. Here, we'll add some Java-Script to the process—in particular, we'll use *JavaScript URLs*. This technique allows us to treat JavaScript statements as a URL; instead of navigating to a new URL, we'll execute those statements.

For example, we could create a new page, Imap2.htm, with the same two hotspots we used in Chapter 6. This time, however, when users click the Microsoft hotspot, we'll execute some JavaScript and display a message asking if they really want to jump to the Microsoft site.

Start this example, Imap2.htm, by setting up the map we'll use:

```
<HTML>
<HEAD>
<TITLE>
A javascript: Example
</TITLE>
</HEAD>
<BODY>
<CENTER>
<H1>
A javascript: Example
</H1>
<MAP NAME = "IMAP">
<AREA NAME = "link1" COORDS = "54,105,118,125" HREF
        = "javascript: ShowMessage()">
<AREA NAME = "link2" COORDS = "104,53,171,75" HREF
        = "http://www.netscape.com">
</MAP>
        .
        .
        .
```

Note that the URL for the Microsoft site has been replaced. Now it reads "javascript: ShowMessage()." This is a JavaScript URL, which means that instead of navigating to a URL somewhere, the browser is instructed to execute the following JavaScript statement.

To complete the page's HTML, we add the image map itself and the text box we'll use:

```
<HTML>
<HEAD>
<TITLE>
A javascript: Example
</TITLE>
</HEAD>
<BODY>
<CENTER>
<H1>
A javascript: Example
</H1>
<MAP NAME = "IMAP">
<AREA NAME = "link1" COORDS = "54,105,118,125" HREF
        = "javascript: ShowMessage()">
<AREA NAME = "link2" COORDS = "104,53,171,75" HREF
        = "http://www.netscape.com">
</MAP>
<IMG SRC = "imap.gif" WIDTH = 240 HEIGHT = 155 USEMAP =
     "#IMAP">
</CENTER>
<CENTER>
<FORM NAME = form1>
<INPUT TYPE = TEXT NAME = Textbox SIZE = 60>
</FORM>
</CENTER>
</BODY>
```

All that's left is to write the ShowMessage() function. In that function, we display the message in the text box this way:

```
<SCRIPT LANGUAGE = "JavaScript">
function ShowMessage()
{
    document.form1.Textbox.value = "Do you really want to
    go to the
        Microsoft site?"
}
</SCRIPT>
```

That's it—open the page, as shown in Figure 10–10, and click the Microsoft hotspot. When you do, the JavaScript ShowMessage() function is executed and places the message in the text box. Now we're using JavaScript URLs.

The code for this page, Imap2.htm, is shown in Listing 10–11.

Now we come to a topic that's popular among programmers (but less so among users): using cookies. We'll explore working with cookies in JavaScript in the following section.

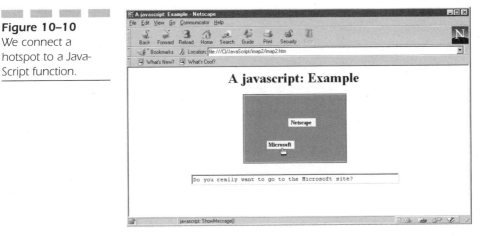

```
<HTML>
<HEAD>
<TITLE>
A javascript: Example
</TITLE>
</HEAD>
<BODY>
<CENTER>
<H1>
A javascript: Example
</H1>
<MAP NAME = "IMAP">
<AREA NAME = "link1" COORDS = "54,105,118,125" HREF
        = "javascript: ShowMessage()">
<AREA NAME = "link2" COORDS = "104,53,171,75" HREF
        = "http://www.netscape.com">
</MAP>
<IMG SRC = "imap.gif" WIDTH = 240 HEIGHT = 155 USEMAP =
    "#IMAP">
</CENTER>
<CENTER>
<FORM NAME = form1>
<INPUT TYPE = TEXT NAME = Textbox SIZE = 60>
</FORM>
</CENTER>
</BODY>
<SCRIPT LANGUAGE = "JavaScript">
function ShowMessage()
{
    document.form1.Textbox.value = "Do you really want to
    go to the
        Microsoft site?"
}
```

continues

```
</SCRIPT>
</HTML>
Sub DoCollections()
    Dim iCollection As New Collection
    iCollection.Add "This is a test", "Test1"
    iCollection.Add "This is a test2"
    MsgBox iCollection.Count
    MsgBox iCollection.Item("Test1")
    MsgBox iCollection.Item(1)
    MsgBox iCollection.Item(2)
    iCollection.Remove (1)
    iCollection.Remove (1)
End Sub
```

Using Cookies from JavaScript

In the next example, we'll store a cookie on the user's computer and retrieve it, all with button clicks. We start this example, Cookie.htm, by displaying two buttons—"Set the cookie" and "Get the cookie"—as well as a text box.

When the user clicks the "Set the cookie" button, we'll set a cookie named "Cookie1" that holds the text "Here's the cookie." in the user's computer. Note that before we do so, the Web browser might warn the user that this is about to happen, depending on the browser's settings. After the cookie is set, we retrieve its text when the user clicks the "Get the cookie" button, displaying that text in the text box.

Start this new example, Cookie.htm, with the button we'll use to set the cookie:

```
<HTML>
<HEAD>
<BODY>
<CENTER>
<H1>
Setting and getting cookies . . .
</H1>
</CENTER>
<FORM NAME = form1>
<CENTER>
<BR>
<INPUT TYPE = BUTTON Value = "Set the cookie" onClick =
    "Set()">  <-
        .
        .
        .
```

Next, add the button we'll use to get the cookie, as well as the text box we'll use to display the cookie's text:

```
<HTML>
<HEAD>
<BODY>
<CENTER>
<H1>
Setting and getting cookies . . .
</H1>
</CENTER>
<FORM NAME = form1>
<CENTER>
<BR>
<INPUT TYPE = BUTTON Value = "Set the cookie" onClick =
     "Set()">
<BR>
<BR>
<INPUT TYPE = BUTTON Value = "Get the cookie" onClick =
     "Get()">
<BR>
<BR>
<INPUT TYPE = TEXT NAME = Textbox>
</CENTER>
</FORM>

</BODY>
```

Now we need to write two functions: Set() to set the cookie and Get() to get the cookie.

Setting a Cookie

In the Set() function, we'll set a cookie with the name "Cookie1" and the text "Here's the cookie.":

```
function Set()
{
   .
   .
   .
}
```

We'll need an expiration time for this cookie; Because this is only a demonstration, we'll set the cookie to last for an hour. To do that, we create a new date object and set its time to an hour from now (the Date object's getTime() method returns the current time in milliseconds):

```
function Set()
{
    var Then = new Date()
    Then.setTime(Then.getTime() + 60 * 60 * 1000)
        .
        .
        .
```

Next, we set the cookie. To do that, we just need to set the document's *cookie* property to the string we want to set. In this case, we give the cookie the name "Cookie1" and set its expiration time by using the keyword *expires* in the cookie string:

```
function Set()
{
    var Then = new Date()
    Then.setTime(Then.getTime() + 60 * 60 * 1000)
    document.cookie = "Cookie1=Here's the cookie.;expires="
        + Then.toGMTString()
}
```

TIP: *The keywords you can set in a cookie's text include expires, path, domain, and secure.*

This sets the cookie, which is now connected to the current document. If the cookie has not expired the next time this same document is read in, we can read it automatically from the document's cookie property. In fact, we'll see how to read the cookie we've set now.

Reading a Cookie

To read the cookie we've set, we simply need to find the cookie in the document.cookie property. We'll do that in the function named Get(), called when the user clicks the "Get the cookie" button:

```
function Get()
{
    .
    .
    .
}
```

TIP: *This function, Get(), can read the cookie as long as it hasn't expired, even if the page is read into the browser at some later time. The whole point of cookies is that they stick around until you want them.*

We start this function by creating a string from the document.cookie property so we can work with that string:

```
function Get()
{
        var cookieString = new String(document.cookie)
             .
             .
             .
```

The string we'll look for in the cookie property is "Cookie1=" because the value of the cookie we set appears immediately after that string. We'll call the string "Cookie1=" the cookie's header:

```
function Get()
{
        var cookieString = new String(document.cookie)
        var cookieHeader = "Cookie1="
             .
             .
             .
```

We find the location of cookie header in the cookie string with the String method indexOf():

```
function Get()
{
        var cookieString = new String(document.cookie)
        var cookieHeader = "Cookie1="
        var beginPosition = cookieString.indexOf(cookieHeader)
             .
             .
             .
```

If the cookie was found, we get the text of the cookie with the String substring() method and display it in the page's text box this way:

```
function Get()
{
        var cookieString = new String(document.cookie)
```

```
var cookieHeader = "Cookie1="
var beginPosition = cookieString.indexOf(cookieHeader)
if (beginPosition != -1){
    document.form1.Textbox.value = cookieString.sub-
  string(beginPosition
          + cookieHeader.length)
}
```

On the other hand, if the cookie was not found, we display an error message:

```
function Get()
{

    var cookieString = new String(document.cookie)
    var cookieHeader = "Cookie1="
    var beginPosition = cookieString.indexOf(cookieHeader)
    if (beginPosition != -1){
        document.form1.Textbox.value = cookieString.sub-
      string(beginPosition
              + cookieHeader.length)
    }
    else{
        document.form1.Textbox.value = "Cookie not found."
    }
}
```

Now open the Cookie.htm example. When the user clicks the button, the browser displays a warning message before setting a cookie, as shown in Figure 10–11.

Figure 10–11
Netscape warns that we are about to set a cookie.

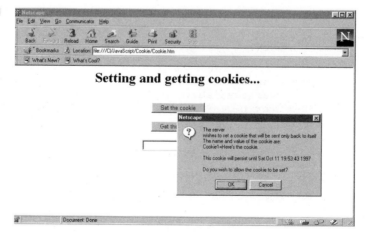

After the cookie is set, we retrieve its text by clicking the "Get the cookie" button, as shown in Figure 10–12, where the program has read the cookie back in and displayed it. Now we're using cookies in JavaScript. The code for this page, Cookie.htm, is shown in Listing 10–12.

Figure 10–12
We retrieve the text of the cookie we've set.

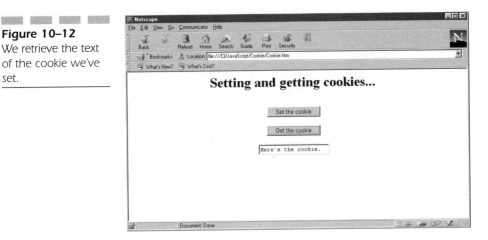

Listing 10–12
Cookie.htm.

```
<HTML>
<HEAD>
<BODY>
<CENTER>
<H1>
Setting and getting cookies . . .
</H1>
</CENTER>
<FORM NAME = form1>
<CENTER>
<BR>
<INPUT TYPE = BUTTON Value = "Set the cookie" onClick =
    "Set()">
<BR>
<BR>
<INPUT TYPE = BUTTON Value = "Get the cookie" onClick =
    "Get()">
<BR>
<BR>
<INPUT TYPE = TEXT NAME = Textbox>
</CENTER>
</FORM>

</BODY>
<SCRIPT LANGUAGE="JavaScript">
```

continues

Listing 10–12
Continued.

```
function Set()
{
    var Then = new Date()
    Then.setTime(Then.getTime() + 60 * 60 * 1000)
    document.cookie = "Cookie1=Here's the cookie.;expires="
        + Then.toGMTString()
}
function Get()
{

    var cookieString = new String(document.cookie)
    var cookieHeader = "Cookie1="
    var beginPosition = cookieString.indexOf(cookieHeader)
    if (beginPosition != -1){
        document.form1.Textbox.value = cookieString.sub-
      string(beginPosition
            + cookieHeader.length)
    }
    else{
        document.form1.Textbox.value = "Cookie not found."
    }
}
</SCRIPT>
</HTML>
```

We will put our cookie knowledge to work now by creating a new page, Welcome.htm, that welcomes users by name to a Web page each time they return.

Using Cookies: The Welcome Page

In the next example, we'll use cookies to store users' names so we can greet them by name when they load the same page again. The first time the user loads the page Welcome.htm, we'll prompt them to enter their name. When they click the OK button, we'll store their name in a cookie. The next time they opens the same page, we'll welcome them by name.

In this example, Welcome.htm, we will name the cookie "Name1." First, we check whether that cookie exists:

```
<HTML>
<SCRIPT LANGUAGE="JavaScript">
    var cookieString = new String(document.cookie)
    var cookieHeader = "Name1="
    var beginPosition = cookieString.indexOf(cookieHeader)
```

.
.
.

If the Name1 cookie exists, the beginPosition variable will hold its position in the cookie string, and we will read the cookie to retrieve the user name. We read the user name from the cookie property like this:

```
<HTML>
<SCRIPT LANGUAGE="JavaScript">
    var cookieString = new String(document.cookie)
    var cookieHeader = "Name1="
    var beginPosition = cookieString.indexOf(cookieHeader)
    if (beginPosition != -1){
        var Name = cookieString.substring(beginPosition
            + cookieHeader.length)
            .
            .
            .
```

Then we display the user's name this way:

```
<HTML>
<SCRIPT LANGUAGE="JavaScript">
    var cookieString = new String(document.cookie)
    var cookieHeader = "Name1="
    var beginPosition = cookieString.indexOf(cookieHeader)
    if (beginPosition != -1){
        var Name = cookieString.substring(beginPosition
            + cookieHeader.length)
        document.write("<BR><BR><CENTER><H1>Hello, " +
    Name + "!</H1><CENTER>")
    }
    .
    .
    .
```

On the other hand, if the Name1 cookie doesn't exist, we display a prompt (as well as a text box and an OK button) asking users to enter their name:

```
<HTML>
<SCRIPT LANGUAGE="JavaScript">
    var cookieString = new String(document.cookie)
    var cookieHeader = "Name1="
    var beginPosition = cookieString.indexOf(cookieHeader)
    if (beginPosition != -1){
        var Name = cookieString.substring(beginPosition
            + cookieHeader.length)
        document.write("<BR><BR><CENTER><H1>Hello, " +
    Name + "!</H1><CENTER>")
    }
```

```
else{
    document.write("<BR><BR>")
    document.write("<CENTER><H1>")
    document.write("Please enter your name and click
OK . . . ")
    document.write("</H1>")
    document.write("<BR>")
    document.write("<FORM NAME = form1>")
    document.write("<INPUT TYPE = TEXT NAME = Name
SIZE = 40>")
    document.write("<BR><BR>")
    document.write("<INPUT TYPE = BUTTON VALUE = 'OK'
onClick
        = 'storeName()'>")
    document.write("</FORM>")

}
```

When users click the OK button, we store their name in a cookie in the storeName() function:

```
function storeName()
{
    .
    .
    .
}
```

We'll give this new cookie a week before it expires, setting up a date object this way:

```
function storeName()
{
    var Then = new Date()
    Then.setTime(Then.getTime() + 7 * 24 * 60 * 60 *
1000)
        .
        .
        .
}
```

All that's left is to set the cookie, as shown here:

```
function storeName()
{
    var Then = new Date()
    Then.setTime(Then.getTime() + 7 * 24 * 60 * 60 *
1000)
    document.cookie = "Name1=" +
document.form1.Name.value + ";expires="
        + Then.toGMTString()
}
```

That's it—now open the Welcome page. The first time users open this page, it asks them for their name, as shown in Figure 10–13.

When users enter their name and click OK, the page stores it in a cookie. The next time users open the same page, we can greet them by name, as shown in Figure 10–14. Our Welcome.htm page is a powerful example of what you can do with JavaScript.

The code for this page, Welcome.htm, is shown in Listing 10–13.

Figure 10–13
We set a cookie storing the user's name.

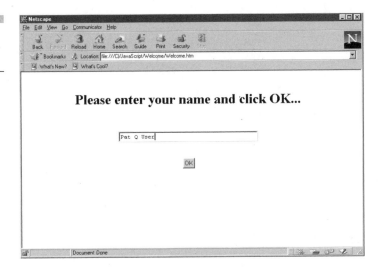

Figure 10–14
We retrieve the user's name from a cookie.

Listing 10–13
Welcome.htm.

```
<HTML>
<SCRIPT LANGUAGE="JavaScript">
    var cookieString = new String(document.cookie)
    var cookieHeader = "Name1="
    var beginPosition = cookieString.indexOf(cookieHeader)
    if (beginPosition != -1){
        var Name = cookieString.substring(beginPosition
            + cookieHeader.length)
        document.write("<BR><BR><CENTER><H1>Hello, " +
    Name + "!</H1><CENTER>")
    }
    else{
        document.write("<BR><BR>")
        document.write("<CENTER><H1>")
        document.write("Please enter your name and click
    OK . . . ")
        document.write("</H1>")
        document.write("<BR>")
        document.write("<FORM NAME = form1>")
        document.write("<INPUT TYPE = TEXT NAME = Name
    SIZE = 40>")
        document.write("<BR><BR>")
        document.write("<INPUT TYPE = BUTTON VALUE = 'OK'
    onClick
            = 'storeName()'>")
        document.write("</FORM>")
    }
    function storeName()
    {
        var Then = new Date()
        Then.setTime(Then.getTime() + 7 * 24 * 60 * 60 *
    1000)
        document.cookie = "Name1=" +
    document.form1.Name.value + ";expires="
            + Then.toGMTString()
    }
</SCRIPT>
</HTML>
```

We've been working with the browser window a lot in this chapter, and there's one more example we'll try. This next example doesn't have to do with navigation directly, but it's still a popular topic in JavaScript: setting the text in the browser's status bar.

Changing the Status Bar Text

In the last example of this chapter, we'll see how to change the text in the browser's status bar, which appears at the bottom of the browser window. With the click of a button, we can change the text in the status bar.

Let's see this in action. Start this page, Status.htm, with the button the user can click to change the status bar message:

```
<HTML>
<HEAD>
<TITLE>
A Status Bar Example
</TITLE>
</HEAD>
<BODY>
<CENTER>
<H1>
A Status Bar Example.
</H1>
</CENTER>
<CENTER>
<FORM>
<BR>
<BR>
<INPUT TYPE = BUTTON Value = "Change Status Bar Text"
      onClick
          = "ShowMessage()">
</FORM>
</CENTER>
</BODY>
```

In the <SCRIPT> element, we start by giving the browser window the original status text, which we place in the window's *defaultStatus* property:

```
<SCRIPT LANGUAGE = JavaScript>
    window.defaultStatus = "Here is the status bar . . . "
        .
        .
        .
```

The button in this page is tied to the function named ShowMessage(). In that function, we just reset the default status text to the new message:

```
<SCRIPT LANGUAGE = JavaScript>
    window.defaultStatus = "Here is the status bar . . . "
    function ShowMessage()
    {
        window.defaultStatus = "Welcome to JavaScript!"
    }
</SCRIPT>
</HTML>
```

Open this page now, as shown in Figure 10–15. You can see the original status bar text displayed in the status bar.

When you click the button in this page, the browser changes the text in the status bar to the new version, as shown in Figure 10–16. In this way, we can dynamically set the text in the browser's status bar.

Figure 10–15
We can set the text in the page's status bar.

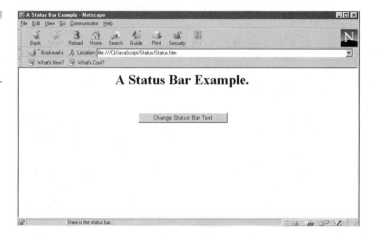

Figure 10–16
We set the status bar text to a specific message.

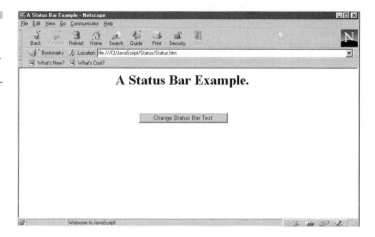

You can also change the status bar text by setting the window's status property. This method just changes the text in the status bar temporarily, until replaced by the default text (if you've set any default text in the status bar).

The code for this page, Status.htm, is shown in Listing 10–14.

Listing 10–14
Status.htm.

```
<HTML>
<HEAD>
<TITLE>
A Status Bar Example
</TITLE>
</HEAD>
<BODY>
<CENTER>
<H1>
A Status Bar Example.
</H1>
</CENTER>
<CENTER>
<FORM>
<BR>
<BR>
<INPUT TYPE = BUTTON Value = "Change Status Bar Text"
     onClick
          = "ShowMessage()">
</FORM>
</CENTER>
</BODY>
<SCRIPT LANGUAGE = JavaScript>
    window.defaultStatus = "Here is the status bar . . . "
    function ShowMessage()
    {
          window.defaultStatus = "Welcome to JavaScript!"
    }
</SCRIPT>
</HTML>
```

CONCLUSION

That example completes this chapter. We've explored the navigator, location, and history objects. We've also learned how to get information about the browser, create a slideshow, jump to a new URL, move forward or backward by using the history object, send information in a URL, use JavaScript URLs, use cookies, create a customized Web page that greets the user by name, and set the text in the status bar. We've gained many new skills in this chapter.

In the next chapter, we'll continue our exploration of JavaScript as we see how to connect it to Java.

11

Connecting JavaScript and Java

In this chapter, we'll see how to connect JavaScript to another Web programming language: Sun Microsystem's Java language. Java and JavaScript will both benefit from the connection because some things that aren't possible in one language are possible in the other.

For example, JavaScript has more control over the Web page than an applet does, so we'll learn how to use JavaScript to rewrite a whole Web page from Java, something not usually possible. On the other hand, Java has more control over other parts of Web programming, such as GUI handling. In this chapter, we'll cover how to control a very visual Java applet from JavaScript. In this way, we'll see how to do things from JavaScript that aren't usually possible in JavaScript—and things from Java that aren't usually possible from JavaScript—all because we can connect the two languages.

> *TIP:* *This chapter requires some knowledge of Java programming techniques.*

We'll cover a lot in this chapter: how to connect to a Java applet from JavaScript, how to pass arguments to that applet's methods, how to receive return values from those methods, how to pass strings to applet methods, how to use Java statements directly in JavaScript (we'll open a window and place a Java text field in that window from JavaScript), and how to use JavaScript from Java to rewrite a Web page (this last technique is especially powerful because it gives applets total control over Web pages, which they don't usually have).

We'll begin by developing a Java applet with several methods that we can reach from scripts in the same page. We'll use and modify this applet throughout the chapter.

The Suspend Applet

Our Java applet will be called "Suspend." This applet displays an animated graphic image—a whirling disk—and two buttons, Suspend and Resume. When the user clicks the Suspend button, the applet stops the disk from spinning; when the user clicks the Resume button, we'll start the disk again. These are the two functions—suspending and resuming the animation—that we'll perform from JavaScript when we connect a script to the applet.

> *TIP:* *We'll use Java 1.0 in this example because at the time of this writing, it's by far the most common Java version; note, however, that using Java 1.1 or 1.2 won't substantially change the following examples.*

Let's start the Suspend example by importing the Java AWT classes and the Applet class in a new file, Suspend.java:

```
import java.awt.*;
import java.applet.Applet;
        .
        .
        .
```

Next, we declare our new class, Suspend, extending the Applet class and implementing the Java Runnable interface (because our applet supports animation and will be multi-threaded):

```
import java.awt.*;
import java.applet.Applet;
public class Suspend extends Applet implements
  Runnable{
      .
      .
      .
```

We'll use four images to support the animation; each one will show a circle divided into four quadrants. A different quadrant will be colored in each image, so when we flash the images onscreen in rapid succession, the result will be a single disk appearing to spin around.

Here's how we load the four images, Wheel1.gif to Wheel4.gif, into an array of Java image objects named "images[]" and add the Suspend and Resume buttons in the init() method:

```
import java.awt.*;
import java.applet.Applet;
public class Suspend extends Applet implements
  Runnable{
      Image images[] = new Image[4];
      Image currentImage;
      Button buttonSuspend, buttonResume;
      public void init()
      {
            images[0] = getImage(getCodeBase(),
"Wheel1.gif");
            images[1] = getImage(getCodeBase(),
"Wheel2.gif");
            images[2] = getImage(getCodeBase(),
"Wheel3.gif");
            images[3] = getImage(getCodeBase(),
"Wheel4.gif");
            buttonSuspend = new Button("Suspend");
            add(buttonSuspend);
            buttonResume = new Button("Resume");
            add(buttonResume);
      }
```

We will also add an action() method to handle the button clicks. In this method, we call a new method, suspend(), when the user clicks the Suspend button, and another new method, resume(), when the user clicks the Resume button:

```
public boolean action (Event e, Object o)
{
      if(e.target.equals(buttonSuspend)){
          suspend();
      }
```

```
     if(e.target.equals(buttonResume)){
          resume();
     }
     return true;
}
```

Now we'll support the animation itself by creating a new thread, thread1. We create and start that thread in the applet's start() method and stop it in the applet's stop() method:

```
import java.awt.*;
import java.applet.Applet;
public class Suspend extends Applet implements
  Runnable{
     Image images[] = new Image[4];
     Image currentImage;
     Thread thread1;
     Button buttonSuspend, buttonResume;
        .
        .
        .
     public void start()
     {
          thread1 = new Thread(this);
          thread1.start();
     }
     public void stop()
     {
          thread1.stop();
     }
```

The actual animation occurs in the run() method, which is called when the new thread starts. Here, we will loop continuously (or until the page is dismissed from the browser, which calls the applet's stop() method), cycling over the images using a variable named "loop_index":

```
import java.awt.*;
import java.applet.Applet;
public class Suspend extends Applet implements
  Runnable{
     Image images[] = new Image[4];
     Image currentImage;
     int loop_index = 0;
     Thread thread1;
     Button buttonSuspend, buttonResume;
        .
        .
        .
     public void start()
     {
```

```
        thread1 = new Thread(this);
        thread1.start();
}
public void stop()
{
        thread1.stop();
}
public void run()
{
        while(true){
            currentImage = images[loop_index++];
            if(loop_index > 3)loop_index = 0;
            repaint();
            try {Thread.sleep(250);}
            catch(InterruptedException exp) { }
        }
}
```

Note that we put the thread to sleep for 250 milliseconds each time through the loop, pausing for a quarter of a second between displaying successive images. Each time through the loop in the run() method, we load a new image into an image object we name "currentImage," and then call the Java repaint() method to display that image. Calling repaint() forces Java to call the applet's paint()method, so we display the image in currentImage in paint():

```
public void paint (Graphics g)
{
        if(currentImage != null){
            g.drawImage(currentImage, 100, 100, this);
        }
}
```

TIP: _We check the currentImage object to see whether it's null before display-ing it because loading the images into the applet is a time-consuming process. Until the images are loaded, we shouldn't try to display them._

That completes the animation. All that's left is to suspend the anima-tion when the user clicks the Suspend button and resume it when the user clicks the Resume button. We'll do that in the suspend() and resume() methods, called when the user clicks the Suspend or Resume buttons:

```
public void suspend()
{
```

```
        .
        .
        .
}
public void resume()
{
        .
        .
        .
}
```

To suspend the animation, use the Java Thread class's suspend() method, and to resume the animation, use the Thread class's resume() method:

```
public void suspend()
{
        thread1.suspend();
}
public void resume()
{
        thread1.resume();
}
```

That's it—our Suspend applet is finished. If we place it in a Web page (after compiling Suspend.java to Suspend.class by using the Java compiler, *javac*), it would look like Figure 11–1. You can see the whirling disk in that figure, as well as the Suspend and Resume buttons. Our Java applet is ready to connect to JavaScript.

The code for this applet, Suspend.java, is shown in Listing 11–1.

Figure 11–1
Our Java Suspend applet.

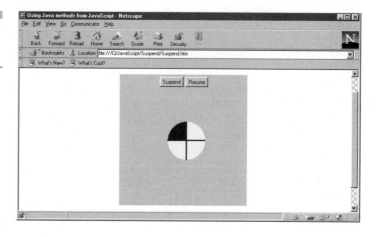

```
import java.awt.*;
import java.applet.Applet;
public class Suspend extends Applet implements
  Runnable{
    Image images[] = new Image[4];
    Image currentImage;
    int loop_index = 0;
    Thread thread1;
    Button buttonSuspend, buttonResume;
    public void init()
    {
        images[0] = getImage(getCodeBase(),
"Wheel1.gif");
        images[1] = getImage(getCodeBase(),
"Wheel2.gif");
        images[2] = getImage(getCodeBase(),
"Wheel3.gif");
        images[3] = getImage(getCodeBase(),
"Wheel4.gif");
        buttonSuspend = new Button("Suspend");
        add(buttonSuspend);
        buttonResume = new Button("Resume");
        add(buttonResume);
    }
    public boolean action (Event e, Object o)
    {
        if(e.target.equals(buttonSuspend)){
            suspend();
        }
        if(e.target.equals(buttonResume)){
            resume();
        }
        return true;
    }
    public void suspend()
    {
        thread1.suspend();
    }
    public void resume()
    {
        thread1.resume();
    }
    public void start()
    {
        thread1 = new Thread(this);
        thread1.start();
    }
    public void stop()
    {
        thread1.stop();
```

continues

```
        }
        public void run()
        {
            while(true){
                currentImage = images[loop_index++];
                if(loop_index > 3)loop_index = 0;
                repaint();
                try {Thread.sleep(250);}
                catch(InterruptedException exp){ }
            }
        }
        public void paint (Graphics g)
        {
            if(currentImage != null){
                g.drawImage(currentImage, 100, 100, this);
            }
        }
    }
```

Now let's connect the applet to JavaScript.

Reaching Java Methods from JavaScript: The Suspend Example

We've seen enough Java for the moment; now let's see some JavaScript. In our next example, Suspend.htm, we'll embed the applet we just created —and some JavaScript—in the same Web page. We'll add two buttons, "Suspend applet" and "Resume applet," to the page.

When the user clicks the "Suspend applet" button, we'll call the applet's suspend() method to suspend the animation; when the user clicks the "Resume applet" button, we'll call the applet's resume() method to resume the animation.

First, we place the Suspend.class applet in the Web page using the <APPLET> tag:

```
<HTML>
<HEAD>
<TITLE>
Using Java methods from JavaScript
</TITLE>
</HEAD>
<BODY>
<CENTER>
```

```
<H1>
Controlling a Java method from JavaScript
</H1>
</CENTER>
<CENTER>
<APPLET
    CODE="Suspend.class" WIDTH="300" HEIGHT="300" MAYSCRIPT>
</APPLET>
</CENTER>
    .
    .
    .
```

Note that we've included the MAYSCRIPT attribute in the <AP-PLET> tag, indicating to the browser that we'll connect this applet to a script. This is a necessary step—you must use MAYSCRIPT before you can reach an applet from JavaScript.

Next, add the two buttons we'll use, "Suspend applet" and "Resume applet":

```
<HTML>
<HEAD>
<TITLE>
Using Java methods from JavaScript
</TITLE>
</HEAD>
<BODY>
<CENTER>
<H1>
Controlling a Java method from JavaScript
</H1>
</CENTER>
<CENTER>
<APPLET
    CODE="Suspend.class" WIDTH="300" HEIGHT="300" MAYSCRIPT>
</APPLET>
</CENTER>
<FORM NAME = form1>
<CENTER>
<INPUT TYPE = BUTTON VALUE = "Suspend applet" onClick =
    "suspend()">
<INPUT TYPE = BUTTON VALUE = "Resume applet" onClick = "re-
    sume()">
</CENTER>
</FORM>
    .
    .
    .
```

We connect those buttons to two JavaScript functions, suspend() and resume():

```
<SCRIPT LANGUAGE = JavaScript>
function suspend()
{
  .
  .
  .
}
function resume()
{
  .
  .
  .
}
</SCRIPT>
```

Now we can connect these functions to the applet.

Reaching an Applet From JavaScript

In the suspend() JavaScript function, we want to call the applet's suspend() method. That's easier than you might think. All we have to do is to use the document object's applets[] collection to reach the applet. Because we have only one applet in this page, we can refer to that applet as document.applets[0], and we can reach the applet's internal suspend() method as shown here:

```
function suspend()
{
    document.applets[0].suspend()
}
```

NOTE: *To reach an applet's methods or properties, those items must have been declared public in the applet.*

TIP: *Just as you can use the applets[] collection to reach the applets in a page, you can use the plugins[] collection to reach plug-ins.*

In the same way, we can connect the "Resume applet" button to the applet's internal resume() method this way:

```
function resume()
{
    document.applets[0].resume()
}
```

Open this new page, Suspend.htm, as shown in Figure 11–2. You can see our new "Suspend applet" and "Resume applet" buttons in that page; if you click the "Suspend applet" button, the whirling disk in the applet stops. If you click the "Resume applet" button, the whirling disk starts again. Now we can reach the internal methods of an applet from Java-Script.

The code for this page, Suspend.htm, is shown in Listing 11–2.

Figure 11–2
Our Suspend page controls an applet.

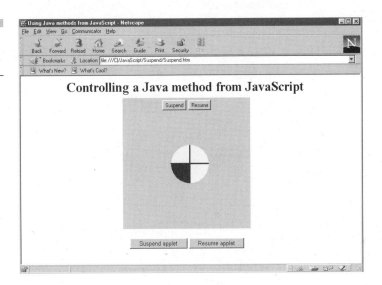

Listing 11–2
Suspend.htm.

```
<HTML>
<HEAD>
<TITLE>
Using Java methods from JavaScript
</TITLE>
</HEAD>
<BODY>
<CENTER>
<H1>
Controlling a Java method from JavaScript
</H1>
</CENTER>
<CENTER>
<APPLET
    CODE="Suspend.class" WIDTH="300" HEIGHT="300" MAYSCRIPT>
</APPLET>
</CENTER>
<FORM NAME = form1>
<CENTER>
<INPUT TYPE = BUTTON VALUE = "Suspend applet" onClick =
```

continues

Listing 15-1.
Continued.

```
        "suspend()">
<INPUT TYPE = BUTTON VALUE = "Resume applet" onClick = "re-
    sume()">
</CENTER>
</FORM>
</BODY>
<SCRIPT LANGUAGE = JavaScript>
function suspend()
{
    document.applets[0].suspend()
}
function resume()
{
    document.applets[0].resume()
}
</SCRIPT>
</HTML>
```

Now we're ready to take the next step—passing arguments to a Java method from JavaScript.

Passing Arguments to Java from JavaScript: The Suspend2 Example

In the next example, we'll pass arguments from JavaScript to Java. In particular, we will change the time the applet pauses between displaying images by passing a new value from JavaScript. Currently, that time is 250 milliseconds:

```
public void run()
{
    while(true){
        currentImage = images[loop_index++];
        if(loop_index > 3)loop_index = 0;
        repaint();
        try {Thread.sleep(250);}
        catch(InterruptedException exp){ }
    }
}
```

In this example, we'll see how to reset that value from a JavaScript function, creating a new version of the Suspend example. This new example, Suspend2, will display one JavaScript button, "Reset spin time."

When the user clicks this button, we'll pass a new animation delay to the applet—50 milliseconds—causing the disk to whirl around faster.

As the Suspend applet is written now, the delay between images is 250 milliseconds:

```
public void run()
{
    while(true){
        currentImage = images[loop_index++];
        if(loop_index > 3)loop_index = 0;
        repaint();
        try {Thread.sleep(250);}
        catch(InterruptedException exp){ }
    }
}
```

Let's place that value in a variable named "time" so we can change it at will:

```
import java.awt.*;
import java.applet.Applet;
public class Suspend2 extends Applet implements
  Runnable{
    Image images[] = new Image[4];
    Image currentImage;
    int loop_index = 0;
    Thread thread1;
    Button buttonSuspend, buttonResume;
    int time = 250;
        .
        .
        .
    public void run()
    {
        while(true){
            currentImage = images[loop_index++];
            if(loop_index > 3)loop_index = 0;
            repaint();
            try {Thread.sleep(time);}
            catch(InterruptedException exp) { }
        }
    }
}
```

Next, we need some way of getting the new delay time from our Java-Script code, so we set up a new method, resetTime(), in the applet. In that method, we're passed the new time (in milliseconds) for the time variable, and we simply load that variable as shown here:

```
public boolean action (Event e, Object o)
{
```

```
            if(e.target.equals(buttonSuspend)){
                suspend();
            }
            if(e.target.equals(buttonResume)){
                resume();
            }
            return true;
    }
    public void suspend()
    {
        thread1.suspend();

    }
    public void resetTime(int x)
    {
        time = x;
    }
    public void resume()
    {
        thread1.resume();

    }
    public void start()
    {
        thread1 = new Thread(this);
        thread1.start();
    }
```

Using the resetTime() method, then, we can reset the applet's animation delay. Now we will write the new Web page, Suspend2.htm, with the
controls and the script that we'll need. Here's how we add the applet and
the "Reset spin time" button to this page:

```
<HTML>
<HEAD>
</HEAD>
<BODY>
<CENTER>
<H1>
Passing Arguments from JavaScript to Java
</H1>
</CENTER>
<CENTER>
<APPLET
    CODE="Suspend2.class" WIDTH="300" HEIGHT="300"
    MAYSCRIPT>
</APPLET>
</CENTER>
<FORM NAME = form1>
<CENTER>
<INPUT TYPE = BUTTON VALUE = "Reset spin time" onClick =
    "resetTime()">
```

```
</CENTER>
</FORM>
</BODY>
```

When the user clicks the "Reset spin time" button, the JavaScript resetTime() function is called, and we can call the applet's resetTime() method, passing it a value of 50 milliseconds:

```
<SCRIPT LANGUAGE = JavaScript>
function resetTime()
{
    document.applets[0].resetTime(50)
}
</SCRIPT>
```

Now open this page, as shown in Figure 11–3, and click the "Reset spin time" button. When you click that button, the disk starts spinning faster. Now we can pass numeric arguments to applet methods.

TIP: *Even though JavaScript is an untyped language and Java is strongly typed, the applet determines what type of variable you're passing to a Java method by checking the declared types of the method's arguments.*

The code for this applet, Suspend2.java, is shown in Listing 11–3, and the Web page, Suspend2.htm, in Listing 11–4.

Figure 11–3
We pass arguments to a Java applet.

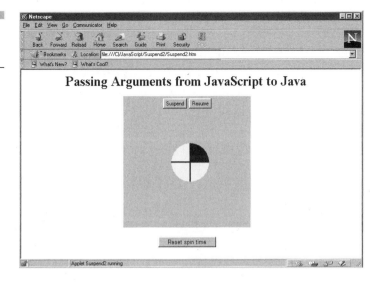

```java
import java.awt.*;
import java.applet.Applet;
public class Suspend2 extends Applet implements
 Runnable{
    Image images[] = new Image[4];
    Image currentImage;
    int loop_index = 0;
    Thread thread1;
    Button buttonSuspend, buttonResume;
    int time = 250;
    public void init()
    {
        images[0] = getImage(getCodeBase(),
 "Wheel1.gif");
        images[1] = getImage(getCodeBase(),
 "Wheel2.gif");
        images[2] = getImage(getCodeBase(),
 "Wheel3.gif");
        images[3] = getImage(getCodeBase(),
 "Wheel4.gif");
        buttonSuspend = new Button("Suspend");
        add(buttonSuspend);
        buttonResume = new Button("Resume");
        add(buttonResume);
    }
    public boolean action (Event e, Object o)
    {
        if(e.target.equals(buttonSuspend)){
            suspend();
        }
        if(e.target.equals(buttonResume)){
            resume();
        }
        return true;
    }
    public void suspend()
    {
        thread1.suspend();

    }
    public void resetTime(int x)
    {
        time = x;
    }
    public void resume()
    {
        thread1.resume();

    }
    public void start()
    {
        thread1 = new Thread(this);
        thread1.start();
    }
```

```
        public void stop()
        {
            thread1.stop();
        }
        public void run()
        {
            while(true){
                currentImage = images[loop_index++];
                if(loop_index > 3)loop_index = 0;
                repaint();
                try {Thread.sleep(time);}
                catch(InterruptedException exp) { }
            }
        }
        public void paint (Graphics g)
        {
            if(currentImage != null){
                g.drawImage(currentImage, 100, 100, this);
            }
        }    }
```

Listing 11–4
Suspend2.htm.

```
<HTML>
<HEAD>
</HEAD>
<BODY>
<CENTER>
<H1>
Passing Arguments from JavaScript to Java
</H1>
</CENTER>
<CENTER>
<APPLET
    CODE="Suspend2.class" WIDTH="300" HEIGHT="300"
    MAYSCRIPT>
</APPLET>
</CENTER>
<FORM NAME = form1>
<CENTER>
<INPUT TYPE = BUTTON VALUE = "Reset spin time" onClick =
    "resetTime()">
</CENTER>
</FORM>
</BODY>
<SCRIPT LANGUAGE = JavaScript>
function resetTime()
{
    document.applets[0].resetTime(50)
}
</SCRIPT>
</HTML>
```

Besides numeric data, we can pass other types of data, such as strings, to Java applets.

Passing Strings from JavaScript to Java: The PassString Example

In the next example, we'll see how to pass string data to applets from JavaScript. For example, we can pass control strings from JavaScript to the applet. If we pass, say, the string "suspend" to the applet, it should stop the disk from spinning. If we pass the string "resume", it should start the applet spinning again. We'll use the same buttons in this example: "Suspend applet" and "Resume applet."

In this example, PassString, we just have to add a new method, read-String(), to the applet. If we pass the string "suspend" to readString(), that method will call the applet's suspend() method; if we pass the string "resume" to the applet, it calls the resume() method:

```
import java.awt.*;
import java.applet.Applet;
public class PassString extends Applet implements
  Runnable{
    Image images[] = new Image[4];
    Image currentImage;
    int loop_index = 0;
    Thread thread1;
    Button buttonSuspend, buttonResume;
    int time = 250;
        .
        .
        .
    public void suspend()
    {
        thread1.suspend();
    }
    public void readString(String inString)
    {
        if(inString.equals("suspend")){
            suspend();
        }
        if(inString.equals("resume")){
            resume();
        }
    }
    public void resume()
    {
        thread1.resume();
```

```
        }
    public void start()
    {
        thread1 = new Thread(this);
        thread1.start();
    }
```

That's all it takes—the JavaScript/Java interface is set up to handle the details. All we have to do is to pass a string to the readString() method. We'll do that in JavaScript in a new page, PassString.htm, starting that page with the "Suspend applet" and "Resume applet" buttons:

```
<HTML>
<HEAD>
<TITLE>
Passing a string from JavaScript to Java
</TITLE>
</HEAD>
<BODY>
<CENTER>
<H1>
Passing a string from JavaScript to Java
</H1>
</CENTER>
<CENTER>
<APPLET
    CODE="PassString.class" WIDTH="300" HEIGHT="300"
    MAYSCRIPT>
</APPLET>
</CENTER>
<FORM NAME = form1>
<CENTER>
<INPUT TYPE = BUTTON VALUE = "Suspend applet" onClick =
    "suspend()">
<INPUT TYPE = BUTTON VALUE = "Resume applet" onClick = "re-
    sume()">
</CENTER>
</FORM>
</BODY>
```

In the JavaScript suspend() and resume() functions, we simply pass the required string to the applet this way:

```
<SCRIPT LANGUAGE = JavaScript>
function suspend()
{
    document.applets[0].readString("suspend")
}
function resume()
{
    document.applets[0].readString("resume")
}
</SCRIPT>
```

Now open the page, as shown in Figure 11–4. When you click the "Suspend applet" button, the JavaScript function suspend() passes the control string "suspend" to the applet and the disk stops whirling; when you click the "Resume applet" button, the resume() function passes the control string "resume" to that applet and the disk starts again. Now we can pass control strings to applets from JavaScript.

The code for this applet, PassString.java, is shown in Listing 11–5, and the code for the Web page, PassString.htm, in Listing 11–6.

Figure 11–4
We pass control strings to an applet.

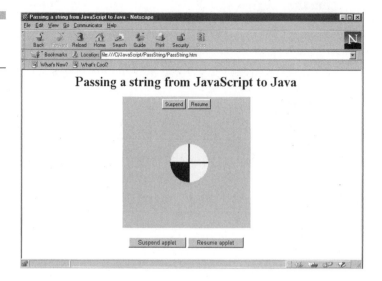

Listing 11–5
PassString.java.

```
import java.awt.*;
import java.applet.Applet;
public class PassString extends Applet implements
 Runnable{
    Image images[] = new Image[4];
    Image currentImage;
    int loop_index = 0;
    Thread thread1;
    Button buttonSuspend, buttonResume;
    int time = 250;
    public void init()
    {
        images[0] = getImage(getCodeBase(),
"Wheel1.gif");
        images[1] = getImage(getCodeBase(),
"Wheel2.gif");
        images[2] = getImage(getCodeBase(),
"Wheel3.gif");
```

```
            images[3] = getImage(getCodeBase(),
    "Wheel4.gif");
        buttonSuspend = new Button("Suspend");
        add(buttonSuspend);
        buttonResume = new Button("Resume");
        add(buttonResume);
    }
    public boolean action (Event e, Object o)
    {
        if(e.target.equals(buttonSuspend)){
            suspend();
        }
        if(e.target.equals(buttonResume)){
            resume();
        }
        return true;
    }
    public void suspend()
    {
        thread1.suspend();
    }
    public void readString(String inString)
    {
        if(inString.equals("suspend")){
            suspend();
        }
        if(inString.equals("resume")){
            resume();
        }
    }
    public void resume()
    {
        thread1.resume();
    }
    public void start()
    {
        thread1 = new Thread(this);
        thread1.start();
    }
    public void stop()
    {
        thread1.stop();
    }
    public void run()
    {
        while(true){
            currentImage = images[loop_index++];
            if(loop_index > 3)loop_index = 0;
            repaint();
            try {Thread.sleep(time);}
            catch(InterruptedException exp) { }
```

continues

Listing 11–5

Continued.

```
            }
        }
        public void paint (Graphics g)
        {
            if(currentImage != null){
                g.drawImage(currentImage, 100, 100, this);
            }
        }
    }
```

Listing 11–6

PassString.htm.

```
<HTML>
<HEAD>
<TITLE>
Passing a string from JavaScript to Java
</TITLE>
</HEAD>
<BODY>
<CENTER>
<H1>
Passing a string from JavaScript to Java
</H1>
</CENTER>
<CENTER>
<APPLET
    CODE="PassString.class" WIDTH="300" HEIGHT="300"
    MAYSCRIPT>
</APPLET>
</CENTER>
<FORM NAME = form1>
<CENTER>
<INPUT TYPE = BUTTON VALUE = "Suspend applet" onClick =
    "suspend()">
<INPUT TYPE = BUTTON VALUE = "Resume applet" onClick = "re-
    sume()">
</CENTER>
</FORM>
</BODY>
<SCRIPT LANGUAGE = JavaScript>
function suspend()
{
    document.applets[0].readString("suspend")
}
function resume()
{
    document.applets[0].readString("resume")
}
</SCRIPT>
</HTML>
```

We've seen how to pass arguments to Java applet methods from JavaScript, but we haven't see how to read the values that such methods return. All we've done so far is pass arguments to Java methods, not read their return values. We'll see how to read these values in the following section.

Returning Values From Java to JavaScript: The RetVal Example

In the next example, RetVal, we'll see how to return a value from a Java method to a JavaScript function. Here, we'll add a new JavaScript button, "Get spin time," to our Web page that reads the current spin delay from the applet.

When the user clicks that button, we can call a new method in the applet—getSpeed()—and we'll display the return value from that method in a text box. In this way, we can get a return value from an applet method and display that value in the Web page.

We start by setting up the getSpeed() method in the applet. All that method does is return the current animation delay, which is stored in the variable named "time." In other words, all we have to do is return that variable from the getSpeed() method:

```java
import java.awt.*;
    import java.applet.Applet;
    public class RetVal extends Applet implements Runnable{
        Image images[] = new Image[4];
        Image currentImage;
        int loop_index = 0;
        Thread thread1;
        Button buttonSuspend, buttonResume;
        int time = 250;
             .
             .
             .
        public boolean action (Event e, Object o)
        {
            if(e.target.equals(buttonSuspend)){
                suspend();
            }
            if(e.target.equals(buttonResume)){
                resume();
            }
            return true;
```

```
    }
    public void resetTime(int newTime)
    {
        time = newTime;
    }
    public int getSpeed()
    {
        return time;
    }
    public void resume()
    {
        thread1.resume();

    }
```

That's it for the Java part of this example. In fact, there's not much more we have to do in JavaScript, either. Here's how we set up the "Get spin time" button in the Web page RetVal.htm:

```
<HTML>
<HEAD>
<TITLE>
Returning values from Java to JavaScript
</TITLE>
</HEAD>
<BODY>
<CENTER>
<H1>
Returning values from Java to JavaScript
</H1>
</CENTER>
<CENTER>
<APPLET
    CODE="RetVal.class" WIDTH="300" HEIGHT="300" MAYSCRIPT>
</APPLET>
</CENTER>
<FORM NAME = form1>
<CENTER>
<INPUT TYPE = BUTTON VALUE = "Reset spin time" onClick =
    "resetTime()">
<INPUT TYPE = BUTTON VALUE = "Get spin time" onClick =
    "getSpeed()">
<BR>
<INPUT TYPE = TEXT NAME = Textbox>
</CENTER>
</FORM>
</BODY>
```

This new button is connected to the JavaScript function getSpeed(). In that function, all we do is call the applet's getSpeed() method and treat the return value as we would one from any other JavaScript function.

That means we can display the current animation delay in the page's text box as shown here:

```
<SCRIPT LANGUAGE = JavaScript>
function resetTime()
{
    document.applets[0].resetTime(50)
}
function getSpeed()
{
    document.form1.Textbox.value = "Spin time = "
        + document.applets[0].getSpeed()
}
</SCRIPT>
```

The Java/JavaScript interface handles all the rest of the details for us. This interface is even more impressive when you consider that Java is a very strongly typed language, with ints, doubles, floats, and so on. Nonetheless, those values are translated into JavaScript variables automatically for us.

Open this page, as shown in Figure 11–5. If you click the "Reset spin time" button, the animation delay is set from 250 milliseconds to 50 in the applet. If you click the "Get spin time" button, we call the applet's get-Speed() method, displaying that method's return value. Now we're retrieving values returned to us from Java methods.

Figure 11–5
We return a value from Java to Java-Script.

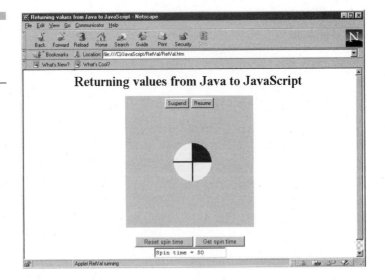

The code for this applet, RetVal.java, is shown in Listing 11–7, and the code for the corresponding Web page, RetVal.htm, is shown in Listing 11–8.

Listing 11–7
RetVal.java.

```java
import java.awt.*;
import java.applet.Applet;
public class RetVal extends Applet implements Runnable{
    Image images[] = new Image[4];
    Image currentImage;
    int loop_index = 0;
    Thread thread1;
    Button buttonSuspend, buttonResume;
    int time = 250;
    public void init()
    {
        images[0] = getImage(getCodeBase(),
"Wheel1.gif");
        images[1] = getImage(getCodeBase(),
"Wheel2.gif");
        images[2] = getImage(getCodeBase(),
"Wheel3.gif");
        images[3] = getImage(getCodeBase(),
"Wheel4.gif");
        buttonSuspend = new Button("Suspend");
        add(buttonSuspend);
        buttonResume = new Button("Resume");
        add(buttonResume);
    }
    public boolean action (Event e, Object o)
    {
        if(e.target.equals(buttonSuspend)){
            suspend();
        }
        if(e.target.equals(buttonResume)){
            resume();
        }
        return true;
    }
    public void suspend()
    {
        thread1.suspend();

    }
    public void resetTime(int newTime)
    {
        time = newTime;
    }
    public int getSpeed()
    {
        return time;
    }
```

```
        public void resume()
        {
            thread1.resume();


        }
        public void start()
        {
            thread1 = new Thread(this);
            thread1.start();
        }
        public void stop()
        {
            thread1.stop();
        }
        public void run()
        {
            while(true){
                currentImage = images[loop_index++];
                if(loop_index > 3)loop_index = 0;
                repaint();
                try {Thread.sleep(time);}
                catch(InterruptedException exp) { }
            }
        }
        public void paint (Graphics g)
        {
            if(currentImage != null){
                g.drawImage(currentImage, 100, 100, this);
            }
        }
```

Listing 11-8
RetVal.htm.

```
<HTML>
<HEAD>
<TITLE>
Returning values from Java to JavaScript
</TITLE>
</HEAD>
<BODY>
<CENTER>
<H1>
Returning values from Java to JavaScript
</H1>
</CENTER>
<CENTER>
<APPLET
    CODE="RetVal.class" WIDTH="300" HEIGHT="300" MAYSCRIPT>
</APPLET>
</CENTER>
<FORM NAME = form1>
<CENTER>
```

continues

Listing 11–8
Continued.

```
<INPUT TYPE = BUTTON VALUE = "Reset spin time" onClick =
    "resetTime()">
<INPUT TYPE = BUTTON VALUE = "Get spin time" onClick =
    "getSpeed()">
<BR>
<INPUT TYPE = TEXT NAME = Textbox>
</CENTER>
</FORM>
</BODY>
<SCRIPT LANGUAGE = JavaScript>
function resetTime()
{
    document.applets[0].resetTime(50)
}
function getSpeed()
{
    document.form1.Textbox.value = "Spin time = "
        + document.applets[0].getSpeed()
}
</SCRIPT>
</HTML>
```

We've been working with our applet a lot in this chapter, but we can use Java methods without even having an applet to work with. Instead, we can use the JavaScript java object.

Using Java Statements in Java-Script: The UseJava Example

In this next example, UseJava.htm, we'll see how to use Java statements without having an applet. We'll execute Java statements directly by using the JavaScript *java object*. Here, we'll display two buttons in a Web page: "Show window" and "Hide window."

When the user clicks the "Show window" button, we'll flash a Java applet window onto the screen with a Java text field holding the message "Hello from JavaScript." In this way, we'll make use of several Java statements without even having an applet in our Web page. Let's start this page, UseJava.htm, with the two buttons "Show window" and "Hide window":

```
<HTML>
<HEAD>
<TITLE>
Using Java From JavaScript
</TITLE>
</HEAD>
<BODY>
<CENTER>
<BR>
<H1>
Calling Java Methods from JavaScript
</H1>
<CENTER>
<FORM>
<BR>
<BR>
<INPUT TYPE = BUTTON Value = "Show window" onClick =
    "showWindow()">
<INPUT TYPE = BUTTON Value = "Hide window" onClick =
    "hideWindow()">
</FORM>
</BODY>
```

These buttons are connected to the JavaScript functions showWindow() and hideWindow():

```
<SCRIPT LANGUAGE = "JavaScript">
    var frameWindow = null
    function showWindow()
    {
        .
        .
        .
    }
    function hideWindow()
    {
        .
        .
        .
    }
</SCRIPT>
```

To show the window, we can use the java object and proceed much as we would in Java. We create a new Java frame window with the title "New window!" in JavaScript (we make this new window, frameWindow, a global object so we can close it in the hideWindow() function):

```
<SCRIPT LANGUAGE = "JavaScript">
    var frameWindow = null
    function showWindow()
    {
```

```
frameWindow = new java.awt.Frame("New window!")
                    .
                    .
                    .

}
```

Next, we create a Java text field and place the text "Hello from Java-Script" in that text field:

```
<SCRIPT LANGUAGE = "JavaScript">
    var frameWindow = null
    function showWindow()
    {
        frameWindow = new java.awt.Frame("New window!")
        var text = new java.awt.TextField("Hello from
    JavaScript")
            .
            .
            .

    }
```

We're almost done—all that's left is to size the window the way we want it and to display it, which we do this way:

```
<SCRIPT LANGUAGE = "JavaScript">
    var frameWindow = null
    function showWindow()
    {
        frameWindow = new java.awt.Frame("New window!")
        var text = new java.awt.TextField("Hello from
    JavaScript")
        frameWindow.add("Center", text)
        frameWindow.resize(200, 200)
        frameWindow.show()
    }
```

At this point, then, a Java applet window is shown on the screen. Now we're using Java directly from JavaScript. To close the window, add code to the hideWindow() function, which is tied to the "Hide window" button:

```
function hideWindow()
{
    .
    .
    .
}
```

After checking to make sure the window is actually open (the user might have clicked the "Hide window" button before clicking the "Show window" button), we close the window using its hide() method:

```
function hideWindow()
{
    if(frameWindow != null){
        frameWindow.hide()
    }
}
```

Open UseJava.htm, as shown in Figure 11–6. When you click the "Show window" button, the program uses Java directly to create a Java applet window and display it. Now we're using Java directly from JavaScript.

As you can imagine, using Java directly from JavaScript is a powerful technique. Many of the aspects JavaScript lacks—such as GUI programming—are supplied in Java. Using the java object helps us make use of Java from JavaScript.

The code for this page, UseJava.htm, is shown in Listing 11–9.

Figure 11–6
We use Java statements to open a window with a Java text field.

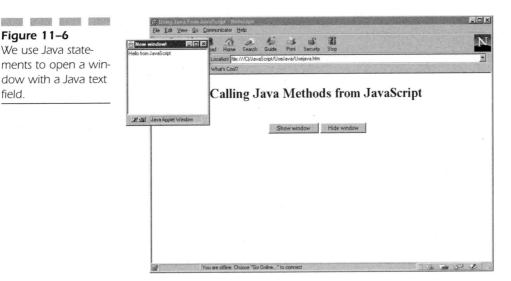

Listing 11–9
UseJava.htm.

```
<HTML>
<HEAD>
<TITLE>
Using Java From JavaScript
</TITLE>
</HEAD>
<BODY>
<CENTER>
<BR>
<H1>
```

continues

Listing 11–9
Continued.

```
Calling Java Methods from JavaScript
</H1>
<CENTER>
<FORM>
<BR>
<BR>
<INPUT TYPE = BUTTON Value = "Show window" onClick =
    "showWindow()">
<INPUT TYPE = BUTTON Value = "Hide window" onClick =
    "hideWindow()">
</FORM>
</BODY>
<SCRIPT LANGUAGE = "JavaScript">
    var frameWindow = null
    function showWindow()
    {
        frameWindow = new java.awt.Frame("New window!")
        var text = new java.awt.TextField("Hello from
    JavaScript")
        frameWindow.add("Center", text)
        frameWindow.resize(200, 200)
        frameWindow.show()
    }
    function hideWindow()
    {
        if(frameWindow != null){
            frameWindow.hide()
        }
    }
</SCRIPT>
</HTML>
```

So far, we've been calling Java from JavaScript, but this transaction can go both ways. We'll see how to use the eval() method now to call JavaScript from Java.

Using JavaScript from Java: The JavaAlert Example
In the next example, JavaAlert, we'll see how to use JavaScript from Java. In this case, we'll present a new button in our page: "Show time." When the user clicks this button, we'll call a new method in the applet, showTime(), that will in turn call the JavaScript alert() function to display the current animation delay.

This example will show us how to call JavaScript from Java. Let's begin this example, JavaAlert, by adding a new method, showTime(), to our applet:

```
import java.awt.*;
import java.applet.Applet;
```

```
public class JavaAlert extends Applet implements
Runnable{
    Image images[] = new Image[4];
    Image currentImage;
    int loop_index = 0;
    Thread thread1;
    Button buttonSuspend, buttonResume;
    int time = 250;
        .
        .
        .

    public boolean action (Event e, Object o)
    {
        if(e.target.equals(buttonSuspend)){
            suspend();
        }
        if(e.target.equals(buttonResume)){
            resume();
        }
        return true;
    }
    public void suspend()
    {
        thread1.suspend();

    }
    public void resetTime(int newTime)
    {
        time = newTime;
    }
    public void showTime()
    {

      .
      .
      .

    }
    public void resume()
    {
        thread1.resume();

    }
    public void start()
    {
        thread1 = new Thread(this);
        thread1.start();
    }
```

When this method is called, we want to display a JavaScript alert box, using the JavaScript window object's alert() method. To use that method, we first need a JavaScript window object, which we get by using the Java *JSObject* class:

```
public void showTime()
{
    JSObject window = JSObject.getWindow(this);
        .
        .
        .

}
```

The JSObject class is a special interface class that lets us reach Java-Script methods and properties from Java.

Using the JSObject Class

The JSObject class is part of Netscape's Java package, which is included with both Internet Explorer and Netscape Navigator. Before using this class, you have to make sure it's in your Java path (set the path statement to include the location of JSObject.class; if you have to, unzip the zipped Java class files that come with the browsers to find the JSObject.class). In our applet, we import the JSObject class this way:

```
import java.awt.*;
import java.applet.Applet;
import netscape.javascript.JSObject;
    .
    .
    .
```

Then we're free to get a JavaScript window object corresponding to the browser window in our applet:

```
public void showTime()
{
    JSObject window = JSObject.getWindow(this);
        .
        .
        .

}
```

Next, we'll create the string we'll display in the JavaScript alert box, which indicates the current animation delay:

```
public void showTime()
{
    JSObject window = JSObject.getWindow(this);
    String displayString = new String("Current
spin time:"
        + String.valueOf(time));
```

.
.
.
.

```
        }
```

Then we can place the alert box onscreen with the JavaScript window object's *eval()* method, which evaluates JavaScript statements. We use eval() to display the alert box:

```
public void showTime()
{
        JSObject window = JSObject.getWindow(this);
        String displayString = new String("Current
spin time:"
                + String.valueOf(time));
        try{
                window.eval("alert('" + displayString +
"')");
        }
        catch (Exception e){}
}
```

That completes the applet for this example. The Web page includes the "Show time" button, as shown here:

```
<HTML>
<HEAD>
<TITLE>
Using JavaScript From Java
</TITLE>
</HEAD>
<BODY>
<CENTER>
<H1>
Using JavaScript From Java
</H1>
</CENTER>
<CENTER>
<APPLET
    CODE="JavaAlert.class" WIDTH="300" HEIGHT="300"
    MAYSCRIPT>
</APPLET>
</CENTER>
<FORM NAME = form1>
<CENTER>
<INPUT TYPE = BUTTON VALUE = "Show time" onClick = "show-
    Time()">
</CENTER>
</FORM>
</BODY>
```

When the user clicks the "Show time" button, we just call the applet's showTime() method, which places the JavaScript alert box on the screen:

```
<SCRIPT LANGUAGE = JavaScript>
function showTime()
{
    document.applets[0].showTime()
}
</SCRIPT>
```

That's all we need. Open the JavaAlert.htm page and click the "Show time" button. This calls the applet's showTime() method, which calls the JavaScript alert() method, displaying an alert box on the screen, as shown in Figure 11–7. Now we're calling JavaScript from Java.

The code for this applet, JavaAlert.java, is shown in Listing 11–10, and the code for the corresponding Web page, javaAlert.htm, is shown in Listing 11–11.

Figure 11–7
We call the JavaScript alert() method from Java.

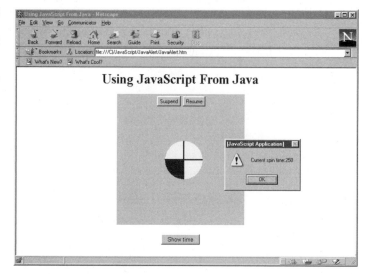

Listing 11–10
JavaAlert.java.

```
import java.awt.*;
import java.applet.Applet;
import netscape.javascript.JSObject;
public class JavaAlert extends Applet implements
  Runnable{
    Image images[] = new Image[4];
    Image currentImage;
    int loop_index = 0;
    Thread thread1;
    Button buttonSuspend, buttonResume;
```

```
    int time = 250;
    public void init()
    {
        images[0] = getImage(getCodeBase(),
"Wheel1.gif");
        images[1] = getImage(getCodeBase(),
"Wheel2.gif");
        images[2] = getImage(getCodeBase(),
"Wheel3.gif");
        images[3] = getImage(getCodeBase(),
"Wheel4.gif");
        buttonSuspend = new Button("Suspend");
        add(buttonSuspend);
        buttonResume = new Button("Resume");
        add(buttonResume);
    }
    public boolean action (Event e, Object o)
    {
        if(e.target.equals(buttonSuspend)){
            suspend();
        }
        if(e.target.equals(buttonResume)){
            resume();
        }
        return true;
    }
    public void suspend()
    {
        thread1.suspend();

    }
    public void resetTime(int newTime)
    {
        time = newTime;
    }
    public void showTime()
    {
        JSObject window = JSObject.getWindow(this);
        String displayString = new String("Current
spin time:"
            + String.valueOf(time));
        try{
            window.eval("alert('" + displayString +
"')");
        }
        catch (Exception e){}
    }
    public void resume()
    {
        thread1.resume();

    }
```

continues

```
    public void start()
    {
        thread1 = new Thread(this);
        thread1.start();
    }
    public void stop()
    {
        thread1.stop();
    }
    public void run()
    {
        while(true){
            currentImage = images[loop_index++];
            if(loop_index > 3)loop_index = 0;
            repaint();
            try {Thread.sleep(time);}
            catch(InterruptedException exp) { }
        }
    }
    public void paint (Graphics g)
    {
        if(currentImage != null){
            g.drawImage(currentImage, 100, 100, this);
        }
    }
}
```

```
<HTML>
<HEAD>
<TITLE>
Using JavaScript From Java
</TITLE>
</HEAD>
<BODY>
<CENTER>
<H1>
Using JavaScript From Java
</H1>
</CENTER>
<CENTER>
<APPLET
    CODE="JavaAlert.class" WIDTH="300" HEIGHT="300"
    MAYSCRIPT>
</APPLET>
</CENTER>
<FORM NAME = form1>
<CENTER>
<INPUT TYPE = BUTTON VALUE = "Show time" onClick = "show-
    Time()">
```

```
</CENTER>
</FORM>
</BODY>
<SCRIPT LANGUAGE = JavaScript>
function showTime()
{
    document.applets[0].showTime()
}
</SCRIPT>
</HTML>
```

Although we can reach JavaScript with the eval() method, there are better ways, as we'll see in the following section when we use the JSObject *getmember()* and *call()* methods.

Calling JavaScript to Rewrite a Window from Java: The Opener Example

In our next example, we'll see how to use JavaScript from Java to rewrite an entire page. Here, we'll modify the Suspend button in the applet to "suspend" not just the applet, but the whole page, by rewriting that page entirely. When the user clicks the "Suspend the whole page!" button, we'll rewrite the page so that it displays only a single header: "Page suspended!" In this way, we'll see how to rewrite a page's HTML from Java, using JavaScript.

To write our code, we'll modify the applet's suspend() method, calling that method when the user clicks the "Suspend the whole page!" button:

```
import java.awt.*;
import java.applet.Applet;
import netscape.javascript.JSObject;
public class Opener extends Applet implements Runnable{
    Image images[] = new Image[4];
    Image currentImage;
    int loop_index = 0;
    Thread thread1;
    Button buttonSuspend;
    int time = 250;
        .
        .
        .
```

```
public boolean action (Event e, Object o)
{
    if(e.target.equals(buttonSuspend)){
        suspend();
    }
    return true;
}
public void suspend()
{
    .
    .
    .
}
```

In the suspend() method, we will rewrite the Web page from scratch. Begin by getting a JSObject corresponding to the browser window:

```
public void suspend()
{
    JSObject window = JSObject.getWindow(this);
    .
    .
    .
}
```

To rewrite the window, we'll need access to the document object, which we get with the JSObject *getMember()* method.

Using the JSObject getMember() Method

We use the JSObject getMember() method to get a property or member object from a JSObject. In this case, we get the document object this way:

```
public void suspend()
{
    JSObject window = JSObject.getWindow(this);
    JSObject document = (JSObject) window.getMem-
ber("document");
    .
    .
    .
}
```

Next, we will call the document's open() method to open the document for writing. We do that with the JSObject *call()* method.

Using the JSObject Call() Method

You use the JSObject call() method to call a JSObject's methods. Here, we call the document object's open() method, passing it no variables:

```
public void suspend()
{
     JSObject window = JSObject.getWindow(this);
     JSObject document = (JSObject) window.getMem-
ber("document");

     document.call("open", null);
          .
          .
          .

}
```

To rewrite the page, we will pass the new HTML for this page to the document's write() method. To do so, we have to store it (like any other arguments we pass with the call() method) in an array of Java objects). Because we'll pass only one argument to the write() method—the new HTML for the page—we set up an array with only one element, the HTML we'll use to indicate the page is suspended:

```
public void suspend()
{
     JSObject window = JSObject.getWindow(this);
     JSObject document = (JSObject) window.getMem-
ber("document");

     document.call("open", null);
     Object[] arguments = { "<HTML><H1><CENTER>Page
          suspended!</CENTER><H1></HTML>" };
          .
          .
          .

}
```

Next, we pass this array to the document's write() method, and then we close the document with its close() method:

```
public void suspend()
{
     JSObject window = JSObject.getWindow(this);
     JSObject document = (JSObject) window.getMem-
ber("document");

     document.call("open", null);
     Object[] arguments = { "<HTML><H1><CENTER>Page
```

```
                          suspended!</CENTER><H1></HTML>" };
                document.call("write", arguments);
                document.call("close", null);
        }
```

That completes the applet; because all the action is in the applet this
time, the Web page just displays that applet:

```
<HTML>
<HEAD>
<TITLE>
Rewriting a Web page from Java
</TITLE>
</HEAD>
<BODY>
<CENTER>
<H1>
Rewriting a Web page from Java
</H1>
</CENTER>
<CENTER>
<APPLET
    CODE="Opener.class" WIDTH="300" HEIGHT="300" MAYSCRIPT>
       <-
</APPLET>
</CENTER>
</BODY>
</HTML>
```

Now open this page, as shown in Figure 11–8, and click the "Suspend
the whole page!" button.

Figure 11–8
We will rewrite this
window from Java.

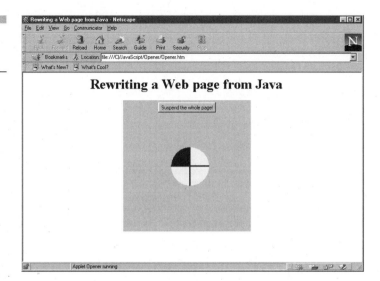

When you click this button, the applet uses JavaScript calls to rewrite the page's HTML, as shown in Figure 11–9. Now we can rewrite whole Web pages from Java using JavaScript.

The code for this applet, Opener.java, is shown in Listing 11–12, and the corresponding Web page, Opener.htm, is shown in Listing 11–13.

Figure 11–9
We rewrote this page from Java using Java-Script.

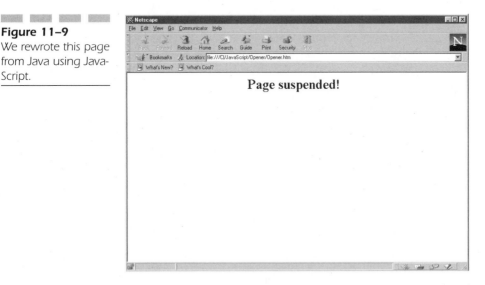

Page suspended!

Listing 11–12
Opener.java.

```java
import java.awt.*;
import java.applet.Applet;
import netscape.javascript.JSObject;
public class Opener extends Applet implements Runnable{
    Image images[] = new Image[4];
    Image currentImage;
    int loop_index = 0;
    Thread thread1;
    Button buttonSuspend;
    int time = 250;
    public void init()
    {
        images[0] = getImage(getCodeBase(),
"Wheel1.gif");
        images[1] = getImage(getCodeBase(),
"Wheel2.gif");
        images[2] = getImage(getCodeBase(),
"Wheel3.gif");
        images[3] = getImage(getCodeBase(),
"Wheel4.gif");
        buttonSuspend = new Button("Suspend the whole
```

continues

Listing 11–12
Continued.

```
page!");
        add(buttonSuspend);
    }
    public boolean action (Event e, Object o)
    {
        if(e.target.equals(buttonSuspend)){
            suspend();
        }
        return true;
    }
    public void suspend()
    {
        JSObject window = JSObject.getWindow(this);
        JSObject document = (JSObject) window.getMem-
ber("document");

        document.call("open", null);
        Object[] arguments = { "<HTML><H1><CENTER>Page
            suspended!</CENTER><H1></HTML>" };
        document.call("write", arguments);
        document.call("close", null);
    }
    public void start()
    {
        thread1 = new Thread(this);
        thread1.start();
    }
    public void stop()
    {
        thread1.stop();
    }
    public void run()
    {
        while(true){
            currentImage = images[loop_index++];
            if(loop_index > 3)loop_index = 0;
            repaint();
            try {Thread.sleep(time);}
            catch(InterruptedException exp) { }
        }
    }
    public void paint (Graphics g)
    {
        if(currentImage != null){
            g.drawImage(currentImage, 100, 100, this);
        }
    }
}
```

```
<HTML>
<HEAD>
<TITLE>
Rewriting a Web page from Java
</TITLE>
</HEAD>
<BODY>
<CENTER>
<H1>
Rewriting a Web page from Java
</H1>
</CENTER>
<CENTER>
<APPLET
    CODE="Opener.class" WIDTH="300" HEIGHT="300" MAYSCRIPT>
</APPLET>
</CENTER>
</BODY>
</HTML>
```

CONCLUSION

That example finishes our chapter on connecting JavaScript and Java. We've covered a lot of material in this chapter: how to call a Java method from JavaScript, how to pass numeric arguments to Java methods, how to pass strings to Java methods, how to read return values from a Java method in JavaScript, how to use JavaScript from Java, and even how to rewrite a Web page from Java using JavaScript statements. We've learned some truly powerful techniques.

In the next chapter, we'll move on to the final topic of this book—how to work with JavaScript stylesheets.

12

JavaScript and Cascading Style Sheets

In this chapter, we'll explore JavaScript *stylesheets*. Stylesheets give you a browser-independent way of formatting text the way you want it. Using stylesheets, you can specify text's size, color, type (such as italic or bold), and more. Because stylesheets are supposed to be browser-independent, they could potentially alleviate the wide variation existing between browsers.

Unfortunately, there's still a variation. Internet Explorer doesn't support JavaScript stylesheets per se. Microsoft has decided in favor of *Cascading Style Sheets* (CSS), not JavaScript stylesheets. However, Netscape Navigator 4.0 can support Cascading Style Sheets, too. Because both browsers agree on this point, we'll cover Cascading Style Sheets, as well as JavaScript stylesheets, later in this chapter.

We'll begin by seeing how to use the STYLE attribute in HTML tags to set an element's style. Next, we'll learn how to create a new style for HTML tags by using stylesheets. Then we'll see how to create style classes, and how to apply styles to HTML elements by ID, how style class inheritance works, how to set styles by using JavaScript style functions, how to set styles dynamically with the click of a button, and more. We'll gain a lot of formatting power in this chapter.

Let's start with an overview of JavaScript stylesheets; later in the chapter, we'll cover Cascading Style Sheets, too.

JavaScript Stylesheets

You create a JavaScript stylesheet with the <STYLE> tag in a Web page, as shown here:

```
<STYLE TYPE = "text/javascript" SRC = "URL">
     declarations
<STYLE>
```

Each of the *declarations* is a style *rule* that looks like this example:

```
tags.H1.fontSize = "48"
```

This style rule sets the font size of the all H1 tags in the document to 48 points by using the fontSize property. The JavaScript stylesheet properties like fontSize, fontStyle, color, and so on are listed in Table 12–1.

Table 12–1

The JavaScript stylesheet properties.

align	backgroundColor	backgroundImage	borderBottomWidth
borderColor	borderLeftWidth	borderRightWidth	borderStyle
borderTopWidth	borderWidths()	clear	color
display	fontFamily	fontSize	fontStyle
fontWeight	height	lineHeight	listStyleType
marginBottom	marginLeft	marginRight	margins()
marginTop	paddingBottom	paddingLeft	paddingRight
paddings()	paddingTop	textAlign	textDecoration
textTransform	verticalAlign	whiteSpace	width

TIP: *You can specify an external file that holds your stylesheet in the*
<STYLE> tag. Doing so is useful if you want to work with different browsers—
or different versions of the same browser—and there are variations in style dec-
larations between the browsers you're targeting. You can test the browser type
and version in code, and then write the HTML to the document that will read
in the appropriate stylesheet file for that browser.

JavaScript Stylesheets and Internet Explorer

Internet Explorer doesn't support JavaScript stylesheets, so you wouldn't
expect to find style properties with names like fontSize and color in Internet Explorer Web pages. However, take a look at this code from Chapter 5, "Keyboard and Mouse Handling," where we set the style of Internet
Explorer hyperlinks when the mouse moved over them:

```
<HTML>
<HEAD>
<TITLE>Emphasizing hyperlinks</TITLE>
</HEAD>
<BODY LINK = 0000>
<CENTER>
<FORM NAME = form1>
<H1>
Place the mouse over a link to emphasize it . . .
</H1>
<A HREF="http://www.server.com" name= link1 onMouseOver =
    "link1Over()"
    onMouseOut = "link1Out()">Here is link 1</A>
<BR>
<BR>
<A HREF="http://www.server.com" name= link2 onMouseOver =
    "link2Over()"
    onMouseOut = "link2Out()">Here is link 2</A>
        .
        .
        .
</FORM>
</CENTER>
</BODY>
<SCRIPT LANGUAGE= JavaScript>
    function link1Over()
    {
        link1.style.color="red"
        link1.style.fontSize=36
    }
```

```
function link1Out()
{
    link1.style.color="black"
    link1.style.fontSize=16
}
function link2Over()
{
    link2.style.color="red"
    link2.style.fontSize=36
}
function link2Out()
{
    link2.style.color="black"
    link2.style.fontSize=16
}
        .
        .
        .
</SCRIPT>
</HTML>
```

As you can see, we refer to properties like fontSize and color here, which certainly look like JavaScript stylesheet properties. What's going on?

In fact, these properties actually represent CSS style properties, which are hyphenated, like font-family and font-size; they are not JavaScript style properties like fontFamily and fontSize (although, confusingly, they have the same name).The problem is that in some scripting languages, hyphens aren't valid in names; therefore, Microsoft was forced to adopt the JavaScript style property names to refer to those properties in code. These properties are properties of Internet Explorer's *style* object, which is a member object of every tag. That object's properties are listed in Table 12–2.

Use the entries in Table 2–2 when you refer to CSS style properties in code in Internet Explorer; in standard Internet Explorer stylesheets, however, you stick to the standard CSS names, which we'll see later in this chapter. So even though it *looks* as though you can use JavaScript style properties in Internet Explorer, you can't actually do so.

The upshot is that the JavaScript part of this chapter is targeted at Netscape Navigator only, and we'll dig into that now, starting with an example that shows how to set styles by using the STYLE attribute in HTML tags.

Table 12-2

Internet Explorer's style object's properties.

background	backgroundAttachment	backgroundColor	backgroundImage
backgroundPosition	backgroundPositionX	backgroundPositionY	background Repeat
border	borderBottom	borderBottomColor	borderBottomStyle
borderBottomWidth	borderColor	borderLeft	borderLeftColor
borderLeftStyle	borderLeftWidth	borderRight	borderRightColor
borderRightStyle	borderRightWidth	borderStyle	borderTop
borderTopColor	borderTopStyle	borderTopWidth	borderWidth
clear	clip	color	cssText
cursor	display	filter	font
fontFamily	fontSize	fontStyle	fontVariant
fontWeight	height	left	letterSpacing
lineHeight	listStyle	listStyleImage	listStylePosition
listStyleType	margin	marginBottom	marginLeft
marginRight	marginTop	overflow	paddingBottom
paddingLeft	paddingRight	paddingTop	pageBreakAfter
pageBreakBefore	pixelHeight	pixelLeft	pixelTop
pixelWidth	posHeight	position	posLeft
posTop	posWidth	styleFloat	textAlign
textDecoration	textDecorationBlink	textDecorationLineThrough	textDecorationNone
textDecorationOverline	textDecorationUnderline	textIndent	textTransform
top	verticalAlign	visibility	width
zIndex			

Using the STYLE Attribute: The StyleAttribute Example

In our first JavaScript style example, we'll make the text in a header blue by setting its color style property to blue. In a new Web page, `StyleAttribute.htm`, we'll set the style of one specific header to blue:

```
<HTML>
<HEAD>
<TITLE>
Using the STYLE Attribute
</TITLE>
</HEAD>
<BODY>
<CENTER>
<H1 STYLE = "color:'blue'">
This header is blue
</H1>
</CENTER>
</BODY>
</HTML>
```

Note the syntax here. We define a style rule for the color style property, followed by the setting we want for that property: blue. That's all it takes —now we've given this header blue text by using a stylesheet.

Open this page, StyleAttribute.htm, in Netscape Navigator, as shown in Figure 12–1; the header is blue (although that's not apparent in this book!). Now we've set a header's style by using the <H1> tag's STYLE attribute, so our first style example is a success.

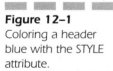

Figure 12–1

Coloring a header blue with the STYLE attribute.

If we wanted to set the header's font size as well as its color, we could use the JavaScript stylesheet property fontSize (note that you separate properties with a semicolon):

```
<H1 STYLE = "color:'blue';fontSize:52">
    This header is blue
</H1>
```

On the other hand, Internet Explorer uses CSS style properties with the STYLE attribute. To set the header's size in Internet Explorer, you would use the CSS style property font-size instead of fontSize:

```
<H1 STYLE = "color:'blue';font-size:52">
    This header is blue
</H1>
```

NOTE: *A stylesheet created with the STYLE attribute is called an inline stylesheet.*

TIP: *Netscape discourages the use of inline stylesheets, preferring to collect all the style information for a page in one location, making it easier to maintain or modify.*

That's it for using the STYLE attribute; the code for this page, StyleAttribute.htm, is shown in Listing 12–1.

Listing 12–1
StyleAttribute.htm.

```
<HTML>
<HEAD>
<TITLE>
Using the STYLE Attribute
</TITLE>
</HEAD>
<BODY>
<CENTER>
<H1 STYLE = "color:'blue'">
This header is blue
</H1>
</CENTER>
</BODY>
</HTML>
```

Now we'll move on, seeing how to work with the tags in a Web page, changing their styles as we like. In this way, we can customize our Web pages with JavaScript styles.

Styling Tags: The StyleH Example

In the next example, we'll see how to modify individual HTML tags with a JavaScript stylesheet. In a new page, StyleH.htm, we'll modify <H1> tags in a page to be 48 point and underlined, and <H2> tags to be 24 point. First, set up the JavaScript stylesheet we'll use:

```
<HTML>
<HEAD>
<TITLE>Customizing header tags</TITLE>
</HEAD>
<STYLE TYPE = "text/javascript">
     .
     .
     .
</STYLE>
```

Then we reset the <H1> elements' font size and font type and underline the text in those elements; note that we underline text with the *textDecoration* style property:

```
<HTML>
<HEAD>
<TITLE>Customizing header tags</TITLE>
</HEAD>
<STYLE TYPE = "text/javascript">
  tags.H1.fontSize = "48"
  tags.H1.fontFamily = "roman"
  tags.H1.textDecoration = "underline"
         .
         .
         .
</STYLE>
```

We adjust the <H2> tag as well:

```
<HTML>
<HEAD>
<TITLE>Customizing header tags</TITLE>
</HEAD>
<STYLE TYPE = "text/javascript">
```

```
 tags.H1.fontSize = "48"
 tags.H1.fontFamily = "roman"
 tags.H1.textDecoration = "underline"
 tags.H2.fontSize = "24"
 tags.H2.fontFamily = "arial"
</STYLE>
```

Now when we use those tags, the new styles will automatically be applied:

```
<HTML>
<HEAD>
<TITLE>Customizing header tags</TITLE>
</HEAD>
<STYLE TYPE = "text/javascript">
 tags.H1.fontSize = "48"
 tags.H1.fontFamily = "roman"
 tags.H1.textDecoration = "underline"
 tags.H2.fontSize = "24"
 tags.H2.fontFamily = "arial"
</STYLE>
<BODY>
<CENTER>
<H1>We've applied a stylesheet to this header</H1>
<BR>
<H2>And to this one too.</H2>
</CENTER>
</BODY>
</HTML>
```

Open this page in Netscape Navigator, as shown in Figure 12–2. As you can see, we've set the styles for the <H1> and <H2> headers.

Figure 12–2
Setting header tag styles

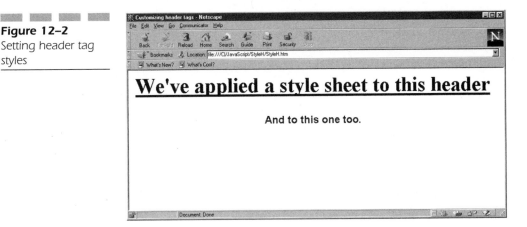

Listing 12–2
StyleH.htm.

```
<HTML>
<HEAD>
<TITLE>Customizing header tags</TITLE>
</HEAD>
<STYLE TYPE = "text/javascript">
 tags.H1.fontSize = "48"
 tags.H1.fontFamily = "roman"
 tags.H1.textDecoration = "underline"
 tags.H2.fontSize = "24"
 tags.H2.fontFamily = "arial"
</STYLE>
<BODY>
<CENTER>
<H1>We've applied a stylesheet to this header</H1>
<BR>
<H2>And to this one too.</H2>
</CENTER>
</BODY>
</HTML>
```

The code for this page, StyleH.htm, is shown in Listing 12–2. Besides working with tags, we can also define style classes.

Style Classes: The StyleUnderline Example

In our next example, we'll see how to use JavaScript style classes to underline text. We begin this new page, StyleUnderline.htm, by declaring a new style class, underline, and setting its textDecoration property to "underline":

```
<HTML>
<HEAD>
<TITLE>Using style classes</TITLE>
</HEAD>
<STYLE TYPE="text/javascript">
    classes.underline.all.textDecoration = "underline"
</STYLE>
<BODY>
<CENTER>
    .
    .
    .
```

Now that we've defined this new class, we're free to use it in HTML elements, as we do here, specifying this <H1> header's class with its CLASS attribute:

```
<HTML>
<HEAD>
<TITLE>Using style classes</TITLE>
</HEAD>
<STYLE TYPE="text/javascript">
    classes.underline.all.textDecoration = "underline"
</STYLE>
<BODY>
<CENTER>
<BR>
<BR>
<H1 CLASS = underline>
Using style classes to underline this text . . .
</H1>
</CENTER>
</BODY>
</HTML>
```

This gives the <H1> element the underline class, which means the text in that element is underlined, as shown in Figure 12–3. In this way, we can set up our own JavaScript style classes and then apply them to the elements in a Web page.

The code for this example, StyleUnderline.htm, is shown in Listing 12–3.

Besides setting styles by HTML tag and by class, we can set JavaScript styles according to the ID of HTML elements.

Figure 12–3

We underline text by using JavaScript style classes.

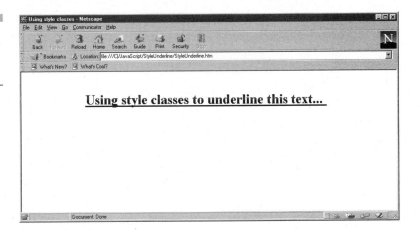

```
<HTML>
<HEAD>
<TITLE>Using style classes</TITLE>
</HEAD>
<STYLE TYPE="text/javascript">
    classes.underline.all.textDecoration = "underline"
</STYLE>
<BODY>
<CENTER>
<BR>
<BR>
<H1 CLASS = underline>
Using style classes to underline this text . . .
</H1>
</CENTER>
</BODY>
</HTML>
```

Setting Styles by ID: The StyleMultiple Example

In our next example, we'll display three lines of <H1> headers. We'll re-define the <H1> tag to display blue text, so the first header will be blue. The next line will use a class that displays red text; specifically, using a class like that overrides our <H1> tag redefinition, so the second line will appear red.

We'll give the last <H1> element that same red class, and we'll add an ID value, setting up the page so all elements with that ID will appear in 48-point type. This combination of <H1> and ID style means that the last line will appear in red, 48-point type.

Let's make this clearer in code. Start this example, StyleMultiple.htm, by setting all elements with the ID "H1Tag" to 48 point:

```
<HTML>
<HEAD>
<TITLE>
Using multiple styles . . .
</TITLE>
<STYLE TYPE = "text/javascript">
    ids.H1Tag.fontSize = "48"
         .
         .
         .
```

Next, we set up a class named "red" that colors its text red, and give the <H1> tags in the page blue text. Note that we declare our red class as classes.red.H1.color so that it will apply only to <H1> elements (if you want to apply this class to all HTML elements, you would declare it as classes.red.all.color):

```
<HTML>
<HEAD>
<TITLE>
Using multiple styles . . .
</TITLE>
<STYLE TYPE = "text/javascript">
    ids.H1Tag.fontSize = "48"
    classes.red.H1.color = "red"
    document.tags.H1.color = "blue"
</STYLE>
    .
    .
    .
```

In this page, then, a simple <H1> tag will appear blue:

```
<HTML>
<HEAD>
<TITLE>
Using multiple styles . . .
</TITLE>
<STYLE TYPE = "text/javascript">
    ids.H1Tag.fontSize = "48"
    classes.red.H1.color = "red"
    document.tags.H1.color = "blue"
</STYLE>
</HEAD>
<BODY>
<H1>
This text is blue . . .
</H1>
    .
    .
    .
```

If we specifically give an <H1> element the red class, however, that overrides the blue default setting, so this line appears red:

```
<HTML>
<HEAD>
<TITLE>
```

```
Using multiple styles . . .
</TITLE>
<STYLE TYPE = "text/javascript">
    ids.H1Tag.fontSize = "48"
    classes.red.H1.color = "red"
    document.tags.H1.color = "blue"
</STYLE>
</HEAD>
<BODY>
<H1>
This text is blue . . .
</H1>
<H1 CLASS = "red">
This text is red . . .
</H1>
        .
        .
        .
```

Finally, we give our last <H1> tag the red class and give it the ID *H1Tag*, which means that header will appear both red and in 48-point type:

```
<HTML>
<HEAD>
<TITLE>
Using multiple styles . . .
</TITLE>
<STYLE TYPE = "text/javascript">
    ids.H1Tag.fontSize = "48"
    classes.red.H1.color = "red"
    document.tags.H1.color = "blue"
</STYLE>
</HEAD>
<BODY>
<H1>
This text is blue . . .
</H1>
<H1 CLASS = "red">
This text is red . . .
</H1>
<H1 CLASS = "red" ID="H1Tag">
This text is red and 48 point . . .
</H1>
        .
        .
        .
```

Now open this page in Netscape Navigator, as shown in Figure 12–4. The page is a success, so now we can set styles by HTML tag ID.

TIP: *One reason style classes are popular is that you can define multiple styles for the same class. For example, here's how to define a class named "bigYellow," which colors the text in <H1> elements yellow and enlarges the text in those elements to 36 point:*

```
<STYLE TYPE = "text/javascript">
        classes.bigYellow.H1.color = "yellow"
        classes.bigYellow.H1.fontSize = "36"
    </STYLE>
```

The code for this page, StyleMultiple.htm, is shown in Listing 12–4.

Classes are powerful style structures; for example, elements inside other elements inherit the outer element's styles, as we'll see in the following section.

Figure 12–4
We set styles by
HTML IDs.

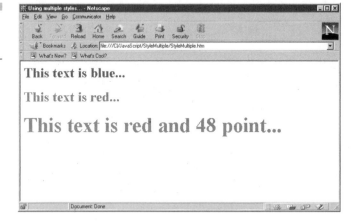

```
<HTML>
<HEAD>
<TITLE>
Using multiple styles . . .
</TITLE>
<STYLE TYPE = "text/javascript">
    ids.H1Tag.fontSize = "48"
    classes.red.H1.color = "red"
    document.tags.H1.color = "blue"
</STYLE>
</HEAD>
<BODY>
<H1>
This text is blue . . .
</H1>
<H1 CLASS = "red">
This text is red . . .
</H1>
<H1 CLASS = "red" ID="H1Tag">
This text is red and 48 point . . .
</H1>
</BODY>
</HTML>
```

Style Inheritance: The StyleDiv Example

If an element contains another element, that inner element can inherit the outer element's styles. For example, if we have a <DIV> element that we've styled to make it appear indented on the page, any other <DIV> elements it contains will also appear indented.

Let's make this clearer in an example, StyleDiv.htm. Start by defining a new class, class1, with a font size of 36 points, and an indentation—which we set with the marginLeft property—of 10 percent of the Web page:

```
<HTML>
<HEAD>
<TITLE>Style class inheritance</TITLE>
</HEAD>
<STYLE TYPE="text/javascript">
  classes.class1.all.fontSize = 36
  classes.class1.all.marginLeft = "10%"
</STYLE>
```

Next, we use that class in a <DIV> element:

```
<HTML>
<HEAD>
<TITLE>Style class inheritance</TITLE>
</HEAD>
<STYLE TYPE="text/javascript">
  classes.class1.all.fontSize = 36
  classes.class1.all.marginLeft = "10%"
</STYLE>
<BODY>
<CENTER>
<H1>Class inheritance . . . </H1>
</CENTER>
<DIV CLASS = class1>
This is the <I>outer</I> element.
<BR>
<BR>
   .
   .
   .
```

This <DIV> element itself contains another <DIV> element, as shown here:

```
<HTML>
<HEAD>
<TITLE>Style class inheritance</TITLE>
</HEAD>
<STYLE TYPE="text/javascript">
  classes.class1.all.fontSize = 36
  classes.class1.all.marginLeft = "10%"
</STYLE>
<BODY>
<CENTER>
<H1>Class inheritance . . . </H1>
</CENTER>
<DIV CLASS = class1>
This is the <I>outer</I> element.
<BR>
<BR>
<DIV>
This is text in the <I>inner</I> element (which has inher-
    ited the outer
element's styles).
</DIV>
</DIV>
```

Figure 12–5

Using style class in-
heritance.

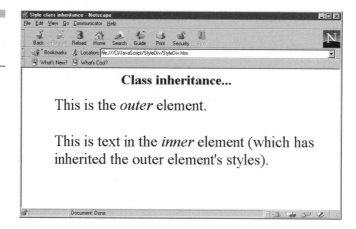

The inner <DIV> will inherit the outer <DIV>'s class, class1, as shown in Figure 12–5, where the text in both <DIV>s is enlarged and indented to 10 percent. In this way, you can build nested style elements in a Web page, passing style classes from element to element.

The code for this page, StyleDiv.htm, is shown in Listing 12–5.

It's also possible to define JavaScript styles with JavaScript functions, as described in the following section.

Style Functions: The StyleFunction Example

You can set styles with JavaScript functions when a page is first loaded, giving us a powerful technique. For example, we can use a JavaScript function to set the style of text depending on the time of day. In this example, we will display the following text in 48 point, unless the time of day is morning, in which case we'll make it 24 point text (so as not to wake the user up too brutally).

Start this page, StyleFunction.htm, with the JavaScript function that will set the <H1> tag's style, depending on the time of day. We'll name this function checkTime(); note that we place this function directly in the <STYLE> element:

```
<HTML>
<HEAD>
```

```
<HTML>
<HEAD>
<TITLE>Style class inheritance</TITLE>
</HEAD>
<STYLE TYPE="text/javascript">
   classes.class1.all.fontSize = 36
   classes.class1.all.marginLeft = "10%"
</STYLE>
<BODY>
<CENTER>
<H1>Class inheritance . . . </H1>
</CENTER>
<DIV CLASS = class1>
This is the <I>outer</I> element.
<BR>
<BR>
<DIV>
This is text in the <I>inner</I> element (which has
     inherited the outer
element's styles).
</DIV>
</DIV>
</BODY>
</HTML>
```

```
<STYLE type="text/JavaScript">
    function checkTime()
    {
        .
        .
        .
    }
```

In this function, we use the date object to check the time of day. If it's morning, we set the <H1> element's font size to 24:

```
<HTML>
<HEAD>
<STYLE type="text/JavaScript">
    function checkTime()
    {
        var currentDate = new Date()
        var currentHour = currentDate.getHours()

        if (currentHour > 6 && currentHour < 12 ) {
            tags.H1.fontSize = "24"
        }
    }
```

If it's not morning, we set the font size to 48:

```
<HTML>
<HEAD>
<STYLE type="text/JavaScript">
    function checkTime()
    {
        var currentDate = new Date()
        var currentHour = currentDate.getHours()
        if (currentHour > 6 && currentHour < 12 ) {
            tags.H1.fontSize = "24"
        }
        else{
            tags.H1.fontSize = "48"
        }
    }
```

Now we apply that function to the H1 tag in the <STYLE> element:

```
<HTML>
<HEAD>
<STYLE type="text/JavaScript">
    function checkTime()
    {
        var currentDate = new Date()
        var currentHour = currentDate.getHours()
        if (currentHour > 6 && currentHour < 12 ) {
            tags.H1.fontSize = "24"
        }
        else{
            tags.H1.fontSize = "48"
        }
    }
    tags.H1.apply = checkTime()
</STYLE>
</HEAD>
```

Now the <H1> tag will be 24 points in the morning, and 48 points otherwise. We use that tag in the page as shown here:

```
<BODY>
<CENTER>
<H1>
    This is styled to 48 point text, 24 point text in the
    morning . . .
</H1>
</CENTER>
</BODY>
</HTML>
```

Figure 12–6
We apply styles that
differ according to
the time of day.

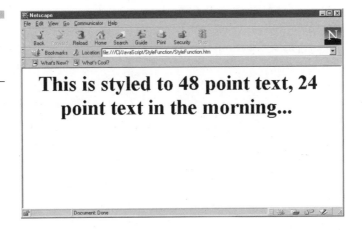

Open this page in Netscape Navigator, as shown in Figure 12–6. The text in that page varies according to the time of day, as we've programmed it to. Now we can use JavaScript functions to set JavaScript styles.

The code for this page, StyleFunction.htm, is shown in Listing 12–6.

We've gotten a good look at JavaScript stylesheets; now we'll turn to Cascading Style Sheets (CSS). CSS is supported by both Netscape Navigator and Internet Explorer.

Cascading Style Sheets

Cascading Style Sheets works much as JavaScript stylesheets do, but you specify a type of "text/css" in the <STYLE> element instead of "text/javascript":

```
<STYLE TYPE = "text/css" SRC = "URL">
    declarations
<STYLE>
```

As mentioned, CSS is supported by both Netscape Navigator and Internet Explorer; the CSS properties are listed in Table 12–3.

Internet Explorer expands the standard CSS property set, as shown in Table 12–4.

Let's start creating some CSS examples.

```
<HTML>
<HEAD>
<STYLE type="text/JavaScript">
    function checkTime()
    {
        var currentDate = new Date()
        var currentHour = currentDate.getHours()
        if (currentHour > 6 && currentHour < 12 ) {
            tags.H1.fontSize = "24"
        }
        else{
            tags.H1.fontSize = "48"
        }
    }
    tags.H1.apply = checkTime()
</STYLE>
</HEAD>
<BODY>
<CENTER>
<H1>
    This is styled to 48 point text, 24 point text in the
        morning . . .
</H1>
</CENTER>
</BODY>
</HTML>
```

CSS Tag Styling: The StyleP Example

In our first CSS example, we'll see that CSS syntax is different from Java-Script stylesheet syntax. Here, we will change the style of <P> tags to 48 point.

In this first CSS example, StyleP.htm, we set the style of the <P> tag to 48 points by using the CSS property font-size:

```
<HTML>
<HEAD>
<TITLE>Specific tag styling example</TITLE>
</HEAD>
<STYLE TYPE = "text/css">
 P {font-size: 48pt}
</STYLE>
```

Table 12–3

The CSS style properties.

background	background-attachment	background-color	background-image
background-position	background-repeat	border	border-bottom
border-bottom-width	border-color	border-left	border-left-width
border-right	border-right-width	border-style	border-top
border-top-width	border-width	clear	color
display	float	font	font-family
font-size	font-style	font-variant	font-weight
height	letter-spacing	line-height	list-style
list-style-image	list-style-position	list-style-type	margin
margin-bottom	margin-left	margin-right	margin-top
padding	padding-bottom	padding-left	padding-right
padding-top	text-align	text-decoration	text-indent
text-transform	vertical-align	white-space	width
word-spacing			

Note that this CSS rule is different from the corresponding JavaScript rule, which would look like this:

```
<STYLE TYPE = "text/javascript">
   tags.P.fontSize = "48"
</STYLE>
```

We're free to use the restyled <P> elements in our Web page now, and the text in those elements will appear in 48-point font:

```
<HTML>
<HEAD>
<TITLE>Specific tag styling example</TITLE>
</HEAD>
<STYLE TYPE = "text/css">
 P {font-size: 48pt}
</STYLE>
<BODY>
<CENTER>
```

Table 12–4

Internet Explorer's CSS style properties.

!important	@font-face	@import	active
background	background-attachment	background-color	background-image
background-position	background-repeat	blendTrans()	border
border-bottom	border-bottom-color	border-bottom-style	border-bottom-width
border-color	border-left	border-left-color	border-left-style
border-left-width	border-right	border-right-color	border-right-style
border-right-width	border-style	border-top	border-top-color
border-top-style	border-top-width	border-width	clear
clip	color	cursor	display
float	font	font-family	font-size
font-style	font-variant	font-weight	height
hover	left	letter-spacing	line-height
link	list-style	list-style-image	list-style-position
list-style-type	margin	margin-bottom	margin-left
margin-right	margin-top	overflow	padding
padding-bottom	padding-left	padding-right	padding-top
page-break-after	page-break-before	position	revealTrans()
text-align	text-decoration	text-indent	text-transform
top	vertical-align	visibility	visited
width	z-index		

```
<P>
The text in this paragraph is styled to 48 point.
</P>
    .
    .
    .
```

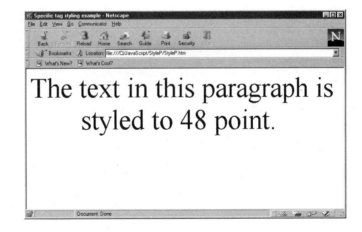

The text in this paragraph is styled to 48 point.

Open this page in either Internet Explorer or Netscape Navigator, as shown in Figure 12–7. As you can see, we've redefined the <P> tag by using CSS styles.

The code for this page, StyleP.htm is shown in Listing 12–7.

TIP: *The way you specify what element—HTML tag, class, or ID—you're defining a style for is by using a style selector.* Cascading Style Sheets provides a new selector: the *contextual* selector. For example, the contextual selector "P B" in the stylesheet rule P B {color:"green"} colors all text green in <B> elements *that are inside* <P> *elements.*

We can also define classes in CSS, just as we can in JavaScript stylesheets.

CSS Style Classes: The StyleClass Example

In this next example, we'll define a CSS class, underlinedText, that when applied to a text element, underlines the text in that element. In CSS, you declare a class by prefacing its name with a dot, so here's how we define the underlinedText class in a new example, StyleClass.htm:

Listing 12–7
StyleP.htm.

```
<HTML>
<HEAD>
<TITLE>Specific tag styling example</TITLE>
</HEAD>
<STYLE TYPE = "text/css">
 P {font-size: 48pt}
</STYLE>
<BODY>
<CENTER>
<P>
The text in this paragraph is styled to 48 point.
</P>
</CENTER>
</BODY>
</HTML>
```

```
<HTML>
<HEAD>
<TITLE>Using CSS classes</TITLE>
</HEAD>
<STYLE TYPE = "text/css">
   .underlinedText {text-decoration: underline}
</STYLE>
<BODY>
   .
   .
   .
```

In this case, we underline text by setting the class's text-decoration property to *underline*. We can apply that class as we did earlier with our JavaScript stylesheet classes:

```
<HTML>
<HEAD>
<TITLE>Using CSS classes</TITLE>
</HEAD>
<STYLE TYPE = "text/css">
   .underlinedText {text-decoration: underline}
</STYLE>
<BODY>
<CENTER>
<H1>
<DIV CLASS = "underlinedText">
This text is underlined.
</DIV>
</H1>
   .
   .
   .
```

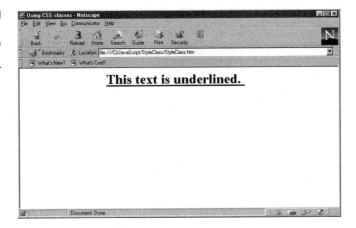

Figure 12–8
We use CSS classes to
underline text.

Open this page now, as shown in Figure 12–8. As you can see, our underlinedText class is at work—we've underlined the text by using that class.

The code for this page, StyleClass.htm, is shown in Listing 12–8.

Just as with JavaScript classes, you can inherit styles from CSS class to class, as described in the following section.

CSS Inheritance: The StyleInherit Example

In this next example, StyleInherit.htm, we'll see how to enclose a <DIV> element inside a <DIV> element, just as we did earlier with JavaScript stylesheets. And just as before, the inner <DIV> element will inherit the outer <DIV> element's styles.

NOTE: *Netscape Navigator doesn't yet allow you to apply CSS styles to <DIV> elements, so this example is aimed at Internet Explorer.*

As we did in our previous JavaScript stylesheet inheritance example, we'll define a class named "class1" that sets the font size to 36 points and indents elements 10 percent. However, this time we use the font-size and margin-left CSS style properties instead of the JavaScript style properties fontSize and marginLeft:

```
<HTML>
<HEAD>
<TITLE>Using CSS classes</TITLE>
</HEAD>
<STYLE TYPE = "text/css">
   .underlinedText {text-decoration: underline}
</STYLE>
<BODY>
<CENTER>
<H1>
<DIV CLASS = "underlinedText">
This text is underlined.
</DIV>
</H1>
<CENTER>
</BODY>
</HTML>
```

```
<HTML>
<HEAD>
<TITLE>CSS class inheritance</TITLE>
</HEAD>
<STYLE TYPE = "text/css">
   .class1 {font-size:36; margin-left:10%}
</STYLE>
<BODY>
```

Now we apply this class to a <DIV> element that contains another
<DIV>:

```
<HTML>
<HEAD>
<TITLE>CSS class inheritance</TITLE>
</HEAD>
<STYLE TYPE = "text/css">
   .class1 {font-size:36; margin-left:10%}
</STYLE>
<BODY>
<CENTER>
<H1>CSS class inheritance . . . </H1>
</CENTER>
<DIV CLASS = class1>
This is the <I>outer</I> element.
<BR>
<BR>
<DIV>
This is text in the <I>inner</I> element (which has inher-
      ited the outer
element's styles)
```

```
</DIV>
</DIV>
        .
        .
        .
```

The result is the same as with our JavaScript style class inheritance example, as shown in Figure 12–9; the inner <DIV> inherits the outer <DIV>'s classes. Now we're supporting class inheritance with CSS.

The code for this page, StyleInherit.htm, is shown in Listing 12–9.

Internet Explorer lets us set style properties on the fly, and we'll take a look at that now as our last example in the chapter.

Changing Styles: The StyleDynamic Example

We can apply CSS classes to HTML elements dynamically in Internet Explorer; for example, our new Web page will have some text in a <DIV> element and two buttons with the captions "Turn text black" and "Turn text red." We'll set up two CSS classes, redText and blackText, in this new example, StyleDynamic.htm. When the user clicks the "Turn text red" button, we'll apply the redText class to the <DIV>, turning the text red.

Figure 12–9
Using CSS class inheritance.

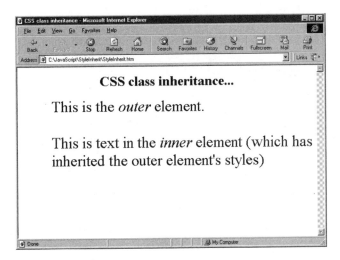

```
<HTML>
<HEAD>
<TITLE>CSS class inheritance</TITLE>
</HEAD>
<STYLE TYPE = "text/css">
  .class1 {font-size:36; margin-left:10%}
</STYLE>
<BODY>
<CENTER>
<H1>CSS class inheritance . .. . </H1>
</CENTER>
<DIV CLASS = class1>
This is the <I>outer</I> element.
<BR>
<BR>
<DIV>
This is text in the <I>inner</I> element (which has inher-
    ited the outer
element's styles)
</DIV>
</DIV>
</BODY>
</HTML>
```

When he or she clicks the "Turn text black" button, we'll apply the black-Text class, turning the text black.

Start this new page with the <DIV> element that encloses the text we'll work on, as well as the two buttons we'll use in our Web page:

```
<HTML>
<TITLE>Coloring text with dynamic CSS classes</TITLE>
<BODY>
<CENTER>
<DIV ID = "Div1">
<H1>
Coloring text with dynamic CSS classes
</H1>
<BR>
<FORM>
<INPUT TYPE = BUTTON Value = "Turn text black" onClick =
    "TurnBlack()">
<INPUT TYPE = BUTTON Value = "Turn text red" onClick =
    "TurnRed()">
</FORM>
</DIV>
</CENTER>
```

Next, we declare the two CSS classes we'll need, redText and blackText, in the <STYLE> element:

```
<STYLE TYPE = "text/css">
 .blackText {color:Black}
 .redText {color:Red}
</STYLE>
```

Finally, in the <SCRIPT> element, we apply those classes to the <DIV> element when the user clicks the matching button:

```
<SCRIPT LANGUAGE = JavaScript>
    function TurnBlack(div1)
    {
        document.all.Div1.className = "blackText"
    }
    function TurnRed(div1)
    {
        document.all.Div1.className = "redText"
    }
</SCRIPT>
```

Internet Explorer will apply the new style to the <DIV> in response to the user's button clicks.

Open this page in Internet Explorer, as shown in Figure 12–10. When the user clicks the red text button, we turn the text red; when he or she clicks the black text button, we turn the text black. In this way, we can apply CSS styles to a Web page element on the fly.

The code for this page, StyleDynamic.htm, is shown in Listing 12–10.

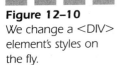

Figure 12–10
We change a <DIV> element's styles on the fly.

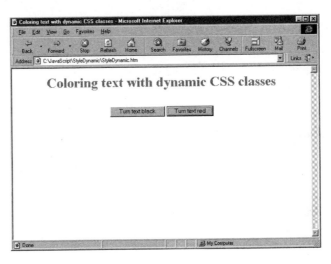

```
<HTML>
<TITLE>Coloring text with dynamic CSS classes</TITLE>
<BODY>
<CENTER>
<DIV ID = "Div1">
<H1>
Coloring text with dynamic CSS classes
</H1>
<BR>
<FORM>
<INPUT TYPE = BUTTON Value = "Turn text black" onClick =
    "TurnBlack()">
<INPUT TYPE = BUTTON Value = "Turn text red" onClick =
    "TurnRed()">
</FORM>
</DIV>
</CENTER>
<STYLE TYPE = "text/css">
 .blackText {color:Black}
 .redText {color:Red}
</STYLE>
<SCRIPT LANGUAGE = JavaScript>
    function TurnBlack(div1)
    {
        document.all.Div1.className = "blackText"
    }
    function TurnRed(div1)
    {
        document.all.Div1.className = "redText"
    }
</SCRIPT>
</BODY>
</HTML>
```

TIP: *You can apply styles to individual words—or even letters in words—in a Web page with the <SPAN> tag.*

CONCLUSION

That concludes our look at JavaScript and CSS style sheets—and that concludes this book. We've come far here, from the basics of JavaScript all the way up to connecting Java to JavaScript, using cookies, rewriting Web pages on the fly, supporting dragging and dropping, creating dialog boxes, using animation, and much more.

We've covered a great deal and been able to add a lot of power to our Web pages. All that remains now is to put JavaScript to work in your Web pages.

Appendix A

This appendix lists the JavaScript and JScript keywords by browser.

Keyword	Netscape Navigator	Microsoft Internet Explorer
$1 . . . $9 Properties		X
/*..*/ (multiline comment)	X	X
// (single-line comment)	X	X
abs	X	X
acos	X	X
action	X	X
Add		X
AddFolders		X
Addition Operator (+)	X	X
alert	X	X
alinkColor	X	X
anchor	X	X
Anchor object	X	X
anchors	X	X
appCodeName	X	X
Applet	X	X
applets	X	X
appName	X	X
appVersion	X	X
Area	X	X
arguments array	X	X
arguments property	X	X
Array	X	X

Keyword	Netscape Navigator	Microsoft Internet Explorer
asin	X	X
asin	X	X
Assignment Operator (=)	X	X
atan	X	X
atan2	X	X
atEnd		X
AtEndOfLine		X
AtEndOfLine Property		X
AtEndOfStream Property		X
Attributes Property		X
AvailableSpace Property		X
back	X	X
bgColor	X	X
big	X	X
Bitwise AND Operator (&)	X	X
Bitwise Left Shift Operator (<<)	X	X
Bitwise NOT Operator (~)	X	X
Bitwise OR Operator (|)	X	X
Bitwise Right Shift Operator (>>)	X	X
Bitwise XOR Operator (^)	X	X
blink	X	X
blur	X	X
bold	X	X
Boolean	X	X
border	X	X
break	X	X
break	X	X

Keyword	Netscape Navigator	Microsoft Internet Explorer
BuildPath	X	X
Button	X	X
caller	X	X
ceil	X	X
charAt	X	X
charCodeAt		X
Checkbox	X	X
checked	X	X
clearTimeout	X	X
click	X	X
close (document object)	X	X
close (window object)	X	X
closed	X	X
Column Property		X
Comma Operator (,)	X	X
CompareMode Property		X
Comparison Operators		X
compile		X
complete	X	X
concat (Array)		X
concat (String)		X
Conditional (trinary) Operator (?:)	X	X
Conditional Compilation		X
Conditional Compilation Variables		X
confirm	X	X
constructor	X	X
continue		X
cookie	X	X

Keyword	Netscape Navigator	Microsoft Internet Explorer
Copy		X
CopyFile		X
CopyFolder		X
cos	X	X
Count Property		X
CreateFolder		X
CreateTextFile		X
current	X	X
Data Type Conversion		X
Date	X	X
DateCreated Property		X
DateLastAccessed Property		X
DateLastModified Property		X
Decrement Operator (−)	X	X
defaultChecked	X	X
defaultSelected	X	X
defaultStatus	X	X
defaultValue	X	X
delete Operator		X
DeleteFile		X
DeleteFolder		X
description	X	X
Dictionary Object		X
dimensions		X
Division Operator (/)	X	X
do . . . while	X	X
document	X	X
domain	X	X

Keyword	Netscape Navigator	Microsoft Internet Explorer
Drive Object		X
Drive Property		X
DriveExists		X
DriveLetter Property		X
Drives Collection		X
Drives Property		X
DriveType Property		X
E	X	X
elements array	X	X
elements property	X	X
embeds array	X	X
enabledPlugin	X	X
encoding	X	X
Enumerator Object	X	X
Equality Operator (= =)	X	X
escape	X	X
eval	X	X
exec		X
Exists		X
exp	X	X
fgColor	X	X
File Object		X
FileExists		X
filename	X	X
Files Collection		X
Files Property		X
FileSystem Property		X
FileSystemObject Object		X

Keyword	Netscape Navigator	Microsoft Internet Explorer
FileUpload	X	X
fixed	X	X
floor	X	X
focus	X	X
Folder Object		X
FolderExists		X
Folders Collection		X
fontcolor	X	X
fontsize	X	X
for	X	X
for . . . in	X	X
Form object	X	X
form property	X	X
forms	X	X
forward	X	X
Frame	X	X
frames	X	X
FreeSpace Property		X
fromCharCode		X
Function	X	X
function		X
GetAbsolutePathName		X
GetBaseName		X
getDate	X	X
getDay	X	X
GetDrive		X
GetDriveName		X
GetExtensionName		X

Keyword	Netscape Navigator	Microsoft Internet Explorer
GetFile		X
GetFileName		X
GetFolder		X
getFullYear		X
getHours	X	X
getItem		X
getMilliseconds	X	X
getMinutes	X	X
getMonth	X	X
GetParentFolderName		X
getSeconds	X	X
GetSpecialFolder		X
GetTempName		X
getTime	X	X
getTimezoneOffset	X	X
getUTCDate		X
getUTCDay		X
getUTCFullYear		X
getUTCHours		X
getUTCMilliseconds		X
getUTCMinutes		X
getUTCMonth		X
getUTCSeconds		X
getVarDate		X
getYear	X	X
Global Object		X
global Property		X
go	X	X

Keyword	Netscape Navigator	Microsoft Internet Explorer
Greater than Operator (>)	X	X
Greater than or equal to Operator (>=)	X	X
hash	X	X
height	X	X
Hidden	X	X
history array	X	X
history object	X	X
host	X	X
hostname	X	X
href	X	X
hspace	X	X
if . . . else	X	X
ignoreCase Property		X
Image	X	X
images	X	X
Increment Operator (+ +)	X	X
index	X	X
indexOf	X	X
Inequality Operator (!=)		X
Infinity Property		X
input Property		X
isFinite		X
isNaN	X	X
IsReady Property		X
IsRootFolder Property		X
italics	X	X
item		X
Item Property		X

Keyword	Netscape Navigator	Microsoft Internet Explorer
Items		X
javaEnabled	X	X
join	X	X
Key Property		X
Keys		X
Labeled		X
lastIndex Property (RegExp)		X
lastIndex Property (Regular Expression)		X
lastIndexOf	X	X
lastMatch Property		X
lastModified	X	X
lastParen Property		X
lbound		X
leftContext Property		X
length Property (Array)	X	X
length Property (Function)	X	X
length Property (String)	X	X
Less than Operator (<)	X	X
Less than or equal to Operator (<=)	X	X
Line Property		X
link	X	X
linkColor	X	X
links	X	X
LN10	X	X
LN2	X	X
location	X	X
log	X	X
LOG10E	X	X

Keyword	Netscape Navigator	Microsoft Internet Explorer
LOG2E	X	X
Logical AND Operator (&&)	X	X
Logical NOT Operator (!)	X	X
Logical OR Operator (||)	X	X
lowsrc	X	X
Math	X	X
max	X	X
MAX_VALUE	X	X
MimeType	X	X
mimeTypes	X	X
min	X	X
MIN_VALUE	X	X
Modulus Operator (%)	X	X
Move		X
MoveFile		X
moveFirst		X
MoveFolder		X
moveNext		X
multiline Property		X
Multiplication Operator (*)	X	X
name	X	X
NaN	X	X
navigator	X	X
NEGATIVE_INFINITY	X	X
new Operator	X	X
next	X	X
Nonidentity Operator (!= =)	X	X
Number	X	X

Keyword	Netscape Navigator	Microsoft Internet Explorer
Object Object		X
onAbort	X	X
onBlur	X	X
onChange	X	X
onClick	X	X
onError	X	X
onFocus	X	X
onLoad	X	X
onMouseOut	X	X
onMouseOver	X	X
onReset	X	X
onSelect	X	X
onSubmit	X	X
onUnload	X	X
open (document object)	X	X
open (window object)	X	X
OpenAsTextStream		X
opener	X	X
OpenTextFile		X
Option	X	X
options	X	X
parent	X	X
ParentFolder Property		X
parse	X	X
parseFloat	X	X
parseInt	X	X
Password	X	X
Path Property		X

Keyword	Netscape Navigator	Microsoft Internet Explorer
pathname	X	X
PI	X	X
Plugin	X	X
plugins	X	X
port	X	X
POSITIVE_INFINITY	X	X
pow	X	X
previous	X	X
prompt	X	X
protocol	X	X
prototype	X	X
prototype Property		X
Radio	X	X
random	X	X
Read		X
ReadAll		X
ReadLine		X
referrer	X	X
refresh	X	X
RegExp Object		X
Regular Expression Object		X
Regular Expression Syntax		X
reload	X	X
Remove		X
RemoveAll		X
replace	X	X
reset	X	X
Reset object	X	X

Keyword	Netscape Navigator	Microsoft Internet Explorer
return	X	X
reverse	X	X
rightContext Property		X
RootFolder Property		X
round	X	X
ScriptEngine Function		X
ScriptEngineBuildVersion Function		X
ScriptEngineMajorVersion Function		X
ScriptEngineMinorVersion Function		X
scroll	X	X
search	X	X
select	X	X
Select object	X	X
selected	X	X
selectedIndex	X	X
self	X	X
SerialNumber Property		X
setDate	X	X
setFullYear		X
setHours	X	X
setMilliseconds		X
setMinutes	X	X
setMonth	X	X
setSeconds	X	X
setTime	X	X
setTimeout	X	X

Keyword	Netscape Navigator	Microsoft Internet Explorer
setUTCDate		X
setUTCFullYear		X
setUTCHours		X
setUTCMilliseconds		X
setUTCMinutes		X
setUTCMonth		X
setUTCSeconds		X
setYear	X	X
ShareName Property		X
ShortName Property		X
ShortPath Property		X
sin	X	X
Size Property		X
Skip		X
SkipLine		X
slice (Array)		X
slice (String)		X
small	X	X
sort	X	X
source Property		X
split	X	X
sqrt	X	X
SQRT1_2	X	X
SQRT2	X	X
src	X	X
status	X	X
strike	X	X
String	X	X

Keyword	Netscape Navigator	Microsoft Internet Explorer
sub	X	X
SubFolders Property		X
submit	X	X
substr		X
substring	X	X
Subtraction Operator (-)		X
suffixes	X	X
sup	X	X
switch	X	X
taint	X	X
taintEnabled	X	X
tan	X	X
target	X	X
test		X
Text object	X	X
text property	X	X
Textarea	X	X
TextStream Object		X
this	X	X
title	X	X
toArray		X
toGMTString	X	X
toLocaleString	X	X
toLowerCase	X	X
top	X	X
toString	X	X
TotalSize Property		X
toUpperCase	X	X

Keyword	Netscape Navigator	Microsoft Internet Explorer
toUTCString		X
type	X	X
typeof Operator	X	X
ubound		X
Unary Negation Operator (-)	X	X
unescape	X	X
Unsigned Right Shift Operator (>>>)	X	X
untaint	X	X
URL	X	X
userAgent	X	X
UTC	X	X
value	X	X
valueOf	X	X
var	X	X
VBArray Object		X
vlinkColor	X	X
void Operator		X
VolumeName Property		X
vspace	X	X
while		X
width	X	X
window object	X	X
window property	X	X
with	X	X
write	X	X
WriteBlankLines		X
WriteLine		X
writeln	X	X

INDEX

G

ABOUT THE AUTHOR

Steven Holzner is a top programmer and one of the most respected authors in the industry. With more than 35 books to his credit, he has taught more than a million people how to program more effectively. Among his most popular titles are *XML Complete* and *Java 1.1: No Experience Required*. Holzner lives in Cambridge, Massachusetts.

SOFTWARE AND INFORMATION LICENSE

The software and information on this diskette (collectively referred to as the "Product") are the property of The McGraw-Hill Companies, Inc. ("McGraw-Hill") and are protected by both United States copyright law and international copyright treaty provision. You must treat this Product just like a book, except that you may copy it into a computer to be used and you may make archival copies of the Products for the sole purpose of backing up our software and protecting your investment from loss.

By saying "just like a book," McGraw-Hill means, for example, that the Product may be used by any number of people and may be freely moved from one computer location to another, so long as there is no possibility of the Product (or any part of the Product) being used at one location or on one computer while it is being used at another. Just a book cannot be read by two different people in two different places at the same time, neither can the Product be used by two different people in two different places at the same time (unless, of course, McGraw-Hill's rights are being violated).

McGraw-Hill reserves the right to alter or modify the contents of the Product at any time.

This agreement is effective until terminated. The Agreement will terminate automatically without notice if you fail to comply with any provisions of this Agreement. In the event of termination by reason of your breach, you will destroy or erase all copies of the Product installed on any computer system or made for backup purposes and shall expunge the Product from your data storage facilities.

LIMITED WARRANTY

McGraw-Hill warrants the physical diskette(s) enclosed herein to be free of defects in materials and workmanship for a period of sixty days from the purchase date. If McGraw-Hill receives written notification within the warranty period of defects in materials or workmanship, and such notification is determined by McGraw-Hill to be correct, McGraw-Hill will replace the defective diskette(s). Send request to:

Customer Service
McGraw-Hill
Gahanna Industrial Park
860 Taylor Station Road
Blacklick, OH 43004-9615

The entire and exclusive liability and remedy for breach of this Limited Warranty shall be limited to replacement of defective diskette(s) and shall not include or extend any claim for or right to cover any other damages, including but not limited to, loss of profit, data, or use of the software, or special, incidental, or consequential damages or other similar claims, even if McGraw-Hill has been specifically advised as to the possibility of such damages. In no event will McGraw-Hill's liability for any damages to you or any other person ever exceed the lower of suggested list price or actual price paid for the license to use the Product, regardless of any form of the claim.

THE McGRAW-HILL COMPANIES, INC. SPECIFICALLY DISCLAIMS ALL OTHER WARRANTIES, EXPRESS OR IMPLIED, INCLUDING BUT NOT LIMITED TO, ANY IMPLIED WARRANTY OF MERCHANTABILITY OR FITNESS FOR A PARTICULAR PURPOSE. Specifically, McGraw-Hill makes no representation or warranty that the Product is fit for any particular purpose and any implied warranty of merchantability is limited to the sixty day duration of the Limited Warranty covering the physical diskette(s) only (and not the software or information) and is otherwise expressly and specifically disclaimed.

This Limited Warranty gives you specific legal rights; you may have others which may vary from state to state. Some states do not allow the exclusion of incidental or consequential damages, or the limitation on how long an implied warranty lasts, so some of the above may not apply to you.

This Agreement constitutes the entire agreement between the parties relating to use of the Product. The terms of any purchase order shall have no effect on the terms of this Agreement. Failure of McGraw-Hill to insist at any time on strict compliance with this Agreement shall not constitute a waiver of any rights under this Agreement. This Agreement shall be construed and governed in accordance with the laws of New York. If any provision of this Agreement is held to be contrary to law, that provision will be enforced to the maximum extent permissible and the remaining provisions will remain in force and effect.